WAKE UP TO YOUR LIFE

WAKE UP TO YOUR LIFE

Discovering the Buddhist Path of Attention

KEN MCLEOD

HarperSanFrancisco
A Division of HarperCollins*Publishers*

HarperCollins books may be purchased for educational, business, or sales promotional use. For information please write: Special Markets Department, HarperCollins Publishers, Inc., 10 East 53rd Street, New York, NY 10022.

HarperCollins Web site: http://www.harpercollins.com

HarperCollins®, ■®, and HarperSanFrancisco™ are trademarks of HarperCollins Publishers, Inc.

FIRST EDITION

Library of Congress Cataloging-in-Publication Data

McLeod, Ken.
  Wake up to your life : discovering the Buddhist path of attention / Ken McLeod
ISBN 0–06–251680–9 (cloth)
ISBN 0–06–251581–7 (paperback)
    1. Spiritual life—Buddhism. 2. Buddhism—Doctrines. I. Title.
BQ4302.M44   2001

294.3'444—dc21   00–046133

01   02   03   04   05   ❖/RRD   10   9   8   7   6   5   4   3   2   1

Contents

Acknowledgments

I thank all my teachers. Without them, this book would never have come into being. I am grateful to Jon Parmenter, Yvonne Rand, and Ruth Gilbert for their substantial contributions. My thanks also to Michelle Bekey, who started the ball rolling; to Tom Lane, Janaki Symon, George Draffan, and Shawn Woodyard for their help in editing and revision; and to Bill Block and Lynn Chu for their assistance and support.

*To my teachers, especially Kalu Rinpoche,
who poured their teachings into me*

*And to my students, whose passion for insight inspired me
to distill and return what was given so freely*

Introduction

I first met my principal teacher, Kalu Rinpoche, at his monastery near Darjeeling, India, in 1970. I had heard that he held a class for Westerners most afternoons. I had also read how teachers tested the motivation of students by putting them through ordeals, so I came to the class with a bit of trepidation. After the translator introduced me, Kalu Rinpoche asked if I had come to Darjeeling as a tourist or because I wanted to study Buddhism.

"To study," I answered.

"Good," he said. "This is no place for tourists."

Abrupt and anticlimactic, his reply left me both relieved and let down—relieved that I wouldn't have to endure an ordeal such as sitting outside the monastery gates for a week, and let down because being accepted seemed too easy. Later I came to appreciate that the path presents its own challenges and a teacher rarely has to add much to the mix.

My own path has been and is a long struggle with very few shafts of light on the way. I'm not even sure that the path has an end. Yet I have had the good fortune to meet and study with a few people who have taken significant steps down that path. Because of their kindness, I've learned something about how to dismantle the wall that separates us from knowing what we are. Even though I teach others, I am still very much a student of the way.

In these pages, you will find no descriptions of alternative states of mind, different realities, or marvelous mystical states. I will not recommend that you retire to a monastery, give up your job, or make other radical changes in the form of your life. Instead, you will find practical tools with which to change the way you experience life.

The methods and perspectives presented here originated more than 2,500 years ago in India with Buddha Shakyamuni. They were preserved and developed in many Asian countries, including the remote mountains of Tibet. They have been transmitted faithfully from generation to generation by individuals who have dismantled the wall that separates us from what we experience and have entered into the mystery of being. They have been taught for generations and have withstood the tests of time.

This book began as series of meditation guides for people who study and practice with me. I use these methods in my own practice and teach them to people who, unable to ignore the separation any longer, are looking for a way to take the wall apart.

The irony is that the separation is a fiction. Existentialist philosophers largely missed this point. Their effort—to live authentically by finding individual meaning in a chaotic universe—presupposes that we are separate from the world we experience. To live authentically, we have to stop trying to avoid suffering and death by looking for meaning. We have to enter into the mystery of life itself.

Suffering points to the mystery of life. Many philosophical and religious traditions seek to explain away the mystery by advancing a set of beliefs that attempt to give meaning to suffering. Belief in meaning is still a belief. It will be betrayed by changes in circumstances. A mother suffers when her child dies in an accident, so she asks, "Why? Why did this happen? It doesn't make any sense." When beliefs we are dependent on are rendered meaningless in the face of tragedy, the only place to go is despair.

Death also points to the mystery. Religions try to mitigate the fear of death by explaining death away with beliefs in heaven or eternal life. When I attended the funeral services for a distinguished teacher in the Tibetan tradition, I was dismayed to hear the lama presiding over the ceremony say, "Do not think of this teacher as having died; instead, think that he has gone into retreat for a while." His statement seemed to contradict the basic teaching of Buddhism that all compounded things are impermanent.

An often-unspoken but deeply held belief is that if a person is morally good, then he or she will live a long life. When a "good" person dies from cancer, however, those who adhere to that belief are devastated. They ask, "How could such a tragedy happen to this person? It doesn't make sense." Their view of life is so shattered that they, too, lapse into a despair from which they may never recover.

Though difficult to do so, we can instead face squarely the fact that suffering and death are part of life and can come at any time to any person, regardless of how good, moral, famous, rich, or respected he or she may be. When death strikes, grief and pain and loss still arise, yet our understanding of life is not shattered, and we are less likely to succumb to despair.

Periodically, someone uncovers a method that precipitates an "instant enlightenment," a momentary opening by virtue of which the sense of separation evaporates. Such methods have formed the basis for numerous religions, psychotherapies, fads, and cults—for example, primal scream, hypnosis, drug cultures, and the like. They proliferate in the New Age community. These devices do not work in the long run because they draw on our system's energy to generate a peak experience. Peak experiences cannot be maintained, and when they pass, the habituated patterns and the underlying sense of separation remain intact.

Peak experiences may open up new possibilities, but they cannot do what a consistent practice or discipline does—instill a deep understanding that expresses itself in life. No quick fix exists. Milarepa, a great Tibetan folk hero who lived in mountain retreats, used to say that to glimpse what is ultimately true is not difficult, but to stabilize that understanding takes years of effort.

> Everything that the human race has done and thought is concerned with assuagement of pain. One has to keep this in mind if one wishes to understand spiritual movements and their development.
>
> *—Albert Einstein*

Buddhism is fundamentally a set of methods through which we wake up to what we are and stop the cycle that generates and reinforces suffering. The forms Buddhism has taken in many cultures, including our own, may suggest that it is a religion. It is not. Buddhism is a collection of methods for waking up from confusion. Over centuries, the original methods were developed, refined, and expanded. Buddhism is fraught with schools of philosophy, cosmological descriptions of the world, and moral and ethical systems, including the various lay and monastic traditions, esoteric initiation systems, energy transformation methods, devotional practices, mindfulness practices, ways to cultivate compassion, pointing-out instructions for insight, elaborate visualization practices based on deities, and meditations on the ultimate nature of being.

We can easily lose our way in all these elaborations. If we forget that the purpose of practice is to move out of the reactive patterns that create suffering, we miss the whole point. All the philosophies, world-views, ethical systems, practices, and rituals have only one intention: to wake us up from the sleep in which we dream that we are separate from what we experience.

CHAPTER 1

The Mystery of Being

One day the villagers thought they would play a joke on Nasrudin. As he was supposed to be a holy man of some indefinable sort, they went to him and asked him to preach a sermon in their mosque. He agreed.

When the day came, Nasrudin mounted to the pulpit and spoke:

"O people! Do you know what I am going to tell you?"

"No, we do not know," they cried.

"Until you know, I cannot say. You are too ignorant to make a start on," said the Mulla, overcome with indignation that such ignorant people should waste his time. He descended from the pulpit and went home.

Slightly chagrined, a deputation went to his house again, and asked him to preach the following Friday, the day of prayer.

Nasrudin started his sermon with the same question as before.

This time the congregation answered, as one man:

"Yes, we know."

"In that case," said the Mulla, "there is no need for me to detain you longer. You may go." And he returned home.

Having been prevailed upon to preach for the third Friday in succession, he started his address as before:

"Do you know or do you not?"

The congregation was ready.

"Some of us do, and others do not."

"Excellent," said Nasrudin, "then let those who know communicate their knowledge to those who do not."

And he went home.

—IDRIES SHAH,
THE EXPLOITS OF THE INCOMPARABLE MULLA NASRUDIN

THE PRINCE AND THE HORSE

In a faraway country, now lost in the mists of time, there lived an old king and queen. Their son, a young prince, though proficient in matters of war and clever enough in the affairs of state, showed little interest in the responsibilities that would one day come his way. As the king was old and his health failing, the queen was increasingly worried about her son and the way he conducted his life. Not knowing what to do, she visited a sorcerer and explained her concerns.

The sorcerer listened in silence and then asked, "What does he like most of all?"

"Horses," said the queen. "He's passionate about horses. They are all he really cares about."

"That will do," said the magician, and he told the queen to walk in the palace gardens the following afternoon.

The next day, after lunch, the queen asked the prince and the court retinue to stroll with her in the palace gardens. Just outside the palace gates, at the end of the garden, stood a beautiful white horse. An old man held the reins. The prince ran to the horse, examined it for a moment, and turned to the old man. "I have to have this horse," he said. "It's a magnificent animal. How much do you want for it?"

The old man bowed and said, "Not so fast, not so fast. You're a prince. I would be foolish to sell you this horse before you ride it. Mount up! If you still want it when you come back, we can discuss the price."

The prince needed no urging. He quickly mounted the horse. The moment he was in the saddle the horse began to gallop. Oh, how that horse could gallop! Faster and faster, they raced through the town and out into the surrounding farmlands. The prince was thrilled. He had never ridden such a swift and powerful beast.

They galloped across the countryside, into the hills, and high into the mountains, over passes and into the next kingdom. The horse never tired. They galloped far beyond any villages and towns, into regions the prince didn't know. Finally, as the sun began to set, the horse slowed to a walk and stopped in the middle of a deep forest.

The prince looked around. He had no idea where he was. He dismounted and led the horse along the path. Evening was coming and the prince was a little worried, but he saw a light in the distance and went toward it. The light came from a small cottage. He knocked on the door, and a beautiful young woman opened it. The prince explained his plight, but she had never heard of his kingdom. Still, night had fallen, so she invited the prince in and introduced him to her father, an old man who still worked as a woodcutter.

The prince stayed the night and set out the next morning to find his way home. He traveled as far as he could and asked every person he met about his home kingdom, but no one knew anything about it or how to help him find his way home. Each night the prince returned to the woodcutter and his daughter. Eventually, he began to help the old man with his work. He learned how to cut wood and grew wise in the ways of the forest. The prince was increasingly attracted to the daughter and she to him, so they married.

The prince settled down into his new life and new trade. Occasionally, when he saw the horse by the house, the prince remembered how he had come there, but he didn't dwell on the matter long. In time, his wife gave birth to a son and a daughter. His life was full. The old man retired, and the prince took over the business. He cut wood, stacked it, and took it to the market. The income wasn't much, but it took care of their needs, and, as they had few other cares, they lived happily and peacefully. The memories of his former life as a prince faded away.

The prince often walked far into the forest. On one of his walks, he came to a glen he had not seen before. In the glen was a pond with water so clear and still you could see all the way to the bottom. The glen, the pond, and the still, clear water drew him for reasons he didn't understand. He went often to the glen, where he would sit, looking into the still depths of the pond.

One day while he sat by the pond, he heard a cry. His two children came running out of the forest. A tiger was chasing them. He had never seen a tiger in the forest before. The prince jumped up to protect his children, but before he could do anything, his children ran into the pond and disappeared. The tiger jumped in and disappeared as well. His wife came running up and ran in after them. She, too, disappeared. The old man came hobbling along and, following the others, disappeared into the water. At that moment, the prince's horse galloped up, leaped into the center of the pond, and disappeared. The waters of the pond became still and clear again, but no traces of his family or horse or the tiger were to be seen.

The prince was dumbfounded. What had happened? In the space of two minutes, everything in his life had vanished. Unable to take in what had happened, he continued to look into the water, perhaps hoping to see something. When the shock of his loss finally hit him, he fell to the ground, his body shaking with sobs, and he cried and cried. Then he felt a hand softly touching his shoulder.

The prince looked up. Above him were the eyes of his mother, the queen, and around him were the concerned faces of the court retainers, the palace gardens, and the horse, standing quietly. The queen was relieved. She told him that as soon as he had touched the horse, he had fallen to the ground. He had been lying there in a trance for two or three minutes.

"No," said the prince. "No! Not two or three minutes. Years. I had a life, a family, a trade, people I loved, a wife and children. I had things that mattered to me. I lived my whole life. It wasn't two or three minutes. That isn't possible." Dazed and bewildered, he stood and walked away.

The old man bowed to the queen, took the horse, and left.

The prince was profoundly moved by this mystery, and his attitude changed. His heart opened to every moment of his life. After his father died, the prince ruled wisely and well, fully present and attentive to the concerns of his people and the welfare of the kingdom.

THE MYSTERY OF LIFE

What is this experience we call life? It is a mystery. Look around you. Look at the room in which you are sitting. Look at the furniture. Notice the play of light and color. Be aware of your body. Note the thoughts and feelings that come and go. Life is just this—what we experience in each moment.

We don't know where experience comes from or where it goes. We don't know how we come to be here or what is going to happen after we die. We live and are aware: we experience thoughts, emotions, and sensations. That's all we really know. Life is a mystery, as the prince learned from his experience.

All of us have felt intimations of this mystery. It may come as a feeling of infinite openness that arises inside yet includes everything you experience. Your definition of who and what you are momentarily crumbles, and you feel that you are falling apart. You react by gripping tighter to your sense of who you are and push away the experience of open emptiness. Rarely do you stop to ask, "What am I holding on to?"

The mystery may make itself felt in a vividness that penetrates the ordinary routine of life. The world momentarily becomes brilliant and alive. You experience a moment out of time, a sense of oneness, a moment of vivid clarity and awareness. You wonder, "Where did that come from?"

Perhaps the mystery makes itself felt as a moment of timeless presence, of being so completely here that you wonder where you've been all your life. The moment passes, however, and a wall goes back up. You realize that you live behind that wall—a glass wall, perhaps, but a wall so impenetrable that it might as well be made of stone. You live with the isolation, but deep inside you wonder, "What is this wall?"

Just as we retreat from the knowledge that we will die one day, we retreat from the mystery of being. The mystery evokes fear—not just the fear of dying, but a deeper fear, the fear that I am not what I think I am. The intimations of the mystery—emptiness, clarity, and presence—challenge the deeply held conviction that "I" exist independently and apart from the world I experience. Yet we hold hard to the individual "I" existing as the subject, with the world as its object. Exactly what "I" am and what the world is are issues we largely ignore, relegating them to the domains of mystics, philosophers, and scientists. We remain confident in the belief that we exist and see little point in examining that belief. Yet all the great spiritual and contemplative traditions regard such a conviction as a fiction or, perhaps more accurately, a misperception.

Separateness

As long as we live in the misperception of being a separate entity, we encounter frustration, confusion, difficulties, and turmoil. Everything we do is slightly out of sync with what is actually happening. We live in a world of ghosts and fantasies. Try though we may to catch up, we never quite make it. In short, we suffer.

The sense of separateness forms very early in our lives. Some people say that it begins before we are born. In either case, we spend our lives sorting out problems that stem from it. Developmental psychologists argue that the sense of separation is a necessary and natural step in becoming a functional person. Perhaps, but the misperception persists and the feeling of separation remains—a seemingly impenetrable wall that separates us from what we really are. Can we break free from the misperception that we are separate from what we experience?

This book describes a way to break down that wall. It describes the tools we need and how to use them in order to take the wall apart.

You might ask, "Why take it apart? My life is okay. Why go to all the trouble?"

If you don't have to do this work, don't. Go and enjoy your life. Few of us, however, escape the problems created by the sense of separation, not knowing who or what we really are. It gnaws at us even as we strive to deny it, shut it down, eliminate it from our lives, or control what we experience so that we never feel it.

The more we avoid the sense of separation, the more our life is consumed by the effort to maintain it, until nothing but the effort remains. Self-perpetuating, this effort continues to function by itself, coercing, consuming, manipulating, and controlling everyone and everything around us. We become predators driven by an insatiable hunger to fill the hollowness inside. We see the world as an object, as food for our hunger. We feed on the world in increasingly desperate attempts to compensate for feelings of incompleteness, separation, and alienation. This is a sorry way to live.

We may come to this work because we want to achieve enlightenment, satori, or cosmic consciousness, but the focus on results, on what "I" will achieve or understand, is just another form of the misperception of separation. Once, when the Dalai Lama gave a talk in Los Angeles, a woman asked how long she would have to practice before she experienced results. The Dalai Lama said nothing and just lowered his head into his hands and cried.

We come to this work because the alternative, being consumed by the effort to ignore the mystery of being, is no longer acceptable.

Do You Need a Teacher?

Can you do this work on your own? Basically, the answer is no. A few individuals spontaneously wake up to the nature of things, but, historically, they are very rare. The vast majority of people who undertake the work of dismantling the misperception of separateness rely on teachers who relied, in turn, on their teachers. So, in starting this work, you enter a lineage in which understanding has been transmitted from generation to generation.

When we start exploring the mystery of being, we are still mired in habituated patterns. Limited in perception to a world projected by these patterns, we do not and cannot see things as they are. We need a person, a teacher, who, standing outside our projected world, can show us how to proceed.

Buddhism, in particular, has always viewed internal transformative work as a path and the teacher as a guide who transmits his or her understanding to others. A guide, however, cannot rely only on what has been taught to him or her. To be effective, the guide must also have made the journey. The guide's own experience invests the understanding with vitality and relevance. The special quality of lineage and transmission lies not just in the understanding that is passed from generation to generation but also in the individual experience of those who have made the understanding their own.

So, when you start on this path, look for a teacher to guide you—one who has done, or at least is doing, his or her own work.

This story from the Sufi tradition illustrates a number of pitfalls that may prevent you from finding or connecting with a teacher.

One dark night two men met on a lonely road.

"I am looking for a shop near here, which is called The Lamp Shop," said the first man.

"I happen to live near here, and I can direct you to it," said the second man.

"I should be able to find it by myself. I have been given the directions, and I have written them down," said the first man.

"Then why are you talking to me about it?"

"Just talking."

"So you want company, not directions?"

"Yes, I suppose that that is what it is."

"But it would be easier for you to take further directions from a local resident, having got so far: especially because from here onwards it is difficult."

"I trust what I have already been told, which has brought me thus far. I cannot be sure that I can trust anything or anyone else."

"So, although you once trusted the original informant, you have not been taught a means of knowing whom you can trust?"

"That is so."

"Have you any other aim?"

"No, just to find The Lamp Shop."

"May I ask why you seek a lamp shop?"

"Because I have been told on the highest authority that that is where they supply certain devices which enable a person to read in the dark."

"You are correct, but there is a prerequisite, and also a piece of information. I wonder whether you have given them any thought."

"What are they?"

"The prerequisite to reading by means of a lamp is that you can already read."

"You cannot prove that!"

"Certainly not on a dark night like this."

"What is the 'Piece of Information'?"

"The piece of information is that The Lamp Shop is still where it always was, but that the lamps themselves have been moved somewhere else."

"I do not know what a 'Lamp' is, but it seems obvious to me that The Lamp Shop is the place to locate such a device. That is, after all, why it is called a Lamp Shop."

"But a 'Lamp Shop' may have two different meanings, each opposed to the other. The meanings are: 'A place where lamps may be obtained,' and 'A place where lamps were once obtained but which now has none.'"

"You cannot prove that!"

"You would seem like an idiot to many people."

"But there are many people who would call *you* an idiot. Yet perhaps you are not. You probably have an ulterior motive, sending me off to some place where lamps are sold by a friend of yours. Or perhaps you do not want me to have a lamp at all."

"I am worse than you think. Instead of promising you 'Lamp Shops' and allowing you to assume that you will find the answer to your problems there, I would first of all find out if you could read at all. I would find out if you were near such a shop. Or whether a lamp might be obtained for you in some other way."

The two men looked at each other, sadly, for a moment. Then each went his way.

—IDRIES SHAH, *TALES OF THE DERVISHES*

You already have a conception of what the mystery of being is, just as the first man has a conception of a lamp shop even though he doesn't really understand what a lamp is or what a lamp does.

Whatever your initial conception, it will change as you accumulate experience through your practice. Some people start with the mistaken notion that waking up is an idyllic state in which you always know exactly what to do or never again experience any difficulty in life. You will probably discover that your initial conceptions of practice, awakening, and the mystery of being are ideas that developed and evolved from the fundamental misconception of separate existence and are quite wrong. If you hold on to them when your teacher's instruction and your own experience contradict them, they become obstacles. This work is experiential, not intellectual, and you can no more rely on a conception of the mystery of being to ease the pain of separation than you can rely on an idea of water to quench your thirst.

You may also feel a degree of uncertainty, which causes you to cling tenaciously to your beliefs about the mystery of being. To travel this path, you must rely on faith, not belief. Faith is the willingness to open to the mystery of experience. It contrasts with belief, which is the attempt to interpret experience to conform with habituated patterns that are already in place, including those inherited from your culture and upbringing.

How do you know whom to trust as a teacher? This is a crucial question. To answer it you must rely on your own intelligence and perception. If you find someone you think can guide you, ask questions. What training does this person have? How did she or he come to teach? What, exactly, does he or she teach? If you smell a fish or your stomach turns, the person is probably not right for you, regardless of his or her reputation, credentials, number of followers, or special abilities.

The key question is whether this person opens up new possibilities for you. From the perspective of the mind-only school of Buddhism, the teacher is how the mystery of being, with its inherent intention of presence, manifests in your experience. The teacher expands possibilities—by raising questions, offering advice, assisting you, or challenging you in ways that don't exactly match the world as you know it. In other words, a teacher brings the mystery of being into your life in a way that you do not ignore.

The Teacher-Student Relationship

The teacher-student relationship is based on a shared aim—your awakening to the mystery of being. It is not based on mutual profit or on emotional connection. The responsibilities of a teacher are three:

- To show you the possibility of presence
- To train you in the techniques and methods you will need
- To direct your attention to the internal patterns that prevent you from being present in your life

Everything else is extra and is usually based on the projections of the student, the teacher, or both.

You, as a student, have two responsibilities:

- To practice what is taught as it is given
- To apply the practice in your life

For the teacher-student relationship to work, the teacher must be concerned only with the student's growth and awakening, and the student must know this to be true. Only when these two conditions are present are you able to go through the process of dying to the world based on the misconception of self and open to the mystery of being.

If you do not trust that the teacher, in the role of teacher, is helping you to wake up, you will inevitably interpret the teacher's actions through the lens of your reactive patterns. For example, if you see the teacher as being cruel, then even if the teacher is not cruel, the student-teacher relationship cannot function fruitfully because you will interpret the demands or actions of your teacher as cruelty, not as pointing you to presence or to your own patterned functioning.

You are entrusting a lot to a teacher, so ask questions and observe until you are satisfied that this person has the experience, the training, and the motivation to teach you. Experience means that he or she has sufficient depth of understanding to open new possibilities for you. Training means that he or she can both teach and guide you in the methods that dismantle the sense of separation. Motivation means that the teacher is sincerely dedicated to your spiritual growth and that no other agenda takes precedence in your relationship.

In making these evaluations, remember that you are not looking for a perfect person. You are looking for a person who can be useful to you in catalyzing real and perceivable change in you.

Does the teacher have the depth of experience to guide you in your practice? In reality, the student-teacher relationship is one of ongoing exploration and deepening. As your own experience deepens, you come to appreciate and understand your teacher's efforts more clearly. On the other hand, you may see that, helpful as a teacher has been, this person's experience is not what you are looking for or she or he is unable to penetrate the questions that burn inside you. Buddha Shakyamuni learned how to cultivate attention from his first teachers, but they could not respond to his inquiry into the origin of suffering.

Training is another matter. Does the teacher have a sufficient mastery and understanding of the techniques he or she is teaching? Does she or he have practical experience in the techniques to guide you through the inevitable difficulties and problems? Is the teacher proficient in showing you how to remove obstacles to the practice of presence and how to generate higher levels of energy to power attention? Is the teacher skilled in introducing you to presence?

The teacher's motivation is one of the essential conditions for a productive relationship. Why is this person teaching—for profit, power, status, recognition, or gratification of personal needs, from an obligation to a teacher or institution, to maintain a tradition, as service to others, or in service to what is true? You can tell something about the motivation of a teacher from what is required of students. Possibilities include money, service, obedience, bringing in new students, dependence, effort in practice, or progress in practice.

If the teacher is interested in you for social, political, or financial reasons, or to satisfy his or her own needs for affection, intimacy, sex, money, recognition, fame, control, or identity, the teacher is merely using you. Sooner or later you will resent the exploitation and feel betrayed. Most people take at least four to five years to heal from this form of betrayal, so pay careful attention to the quality of your relationship with your teacher.

Don't blindly accept appeals to a higher wisdom or deeper insight as justification for behaviors that you see as fundamentally wrong or inappropriate. Ask questions and discuss your experience of the relationship with your teacher when you are confused. Like all relationships, the relationship between student and teacher has its share of challenges. Only by exploring your own experience will you be able to determine whether your perception is due to habituated patterns operating in you or to a weakness in your teacher. If the former, you know the next step in your practice. If the latter, you have to decide whether the perceived weakness is sufficient to obstruct the fundamental aim of the relationship: your awakening to the mystery of being.

Remember, the point is to see things as they are, not as you would like them to be.

Frequently, problems begin on either the student's or the teacher's side with a poorly developed ability to set or maintain appropriate boundaries. In this culture, lacking the checks and balances on the teacher-student relationship developed in other cultures, idealization and projection become highly problematic. Teachers are relatively isolated in this culture and receive little support or appreciation from society. They often compensate for their isolation by overburdening the one community they have—students—with their needs for appreciation, recognition, or support.

Students in this culture have a tendency to give themselves away to their teacher, often as a result of family conditioning or similarly based needs for affection, appreciation, or security. The student may idealize the teacher and project onto the teacher the student's own conception of perfection. The student may then take the position that association with perfection is sufficient and make little further effort in his or her own practice. Or, if the association seems insufficient, the student finds fault with the teacher and is unable to accept instruction.

A crucial task for you as a student is to be clear about your own intention. If you don't clearly understand what you are looking for in a teacher or in internal work, you will inevitably accept someone else's agenda as your own. While you may start internal transformative work on the suggestion or advice of another person, at some point your practice has to become a response to your own questions about life and being. Your own suffering, however it manifests, is the basis and motivation for your practice. To lose sight of it is to lose connection with your reason for practicing. Another person's experience can never answer your own questions. You have to know what you want from your practice. Then you can know what you want in a teacher.

Some teachers and groups place too much emphasis on ascent—gaining access to high states of energy with corresponding experiences of bliss, emptiness, or clarity. The high-energy states are taken as the goal of practice. Since only lip service is paid to dismantling the habituated patterns that obscure presence, the high-energy states are inherently unstable. They require more and more effort to maintain, and imbalances in life and personality become progressively greater. Little attention is given to how to live in presence, so teachers and students often exhibit clearly reactive behaviors outside the practice environment.

Other teachers place too much emphasis on descent—working mainly on habituated patterns and reserving instruction and teaching on what is ultimately true for a selected group of students. This approach tends to create inner and outer circles of students, privileged access to the teacher, and dependency based on gaining or losing the teacher's favor.

Examine also how a teacher responds to questions. Do answers expand the scope of the student's understanding? Do the answers relate to your own experience? A good teacher avoids pat or rote answers and will often answer the same question from different students in different ways.

Observe how the teacher handles mistakes. Are mistakes never acknowledged? Are they justified as manifestations of the teacher's supposedly higher or concealed level of understanding? Does the teacher become defensive, attack or criticize the student, or become inaccessible?

A teacher's students reveal a lot about the teacher. A common set of habituated patterns in a group of students indicates that the teacher is ignoring at least one aspect of presence. Observe the group with the following questions in mind. A yes answer to any of them is usually a sign that things are not right:

- Does the group feel that it is special or that it is going to save the world, or does it insist that this is the one true teaching?
- Are students restricted in the use of their own intelligence and judgment?
- Are questions and discussions inhibited or restricted to certain topics?
- Do students have to climb a staircase of escalating fees, donations, or service in order to receive instruction and guidance?
- Does the group exploit students for its own functioning?
- Do students show no appreciable progress over the long term?
- Does the group require severing connections with family, friends, and other long-term relationships?

Like all things, relationships are impermanent, so you know that your relationship with your teacher will end. It may end only when your teacher or you die, or it may end earlier for any number of reasons. The point is not to make the relationship last forever, because it can't. Serve the intention of the relationship: wake up to the mystery of being. When that intention is no longer being served, the student-teacher relationship ends. The determination is ultimately up to you. Then another relationship, with a different basis, may form. Serious problems often arise when, for whatever reason, you do not recognize or acknowledge that the student-teacher relationship has ended.

To appraise your own progress as a student is very difficult. A week or a month is insufficient for gauging progress. However, if, after a year, say, you can discern no change in the quality of your practice, in how you see and experience the world, or in your abilities and behaviors in daily life, then you need to discuss your practice with your teacher and possibly reconsider what you are doing. Generally speaking, from year to year you should be able to observe changes in your life that you can attribute to your practice and to what you have learned.

TRANSMISSION

For many years, a monk studied and practiced under the guidance of his teacher. One day, his teacher came to him and said, "Your training is finished. The time has come for you to leave the monastery and teach others."

The teacher accompanied the monk to the monastery gates, where he bid him farewell and set him on his way with his robes, his begging bowl, and a few necessities.

Going on foot, the monk traveled far and wide. He relied only on what people gave him for food and conversed happily with those who sought out his guidance or counsel. One day, he came to a wide river where he decided to end his wanderings. He continued as before, relying on what people offered and helping them as best he could. Living modestly, he put aside what he didn't need from the offerings and gifts of passers-by and eventually saved enough to build a boat. He became a ferryman, taking people back and forth across the river.

Time passed. As a ferryman, he met people from many different walks of life—the rich, the poor, the famous, the obscure, traders, farmers, nobles, and peasants. Those who were well off he charged a modest fee. Those who were not he ferried across for free. He treated them all with the same respect and courtesy. Nobody knew that he had once been a monk or anything else about him. They only knew him as a ferryman and felt safe with his capable hands at the oars.

One day, a young monk asked to be taken across the river. As the ferryman rowed, he asked the monk a few questions about his training. At first the monk had little interest in talking with this obscure person. Yet the questions were probing and made the monk a little uneasy. Who was this ferryman?

For his part, the ferryman soon determined that the young monk showed promise. In the middle of the river, he asked the monk, "What is your mind?"

"Mind is no thing," said the monk, "infinite like the sky, it has no center or perimeter, and is beyond coming and going, birth or death, many or one."

"Hmph," grunted the ferryman, "fine words. Now tell me, what is your mind?"

Before the monk could answer, the ferryman tipped over the boat.

The monk thrashed his way to the surface spluttering with shock and rage. "What are you doing? We're in the middle of the river! What kind of crazy ferryman are you?"

The ferryman calmly lifted up an oar and brought it crashing down on the poor monk's head.

"What is your mind?" the ferryman demanded as he pushed the monk under the water.

This time, when the monk rose to the surface, his face was clear and radiant. He had seen into the nature of mind. Flooded with the clarity of original mind, he silently bowed his head to the ferryman.

"Now I have repaid the kindness of my teacher," said the ferryman, and he slipped beneath the waters and drowned.

This story, in contrast to the story about the lamp shop, shows how teacher and student fulfill their respective responsibilities.

The ferryman lives simply, engaged in his work and open to what arises. He is not concerned with becoming happy, rich, famous, or respected; he is free from attachment to conventional success. He is not concerned with gathering students in order to enhance his status in the world or to satisfy his emotional needs.

The story does not tell us what the ferryman and monk talked about in the boat, but, clearly, the monk's initial projections fell apart in the conversation. He became intrigued by this seemingly simple ferryman. As you work with a teacher, inevitably, you project your own ideas and patterns onto the teacher. The teacher receives these projections and uses them to dismantle the corresponding patterns in you. You begin to sense the mystery of being. The teacher's questions and demands impinge increasingly on your life. At some point, you react, relying on what you think you know, just as the monk relied on his academic training.

The teacher isn't satisfied. He or she tips over the boat to show you presence. Everything you thought you knew is useless at this point.

In the story, the monk first misses what the teacher is pointing to. He goes straight back into habituated patterns, seeing this strange person as a crazy ferryman. Undeterred, the ferryman directs the monk's attention to the habituated patterns by hitting him with the oar. He instructs the monk in technique by telling him again to look at his mind. For his part, the monk now practices exactly what the ferryman gives him. He looks at his mind even though he's swimming in the river, wakes up, and, realizing the significance of the experience in his life, expresses his appreciation to the ferryman.

The teacher has done his job, so his relationship with the young monk is finished. At the same time, he has completed his relationship with his own teacher. Nothing is left to be done, so he dies.

This last point is important. You cannot repay your teacher directly. The teacher, in teaching, is fulfilling his or her own relationship with the mystery of being. The only way to repay a teacher for freeing you from the confusion of habituated patterns is to pass on what you have come to understand to another person. In a larger sense, the transmission of understanding from one person to another is the natural expression of original mind. Every moment in which you are present opens the possibility of presence in those around you. In other words, the practice of presence, itself, is how you repay the kindness of your teacher.

We are what we experience. Presence is knowing, directly in the moment, that we are what we experience. The path described here does not promise quick results. It does not rest on fictions, beliefs, or peak experiences. It consists of taking apart, brick by brick, the wall that prevents us from knowing what we are. To dismantle that wall is the work of a lifetime. It requires an *outlook* to show us a way, a *practice* to develop the abilities we need, and a *way of living* that brings the practice into life.

The outlook is no separation: we are what we experience, nothing more and nothing less. The practice is attention: cultivating attention and using it to dismantle the sense of separation. The way of living is presence: we live in attention, aware and awake in the mystery of being.

THE CENTRAL ROLE OF ATTENTION

The essential tool is attention—not the weak, unstable, reactive attention that is part of our autonomic functioning, but the strong, stable, and volitional attention cultivated in such disciplines as meditation. Active attention, composed of mindfulness and awareness, is the key. Attention, in this sense, is not intellectual or physical. It is energy, the same kind of energy that powers emotions.

Attention is used to dismantle the wall that separates us from what we are. This wall consists of conditioned patterns of perception, emotional reactions, and behaviors. The wall has many components: conventional notions of success and failure, the belief that I am a separate and independent entity, reactive emotional patterns, passivity, an inability to open to others, and misperceptions about the nature of being.

Dismantling these habituated conditioned patterns is not a smooth process. Things don't unfold in a neat progression. Attention is the one principle on which we can always rely. We meet every problem encountered in practice (and there will be many) in the same way: do the practice and bring attention to what arises in experience.

In Florence, Michelangelo's statue of David stands at the end of a long hall. Twelve roughly hewn blocks of marble line the hall, six on each side. The twelve blocks are unfinished sculptures of the twelve titans from Greek mythology. Each block contains a rough human form, crouched, back bent, powerfully flexing its muscles. When I looked at the unfinished sculptures, I felt the power in the forms. Extra marble separates the figures from who and what they are. I had the impression that their flexing muscles had broken off chips of marble and would continue to break off more marble until the beings inside were free. The life and vitality in the rough forms are remarkable.

Like these titans, what we are lies buried under the marble of our conditioning. By cultivating attention, we break apart the marble, dismantle the wall, and enter into the vitality of being.

Attention acts on the wall of habituated patterns in the same way that the energy of sunlight acts on a block of ice. Heat from the sun raises the level of energy in the water molecules until they can no longer remain in the compact crystalline structure of ice. The crystal breaks up, and ice melts into water. In the same way, attention penetrates habituated patterns and raises the level of energy so that the patterns have to break up. The energy locked up in the patterns is released and is used to power attention to higher levels. Step by step, attention increases in energy until even the sense of separation dissolves and we open to the mystery of being.

This process lies at the heart of all the great world religions, but in institutional settings, the vitality and immediacy of lived experience is gradually covered over and lost. As the Catholic contemplative David Steindl-Rast once pointed out, direct experience of the mystery of being manifests in three ways: a practice that supports opening to the mystery, a celebration of the experience, and a way of life that arises out of understanding and insight. The practice becomes a body of teaching, the celebration is expressed in ritual, and the way of life is formulated in precepts. As time passes, traditions accumulate accretions, and the teaching becomes dogma; rituals become empty forms; and precepts originally intended to guide become restrictive moral codes.

From time to time, traditions go through periods of great turmoil, shedding the accretions of the centuries and finding fresh expressions of the mystery of being. Buddhism has gone through such a process many times in many countries. Zen originally arose as Chan Buddhism in the seventh century C.E. in response to the increasingly rigid moralistic and ritualistic approaches then prevalent in China. Nineteenth-century eastern Tibet saw the flowering of the Rimé approach, which revitalized a practice that had become increasingly stuck in academic posturing. A similar revitalization is now taking place in the West.

My own training is in the Kagyu tradition of Tibetan Buddhism. I immersed myself completely in the tradition—learning the Tibetan language, studying the texts, learning and practicing the rituals, and spending seven years in a traditional training retreat. I learned more than I ever considered possible. Like many of my friends and colleagues, I encountered painful and seemingly intractable obstacles in my practice. In confronting these obstacles, I saw that, though powerful and potent, Tibetan Buddhist methods cannot easily be practiced in the classical manner in the context of contemporary American life. So I set about reexamining everything I had learned and practiced.

I came to understand the central role of attention in internal transformative work, and I saw how all aspects of Buddhist practice (and all forms of internal transformative work) can be described in terms of the operation of attention.

Buddhism is more a set of tools for waking up to our original nature than a system of beliefs. For this reason, many of its tools are used by adherents of other religious traditions. With attention as the central element of practice, the spiritual principles involved in different methods of practice can clearly be discerned. The process of spiritual awakening becomes clear so that you, the reader, can recognize your own process and practice. The methods presented here are relevant regardless of your background or tradition. You can use them to deepen your own work.

Even when the ideas presented here resonate with your own experience, you need time to absorb new perspectives. Instead of leafing through a few pages late at night, read carefully and slowly when you are clear and awake. In short, regard reading the book itself as an exercise in attention.

CHAPTER 2

Buddhism in a Nutshell

Nasrudin was sent by the King to investigate the lore of various kinds of Eastern mystical teachers. They all recounted to him tales of the miracles and the sayings of the founders and great teachers, all long dead, of their schools.

When he returned home, he submitted his report, which contained the single word "Carrots."

He was called upon to explain himself. Nasrudin told the King:

"The best part is buried; few know—except the farmer—by the green that there is orange underground; if you don't work for it, it will deteriorate; there are a great many donkeys associated with it."

—IDRIES SHAH,
THE EXPLOITS OF THE INCOMPARABLE MULLA NASRUDIN

Approximately 2,500 years ago, Siddhartha, a prince of the Shakya clan in northern India, abandoned his royal heritage to seek the source of human suffering.

Sheltered by an overly protective father who wanted his son to succeed to the throne, Siddhartha grew up in the greatest luxury that his time could provide. Not until his twenties did the prince venture beyond the palace grounds. His illusions about life were quickly shattered as he encountered illness, old age, and death among his subjects. Soon afterward, Siddhartha saw an old religious mendicant who was utterly present and at peace. How could that be? How could anyone be at peace in the midst of all that suffering?

No matter how we grow up, in wealth or poverty, in love or adversity, we form a view of life. Everything we do subsequently is based on the belief that that view of life is how things are. Perhaps you grew up in an environment in which you could easily trust everyone not to hurt you, but then you encounter a person who, for no reason you can imagine, is intent on doing you harm. Perhaps you grew up learning to trust no one and can't imagine trusting another person with anything that is important to you. We first encounter the mystery of being when our view of life is called into question. All too often, we react by ignoring, closing down, manipulating, or controlling what arises in experience to avoid questioning that view of life and what we feel we are.

Siddhartha could not ignore what he had seen. Power, wealth, and position became meaningless to him in the face of illness, old age, and death. His conceptions of life and what he was were turned upside down and inside out. He saw another possibility, however, in the presence and peace of the religious mendicant.

The first encounter with the mystery of being momentarily shatters the structures of ordinary life. When everything falls away, a moment of opening takes place. In that moment, we are free—free from the fetters of beliefs and ideas about who and what we should be. In other words, in the midst of the destruction of our illusions about life, we experience being what we actually are—free, open awareness. Most of the time, we don't notice that freedom and open awareness. We're too busy putting our view of life back together. Even if we do notice it, we don't stay there for long. But, like Siddhartha, we have encountered the religious mendicant and the possibility of presence.

Siddhartha soon left the court life he knew to examine the issue of suffering. Why is there suffering? Where does it come from?

His first step was to turn to the religious teachers of the day. He quickly learned everything they had to teach: their philosophies, meditation techniques, and codes of conduct. He practiced what he was taught, and he gained abilities equal to those of his teachers. Yet his questions remained unanswered.

The mystery of being often makes itself felt in our lives in the form of questions. We turn to institutions, traditions, and respected teachers, hoping to find answers to our questions. We study and practice, learning much that is helpful. When we really listen to our own questions, however, we know that we can never receive answers to them from an institution, tradition, or another person. The answer can come only through our own experience. At some point, we take what we have learned and apply it to our own questions. We have to make the practice our own.

Along with five companions, Siddhartha began a life of extreme asceticism in order to understand the source of human suffering.

Tradition records that for six years he ingested only one sesame seed, one grain of rice, and one drop of water each day.

In a museum in India, I once saw a sculpture of Siddhartha at that point in his life. The sculpture depicts a person sitting in meditation who is nothing more than skin draped over a skeleton. I can't adequately express my reaction to seeing this vision of a heart-wrenching intention to know the source of suffering, an intention so powerful that it would not let physical death get in the way.

When they discover that their approach to life is based on an illusion, many people react by pursuing wealth and power. In pursuing asceticism, Siddhartha was taking an approach to life that was the opposite of the one that most people adopt. He had learned that wealth and power were meaningless. Perhaps the answers to his questions could be found in poverty and austerity.

Whether we pursue wealth or austerity, our lives are still based on the same conditioning; we're just running in one direction or the other. Which direction the conditioning runs makes no difference. Like a train that has been going the wrong direction, we stop, turn around, and go the opposite way, but we are running on the same tracks. The same ideas and assumptions are still operating. To enter the mystery of being, we have to step off the tracks.

After six years of starving himself, Siddhartha could no longer keep his mind clear. He concluded that the practice of asceticism for its own sake would not lead him to understand suffering. Siddhartha stopped his regimen and began to eat normally, despite being rejected by his companions.

With his body restored, he sat under a tree and resolved not to move until he understood the source of suffering. He let his mind rest in attention, undistracted, not trying to make anything happen, not trying to cultivate any particular quality or ability. He stopped everything and simply sat with his question: what is the source of suffering?

How do we step off the tracks? We stop trying to avoid, close down, manipulate, or control what arises in experience. When we do stop, we are inevitably regarded with suspicion, and even rejected, by those who continue to live their lives based on patterns and conditioning. We go forward alone.

That evening, Siddhartha entered progressively deeper states of attention. The traditional accounts describe how Mara, the demon of obsession, tried to distract Siddhartha and bring him back into the realm of reaction and confusion, where Mara held sway. He first tried to distract Siddhartha with desire by sending his daughters, in the form of beautiful women, to seduce him with affection, relationships, and sexual pleasure. Understanding that all experience, no matter how pleasurable, comes and goes, Siddhartha remained in attention. Mara tried anger next, sending armies of demons to the attack. Siddhartha saw the demonic armies as the play of mind, so the rain of weapons arose in his experience as a rain of beautiful flowers. Siddhartha then saw that the source of suffering was emotional reaction to what arises in experience. He saw that reactivity is based on the misperception that the "I" exists apart from experience. When he saw through the misperception, it dissolved completely. In that moment, Siddhartha became a buddha, a person who has awakened from the sleep of unawareness and reactive patterning. Mara had one final challenge for him and demanded an external validation of his experience. Buddha Shakyamuni smiled, touched the earth, and said, "The earth is my witness." That was the end.

To wake up is hard. We must first realize that we are asleep. Next, we need to identify what keeps us asleep, start to take it apart, and keep working at dismantling it until it no longer functions. As soon as we make an effort to wake up, we start opening up to how things are. We experience what we have suppressed or avoided and what we have ignored or overlooked. When that happens, the reactive patterns that have run our lives, kept us in confusion, distorted our feelings, and caused us to ignore what is right in front of us are triggered. They rise up strongly to undermine the attention that is bringing us into a deeper relationship with what we are and what we experience. When we can see those patterns and everything that is constructed out of them as the movement of mind and nothing else, we begin to wake up.

The final challenge posed by habituated patterns is to question direct experience. How do we know? How can we trust this knowing, which is totally beyond the ordinary conditioned experience of life? Like Buddha Shakyamuni, we turn to no external reference and live in the knowing. We live in presence, in the mystery itself.

After his awakening, Buddha Shakyamuni spent the next seven weeks quietly digesting what had happened. His initial assessment was that no one else could possibly understand what he had discovered. Eventually, however, the Buddha decided he had a responsibility to try to communicate his understanding to others. He set off for Benares, a major city a few miles away.

When we see how things actually are, our whole system experiences a profound shock. We are not what we thought we were. All our struggles to define who and what we are are revealed as pointless, fruitless, and self-defeating. At first, we have no idea what to do or how to function, but we are still breathing. Life goes on, but now what? Our natural human impulse is to share our knowledge and understanding with others. This impulse manifests in life as compassion, which is a response to the circumstances of the moment.

In the village of Sarnath, a suburb of Benares, Buddha encountered his companions in asceticism. At first, they didn't want to have anything to do with him and resolved to ignore him. As Buddha approached, however, they felt an extraordinary presence and spontaneously rose to greet him. They were so awed by his presence that they asked him to explain what had happened. Buddha Shakyamuni started with the existence of suffering and explained what he now knew.

For Buddha, the circumstance of the moment was this chance meeting with his former companions. All of them had been motivated originally by the question of suffering, so he gave his first teaching, the four noble truths.

THE FOUR NOBLE TRUTHS

Buddha Shakyamuni's way to presence was through the problem of suffering. What is it? How does it arise? Can it be ended? How do we end it? When other spiritual teachers and philosophers asked Buddha to describe his teaching, he usually answered, "I teach one thing and one thing only, suffering and the end of suffering."

In his first teaching, Buddha formulated his understanding as the four noble truths: suffering, the origin of suffering, the cessation of suffering, and the path to cessation. Stated baldly, the four truths seem a bit enigmatic. They are, in fact, based on a simple problem-solving model, a model that dates far back in Indian philosophy and medicine.

- What is the problem?
- What is the root of the problem?
- Is there a solution?
- How do you put the solution into effect?

Suffering

The first noble truth is the truth of suffering: there is suffering. Suffering is the central problem of human experience. Buddha did not ignore suffering or try to explain it away as an unfortunate side effect of a divine plan or cosmic order. Suffering was, for him, the central issue.

And it is still the central issue today. So, what is suffering? The Sanskrit term is *dukha,* a term that refers to the unsatisfying quality of experience. It is a general term that covers everything from vague feelings of unease to extreme physical and emotional agony. Suffering, as it is used in the first noble truth, refers to any sense of discomfort. We all experience discomfort, whether it is the slight uneasiness of embarrassment or the intense pain of bone cancer. When discomfort arises, our first impulse is to put an end to it, to stop it any way we can. We are, in effect, trying to separate from what we are experiencing, and, by doing so, we separate from life and from the mystery of being. The first noble truth is basically an injunction not to ignore or dismiss what we experience.

Suffering arises in three ways: from pain, from change, and from existence itself.

The first kind of suffering is *the suffering of physical or emotional pain.* When we encounter physical pain, we reactively try to avoid, control, or stop it. Burning a finger on a stove is very painful. We plunge the finger into cold water so that it will stop hurting.

The second kind of suffering is *the suffering of change.* When change takes place in our lives, internal and external structures are dismantled, either by choice or by force of circumstances. A relationship comes to an end. Our children go to college. We take on a new job with new responsibilities.

Even when we welcome change because it creates new possibilities, we still feel discomfort as the old structures come down. At first, the new job is exciting—more responsibility, more money, better opportunities. At the same time, all that is familiar is gone—it's a new office, with new people, new pressures, and new expectations we aren't sure we can meet.

The discomfort we feel in the face of change is the suffering of change.

The third kind of suffering is *the suffering of existence itself.* We believe that we exist, yet if we ask, "What am I?" we find no answer beyond the roles and functions that we fill in life. We feel empty inside or separate from what we experience, and we react with fear and doubt.

Even when everything is going well in our lives—when we are happy and fulfilled with our family and our work—a small doubt or fear lingers. Is this who I am? Is this all there is to life? Am I really all alone? The suffering of existence is the discomfort we experience from our fears and doubts about what we are or are not.

The first noble truth says that suffering is pervasive. It invites us not to ignore or avoid it, but to look at it, know what it is, and understand how it arises.

The Origin of Suffering

Buddha Shakyamuni's second insight involves the origin of suffering. Suffering comes from emotional reactivity.

All experience is pleasant, unpleasant, or neutral. The three fundamental emotional reactions to experience are attraction, aversion, and dullness or indifference. *Attraction* is the emotional reaction to what is pleasant. *Aversion* is the reaction to what is unpleasant. *Indifference* is the reaction to what is neutral. These three reactions are called *the three poisons* because they poison our experience of life.

Suppose that you are having a good time at a party and you wish you could always feel this way. Your desire to hold on to the good feeling subverts your enjoyment. Attraction has poisoned your experience of the party.

Suppose that you are hungry but you won't eat the only food available because you don't like it. Hunger gnaws at you, and you become more and more irritable. Aversion has poisoned your experience of eating.

Suppose that you have an open afternoon but you can't think of anything interesting to do. You sit around, bored and discontented. Indifference has poisoned your experience of peace.

In each case, the emotional reaction separates us from what we are actually experiencing (company, nourishment, peace) and leads us to interpret the experience as negative. The negativity is not in the experience itself but in the way we react to it.

If we examine the experience of suffering, we will see that it has two components: pain and emotional reaction to the pain. Pain is simply what happens. We drop a hammer on our foot. It hurts. Suffering is an emotional reaction to the pain. We yell at the hammer, berate our spouse for leaving it precariously balanced on a shelf, or fume at ourselves for being careless.

One day, I was skiing just outside Los Angeles. A number of families had brought their young children up the ski lift for their first experience of snow, but the ride was chilly because of an unusually strong wind. I remember a small child, about six or seven, who clearly had never experienced such cold before. Even though he was now in the warmth of the cafeteria, the child still cried and continued to cry and jump around for twenty minutes. His parents could do nothing to console him. The child was suffering terribly, caught up in his own reaction to the cold and unable to feel the warmth of the fire in front of him.

Another example is anxiety. We feel anxious about a job interview. Because we want to do well in the interview, we do not want to be nervous, so we start to feel anxious about feeling anxious. The cycle of reaction feeds itself, causing anxiety and fear to escalate quickly.

Reactions are patterns of emotions and behaviors, formed by conditioning, that run automatically when they are triggered by internal or external events. They are the cumulative result of a complex interaction among emotions, behaviors, and perception. Significant sources of conditioning include the needs of the body and the basic human need for love, affection, and other forms of attention. We can add family history and values, childhood and adult experience, and social and cultural influences. Reactive patterns also develop from biological propensities and such evolutionary traits as the flight-or-fight response. In Buddhism, the formation of patterns and their role in shaping what we experience is called karma, a topic explored in chapter 5.

Think of reactive patterns as mechanisms. They are preestablished by conditioning, are triggered by external and internal events, and, once triggered, run only according to what has been conditioned. Such mechanisms may appear to be aware or responsive, but they are no more responsive than a computer program. Sufficiently complex machines, such as IBM's Deep Blue chess computer, may give the impression of being able to think and decide. Deep Blue's programmers state clearly, however, that it doesn't think and isn't aware. It only reacts to the other player's moves by calculating its next move from complex algorithms and preestablished criteria of acceptance or rejection. Reactive emotional patterns may be explained as beliefs, myths, metaphors, or teaching methods or they may be personified as Mara or demons or some other conscious entity, but for our purposes they are mechanisms.

The second noble truth tells us that the origin of suffering is emotional reactivity. What do we do to end this suffering? We dismantle the patterns of emotional reactivity.

The End of Suffering

Is it possible to disengage from reactivity? The third noble truth is Shakyamuni's powerful answer, *yes*. He saw that the sense of self, of

"I," is the basis of emotional reaction, and that "I" as a separate entity doesn't exist. In other words, when the conditioning that underlies the sense of separation, the false duality of subject and object, is dismantled, suffering ceases.

We cannot and do not end pain, but we can and do end suffering. We end suffering by ceasing to identify with what we are not: a pattern that interprets experience as separate and other and then operates to control or justify its own imagined existence.

Attention is the ability to experience what arises without falling into the conditioned reactions that cause suffering. Attention is always present in potential but is unable to function because of conditioning. Most of us have experienced spontaneous attention. A person attacks you verbally, but instead of reacting to the insults, you see how upset and angry the person is, and you respond appropriately, perhaps by simply asking what is upsetting him. Your response takes you both by surprise, too, because it is different from the way you usually react.

In the account of Buddha's awakening, Mara, the demon of obsession, and his army represent patterns and conditioning. Buddha Shakyamuni rooted in attention, undistracted and undisturbed by the ploys and attacks of Mara. His attention penetrated Mara and his army so that he saw them and experienced them for what they are: movements in mind. They fell apart and ceased to function. The fetters of conditioning fell away. All that remained was original mind, pristine awareness. When Mara, the sense of "I," demanded an external authority for pristine awareness and direct experience, Buddha knew none was necessary, so he simply touched the earth, saying, in effect, "Here's your authority. That's it."

In *pristine awareness,* awareness and experience are not separate. Gone is the sense of separation, of internal emptiness, or of not being quite present. We are awake and present. We may not be able to say exactly what we are or what the experience is—hence, the mystery of being—but in the moment of presence, questions about origin, meaning, value, and purpose do not arise. We know, and that's it.

Most of us have experienced moments of pristine awareness. In a conversation with a close friend about a tragedy, time stops, yet the conversation continues. Although you may not remember what was said, the experience of presence remains with you. It becomes a treasured memory in the middle of the tragedy. It may even awaken a curiosity about this mystery we call life.

Our intuition is correct: we don't exist in the way that we habitually think, feel, and perceive that we do. For most of us, the experience of not existing as a separate entity is terrifying. Our attention is too weak for us to stay present in the experience. Reactive patterns form to keep us from experiencing it. The reactive patterns that maintain the feelings of separateness, incompleteness, and lack of presence all arise from the fear of nonexistence. These conditioned reactions maintain a world of illusion, a world of subject and object, which prevents the direct experience of being. Layer upon layer of reactive patterns form to maintain the illusion that each of us is a separate entity. Suffering is the subjective experience of all this emotional reactivity.

Buddha Shakyamuni could say unequivocally that there is an end to suffering because he developed such a high level of attention, diamondlike attention, that he could rest in the mystery of being, the experience of not existing as a separate entity, with no fear and in complete clarity. At that level of attention, the experience of not existing as a separate entity is known for what it is and ceases to be a basis for fear and emotional reactivity. The key effort in the third noble truth is to come to this understanding ourselves. Suffering ends when we have sufficient ability in attention to be present in all experience—even the experience of not being a separate entity.

The Path

In the fourth noble truth, we are introduced to the path, the way of life, that leads to freedom from suffering and the reactive patterns that generate it.

Reactive patterns have been in place for a long time. Much of life is the product of their operation. To dismantle these patterns we must take apart our lives. Attention works to dismantle patterns the way the energy of the sun melts ice. The directed energy of attention dissolves the structure of patterns, releasing the energy locked in them. We experience the freed energy as awareness and presence.

To cultivate and apply attention, we travel the eightfold path: right speech, right action, right livelihood, right effort, right mindfulness, right attention, right view, and right cognition.

How, for instance, do we practice right speech? Right speech does not mean saying the "right" thing. Ideas about the "right" thing usually come from conditioning. As a teacher, I field a lot of questions from students about different aspects of practice. I can easily fall into the habit of giving stock answers. If I give a stock answer, however, I am operating out of habituation, not presence. I am not really paying attention to the student, how he or she is asking the question, or how the question arises in the context of the student's practice. A stock answer is not the practice of right speech, even though the answer may be "right" in a technical sense.

To cultivate right speech, listen as you talk so that you hear, with your own ears, exactly what you say and how you say it.

When I listen to my voice as I answer a student's question, I quickly become aware if I am slipping into a stock answer. When I am, my tone is flatter and less animated than usual. When I return to attention, what I say comes out in a different way. Even though the words may be exactly the same, attention is operating as I speak. Attention dismantles the impulse to give a stock answer, dismantles the concern to be seen as the knowledgeable teacher, and dismantles any resistance to being present with the student.

As we make this effort over and over, we will find that we speak differently: we speak from attention. The practice of right speech is speaking in attention.

One of my students is a consultant for corporate training. When he started to listen to the way he talked with prospective clients, he noticed that in order to win their business he dropped into a sales patter and told them what he thought they wanted to hear. He realized that the practice of right speech would change the way he did business. He took more time with each client, determining what the client's needs really were and communicating clearly what advice and services he could provide.

To travel the eightfold path, we make the same effort in each of eight areas. In addition to bringing attention to how we speak, we bring attention to how we act and behave, to what we do for a living, to the way we direct our efforts in practice and in life, to how we practice mindfulness and cultivate attention, and to how we look at the world and how we think.

In the context of the eightfold path, *right* does not mean right as opposed to wrong. The path is not a prescription for behavior that is deemed "right" by any authority. An action is right, in terms of the eightfold path, when the action comes from attention and presence rather than from reaction.

The Buddhist path is the path of attention. Attention is cultivated through *meditation*. As attention breaks up our habituated patterns of perception and reaction, the *wisdom* of original mind is progressively uncovered. That wisdom expresses itself in *morality,* how we actually live our lives. We now turn to these three disciplines: morality, meditation, and wisdom or understanding.

THE THREE DISCIPLINES

Understanding arises naturally from the dismantling of the patterns that prevent us from knowing what we are. To dismantle reactive patterns we need to cultivate attention, and to cultivate attention we need to bring order into our lives. Although the earliest formulation of Buddha's teachings, the four noble truths, describes the essential steps to freedom, the actual practice is usually discussed in terms of three disciplines: morality, or how to bring order to our lives; meditation, or how to cultivate attention; and wisdom, or how to develop understanding.

Fundamentally Buddhism is not a system of beliefs; instead, it is a set of instructions for entering the mystery of being. In the Buddha's original formulation, these instructions are the eightfold path. The three disciplines—morality, meditation, and wisdom—show how the different elements of the eightfold path interact and provide a clear view of the central elements of practice.

The first three elements—*right speech, right action,* and *right livelihood*—constitute the discipline of morality. The practice of morality has two aspects. First, by bringing attention to how we speak, act, and live, we create the conditions needed in order to practice. Second, how we live is the expression of what we understand through practice. Therefore, in Buddhism, morality is a matter not of observing rigid moral principles but of giving expression to the wisdom of original mind.

Right effort, right mindfulness, and *right attention* constitute the discipline of meditation. In this context, meditation means stable attention. We begin with the effort of resting with the breath. We develop mindfulness first, then awareness, then stable attention. Attention is the heart of Buddhist practice. Although we use formal meditation to cultivate attention, the critical practice is to live in attention all the time.

The third discipline, wisdom or understanding, involves *right cognition* and *right view.* Right cognition means that we bring attention to the thinking process. We use cognitive processes to uncover and correct problems in our practice and in our lives. Right view is seeing things as they actually are. By bringing attention to how we see things, we step out of the projected "realities" of conditioning.

Morality, meditation, and understanding are closely connected. Most traditions start with morality, since discipline in our behavior prepares us for the discipline of meditation. As meditation practice develops, understanding unfolds.

In my work with students, I have found that meditation is the best place to start. The discipline of meditation leads directly to a clearer understanding of what we are and what life is. Understanding in this sense does not come from theory or speculation. It comes from the direct experience of being. It changes how we think, feel, and behave. If understanding doesn't change how we think, feel, perceive, and act, it isn't really understanding.

A highly competitive businessman came to me because he was both curious about Eastern disciplines and concerned about his level of stress. An angry and volatile person, he went through secretaries quite regularly, dismissing them as weak people who could not cut it in the business environment. His energy and drive served him well in his meditation practice. He never missed a day and soon started to relax a little, mentally and physically. As he relaxed, he began to understand how much stress his anger and volatility generated. He made a discipline of putting his attention on his breath whenever he felt angry. One day, he had once again chewed out his secretary for an error in a letter. Back in his own office, he put his attention on the breath and realized how angry he had been and how unproductive the anger was. He went back to his secretary and apologized. Much to his consternation, she simply replied, "Oh, that's just what I expect. You're

You might begin by bringing order into your daily life, especially by noticing all the disorder in relationships through looking without judgement at what you are actually doing. This would help to bring your mind into a more orderly, quiet state, a state more conducive to intelligence. So that is one thing you can do—become aware of the general disorder in your thoughts and in your daily life.

—*David Bohm*

basically abusive." When he heard that comment, he understood for the first time how his behavior was perceived by others.

His experience demonstrates how the three disciplines work. Attention from meditation led him to understand the actual effects of his anger. When he acted on this understanding and not from his conditioned patterns, his secretary dramatically corroborated his conditioning. Now that he saw more clearly how his world was affected by his anger, he naturally worked to change how he behaved.

The Discipline of Morality

Morality governs behavior. Like most spiritual traditions, Buddhism includes many moral codes that specify which actions are moral.

In Buddhist practice, the intention of morality is to be aware of the ways in which habituated behaviors undermine the effort to be awake and present in life. The role of morality is to provide a suitable psychological environment for training the mind. The crucial question in the practice of morality in Buddhism is not "Is this action right or wrong?" but "Does this action come from attention or reaction?" If it comes from reaction, what is being served?

Moral training in Buddhism rests on three principles: avoid harming others, act to help others, and refine the way we experience the world. These three principles are summarized in the well-known verse:

> Cease to do evil.
> Learn to do good.
> Train your own mind.
> These are the Buddha's teachings.

Morality works on three levels: action, motivation, and view of self. We train in morality by bringing attention to our actions. We soon become aware of the emotional reactions that motivate actions and the self-images around which those reactions are organized.

The ultimate intention of the practice of morality is to dismantle conditioned self-images so that we are free from the fetters of habituated patterns. Then our actions do not serve conditioned agendas and we are able to act in ways that serve the reality of the situations we encounter in life.

The three principal codes in Buddhism are the individual-freedom code (Sanskrit: *pratimoksha*), the awakening-being code (*bodhisattva*), and the direct-awareness code (*vidyadhara*).

Individual Freedom

The individual-freedom code is concerned primarily with actions that cause harm to others. By ceasing such actions, we create the freedom (internal and external) that we need to cultivate attention and experience the mystery of being. The code of individual freedom is based on five precepts:

- Not to take the life of a human being
- Not to take anything of value that is not given
- Not to lie about spiritual attainment
- Not to have inappropriate sexual relations
- Not to drink anything that is fermented

The first four precepts keep the practitioner free from complications in life and from conflicting, distracting, and disturbing thoughts and feelings. The last keeps the mind clear. The five precepts developed into the hundreds of vows that govern the behavior of monks and nuns. According to early texts, the number of vows was increased for two reasons: to provide guidelines for governing groups of practitioners and their relationship with society, and to exclude explicitly a wide range of behaviors because individuals frequently looked for ways around the basic precepts.

Awakening Being

The awakening-being code is aimed at waking us up to the groundlessness of all experience. In the Tibetan tradition, the awakening-being code is a declaration of intent to follow the training of those who have awakened before. In the Zen tradition, it is expressed in the four vows:

Sentient beings are numberless; I vow to free them all.
Reactive emotions are endless; I vow to uproot them all.
The doors to experience are limitless; I vow to enter them all.
The way is infinite; I vow to attain it completely.

The awakening-being code is less concerned with specific actions and more concerned with embracing compassion and emptiness. Through emptiness, we awaken to the nature of experience; through compassion, we awaken to experience as it arises. Without compassion, we are unable to open to the totality of experience. Without emptiness, we can't be free of habituated patterns. The essence of the awakening-being commitment is twofold: never to despair about awakening and never to dismiss a sentient being as unable to wake up. The former is the commitment to emptiness. The latter is the commitment to compassion.

Direct Awareness

The direct-awareness code is very subtle. It starts with the experience of original mind, the union of compassion and emptiness. The direct-awareness code is the intention to experience everything as an arising and subsiding in original mind. In other words, the commitment of the code is to be awake in every moment of experience. Whereas the individual-freedom code is primarily about actions and the awakening-being code is primarily about motivation, the direct-awareness code is primarily concerned with intention. When we are awake and present in the mystery of being, intention is determined not by conditioned agendas but by direct awareness that knows the situation. The direct-awareness code involves knowing and acting on the intention of the present.

The Discipline of Meditation

Meditation is the method used to cultivate attention. The first effort is to establish a formal practice—practicing the cultivation of attention free from other forms of activity. In other words, we set aside a regular time for meditation. We don't answer the phone, talk to friends, exercise, write, or do any other activity during that time. The second effort is mixing attention with the activities of daily life. The third effort is to live in attention all the time.

Formal Practice

Meditation techniques for formal practice fall into three categories: the practice of presence, energy transformation, and the removal of obstacles to presence.

The practice of presence is not usually a beginning practice. Properly speaking, it is the goal at which all other forms of meditation are aimed. It is resting in the mystery of being. The practice-of-presence methods, some of which are covered later in this book, are usually very simple. In the Theravadan traditions of Southeast Asia, they are known as the practice of bare attention. In the Tibetan tradition, they include mahamudra and dzogchen. In Zen, the principal technique is shikantaza. The intention is to be present with experience as it arises without trying to analyze it, understand it conceptually, or change it in any way. The two key abilities for the practice of presence are the ability to maintain attention without distraction and the ability to relax. Training in presence methods starts with training in attention. The breath (or some other suitable object) is usually used as a basis for developing attention. As attention develops, the basis of attention is shifted from the breath to awareness itself. Resting attention in awareness is the practice of presence.

Energy transformation methods are very different. They often involve visualizations that are combined with physical exercises, both of which move energy through the body. Tai chi, chi kung, and certain forms of yoga are examples of transformation methods. They are used to transform the natural energies of the body into increasingly higher and more powerful levels of attention. Because these methods draw on the energies that govern our physical and emotional functioning, they can lead to serious physical and mental disturbances if they are not practiced properly. In addition, if we do not have a clear intention to use the energy to open to deeper levels of experience, the energy raised by these methods inevitably flows into, and reinforces, habituated patterns. For these reasons, such methods are taught only when the teacher is confident that the student will benefit from their practice. Energy transformation methods can be learned and used at any level of practice. They are particularly important in the actual uncovering of original mind, so ecstatic opening, a straightforward and relatively safe method, is described in chapter 9.

Probably the largest category of meditation methods consists of ways to remove obstacles. The obstacles to presence are the conditioned patterns that undermine attention and produce distraction, confusion, and reaction. Meditations on death and impermanence, the four immeasurables (love, compassion, joy, and equanimity), and visualization methods such as the deity practices in the Tibetan tradition all fall into this category. The meditations on impermanence and death dismantle the reactive patterns that are related to attachment to conventional success. The meditations on the four immeasurables move us out of ordinary reactive emotions. The complex symbolic meditations of deity practice in Tibetan Buddhism dismantle attachment to the conditioned personality.

Extending Attention to Daily Life

The second effort in meditation is to extend attention to daily life outside formal practice. We practice by mixing attention with the activities of life. The intention is to maintain attention as we go about the day. We begin with simple activities such as walking or other exercises and simple manual tasks such as washing dishes and washing the car. We then extend the practice to more complex activities, such as conversation. Step by step, we bring attention to the various activities of life, noting the areas in which we habitually lose attention and fall into reaction. We make those areas the focus of our practice of attention during the day. The work of internal transformation comes alive as the abilities and experiences developed in formal practice are exercised in daily life. We move out of habituated patterns of behavior. What happens, for instance, when another driver zips into a parking spot in a crowded mall just as you are about to back into it? Can you observe the arising of your reaction as the movement of mind, or do you jump out of your car and let the other person have it?

Living in Attention
The third effort in meditation is to live in attention. The practice of attention and the operation of habituated patterns are incompatible. As we practice attention, we see the conditioning that runs our lives more and more clearly. We see how our reactions and conditioned behaviors create difficulties and suffering for everyone, including us. At first we are not able to change our behavior, but continued work in cultivating attention eventually opens up the possibility of acting differently. One day, instead of reacting to a situation, we see another possibility and do it. Everything changes. With this first cut into a pattern of reactive behavior, we realize that we can live and function in the world without relying on conditioned behaviors and the self-images underlying them. We can live in attention. Now, as soon as we are aware that habituated patterns are operating, we use attention to cut through them and then do what the situation requires.

At this stage, the discipline of attention merges with the discipline of morality and the discipline of understanding and develops into the practice of presence.

The Discipline of Understanding

The third discipline is understanding or wisdom. Here, the three levels are conventional understanding, understanding that the "I" does not exist independently, and the understanding of presence.

Understanding at the conventional level involves comprehending how meditation practice and Buddhist perspectives on life reduce stress and reactive behaviors and help us be more effective in our lives. This understanding is primarily intellectual. When a relationship comes to an end and we suffer, we recall, for instance, the first noble truth—there is suffering. This first noble truth helps us differentiate between the pain of the separation and our emotional reaction to it. Conventional understanding of meditation includes how to use meditation to relax, to let go of reactions, to work through feelings and disturbances, and to gain insight into situations.

The second level is the experiential understanding that we do not exist in the way we ordinarily think we do. This level of understanding is not intellectual. Through meditation and practice, we have the direct experience of seeing that there is no such thing as "I." The illusion of a permanent, independent thing called "I" is exposed. The patterns of fear and reaction based on preserving the misconception of "I" are dismantled. We are freed from the burden of defining who and what we are. Attachment to "I" no longer distorts our experience of life. Descartes's "I think, therefore I am" is true, but it is not a proof of existence. It is merely a description of the thinking processes. The "I" is a product of thinking.

The third level is the understanding of presence. It is the direct knowing that all experience is groundless; it simply arises and subsides. Here is where we open to the mystery of being. We begin by asking, "What is experience?" Experience consists of thoughts, feelings, and sensations, all of which arise in the mind. Therefore, we ask the next question, "What is mind?" Nothing is seen, but in that nothing, the clarity of awareness is present. Mind is not simply nothing. It is empty, no thing, and clarity at the same time. Nothing impedes the arising of experience. The three aspects of mind—emptiness, clarity, and unimpeded experience—are the real mystery of being. In the open space of awareness, experience arises and subsides, but what arises is not separate from awareness. Presence is resting in awareness, knowing that mind nature is empty, clear, and unimpeded, and knowing no separation from what we experience.

To get a better idea of these three levels of understanding, pick up an ice cube. What is it? At the conventional level, an ice cube is water that has been frozen in the shape of a cube. It can be used to cool drinks or to apply a cold pack to a strained muscle.

Put the ice cube in the palm of your hand. What is it now? Your hand gets colder and colder, and the feeling of cold becomes more and more intense until it feels almost like burning. "My hand is so cold it hurts," you say, but what is this "my"? What is the "I" that has a hand? When you look, you see no thing. The sensations of cold are present. So are the sensations of unpleasantness, the concepts of cold and ice cube, pain, feelings of uneasiness, anxiety, dislike, and fear, and consciousness of all the above. Where is the "I" that owns the hand? No such "I" exists, but you feel very strongly, "I am in pain." If you rest attention in the sensations in your hand, letting go of the attachment to "I" and all your reactions to the cold, the threat and fear subside, leaving only pure experience.

For the third level of understanding, ask, "What is this experience, this sensation of cold?" Look closely to determine exactly what the experience is. You will find that it dissolves in your attention. Your finger hurts with the cold. Pain arises in the finger, but the pain is not actually felt by the skin, the bone, or the muscle of the finger. It is not felt by the brain or in any part of the nervous system that connects the brain and the finger. You can find nothing that feels the sensation of pain, so where is the pain?

Yet the pain is there! Pain is a sensation that arises in experience. Experience arises in the mind. If you look at the mind that experiences the pain, you still see nothing, yet the experience remains vivid. How strange and mysterious! Imagine what your life would be like if you experienced every moment with the vividness with which you experience the cold of the ice cube, and you simultaneously saw and knew that what you were experiencing was neither more nor less than an arising in your mind.

Intention in the Three Disciplines

The three disciplines of morality, meditation, and understanding act as a bridge that connects the activity of life with our intention in practice. We begin with the intention to achieve individual freedom, and we adopt a way of life, the code of individual freedom, consonant with that intention. As understanding deepens, intention changes to waking up to the nature of experience, and we move into the code of the awakening being. Finally, intention shifts to resting in presence—the direct awareness that is our human heritage—and we move into the code of the awareness holder.

At the conventional level, we observe morality because it is part of the social structure in which we live. If we practice meditation, we do so for personal benefits such as relaxation, stress reduction, or greater effectiveness. Understanding at the conventional level also includes the learning we pursue for personal reasons: we want to be more effective, we need to learn a skill related to our work, or we want to learn about a subject for our own enjoyment.

Interest in individual freedom leads to a different relationship with morality. We act morally because to do so reduces emotional disturbance. We are less concerned with acting appropriately as a member of society and more concerned with creating an internal environment that supports our efforts in meditation and understanding. The meditation practices of individual freedom cultivate sufficient attention to penetrate the habituated patterns associated with a sense of self. Understanding arises when we see and know directly that the sense of self, the "I," is a misperception and that suffering comes from the emotional reactivity associated with this misperception. When this understanding is stabilized in experience, we are freed from the reactive process.

The awakening-being level of practice is about awakening to all that we experience. The vow of intention expresses a commitment to wake up. Compassion and emptiness are key tools to open to what arises in experience and to what experience is. Meditation consists of methods of cultivating compassion and understanding emptiness. Compassion is realized when the level of energy in our attention is higher than the energy of emotional reactivity. We then access the higher or impersonal emotions (love, compassion, joy, and equanimity). Emptiness is known when we see that all experience has no ground.

Understanding at the awakening-being level is the end of two illusions: the illusion that things are real and the illusion that things aren't real. We see that all that arises is apparently real but that ultimately there is only the arising and that what we experience has no independent reality. The understanding of how things are finds natural expression in compassion. The experience of compassion and emptiness together is the essence of awakening-being practice.

The direct-awareness level starts from the understanding that what is apparently true and what is ultimately true are one and the same; experience and awareness cannot be separated. Morality consists of doing what is required by the situations we encounter in life. We could call this morality "radical situational ethics"—radical because it is based not on social considerations but on direct awareness. Intention is the only reality, but not the intention of the conditioned personality. In direct awareness, a deeper intention arises as the knowing that is present in each moment. Meditation practice consists of cultivating attention to such an extent that we live in attention. When we live in attention, we are present and can know the intention of the moment. Understanding at the direct-awareness level is presence, knowing the intention of the moment.

THE THREE DISCIPLINES AND INTENTION IN PRACTICE

THE THREE DISCIPLINES	CONVEN-TIONAL LIFE	INDIVIDUAL FREEDOM	AWAKENING BEING	DIRECT AWARENESS
morality	social and cultural morality	for internal peace	opening to all experience	acting on the intention of the present
meditation	for personal benefits	attention to penetrate "I"	compassion and emptiness	living in awareness
understanding	effectiveness in life	end of suffering	end of illusion	presence

KARMA

Karma is a difficult topic even in Asian cultures. I recall an incident that one of my teachers, Dezhung Rinpoche, related to me.

When he was a young monk in Tibet, Dezhung Rinpoche trained with the Sakya master Ngawang Lekpa. On one occasion, Ngawang Lekpa asked Dezhung Rinpoche, "Do you understand karma?" Dezhung Rinpoche answered enthusiastically, "Oh, yes, I believe it completely!" Ngawang Lekpa quietly replied, "You are very fortunate—I find karma very difficult." Dezhung Rinpoche was startled by his teacher's candor and realized that something more than simple belief was required.

Karma is a Sanskrit word that means "action." In Tibetan usage, the term is often expanded to "action-seed-result." The basic idea is that karma is a process in which actions develop into experiences in the same way that seeds develop into plants that bear fruit.

Karma is not a static process, with one action producing one result. It is not a simple cause-and-effect process such as pushing down on the brake pedal to bring a car to a stop.

Karma is a more complex growth process. Every action establishes a predisposition to similar actions and perceptions. Repeated patterns of behavior evoke reactions from others and even affect our sensory experience of the world. The growth of reactive patterns has no inherent dynamic that leads to their dissolution. In other words, we can spin forever in our own karma. As Gampopa writes in his *Jewel Ornament of Liberation,* the cycle of existence is notorious for being without end.

According to classical teaching, an action becomes a karmic seed when four conditions are met: activation, execution, object, and completion.

Activation means that the action is premeditated; we first think of acting and then prepare to act. For example, a would-be thief sees a person leave an ATM with a handful of money, thinks about stealing the money, and then looks around to see that no one is watching before approaching the bank customer. Action that takes place without premeditation does not have the same karmic result. The distinction is recognized by our legal system in the difference between murder and manslaughter.

Execution means active participation; we actually perform the action or cause another person to perform the action. In the ATM example, the thief either steals the money himself or directs another person to steal the money for him.

Object means the action affects another person. The person from whom the money is stolen is affected. Stealing in your imagination or in a dream is not significant karmically, since no person is affected.

Completion means that the action is completed; we experience the completion of the action. When the thief has the money in his hands or in his control, the action is completed. If the thief is shot and killed before actually taking possession of the money, the action is not completed, since the thief doesn't experience having the money.

When these four conditions are present, an action is like a seed planted in the stream of experience. The seed grows, affecting how we experience the world in four different ways. To return to the thief example, the first result is that greed consumes the thief. He can never have enough money. The second result is that people guard their possessions when he is around and avoid him or refuse to interact with him. The third result is that he believes that the only way he can survive is by stealing. The fourth result is that the world appears to him as a wasteland, devoid of opportunities, wealth, and enjoyment.

The vicious cycle of action and experienced result reinforces the behavioral pattern. To step out of the cycle, we stop letting reactive patterns drive behavior. The key, of course, is attention. By learning to think, speak, and act in attention, we see more and more clearly how actions reinforce conditioned ways of thinking, feeling, and behaving and how conditioning forms and shapes what we experience. As attention develops, we step out of patterned existence and into the mystery of being. We respond to situations instead of reacting and act volitionally instead of habitually. We experience more and more freedom rather than a downward spiral of ever stronger conditioning.

Traditionally, the four results of karma are said to mature over the course of lifetimes. That view raises the issue of rebirth and such questions as "What is reborn?" and "How are karmic propensities carried from one life to the next?" Many people hold that belief in rebirth is necessary to practice Buddhism, but I disagree. The essence of karma is that actions determine experience: actions based on reactive patterns reinforce patterns and lead to suffering; actions based on attention and presence dismantle patterns and lead to opening. When we understand how behavior affects experience, we understand karma. Belief in past and future lifetimes isn't an issue. Appreciation of karma does not come from intellectual understanding or belief. It comes from seeing directly how patterns and conditioning operate, a seeing that comes about only through cultivating attention and uncovering awareness. This is the subject matter for the chapters that follow.

> It is a misconception to think
> That I shall experience
>   [suffering in a future life],
> For it is another who will die
> And another who will be born.
>
> —*Shantiveda, A Guide to the Bodhisattva's Way of Life*

Before we address these issues, however, let's look at how Buddha Shakyamuni is regarded in Buddhism. Is he God? Is he a god? Are his teachings regarded as literal truth? Are present-day teachers pale reflections of Buddha Shakyamuni? What weight does their experience carry?

THE THREE JEWELS AND REFUGE

In Buddhism, we start with the experience of suffering. Unlike most religions, Buddhist practice does not posit a creator or an arbitrator of divine justice. Speculation about why a supreme being would create suffering is unnecessary, since there is no such being. Questions about the justness or fairness of life don't arise, because there is no individual, agency, or power whose role is to make life fair. We come to

Buddhist practice because of a feeling of separation, emptiness, or lack of presence in life. Standing outside the vibrancy of life is no longer an option. We want to enter directly into the mystery of being.

The Three Jewels

Even though Buddhism posits no creator, when you enter a Buddhist temple you often find statues of Buddha Shakyamuni or other teachers. You may observe people bowing to these statues or bowing to a shrine. If Buddha isn't a supreme being, then what is going on?

Buddha

Buddha Shakyamuni is not a god or a supreme being in the usual religious sense. He was a person who lived approximately 2,500 years ago, who, through his own efforts, came to understand that suffering arises from the emotional reactions associated with a sense of self—a sense of self that separates us from the mystery of being, leaving us feeling incomplete, not fully present, and isolated.

When the Buddha saw and understood that the sense of self is a misperception, the reactive processes of suffering just fell apart. Therefore, Buddha Shakyamuni is regarded as a teacher rather than a god. A teacher is an individual who gives instruction. Buddha Shakyamuni discovered how to bring an end to suffering and gave instructions in how to do so.

Dharma

The teachings and instructions of Buddha Shakyamuni are known as the Dharma. Whereas Buddha is the teacher, the Dharma is the way. The term *Buddhism* is unfortunate, since the suffix *-ism* is usually used to denote a set of beliefs and does not carry the sense of instruction that characterizes the Dharma. In Tibetan, for instance, the phrase for the Dharma means "instructions for awakening internally." No set of beliefs is implied.

Historically, Buddha's teachings were first transmitted orally from teacher to student. Only after several hundred years were they put into written form. Over the centuries, numerous masters, working from their own experience and insight, have revised, refined, and reformulated the teachings. Variations in interpretation, emphasis on one practice or another, and circumstances in different countries gave rise to the large number of traditions and schools that constitute Buddhism today. The Dharma consists of the teachings of Buddha Shakyamuni, canonical scriptures written at later dates, and commentaries composed by masters, with all their texts, oral instructions, guidelines, and sayings.

Although the original scriptures, the sutras and tantras, are greatly revered and studied carefully to this day, Buddhism has consistently resisted a common religious tendency to enthrone one set of teachings as the one and only truth. Buddhism has always recognized the experience and teachings of contemporary masters as equal in validity to the teachings recorded in traditional scriptures. In each generation, teachers rely on their own experience to explain how to wake up in terms relevant to the students in front of them. The Dharma is not a static body of teaching. It is constantly evolving and developing according to the needs of students in each generation and culture.

Sangha

Traditionally, the Sangha refers to those individuals who have made the practice of the Dharma their life, that is, ordained monks and nuns. The monastic tradition, historically, has been the backbone of Buddhism. Monastics have faithfully transmitted the teachings from generation to generation for over two millennia.

More generally, the Sangha consists of all individuals who practice the Dharma with the intention of waking up into the mystery of being. The Sangha is a community based on shared intention, not on mutual dependence. Just as the term *Buddhism* incorrectly implies belief, so does the term *Buddhist* incorrectly imply believer. A person who practices the Dharma is, more accurately, a follower or traveler of a path, the path that Buddha Shakyamuni discovered.

The path is far from easy, and the difficulties and challenges are considerable. Fellow travelers, companions in the path, provide us not only with support but also with the benefit of their own experience and understanding. When a colleague of mine was asked why he thought the Sangha was important, he replied, "Because this path is so damn difficult we need all the support we can get."

Collectively, the Buddha, the Dharma, and the Sangha are known as the three jewels. Like jewels, they are rare and precious. The three jewels are deeply revered in Buddhism, but not because they have supernormal or magical powers or because we will be rewarded by revering them. We revere Buddha Shakyamuni because he demonstrated that it was possible to step out of the confusion of ordinary reactive existence. We revere the Dharma because it provides us with a way to open to the mystery of being. We revere the Sangha because these individuals have, through their efforts, made our own practice possible.

When we bow to the Buddha, we are not bowing to a supreme being; we are acknowledging our own potential to wake up into presence. When we bow to the Dharma, we are not bowing to sacred books; we are acknowledging that these teachings provide us with a path out of our own confusion. When we bow to the Sangha, we are not bowing to them because we feel they are holier or more powerful than we are; we are simply acknowledging that we share the same intention to follow this path.

Refuge

The original Buddhist metaphor for entering the path of awakening is refuge. Buddha Shakyamuni faced the mystery of being in order to understand the nature of suffering. In his awakening, he uncovered the possibility of presence.

When we set out on our own path of practice, we need a direction. In Buddhism, the direction is described by the phrase "taking refuge in the three jewels."

Where do we turn for peace? Where do we turn to become free of suffering? Where do we turn to understand the mystery of life? Many people take refuge in money, beauty, power, fame, relationships, or achievements. They think or feel that if they can get enough money or whatever, they will be happy and will suffer no more. In other words, they look outside for an end to suffering. The central insight of Buddhism is that we cannot bring an end to suffering by looking outside. We must look inside.

Refuge takes on multiple levels of meaning in the course of practice. We first take refuge by acknowledging the example of Buddha Shakyamuni. We take refuge in Buddha as the teacher, the one who showed the way. We take refuge in the Dharma as the instructions for practice. We take refuge in the Sangha because the members of the Sangha provide inspiration, guidance, and support on the path.

As experience and understanding grow, we move to a more internal sense of refuge. When we see that suffering does not come from outside but from our own reactive patterns, we see that to take refuge in the Buddha means that we take refuge in the possibility of presence, being free from the turmoil of reactive patterns. We see that to take refuge in the Dharma means that we use the instructions to cultivate attention and insight so that we experience presence. To take refuge in the Sangha means that we work with our teachers and companions in the practice of presence.

When, through our efforts, we begin to experience presence and original mind, we discover yet another level of meaning in refuge. As mentioned above in the discussion on the three levels of understanding, our mind is originally empty, clear, and unimpeded. To take refuge in the Buddha is to rest in the emptiness of original mind, free from any reference or defining characteristic. To take refuge in the Dharma is to experience the clarity of original mind, the natural awareness that knows what experience is and how experience arises. To take refuge in the Sangha is to be one with the unimpeded arising and subsiding of experience, free from the three poisons of attraction, aversion, and indifference.

How does one take refuge? The words are very simple:

> *I take refuge in the Buddha.*
> *I take refuge in the Dharma.*
> *I take refuge in the Sangha.*

This prayer is repeated daily by Buddhists all over the world, who wish to keep in mind the path they have chosen and what following it means.

WHAT TO TRUST?

Buddhism relies on direct experience to such an extent that in the Tibetan tradition a short verse summarizes how to approach a teacher, how to understand what is taught, and what understanding is important.

> *Do not rely on the human individual; rely on the teaching.*
> *Do not rely on the words; rely on the meaning.*
> *Do not rely on the apparent meaning; rely on the real meaning.*
> *Do not rely on ordinary consciousness; rely on pristine awareness.*

The first line is a reminder that the teacher is human and may not always act as an exemplar of the teaching. The shortcomings and weaknesses of a teacher in no way diminish the power and effectiveness of the teachings. Remember that the teacher isn't there to save you. He or she is there to teach you. Learn everything you can, and then practice to make the teachings your own.

The second line is a warning against literalism. Buddhism has been practiced for over two thousand years in cultures ranging from the

Caspian Sea to the Philippines, and now throughout Europe and North and South America. The words used to express the teachings in one culture may have a different, even contradictory, meaning in another culture. Instead of relying on the words, strive to understand what the words mean as lived experience.

The third line is a reminder that the teachings have many levels of meaning. The intention of teaching in Buddhism is to point the student toward the experience of original mind. Sometimes a student misses the intention of an instruction and attaches to the instruction as having meaning in and of itself. When that happens, the teacher is like a person pointing at the moon with his finger, while the student is like a person who focuses on the finger and never looks at the moon.

Finally, the fourth line is an instruction to rely on original mind, pristine awareness, and not on ordinary consciousness, which works only through ideas, notions, concepts, reactive emotions, and subject-object dualism. Pristine awareness, our human heritage, is pure awareness. Everything presented in the following pages is aimed at removing the reactive patterns and confusion that prevent pure awareness from manifesting in our lives.

Remember these four lines as you read. Remember them as you practice. Remember them again if you ever teach others.

CHAPTER 3

Cultivating Attention

"I will instruct you in metaphysics," said Nasrudin to a neighbour in whom he saw a spark of understanding, albeit a small one.

"I should be delighted," said the man; "come to my house any time and talk to me."

Nasrudin realized that the man was thinking that mystical knowledge could be transmitted entirely by word of mouth. He said no more.

A few days later the neighbour called the Mulla from his roof. "Nasrudin, I want your help to blow my fire, the charcoal is going out."

"Certainly," said Nasrudin. "My breath is at your disposal—come over here and you can have as much of it as you can carry away."

—IDRIES SHAH,
The Pleasantries of the Incredible Mulla Nasrudin

Imagine that you are in a wooden boat in the middle of the ocean. The boat is sinking, and sharks are circling around you. You realize that you have to build a new boat out of the old, leaky boat, and you have to do it without sinking. How do you do it?

We come to meditation for many reasons. Fundamentally, however, we come because the boat is sinking—we can't go on living as we have before. The sharks, the habituated patterns, are circling.

Perhaps stress in your life has reached the breaking point and you know that you have to change or die. Perhaps, in the face of a major change—divorce, illness, a career shift, retirement—you realize that you can't function the way you used to. You may have been touched by an experience that dropped the bottom out of your life. Perhaps you wake up one day feeling no connection to your life and realize that you are one of the walking dead. No matter what brings us to meditation, we start to practice because we want to change the way we live.

Change comes about in one of two ways: by force or by choice.

An attorney, for instance, is pressured to take on more cases to increase his billable hours. He spends more time in case preparation and settlement negotiations, less time relaxing with his wife and family. He disregards the growing tension and rigidity in his body, relying on muscle relaxants to keep him functioning at work and sleeping pills to put him to sleep at night. The drugs are increasingly ineffective, however, and the attorney's health deteriorates until he collapses and can no longer function. This scenario is an example of forced change.

Forced change happens when we are not present in our lives. We dismiss signs that something is wrong and push forward until established structures break down. In the case of the attorney, he ignored the tension in his body until he collapsed and could no longer work. Of course, he can continue to ignore his body and keep working until he dies. Either way, he changes.

Forced change is the consequence of being locked into a set view of who and what we are, regardless of circumstances. As conflict between actual circumstances and our set view of things intensifies, something has to give. Change takes place, often violently and tragically. Ignoring symptoms causes health to deteriorate, obsession with work causes marriages to fail, and ruthless competitiveness leads to ineffective action, causing careers to be lost.

When change takes place by force, we have no say in which part of our life collapses. That is determined by forces outside our intention. We are stuck in habituated patterns and cannot see the needed changes or the inevitable consequences of our behavior. We are, in effect, victims of our own patterned behavior, and we remain so until we wake up to what is happening and take responsibility for making changes in our lives. Forced change, even when the stakes are a matter of life and death, does not, by its nature, lead to heightened awareness or any sort of internal transformation. Health, relationships, careers, businesses, and countries may fall apart, and the same blind patterns keep operating in the ruins.

Change by choice, however, is transformation. As long as patterned behaviors consume our energy and attention, change is impossible. Habituated patterns remain intact and bring back again and again the discomfort and problems we experienced before. Change by choice becomes possible only when we have free attention, a level of attention that is not completely absorbed by conditioning. The ability to act and respond (rather than react) depends on the ability to maintain such a level of attention.

Internal transformative work is primarily destructive. Those parts of our lives that result from and depend on habituated patterns will fall apart. In other words, to do this work, we must be willing to die to the life we have known. The essence of the dismantling process is the ability to maintain attention in the face of habituated reactions and not be consumed by them. Therefore, the initial work of internal transformation is cultivating attention, and meditation practice is one of the oldest and most reliable methods.

The essence of all internal transformative work is original mind—the open, natural awareness that is our human heritage. Conditioned patterns of perception and behavior prevent this natural awareness from manifesting in our lives. Internal transformative work consists of dismantling habituated patterns that cause us to ignore what is taking place inside and around us. Attention is the primary tool. As the Vietnamese Zen teacher Thich Nhat Hanh once said, "The practice of meditation is the study of what is going on. What's going on is very important."

WHAT IS ATTENTION?

What happens when you look at a flower? Perhaps it triggers a memory and the memory replays itself in your mind. Where did the flower go? Oh, yes, you are holding it, but you aren't aware of it as the memory replays itself. Perhaps you are entranced by the delicate colors and the shape of the petals. Again, what happens to the flower? In both cases, the flower disappears and only the reaction remains. This is called *passive attention*.

When an experience absorbs emotional energy, whether the experience is a flower, a thought, a feeling, or a belief, attention goes passive and we are less present with what's going on. Emotional energy shifts to a lower level. We are, in effect, passive participants in the experience. We say, "That flower caught my attention," making it, not us, the active agent. Passive attention is unstable, reactive, and involuntary. We don't stay with the flower but are quickly caught by memories, associations, or details. The whole process is a reaction—"flower, white, white dress, prom date, happiness, oh, that was such a long time ago, I wonder what happened to him"—a sequence of thoughts and feelings triggered by the flower, a sequence that flows automatically with no intention on our part and, once started, has nothing to do with the flower.

Suppose you look at the flower, and your experience of seeing it is vivid and clear. Thoughts triggered by associations arise, but you aren't distracted by them. Perhaps the flower does stimulate a poignant memory and you feel a surge of emotion. You feel it, but you aren't lost in memories or feelings. You remain vividly aware of the flower in your hand and all the memories and feelings associated with it. That is *active attention.*

When attention remains directed at an object and there is a shift in clarity and vividness, we experience active attention. Two points are important. First, active attention is not an intellectual function. It has power for the same reason that emotions have power—energy. Second, active attention is a function of levels of energy. To be in attention means that the energy directed at what is experienced is at a higher level than the energy in the reactive patterns triggered by that experience.

Active attention is volitional, stable, and inclusive. We choose to direct attention; we aren't simply reacting to a stimulus. Active attention is not disrupted by sounds, thoughts, sights, or other events in our experience. Active attention is inclusive, allowing us to be aware not only of the object at hand but also of whatever else we are experiencing at the moment. Because active attention is not disrupted by habituated patterns, the more we live in attention, the less we fall victim to the reactive processes that are operating in us.

Active attention is the door through which we step out of a life of reaction and habituation and into a life of presence. The energy of active attention penetrates patterns, disrupts their operation, and eventually dismantles them.

Cultivating Attention and the Mystery of Being

Many people initially approach meditation thinking that they will learn to control the mind. Control is an illusion; we cannot even direct what our next thought will be.

Pound for pound, the amoeba is the most vicious animal on earth.

What do amoeba have to do with meditation? Nothing, of course, but did you expect to be thinking about amoeba when you chose to read this book? We cannot and do not control what will happen in the next moment or tomorrow, much less in the course of life.

Life is a mystery. Life is what we experience, and we cannot and do not know what the next moment of experience will be. While we live in a mystery, we reactively and automatically try to control what we experience. To be present in our lives, we have to let go of the illusion of control, and that is exactly what we do in meditation.

Attention is not a concrete object that we can manufacture or reproduce. Attention is an ability that can be developed, just as physical stamina or flexibility can. Attention is cultivated by repeatedly exercising it, just as flexibility is developed by repeated stretching. In meditation, we first exercise attention in a small way, by experiencing the breath—feeling the coming and going of the breath in attention. As attention grows, it becomes stronger and can operate at higher and higher levels of energy. As a result, we become progressively more present in our lives.

Cultivating attention is like growing a plant. Nobody makes a plant grow. A seed grows into a plant by itself when conditions are right. In meditation practice, we provide the right conditions for the seed of attention to grow.

We all have the seed of attention already. The seed is natural awareness, or original mind. Natural awareness is present in every moment of experience but is usually obscured by conditioned patterns. For attention to grow, the operation of habituated patterns has to be interrupted, at least temporarily. A formal meditation practice is a crucial element in the effort to interrupt the operation of those patterns.

Meditation: Cultivating Attention

There is really only one way to cultivate attention: take a simple activity that requires attention but not much intellectual effort, and do it again and again. Whenever attention lapses, bring it back to the task and continue. The activity, whatever it is, serves as the basis for attention. In this case, we use the activity of breathing.

Meditation comes down to one key principle:

Return to what is already there and rest.

This principle is applied in three ways: to our physical posture, to the way we breathe, and to the way we direct the mind.

Body

Take a moment right now, and imagine sitting in attention. As soon as you pay attention to the body, you become aware of a natural straightness in the body. Let the body move to express that natural straightness.

Notice how your chin drops a little, how your neck and spine straighten and lengthen, and how the rest of your body falls into line. Keep your eyes slightly open—not expressly looking at anything, but open. Notice how you are more present and awake in this posture. Once you recognize the feeling of natural straightness in the body, you realize that it is always there. All you have to do is let this natural straightness express itself in your posture.

The first application of the key principle is to physical posture: *whenever you notice that you have lost the natural straightness of the body, return to it and rest.*

Natural straightness is not tense or strained, but the body, burdened by years of conditioning, may be unused to expressing it. Consequently, you may experience discomfort in the limbs and back for a while as the body adjusts to the sitting position. Depending on how burdened the body is, the adjustment may take a few weeks or even months. By bringing attention to how you sit, you move out of the physical expression of reactive patterns. Sitting becomes easier as the body relaxes and lets go of its conditioned rigidity and tension.

Traditionally you sit cross-legged. A meditation cushion is used to raise the buttocks off the ground so that the back is naturally straight, but physical limitations may make a meditation bench or a chair a better choice. You should be reasonably comfortable when you sit to practice meditation. Straining, tension, and constant pain are not conducive to cultivating attention. Gently yet consistently apply the principle: return to natural straightness in the body and rest. Allow the body to make its own adjustments.

The physical posture is also a symbol of the intention of practice. Sitting expresses the intention to be stable and present. Not leaning against anything expresses the intention to rely on your own capabilities. Keeping the eyes open expresses the intention to be present in the world without distraction.

Breath

Take another moment. Sit in natural straightness, and imagine breathing with attention. Immediately, the breath becomes natural, unforced, relaxed. Breathing with attention involves letting the body do the breathing.

Don't try to control the breath. You may experience tension between the body and the breath. The tension indicates that you are no longer breathing naturally. It is often the result of an emotional pattern that has been triggered and is undermining your effort in attention.

The second application of the key principle is to breathing: *whenever you notice tension between the body and the breath, return to what is already there—the natural relaxed breathing the body knows how to do*. Let go, let the body breathe, and rest.

Many meditation and energy transformation techniques use special ways of breathing. These methods have their uses but are not our concern here. Our concern is to cultivate attention so that it becomes a natural and uncontrived aspect of our lives.

Because we use the breath in formal practice, we also use it to reconnect with attention amid the ups and downs of daily life. A Zen teacher, when asked how he practiced presence in his life, replied, "Sometimes my mind gets so confused with thoughts and feelings that I don't know which way to turn. But then I remember my breath, and I am one with my treasure once again."

Mind

The third step in the formal practice is to bring the mind to the breath. What is mind? Mind is experience. Mind is all the thoughts, feelings, and sensations that constitute our experience of life. To bring the mind to the breath means that we pay attention to the experience of breathing.

First, we place attention on the breath.

As before, take a moment to feel the natural straightness in the body. Feel the natural flow and rhythm of the breath. Now, put a slight emphasis on the exhalation—a slight emphasis, not enough to disturb the rhythm of the breath.

Thoughts stop and you are just aware of the breath. You are not thinking about the breath; you are just aware of it going out. Placing with intention cuts through passive attention. Attention becomes active, and you volitionally experience the breath.

Second, let attention rest on the breath.

Once you have placed attention on the breath, let it rest there. There is nothing more you need to do. Breathe, resting the attention on the breath, feeling the breath going in and out.

Attention is clear, stable, and natural. Thoughts and feelings arise, but they are of no consequence. Sit, intentionally experiencing the breath coming in and going out.

At some point, of course, active attention decays into passive attention and you become involved in a thought, memory, or image or slip into a dull or sleepy state. A moment, a few seconds, or several minutes later you suddenly become aware that you are no longer resting on the breath. The thought, feeling, or sensation has gone and you are once again aware of what you are doing—practicing meditation. Breathe out to return attention to the breath.

To help identify distraction, say "thought" or "thinking" as soon as you wake up from whatever distracted you. Of course, you could tell yourself that you aren't meditating properly or that you are a failure at meditation or that meditation doesn't work or that the time is going unbearably slowly or that you are uncomfortable and want to do something else. But all such internal chitchat is just more thinking, more thoughts, more distraction.

In the moment of recognition, the distraction is already gone. All that remains is to return to the breath.

The third application of the key principle is to mind: *whenever you realize that you have been distracted, return to the clear, stable attention that rests on the breath.*

Meditation, in the way that I'm describing it, does not mean concentration on the breath. The effort to hold attention by concentrating creates tension. Attention keeps falling off the breath, no matter what you do. Tension only makes it fall off more often. You end up tired and frustrated, not relaxed and awake.

Instead of trying to concentrate, rest, feeling the breath coming and going. The number of disturbances is not important. Neither is what distracts us. Michael Conklin, a friend and colleague of mine, says:

> We can't control how many thoughts we have in a period of meditation. We can't control what our next thought will be. We can't control whether the next thought will distract us from the breath. And we can't control how long we will be distracted. All we can do is return to the breath when we recognize that we have been distracted.

The essence of meditation is returning to what is already there and resting. Return to the natural straightness of the body and rest. Return to the natural rhythm of the breath and rest. Return to the natural awareness of the breath and rest. Don't think of meditation as holding attention on the breath. Think of it as placing attention on the breath and resting, over and over again.

Three qualities will serve you well: patience as you realize that you keep falling into distraction, gentleness as you realize that you can't avoid some distraction, and a sense of humor as you observe that the mind is like a monkey.

Commentary

Practical Points on Eyes and Intellect

First, although I explicitly advise my students to meditate on the breath with the eyes open, the question of eyes opened or closed comes up again and again. There is no right or wrong way here. The northern schools of Buddhism generally recommend eyes open, while the southern schools recommend meditating with eyes closed. The difference is in philosophy: the southern schools traditionally emphasize withdrawing from the distractions of engagement with the world, while the northern schools stress waking into presence in each moment.

When the intention is to be present in the world, I have found that meditating with the eyes at least partially open works better. We tend to be more awake, the internal movement of thought is noticed sooner, and attention is more easily extended to daily life. Double vision, blurred vision, watery eyes, and other minor discomforts are experienced initially. After a week or two, however, the conditioned link between attention and looking begins to weaken. The eyes are open, but you don't look through them as you rest with the breath. As the eyes come to rest, so does the mind.

> Somewhere in this process, you will come face-to-face with the sudden and shocking realization that you are completely crazy. Your mind is a shrieking, gibbering madhouse on wheels barreling pell-mell down the hill, utterly out of control and hopeless. No problem. You are not crazier than you were yesterday. It has always been this way and you never noticed.
>
> —*Henepola Gunaratana*

Second, does meditation involve the intellect? No. Meditation is experiential, not intellectual. Buddhism talks endlessly about mind, but in Sanskrit and Tibetan *mind* does not mean intellect; instead, mind is everything we experience. Mind includes sensations, feelings, and the heart as well as thoughts and the intellect.

The use of the word *mind* has introduced an intellectual and cognitive bias in English, which is neither valid nor helpful in this context. "Put the mind on the breath" does not mean "Think about the breath." It means "Experience the breath" or "Feel the breath with your heart."

The Backdoor Approach

The key principle of meditation is to return to what is already there and rest. This explicit and direct instruction is the front-door approach. Sometimes it is better to go through the back door and elicit the appropriate effort while avoiding the confusion often generated by a set of explicit instructions. Here is a set of backdoor instructions from the mountain hermit tradition of Tibet:

> *Body like a mountain.*
> *Breath like the wind.*
> *Mind like the sky.*

Let the body be like a mountain, effortlessly still, and you return to the natural straightness of the body.

Let the breath be like the wind, free, with no sense of restriction, and you return to the natural rhythm of the breath.

Let the mind be like the sky, open and clear, including but undisturbed by thoughts, feelings, and sensations, and you return to attention and natural awareness.

Meditation is a constant returning to natural wakefulness and original mind.

Purpose, Methods, Effects, and Results

Many problems in meditation practice come from confusion about what we think should happen, what we want to happen, and what actually happens. One way to clear up this confusion is to be clear about the purpose, method, effects, and results of meditation practice.

The *purpose* of meditation practice is to cultivate attention. The *method* is what we do to cultivate attention—place attention on the breath and rest. *Effects* are the experiences that arise during meditation practice. *Results* are the qualities and abilities that develop from doing the practice.

Consider the same four categories in the context of running. The purpose of jogging is to be physically fit. The method is to regularly run a set distance or time at a set pace. The effects of running vary. You are energized and invigorated on some days, tired and worn out on others, stiff or sore on some days, flexible and relaxed on others. The effects vary from day to day, on some days positive, on other days negative. The results are increased strength, muscle tone, endurance, and general fitness.

The same distinctions apply to meditation. The purpose is to cultivate attention. The method is placing and resting attention on the breath. The effects are varied. On some days meditation is like a peaceful rest in infinite open space. On other days it is more like a struggle through a howling storm. On some days attention is clear and stable. On other days all we experience is distraction and pain. The results are an increase in the level of attention, the ability to stay in attention in both formal practice and daily life, and less reactivity in our lives.

One common form of confusion is to take the positive effects or the results of practice as the method of practice.

New students often tell me how frustrated they are with meditation. They've read a book or two, and the instructions include such phrases as "Open your mind," "Be centered," "Let your mind be empty," or "Be one with your body." They can't figure out what to do because these "instructions" are effects of practice, not methods.

When students sit down and try to feel centered, try to open their minds, and try to be one with their bodies, nothing happens and they end up feeling frustrated.

Tell a tense person to relax, and he will usually become tenser in the effort. He is tense because he doesn't know how to relax. Tell him to take a deep breath, let it out slowly, then take another breath, and let it out slowly. Then he will relax. The method is breathing slowly and deeply. The result is relaxation. In meditation, the method is resting attention on the breath. When you do this, you will at some point feel centered, your mind will open and relax, and you will feel more connected with your body.

Another common confusion is to take effects as purpose.

People often come to meditation with the hope of feeling centered or of experiencing a clear mind, free from thoughts. After a week or two of practice, they are frustrated or disappointed. "I can't meditate," they say. "My mind is all agitated, and when it's not agitated, I fall asleep. This obviously doesn't work." They have confused the purpose of practice with the effects. They haven't yet appreciated that meditation requires effort in repeated returning to the breath and working through distractions such as agitation and dullness. Clear, stable attention develops from practice, not just because you decide to have a clear mind. To view turbulence as an error rather than something to work with is to confuse effects with purpose. Such an attitude undermines confidence and prevents attention from developing.

To avoid such problems in meditation or in any other discipline, be clear about these elements. Know the purpose, understand what to do, and do just that. Observe what arises, but don't get caught up in experience, and be patient and consistent in the practice. Let the results develop over time.

PURPOSE, METHOD, EFFECTS, AND RESULTS

CATEGORY	DEFINITION	MEDITATION	EXAMPLE
purpose	the aim of the practice	cultivating attention	staying fit
method	what you do	return to what is already there and rest	jog
effects	experiences that arise as you practice	dull, distracted, relaxed, clear, stable, anxious	energized, invigorated, stiff, sore, tired
results	abilities that develop over time	increased clarity and stability in attention, less reactivity	increased strength, stamina, and muscle tone

SIX SUPPORTS FOR MEDITATION PRACTICE

Like a stone thrown into a pond, meditation practice creates ripples that radiate throughout life. Meditation does not, however, magically change your life. Your life changes only when the attention you develop in meditation operates in the course of day-to-day living. The first effort is to make meditation practice a stable element in your day. This effort can be summarized in six points: conducive space, basic needs, contentment, manageable life, ethical behavior, and letting go of drama.

Conducive Space

Clearly, you have to have a place where you can actually sit down and practice meditation. It needs to be safe, quiet, and free from disturbances such as loud, unexpected noises or a strong source of light directly opposite your sitting position. Don't meditate in total darkness or with only a single light source such as a candle. The lighting should be even and not too strong, like the natural light of early morning.

Complete silence is not necessary. After all, the aim is to be present in our lives without distraction. The rustle of the wind, the sounds of the street, or background noise from around the house actually serves to increase your ability to rest in attention.

The choice of practice space reflects your attitude toward meditation. A clean, tidy area reflects the value placed on meditation. When meditation practice is relegated to a closet or bathroom, you are really squeezing it into your life. If you have to squeeze meditation into your life, other priorities soon squeeze it out. The priority given to practice is reflected in where and when you meditate. Meditation needs to be approached directly and unambiguously: either you make it a priority and practice, or you don't and it falls by the wayside.

Practice takes time. I recommend starting with a half-hour session. The surface level of tension and disturbance typically takes fifteen to twenty minutes to dissipate. Only then do you begin to experience what is underneath. Fifteen or twenty minutes of meditation are still highly beneficial, but a half-hour session makes a qualitative difference in the cultivation of attention. As ability, confidence, and interest increase, you can increase the practice session to forty minutes or an hour.

The time of day you practice is not as important as consistency. Practice meditation every day. Most people find that the early morning works best. Other times are before lunch, at the end of the workday, or in the evening, each of which has advantages and disadvantages. Whatever the choice, meditation time needs to be an inviolate time that is free from all other demands, a time when you don't need to answer the phone or attend to someone else, a time when you can sit, place attention on the breath, and be there completely.

On the practical level, you will make better progress if you eliminate all choice or decision making in connection with meditation practice. Practice at a set time for a set period of time. Use a timer. Before clocks came to Tibet, people timed their meditation by putting a lighted stick of incense between their toes. When the incense burned down, the period was over. A timer eliminates burned toes. It also eliminates both the need to check the time and the temptation to cut the session short. If the session is difficult, sit until the timer goes off and learn to sit through difficulty. If the session is pleasurable, stop at the designated time and learn not to cling to special states or experiences. A timer also removes the need to check the time during a meditation session so you can let go any worries that you will be late for a meeting or taking the children to school.

Basic Needs Met

Basic needs are food, clothing, and shelter. When these needs aren't met, your survival is threatened and you become reactive, edgy, and anxious. To practice meditation, you need a solid foundation, free from such primal worries, so that you can sit, relax, and rest with the breath.

When engaging in internal transformative work, you still need to eat and sleep. As Buddha Shakyamuni learned after starving himself for six years, he needed to take care of his body and mind. Energy and clarity are needed to dismantle habituated patterns and open to the mystery of being.

Spiritual traditions are full of stories about people who leave society and live only on what comes to them through gifts or donations. Their foundation is a strong and stable determination to accept and work with uncertainty. Because of their strength of mind, they can practice effectively even in uncertain or harsh conditions. Most of us don't have that strength of mind. We need a more concrete foundation: food to eat, clothing to keep us warm, and a place to rest our heads.

Contentment

Contentment means knowing what's enough. How much money is enough? How much beauty? How much fitness? How much status? How much fame? How much power? How much knowledge? How much love? How much happiness? How much security?

Can you at least imagine having enough money, power, status, or whatever else you desire? If not, you are facing a black hole of insatiable need that drains energy from practice and life. No one can sit in attention when driven by insatiable need. You are, in effect, taking refuge in an object of obsession, acting on the feeling, "If I can get enough of this, then everything will be all right; I will be okay." The attitude is pure delusion. Anything that comes from outside you can be taken away. Where is the security in that?

As attention develops, the objects of desire and obsession are seen more clearly for what they are—objects that have little or nothing to do with the effort to be present in life.

Manageable Life

A manageable life is one in which you can breathe. Your life is not so full that you have to be concerned with one matter or another all the time. You need to be able to sit and rest, at least for the period of formal practice. You will know soon after you start a meditation practice whether your life is manageable by how frequently you meditate and what distracts you during your meditation sessions. When you see how your life takes all your time and energy, the first impulse is to cut down on activities and responsibilities. Where do you start? What do you cut? When you are just beginning to practice, don't start eliminating things immediately, because you may be unable to tell what to let go and what to keep.

Use the practice of meditation to organize your life. Because you have decided to sit every day, you have to make time for practice. Tighten up your life a little. Cut a few minutes here and a few minutes there until you have the half hour of meditation time.

As attention develops, your relationship with life changes. You will know clearly and directly what is important and meaningful. Then simplification takes place naturally.

Ethical Behavior

Let's keep the ethics discussion simple. Forget about the list of do's and don'ts of most ethical and moral codes. Rely on your own experience.

Imagine that you are in a situation and you know the right thing to do. You hesitate because it's going to cost you something to do it. You may lose some money, prestige, influence, or even respect. You overcome your hesitation and do it anyway. How long do you think about it afterward?

Imagine the same situation again. You know the right thing to do, and you don't do it. Now how long do you think about it afterward?

For most of us, the answer to the first question is "not very long" or "not at all," while the answer to the second question is "a long time." That difference is the essence of ethics in this approach to practice. When we act ethically, we have less on our mind. With less on our mind, we sit in attention more easily.

Letting Go of Drama

Finally, is everything a big deal, or can you let go of emotional reactivity? Emotional reactivity takes many forms: stubbornly maintaining set positions, compulsively clinging to emotional connections, desperately consuming every experience in your life, spinning elaborate rationalizations to justify your actions, or falling to pieces under the slightest pressure. If you can't step out of reactivity for even a moment, you won't meditate. You will be too busy reacting to the current crisis. To meditate, you have to let go of confusing emotional reactions long enough to sit for at least a few minutes.

Constant vigilance is necessary if you are going to recognize how emotional reactions are operating. Reactive patterns can even use elements of a meditation practice to maintain their operation. One person worked independently as a consultant. She was a bit short of work but had enough to live for several months, yet her meditation practice was inconsistent—a day here, a day there. Whenever a potential client appeared, she worked day and night on a presentation, justifying her neglect of practice with the rationalization that she had to have her basic needs met. In her case, a pattern (never feeling that she has enough) used an element of the practice (attention to basic needs) to disrupt her effort in attention. We can easily fall into the drama of our reactive lives. Constant vigilance and a certain ruthlessness with internal material serve us well.

Meditation practice will definitely reinforce these six basic supports. The initial effort, however, has to come from your intention to change the way you live by putting these six supports in place. Without them, practice quickly becomes an inconvenience and is soon forgotten.

DEVELOPING ATTENTION

Mindfulness

In the beginning, meditation is a struggle with too many thoughts. For some people, the experience is so shocking that they think they have gone crazy. Others think that meditation has caused them to have more thoughts and be more distracted than they are normally. Welcome to "the monkey mind"—a Buddhist term for the capricious activity of thinking. Actually, the thoughts have been going on the whole time, but we never noticed how active our minds were.

Imagine that you are having coffee with a friend at a sidewalk café. While you sit and talk, you pay no attention to the cars on the street. When you finish your conversation and start to cross the street, however, you notice exactly how many cars are coming and going. Obviously, your standing on the curb and looking at the street didn't cause more cars to drive by.

Technically, mindfulness means being present with the object of attention—in this case, the breath. After you've been practicing for a while, a miracle happens. You just rest with the breath. Maybe the resting lasts for only two or three breaths, but the experience of attention is unmistakable. Congratulations. You have just experienced mindfulness.

Of course, the first time this happens, you immediately think, "Oh, good, I'm resting on the breath," and fall once again into distraction. You now know, however, from personal experience what resting in attention with the breath is, what it feels like, and that it is possible. Thinking isn't necessary. Concentrating isn't necessary. Mindfulness is very simple: all you have to do is rest, feeling the breath going in and out.

The experience of mindfulness has three distinct results: confidence increases, the possibility of presence begins to make sense, and attention during the day becomes possible.

With the experience of mindfulness, meditation practice begins to acquire momentum. Confidence in your ability to practice helps you cut through doubts and hesitation. But beware. If you attach to the experience of mindfulness, the momentum will quickly dissipate. At this point, mindfulness is the result of practice, not the method. The method of practice is to return attention to the breath.

Mindfulness is the first experience of any degree of presence. With mindfulness, you discover the possibility of being in attention. You now know, through experience, the difference between confused reactive thinking and attention, and how much more present you feel when you are not lost in reactive thinking.

Now that you have developed mindfulness in meditation, extend it, bringing attention into your daily life. To live in the mystery of being, you must live in attention, so extending the practice of attention to daily life is an important step. In the big picture, practice has two components: formal practice and the rest of your life. During the formal sitting period, you practice attention unmixed with other activities. During the rest of the day, you practice attention by mixing it with the activities of life—talking, listening, working, and playing.

For instance, sit down at the dinner table and notice what is on the plate in front of you. If thoughts or feelings come up and carry you away, return attention to the food, experiencing the colors, shapes, and aromas. Pick up the fork, feeling its weight and balance. Feel the resistance, weight, and texture of the food as you push the fork beneath it or slice through it. When you put the food in your mouth, experience the first rush of taste and sensation, then the ebbing and flowing of different flavors as you chew. Before taking the next mouthful, swallow the food completely and then return full attention to the plate in front of you.

In walking, the object of attention is walking—the movement of the body, the sensations of muscles contracting, the shifting of weight from foot to foot, from heel to toe, and the sights, sounds, and other sensory impressions you experience. Whenever you realize that attention to walking has faded and you are thinking about the destination, what you're going to do once there, or something that happened yesterday, then return your attention to what is already there, the experience of walking, and rest attention in that.

Start with a simple activity such as walking or running, or select some other form of repetitive exercise. Any activity that involves a simple physical process and not a lot of intellectual effort is suitable: washing dishes, sanding a piece of woodwork, gardening, working out, or sweeping the floor.

One caveat should be included here. Being mindful doesn't mean simply doing what we normally do in slow motion. To do things slowly is an excellent way to train attention in activities that we habitually do mindlessly. The intended result, however, is not life in slow motion but life in attention.

Awareness

Mindfulness becomes stronger and more stable with continued meditation practice. One day, you again experience a shift—a sense of opening into a larger space, of relaxing, of resting with the breath with much less effort. Meditation is suddenly surprisingly easy. You are relaxed and aware.

This shift marks the development of awareness, the quality of clarity in attention. The definition of *awareness* is knowing what is going on. *Mindfulness* is being present with the object of attention, but awareness enables you to know what is happening.

Suppose that you have to carry a glass of wine across a room full of people. Attention works in two ways. One way is focusing on the glass to avoid spilling its contents. This aspect corresponds to mindfulness. The second is knowing where people are in relation to your own position so that you avoid bumping into them. This aspect corresponds to awareness.

In meditation, the wineglass is the breath. Mindfulness is resting attention on the breath. Awareness is being aware of everything else—thoughts, feelings, and sensations—without being distracted.

Awareness has an inclusive quality that is essential to opening to the mystery of being. To generate the feeling of inclusive awareness, put a small object such as a pen in front of you. Rest your attention on it. Without taking your eyes or attention away from the pen, let your field of vision expand to include what is near it—the top of the desk and the objects on it. Let your field of vision continue to expand without taking your eyes away from the pen until you can see everything in your field of vision.

Meditate on the breath in the same way. The breath is the pen. Initially, you develop the ability to rest attention on the breath, which is mindfulness. Next, expand to working with awareness, including, but not being distracted by, the coming and going of thoughts, feelings, and sensations. You are mindful of your breath while also being aware of the rest of your experience.

Remember that the development of attention is not linear. Attention grows. While, for the most part, people move from immature to mature behavior as they grow up, a child sometimes exhibits mature behavior and an adult sometimes exhibits immature behavior. As you practice meditation, your ability in attention will increase, but it will be clearer and more stable on some days than on others. Consequently, do not take the experience of any given meditation session as an absolute indication of problem or progress.

Active attention is characterized by two qualities: stability and clarity. *Stability* in attention is called mindfulness. *Clarity* in attention is called awareness. *Active attention* consists of mindfulness and awareness together.

Awareness as a quality of active attention is different from the natural awareness mentioned in chapters 1 and 2. *Natural awareness* refers to original mind, the pristine awareness that is our human heritage. It is naturally present under all the patterns of habituation and conditioning. The aim of practice is to dismantle conditioned patterns and uncover natural awareness.

Awareness as a quality of active attention is a form of knowing that develops from mindfulness. The two usages are related in that the awareness of active attention is how we first experience the possibility of natural awareness, or original mind.

Relaxing and Energizing

Once mindfulness and awareness have developed, we start to appreciate different degrees of distraction and inattention. At one end of the spectrum is daydreaming, being totally absorbed in dreaming about what was, what might be, or what might have been. You wake up from these daydreams wondering where you are. Next is the busy mind, in which thoughts keep absorbing attention despite efforts to rest with the breath. Then comes the subtle busy mind, in which you feel that you are resting with the breath but background distraction persists, like a conversation that you can hear but can't quite follow because it is too far away.

At the other end of the spectrum is sleep, the ultimate distraction. Meditation is constantly interrupted by unintended naps. My teacher told me that he used to meditate while sitting on a window ledge to counteract this problem in his practice. Every time he fell asleep, he fell off the ledge! There is also the dull mind. When you are dull minded during meditation, you feel thick, woolly headed, foggy. Your body feels heavy and sluggish. Attention is weak. Next comes the subtle dull mind, which is like looking at a person on a foggy day: you can make out the outlines but not the features. You rest with the breath, but the resting has no clarity or vitality.

In busyness, you become occupied with thoughts or images, and the body feels uncomfortable and agitated. When you notice these experiences, your first impulse is to try to force stability. This impulse is part of the reactive process and only leads to further decay in attention and a corresponding increase in busyness. You are soon engaged in a self-reinforcing cycle. The appropriate effort is to relax. Since you are using the breath as a basis for attention, relax into the breath. Imagine coming home from a hard day's work and flopping down in your favorite chair with a big exhalation, "A-a-a-a-ah."

Put the emphasis on resting, letting all the busyness and activity swirl around like dust devils. Remember the hermit instructions: *body like a mountain,* resting effortlessly, and *mind like the sky,* undisturbed by winds and storms. Just feel the breath go out, and relax into it. Relaxation doesn't immediately counteract the busyness, but it moves you out of the reactive cycle. As you continue to breathe, relaxing into the breath, the busyness begins to subside.

We often become agitated because we forget about resting with the breath and try to make something happen in meditation. When we relax and rest with the breath, stability is restored.

In dullness, the dissipation of attention is experienced as a loss of clarity. A physical or emotional block absorbs the energy of attention, and you become sleepy, dull, listless, and sluggish. The instinctive reaction is just to rest, and when you do, you end up having a nice nap! The appropriate effort is to energize. Renew the posture, focus on the details of the sensations associated with the breath, and follow the breath carefully with attention. In other words, put more energy into the practice.

Active attention has two qualities: stability and clarity. Mindfulness develops stability; awareness develops clarity. Busyness and dullness are subjective experiences that signal the decay of active attention.

Stability is undermined by busyness. Busyness is the result of a reactive process that drains energy away from mindfulness. The reactive process works to distract us from the object of attention by bringing up other objects that absorb energy. The remedy is to relax, to let things be as they are, and not to react to the thoughts and images that fill the mind.

Clarity is undermined by dullness. Dullness is the result of a reactive process that drains energy away from awareness. The reactive process works to dull our ability to be aware so that we don't know what is going on. The remedy is to energize, to see what is happening, and to avoid falling into the dull state that is presented to us.

Meditation practice is a bit like riding a bicycle. At first you can't balance at all. How can anyone ride such a contraption? Then, after repeated efforts and a number of spills, you discover that as long as you keep moving you don't fall over. Similarly, when you establish consistency in meditation practice, you don't fall off practice despite the ups and downs.

Once you can stay upright on a bicycle, you remain that way for longer and longer periods by constantly making little adjustments, leaning slightly to the left or right or turning the handlebars a little to the left or right as needed. Rather than struggling to maintain a static balance, you become adept at sensing and correcting imbalance. Eventually, riding on a bicycle becomes completely natural, and even after years of not riding, you can easily ride again without going through the whole learning process.

In meditation, relaxing and energizing correspond with the shifts to the right and left in bicycle riding. The basic principle is to relax when you experience busyness and to energize when you experience dullness.

Energy Transformation

As you practice meditation, the level of energy in attention rises and you become increasingly aware of the richness of experience that makes up your life. When you first sit and put attention on the breath, you become aware of your body and the sensations associated with breathing. Bodily sensations, itches, pains, and discomfort are as distracting as thoughts. You may notice that many of the thoughts are connected with physical sensations. In the diagram below, the dashed downward arrows indicate the operation of attention.

ENERGY TRANSFORMATION AND
THE FOUR FOUNDATIONS OF MINDFULNESS

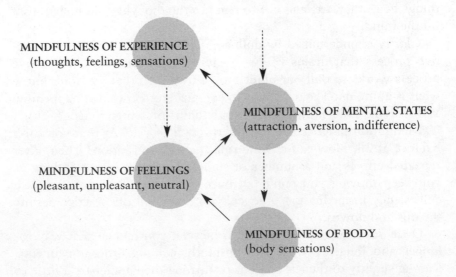

MINDFULNESS OF EXPERIENCE
(thoughts, feelings, sensations)

MINDFULNESS OF MENTAL STATES
(attraction, aversion, indifference)

MINDFULNESS OF FEELINGS
(pleasant, unpleasant, neutral)

MINDFULNESS OF BODY
(body sensations)

In the lowest circle, the attention on the breath brings attention to the body. As you are able to stay present with physical sensations, the energy that would ordinarily be dissipated in reaction and distraction is transformed into attention. Now, when you rest attention on the breath, you are aware of the pleasant, unpleasant, and neutral feeling tones associated with sensory experience.

With continued practice, the level of attention rises and you experience the three feeling tones without being distracted by them.

Awareness of the feeling tones leads to a still higher level of attention, awareness of emotional states of mind that form as reactions to the feeling tones. The three fundamental reactions are the three poisons, attraction, aversion, and indifference.

When attention develops to the point that the three poisons don't absorb all the energy, you experience the three poisons and other emotional states as emotions, not as what is. Now you become aware of all experience as experience—thoughts, feelings, and sensations—free from distraction and distortion.

The four stages are known traditionally as the four foundations of mindfulness.

BUILDING MOMENTUM

As we cultivate attention through a steady meditation practice, ability and momentum build. At first, attention is momentary and fleeting. Next, you experience periods of attention that are disrupted frequently by thoughts and reactions. Attention gradually becomes more continuous, and you are able to stay present in the movement of both thought and emotions. Eventually, attention operates without any express effort, and you remain in attention, both in formal practice and in life.

A stream begins as a small trickle high in the mountains and develops volume and momentum until it becomes a powerful river and merges with the vastness of the ocean. Attention develops momentum in a similar way, and, using the metaphor of a river, we can distinguish five stages in its development.

Stage 1: Cascade Down a Rock Face

As water cascades down a rock face, it splashes from rock to rock. At this stage of meditation, the subjective experience is chaos. Thoughts bounce all over the place. There is no sense of flow or continuity in attention.

The first stage of meditation is called the recognition of thoughts. When placing attention on the breath, you abruptly become aware of how active the mind is.

People new to meditation often react to this first stage by assuming that they are not suitable candidates for meditation or that they are doing something wrong. The first stage is the recognition of thoughts. The fact that they see the chaotic mind demonstrates that they are practicing correctly. This initial experience can be very discouraging, but the only thing to do is to continue to practice.

Many years ago two psychologists, a man and a woman, came to me to talk about meditation and I invited them to attend a weekly class. They both attended the first class, but after that, only the woman came. I never saw the other psychologist again. After several meetings, I asked her what had happened to him. "Oh," she replied, "those two meditation periods we did in the first class were the most hellish experiences of his life. He couldn't face anything like that again. I told him that things would change and he should just stick with it, but he wouldn't listen."

Thoughts are not caused by meditation. They are there all the time. Only when we place attention on the breath do we become aware of them.

Practice consists of returning attention again and again, resetting posture, returning to natural breathing, and returning attention to the breath. After a while, attention begins to stay with the breath for short periods, but practice still feels very chaotic.

Stage 2: A Torrent in a Gorge

Mindfulness begins to form, and we experience a direction in practice. Attention is like water in a gorge. Though roiled and turbulent, the direction of flow is clear. At the beginning of this stage of practice, the subjective experience is short periods of mindfulness interrupted frequently by distractions. A sense of continuity in practice begins to develop. We notice thoughts, feelings, and sensations before they distract us. We can now place the mind fully on the breath.

Periods of mindfulness become longer while interruptions and distractions are shorter. Though it is rough, raw, and far from stable, attention is forming.

Stage 3: River with Rapids

As mindfulness stabilizes, awareness develops. We feel as if we've suddenly stepped into a large room or an open field. We relax and rest with the breath. A common reaction is, "Oh, I like this. I can meditate!"

The relaxation and spaciousness in meditation are like a river coming out of a gorge. It flows quietly for a time and then goes over some rapids. After the rapids, it flows quietly again until it hits the next set of rapids. Busyness and dullness still arise, but we know how to return to attention.

Awareness forms and the unruly monkey mind is tamed. With mindfulness and awareness, we are now capable of active attention.

Consistency is what counts at this point. When you experience the calm flow of attention, you may feel that practice has become boring. Boredom is excess attention with insufficient intention. It brings us directly in touch with the conditioned need for constant stimulation. The lack of stimulation and distraction is unsettling. You don't know who you are without something to bounce off. Boredom is the next challenge in moving out of reactive patterns. Recall that your intention is to open to the mystery of being. The calm flow of attention is the first intimation of the open space of original mind. This is boring?

Calm and peace in the mind allow you to see things more clearly. While you sit in meditation, insights into interactions with people, business affairs, or personal problems arise spontaneously. Creative ideas and images arise from nowhere. Thoughts and thinking don't really disturb the quality of attention. Instead of only resting with the breath, you feel that you can use meditation to be more creative, to solve problems and generate insights, and that you can do all that without disrupting attention.

You are wrong.

This is a critical point in practice. If you are to continue cultivating attention, any engagement with thinking in formal sitting practice, even the most helpful insights or creative ideas, must be regarded as a distraction. The content is not the problem. The problem is the thinking process itself. You must let go of it.

If you pursue insights and creative ideas during meditation practice, attention stops developing. You may come up with an idea for a great painting, the next great novel, or a way to end world hunger, but you won't develop attention or open to the mystery of being. The energy of practice flows from attention into habituated patterns. In the absence of a practice of attention, habituated patterns become more fixed than they were originally. I usually suggest to students that if they want to explore such insights, they should set up two practice sessions, one to cultivate attention and the other to explore what arises.

At the beginning of this phase, you could stay present in the face of thoughts and some reactive emotions. By its end, you can stay present in the face of strong reactive emotions.

Stage 4: Lake with Waves

In a lake the river is at rest. When the wind blows, waves form, but the waves don't stop the water from resting. We begin to experience thoughts and feelings as the movement of mind, not as a distraction from the breath. Dullness and busyness come up but are calmed without trouble or effort.

At this stage reactive emotions arise, are experienced, and subside by themselves. The strength and duration of the experience depend on the emotion and the circumstances. Attention is now at a sufficient level of energy that reactive emotions don't disturb it. Meditation practice is now an integral part of our lives. We clearly recognize its influence in the way we function in difficult situations: we are more present, less reactive, and able to let go of unnecessary concerns more easily. Mindfulness and awareness are fully developed in formal practice and are showing up in daily life regularly.

Stage 5: Ocean Without Waves

The ocean is vast and deep. At this stage, the mind feels as vast as space and as deep as the ocean. No effort is necessary. The mind rests with clear, stable attention.

The final stage is the full development of attention. Previously, an effort had to be made to meet the object of attention. At this stage, the object comes to us. Wherever we direct attention, it rests effortlessly and undisturbed. Continued practice produces blissful sensations, first mental and then physical. These sensations are not enlightenment or insight; they are experiences of pleasure that naturally occur when mind and body are both at rest and fully coordinated.

ROADBLOCKS

Internal work is hand-to-hand combat without hands. As attention grows, we become more and more aware of the habituated patterns that run our lives. One student said to me, "I was aware of all these issues before I started practicing meditation, but now I'm intolerably aware of them."

Attention and patterns are in direct conflict with each other. Patterns function for one purpose and one purpose only: to decay attention so that the emotional core of the pattern is never sensed, felt, or known experientially. To be present in life, we must engage these patterns in combat. To avoid this conflict is to give our lives to the patterns.

Traditional Buddhism applies the title Foe Destroyer (Sanskrit: *Arhat*) to those who engage in this conflict and dismantle the patterns that obscure awareness and presence. The only weapon against the operation of patterns, the only weapon that makes victory possible, is active attention.

The road to awareness and presence is barred by numerous roadblocks created by reactive patterns. We can't negotiate with them, but we can generate sufficient momentum in attention to dismantle them. In cultivating attention, we encounter five roadblocks: unwillingness, forgetfulness, confusion, not making an effort, and trying too hard. To build momentum, we use eight tools: interest, effort, confidence, competence, mindfulness, awareness, restoring balance, and equanimity. We have already encountered mindfulness and awareness, and the other tools will be introduced shortly.

Going through these roadblocks does not mean ignoring them or bashing your way through. The operative word in *breakthrough* is *break*, not *through*. When we ignore and continue blindly, things break inside and we often have to spend as much time and effort repairing the damage done as it would have taken to dismantle the roadblock in the first place. Dismantling these roadblocks requires taking them apart, which is done with active attention. The various methods described below are not so much remedies as methods for increasing intention and attention sufficiently to penetrate the operation of these roadblocks so that they fall apart.

Unwillingness

The first and possibly most difficult roadblock is unwillingness. Unwillingness is often viewed as mere laziness, but to tell yourself that you are lazy doesn't help you understand the roadblock or how to remove it.

We avoid meditation for very specific reasons. To discover the reasons, first establish a definite time and place for meditation. Every day at the set time, go to where you practice and stand there until one of two things happens: either you know exactly why you aren't going to practice that day, or you sit down and practice. In a week or two, this simple (but not easy) exercise will expose at least one of the reasons underlying your unwillingness to practice. When you learn what it is, you can take it apart by using any or all of the following four tools: interest, effort, confidence, and competence.

Interest
When a person comes to see me, the first question I ask is "Why are you here?" Often, the response is along the lines of "I want to develop a spiritual dimension in my life" or "I want to be more focused and less distracted" or "I'm interested in Eastern ideas and want to see what they have to offer."

Vague ideas about a spiritual dimension to life, expectations of specific benefits, naive curiosity—these motivations are not sufficient to hold us when the inevitable battle with the internal material begins. Probing more deeply into our motivations, we discover that interest in internal work is always based on discomfort. Discomfort of one sort or another is the fundamental reason to change anything: the position in which we sit, our job, or how we experience life.

The touchstone for interest in meditation ultimately comes from the discomfort of feeling separate, incomplete, or asleep to the vitality of the world. When you feel that discomfort, you are in touch with the reason you came to meditation. Practice becomes personally relevant, and you face unwillingness squarely. You dismantle the roadblock by implementing the intention to maintain practice in the face of unwillingness. As you just sit and breathe, regard the various manifestations of unwillingness as the play of monkey mind, and keep practicing.

Meditation practice is tough. It throws us right up against habituated ways of functioning and shows us that they don't work. As Trungpa Rinpoche once said, "Meditation practice is one insult after another."

Effort
The second tool is effort, not the nose-to-the-grindstone, grin-and-bear-it kind, but the natural flow of energy that comes with enthusiasm for what you are doing. Despite difficulties or setbacks, we pour energy into practice because we feel good about what we are doing. How do we develop such enthusiasm for a practice that is so difficult? Choicelessness.

After about two or three months of sitting practice, the initial enthusiasm fades. Students then often ask how much time is needed to work through such and such a pattern. They are looking for assurances that things will get better. There are no such assurances. The only sure thing is that if you don't cultivate attention, your life will continue to be consumed by habituated patterns.

At this point I may ask, "Now that you have uncovered this pattern and you see how it prevents you from being present in your life, how it prevents you from experiencing the only life you have, what would you do if I told you that you might have to work on this one pattern for the rest of your life?" And they invariably reply, often with a sigh or a grudging smile, "Work on the pattern."

Hope undermines effort because it takes us away from the present. By coming back to what is right here in front of you right now, you see that meditation and internal transformative work are the best and most direct paths toward being present in life. Energy flows into practice because you see that you have no choice.

Confidence

The third tool for counteracting unwillingness is confidence. Confidence is trust in our own potential for waking up. We don't have to be a saint, great master, spiritual adept, or special person. Original mind is our human heritage. Meditation practice is based on the confidence that the seed of attention—natural awareness, or original mind—is present in everybody. Our work is to provide the conditions in which that seed can grow.

Confidence is based on faith, not beliefs. Beliefs are ways of interpreting and understanding experience that conform to preestablished patterns of perception. As such, they are used to justify conditioned behavior. Faith, however, is the willingness to open to the mystery of being, to meet whatever arises in experience. Faith sets no conditions on what is right or wrong, good or bad, acceptable or unacceptable.

Confidence comes through direct experience. As attention grows, you experience resting in attention with the breath. The more you remain in attention, in formal practice and daily life, the less opportunity reactive patterns have to run. You experience directly an increased capacity to respond, not react, in situations. Doubt and hesitation about practice evaporate. You don't need to trust what someone else has said or written. You know through your own experience that practice is effective. Such confidence comes only from the direct experience of practice, so keep practicing.

Competence

Competence is the fourth tool that takes apart unwillingness. Competence is just old-fashioned know-how, nothing fancy. The meditation technique we use, while very simple, is not easy. Like confidence, competence comes through practice, from learning how to negotiate the various difficulties and pitfalls of meditation. Two common pitfalls are the assumption that a noisy, chaotic mind means that meditation practice has gone wrong, and the assumption that a peaceful, quiet mind means that our practice is correct.

I've done a little sea kayaking. It's quite exciting to ride in a small boat in a five-foot swell. The person in the next boat may be only a few yards away, but one moment he's ten feet above me and the next he's ten feet below me.

When the ocean is calm, my kayak is stable and I move through the water easily. On other days, a gusty wind makes the ocean choppy and waves come from two different directions. When the sea is like that, I have to put my attention into keeping my balance, being neither too rigid nor too loose. Paddling is difficult, and I often feel that I'm making no progress.

When I'm in the middle of the ocean in a kayak, my first priority is to keep the kayak upright and me in it. That's the measure of my competence as a kayaker. I'm not at all concerned about keeping the kayak still, and a bit of chop and a few waves help to develop competence.

The same holds true for meditation. Competence in meditation is to keep an effort in attention going even when everything is noisy and chaotic inside. Periods with a lot of internal turmoil are sometimes more helpful in learning how to stay present than peaceful sessions. You are bringing attention right into the confusion and reactivity of the moment.

Competence means being able to make the effort, not having this or that experience. As competence develops, you learn how to work with the choppiness of thoughts and the swells of emotions. The point is not to have a smooth ride; the point is *to stay in the boat.*

Obviously, the four tools reinforce one another. Interest is the seed, which, nurtured by effort and confidence, matures and becomes competence. With increased competence, the roadblock of unwillingness becomes just another experience. We go through it whenever it arises.

By way of analogy, let's apply these four qualities to the activity of swimming. A person who isn't interested in swimming will be unwilling to dive into the water. He has to have some motivation, whether it is exercise, enjoyment, or an emergency. If he doesn't enjoy swimming or doesn't believe that it is worthwhile, he will do it halfheartedly if at all. If he has no confidence in his ability to swim or to learn how, he won't go swimming. Finally, if he doesn't know how to swim, he will be very unwilling to jump into the water.

Employ these countermeasures whenever you need to—before, during, or after meditation. If you have difficulty sitting down to meditate in the morning, start by sitting down and taking a few minutes to recall exactly why you originally decided to practice, or recall the discomfort you experience because of lack of presence. If you have difficulty finishing a meditation session, apply any of the four countermeasures during the meditation session. Shift your attention from the breath, and connect with your sense of confidence or enthusiasm— "Yes, despite all the chaos, I can do this" or "It doesn't matter that it's difficult. I'll keep going."

All four of the above countermeasures work naturally. When you connect with your intention in practice, you step out of the reactive patterns that cloud the mind. When you put energy into practice, reactive patterns can't hold. When you feel confidence in your potential for attention and presence, you rise above the level of reactivity. When you are grounded in the knowledge of how to practice, you cannot be shaken.

Forgetfulness

How many times have you said, "I forgot what I was going to say" or "I forgot why I came here"? In the context of meditation, there are three levels of forgetfulness: forgetting to practice, forgetting how to practice, and forgetting the breath.

Forgetting to practice happens all too easily. You wake up in the morning, belatedly remember that you have an early meeting, and start preparing for the meeting before meditating.

Often, the only warning that you are neglecting practice is a fleeting thought: "I don't feel like practicing today." Practice is forgotten, and you don't sit. The same thing happens the following day, and the next thing you know several days, weeks, or months have passed since you last practiced meditation. Meditation happens only if you make it a top priority. The best way to counteract forgetting to sit is to make practice a nonnegotiable element in your daily routine. In other words, meditate every single day.

Forgetting how to practice is another matter. One day we experience a wonderfully calm and clear state of mind, so the next day we try to duplicate that state of mind instead of just placing attention on the breath and feeling it go in and out. Gradually, the meditation practice goes sour, but we don't know why. We forget how to practice.

One of my students had a problem with her practice. Despite her explanations, I couldn't identify what was causing it, so I asked her to instruct me in meditation. She explained everything correctly except for one point. I recognized that the point she had left out was the point behind her problem. We discussed it, and I asked her to instruct me again. She left out the same point. That is how forgetfulness operates.

Forgetting the breath happens all the time in meditation. You sit, feeling the breath coming and going, and then suddenly realize that you have been thinking about something else. You forgot the breath.

Forgetfulness can be a powerful roadblock in practice. When you forget what you are doing, habitual patterns operate freely. Without mindfulness, your life is run by reactive processes.

Mindfulness

Mindfulness is what we use to dismantle forgetfulness. You will recall from the earlier discussion that mindfulness is being present with the object of attention. In other words, mindfulness is remembering. You remember to practice, you remember how to practice, and you remember the breath while practicing. Mindfulness works as sand in the gears of a pattern's operation. You simply cannot function automatically and be mindful at the same time. At first you experience the interruption of reactive processes as inconvenient and unsettling because it disrupts your usual way of living. Eventually, however, you see that mindfulness saves you from being consumed by reactive patterns.

Confusion

After the roadblock of forgetfulness, you run into the roadblock of confusion. In one moment you are resting with the breath, and in the next you are either asleep or recalling a conversation with a friend. Attention is only partially formed, so when mindfulness decays, you are right back in the operation of reactive patterns. As we saw earlier, the two most common causes of loss of attention are busyness and dullness.

Initially, you have to deal with the monkey mind and other forms of busyness. As attention develops, the mind joins with the object of meditation (in this case, the breath), and both body and mind relax. Dullness and sleepiness now become the main problems. You go back and forth, from busyness to dullness, with patches of mindfulness in between. The whole experience is very confusing.

Awareness

Awareness, the spacious inclusive quality of attention, provides the means to go through the roadblock of confusion. With awareness you know whether the mind is clear or dull, stable or busy. Awareness prevents you from falling into confusion, which often manifests as emotional turbulence.

When we are aware, we start to appreciate differences in meditation and daily functioning that we couldn't distinguish before. We experience a clear difference between being lost in a train of thought and being present with the breath. We know how eating or walking in attention is different from going about our lives lost in a whirlwind of thoughts and feelings. We see the difference between reaction and response.

A retired businessman who had been practicing meditation for some time received a call from his exwife. Phoning from France, she told him that thieves had broken into her hotel room and had stolen both her passport and her travelers' checks. "No problem," he said. "Go to the American consulate, and they will issue you a temporary passport. Then go to American Express with the yellow receipt you removed from your travelers' checks, and they will reissue them."

"The yellow receipt was still with the travelers' checks," she replied. "I didn't take it out."

Because of his mindfulness practice, he observed all the old frustrations rising up and the urge to tell his wife how stupid he thought she was. Then, because of awareness, he knew that what was arising was a reactive pattern that had nothing to do with the present situation. He let the reaction arise and subside and then asked, "What do you need?"

Without awareness, you cannot cut through the confusion of dullness and busyness. In the absence of a consistent practice, mindfulness will never give rise to awareness.

Not Making an Effort

The next roadblock is not making an effort. Even though we know, through awareness, that attention is decaying into confusion, we let confusion take over.

In daily life, we run into the same obstacle. You know you are coming down with the flu but don't take time to rest. You have an important deadline coming up on a project, yet you still tend to less urgent matters. In both cases, you know a problem is developing but don't take any action to stop it. In meditation, not making an effort means that you do nothing to return to active attention when you know you are slipping into the confusion of dullness and busyness.

Restoring Balance

To go through the roadblock of not making an effort, restore balance by relaxing and energizing, as I described earlier. To relax, take a deep breath, let it out slowly, then take another breath and let it out slowly. Relaxing in attention undermines the tension that generates busyness. To energize, reset your posture and focus on the details of the sensations associated with the breath, and follow the breath carefully with attention. Energizing in attention counteracts the lassitude that produces dullness.

The "one-breath meditation" combines relaxing and energizing. It cuts through both busyness and dullness. The essence of this method is to cut once and rest. Imagine that the breath is like a sword. As you breathe out, feel that sword cutting through busyness or dullness. With one breath, you cut through all busyness and dullness and rest in clear, stable attention. Your intention to be present is so strong that at the end of this one exhalation, you are completely clear and relaxed. Now rest, feeling the coming and going of the breath. Breathe naturally, and be totally present in the breath.

If the dullness or busyness is particularly strong, practice cutting once and resting ten or fifteen times in succession. Each cut must be complete or you will be left with some residual dullness. Resting with the breath after each exhalation is essential or you will just generate a lot of tension and more busyness.

Trying Too Hard

The final roadblock is trying too hard. You are resting in attention, and thoughts come and go while your attention remains undisturbed, but you aren't satisfied. It has to be perfect all the time!

In the early stages of meditation practice, the play of clarity and stability will be a bit rough. We swing from one to the other. The temptation is to try and hold the attention exactly at the balance point, but we can't. We inevitably veer off into dullness or busyness. To return to the bicycle example, even when we are moving at speed, the bicycle tips back and forth a little. The bicycle never stays exactly in balance. The momentum of the spinning wheels has a gyroscopic effect and acts to return the bicycle to the vertical. If you try to hold the bicycle perfectly in balance, you expend a lot of useless effort and prevent the gyroscopic effect from operating. You crash.

To hold both clarity and stability means to rest when they are both present. As attention accumulates momentum, it becomes self-sustaining. Trying too hard comes from a pattern of trying to control. The pattern comes from feeling separate from what you experience, and it prevents the development of self-sustaining attention.

Equanimity

To go through the roadblock of trying too hard, rely on equanimity. Equanimity is the ability to let things be as they are. For instance, when a child grows up, her parents have to let go and trust that she has learned how to meet the challenges of life. Letting go and trusting are the essence of equanimity. Once you experience resting in attention with the breath, you must trust that resting with the breath in clear and stable attention is enough for attention to grow and become self-sustaining.

Active attention is not a balance between clarity and stability. It is a higher level of directed energy in which both clarity and stability are present. You move into the higher level of energy by holding both clarity and stability. You will feel the shift. When clarity and stability are both present, rest. Don't do anything more. Even when thoughts arise, if they do not disturb the clarity and stability, don't try to get rid of them. They won't stay long. When you feel the quality of attention decay (characterized by a loss of clarity or a loss of stability), apply the appropriate countermeasures. If the attention is clear and stable, however, just rest. Rest in attention and let the momentum of attention accumulate.

WORKING WITH REACTIVE EMOTIONS

A husband and wife plan to go out to dinner. Because he has a lot of pressure at work, the man asks his wife to make reservations. Delayed by traffic, they arrive a little late and can't find a parking place. The husband starts to get upset, but his wife is unperturbed. She keeps driving around until a space opens up. By then, however, her husband is furious. A light rain starts to fall, and they must walk an extra block to get to the restaurant. Fortunately, their reservations hold, so they are soon seated. He knows he is overreacting but can't let go of it. She, however, can't understand why he's upset. They sit together, eating in stony silence.

Reaction is always based on past experience. Elements of any present situation resonate with the past and trigger habituated patterns that formed and developed on the basis of past experience. When patterns are triggered, attention goes out the window. What we see, what we feel, and what we do are shaped by the complex interactions of conditioned patterns from the past.

When the husband later examined his reaction, he first identified how exasperated he felt because his wife hadn't arranged for parking in advance or at least had a backup plan. "That's what I would have done," he said. When asked why the lack of parking arrangements was so upsetting, he smugly replied that he always made sure that any eventuality was covered in at least two ways, a skill that served him well as a business manager. Further inquiry revealed that he really felt unsafe if anything was left to chance. His whole life was based on controlling outcomes as much as possible.

His pattern of control prevented him from appreciating that his wife had her own way of handling situations and that she was patient, resourceful, and flexible. Despite the fact that nothing had really gone wrong, his reaction to the lack of backup arrangements stopped him from enjoying the rest of the evening. He was a victim of his own reactive patterns.

Reactive emotions play a big part in the way we experience life. Probably the most frequently asked question in meditation practice is "How do I use meditation to deal with emotions?" In subsequent chapters, specific techniques with which to dismantle reactive emotional patterns are explained. Here, the attention developed in meditation practice is used to step out of reactive emotional states.

How do emotional reactions operate? Emotional reactivity is a process that is initiated by a stimulus, proceeds through several internal stages, and culminates in an expressed reaction.

Let's take an example. As part of a team, you present your idea for the current project. A co-worker on your same team says angrily, "If we go with that stupid idea, we'll have to redo everything."

How do you react? One possibility is to take the comment as an insult and retort in kind. Another is to swallow your own anger and have it churn inside you for the rest of the day. The process can be broken down into five steps (corresponding to the five skandhas).

1. The first experience is the sound of the co-worker's voice.
2. It is accompanied by an unpleasant feeling.
3. The sound, tone, and words are interpreted as insulting and offensive.
4. Anger arises as an emotional reaction.
5. The anger is expressed or repressed: you deliver a stinging retort or swallow the anger and say nothing.

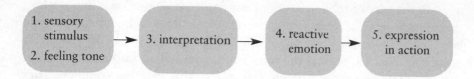

As you practice meditation, you see the possibility of an opening between steps 4 and 5; you see a difference between the reactive emotion of anger and the expression of that anger in action. Attention enables us to differentiate between the feeling and the expression of feeling. In actual situations, most people have difficulty in taking advantage of that opening because, by step 4, the reactive process has built up too much momentum.

As you continue to practice, active attention penetrates the reactive process more deeply and allows you to pick up the transition from step 3 to 4, from interpretation to reactive emotion. Stepping out of the reactive process at this point is easier because the energy in the reaction is at a lower level. It doesn't have as much momentum. The first few times you do this, however, you may be surprised by a second process that you weren't aware of up to that point.

When you become aware of the transition from interpretation to reactive emotion and step out of the reactive process, you experience accumulated conditioning associated with that particular interpretation. The conditioning includes similar past experiences and the reactive emotions generated by those experiences. You feel like you've been hit by a wave that came out of nowhere. Even though the emotional associations are not connected with the present situation, they often push you back into the reaction. As attention develops, you can increasingly distinguish past associations from the present, let them go, and not react.

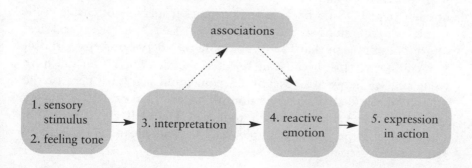

In the case of the angry comment from the co-worker, your work in attention lets you know you are upset. As you feel anger arise, you realize that you are upset about being called stupid. You know you aren't stupid. You know that the idea isn't stupid. You know that the co-worker routinely puts down new ideas and that his comment isn't really directed at you. Yet you still feel angry. As you stay in attention with the anger, you feel old anger and frustrations from being called stupid and not being understood in other situations having nothing to do with this one.

Continued cultivation of attention enables us to pick up the reactive process even earlier. A feeling tone, whether pleasant, unpleasant, or neutral, arises with every sensory experience. The feeling tone triggers one of the three basic reactive patterns: attraction, aversion, or indifference. When you experience the feeling tone in attention, you don't fall into the corresponding reactive pattern. You experience pleasure when you see a flower in a meadow and do not have to pick it and make it yours.

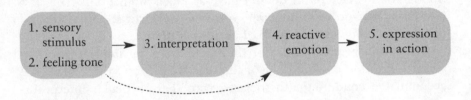

Most people want to apply meditation practice to the last stages of this process—that is, when they feel the anger and don't want to express it inappropriately. Unfortunately, by that time the emotional reaction has usually built up too much energy to be stopped. The benefit from meditation practice and attention is that we pick up the process much earlier.

If you have enough energy in attention, a new possibility opens up at each step. Let's go back to the co-worker and his offensive comment. Between steps 4 and 5, you could say, "Just because I feel angry doesn't mean that I have to retaliate." Between steps 3 and 4, you could say, "Just because he rejected the idea doesn't mean I have to be angry." Between steps 2 and 3, you could say, "Just because the comment sounded unpleasant doesn't mean I have to take it as a rejection." Steps 1 and 2 occur together. The shift at this point is, "Just because the sound is unpleasant doesn't mean that I have to react with aversion."

Choice depends on being able to perceive an alternative. If you are unable to perceive an alternative, the notion of choice is meaningless. When the reactive process is running, there is no awareness. To act differently, you have to have free attention. Free attention is energy that is not consumed by habituated patterns. With it, you see and experience events differently. New possibilities of action open up.

Reactive processes operate in two principal ways: expression or repression. The reactive emotion is either pushed out into action or pushed back out of conscious awareness. In neither case do we feel the reactive emotion or the reactive process.

When we express or push the emotional charge out into action, the emotional charge is dumped into the world and affects those around us. When we repress or push the emotional charge back, it goes into the body and produces illness or compensating behaviors such as addiction.

Attention opens a third way of working with reactive emotions. We hold them in attention, neither expressing nor repressing the reaction. When we feel the emotion completely, the energy of the emotion is transformed into attention.

How do you transform reactive energy into attention? When a strong emotional reaction arises, rest attention on the breath and include the experience of the emotion. Two mistakes are commonly made: focusing on the emotion itself and focusing on the breath to the exclusion of the emotion. If you focus on the emotion itself, more energy tends to flow into the reactive pattern and you end up reacting even more strongly. If you try to exclude the emotion from attention, you end up repressing it.

Instead, rest attention on the breath, and include as much of the sensation of the emotion as you can without falling into busyness or dullness. When you can rest with the emotion a little bit, include more of the feeling in your attention. Next, include all the physical, emotional, and cognitive reactions to the initial emotional reaction. Eventually, you will experience a shift and be able to rest calmly and at ease even when you recall the original situation. You will feel clearer and more present. At that point, the reactive process has been transformed into attention. You have begun to break down the conditioning connected to the underlying patterns.

Finally, there is one pitfall in meditation practice that you must avoid. Meditation practice raises the level of energy in your system in the form of active attention. The higher level of energy inevitably brings you into contact with reactive emotional patterns. If you now become selective and repress certain emotions, pushing them out of attention, two things happen. The higher level of energy in your system flows into the reactive pattern, making it stronger. The higher energy also flows into the repressing pattern, making that stronger. Both the reactive patterns of the emotion and the repression are reinforced. You end up splitting in two. One part of you is capable of attention and response. The other part becomes increasingly rigid and inflexible. It takes over unpredictably whenever the repressed emotion is triggered by events or situations. Typically, a person becomes more arrogant and self-indulgent, obsessed with power, money, sex, security, or other fixations, and acts in ways to control or amass the object of the obsession. Long-term practitioners and teachers who protect areas of their lives from their practice frequently run into this problem with unfortunate and sometimes tragic results. We run the risk of a similar fate if we protect any area of our personality or lives from the increased awareness that develops in meditation.

To guard against this problem, always have at least one person, a teacher, colleague, or friend, with whom you discuss all aspects of your practice and your life. The person needs to be someone you trust and to whom you will listen regardless of the state of mind you are in or what he or she says. The *only* way to be sure that you will not protect an area of your habituated personality from the effects of practice is to have such a person in your life.

SUMMARY

Active attention is essential for any internal transformation work. Only through attention do we step out of reactive processes that run our lives. Attention is essential if we are to uncover the natural awareness that is our human heritage.

The apparently simple method of returning to what is already there is based on the perspectives and methods of the direct awareness schools of Tibetan Buddhism. Simple does not mean easy. As we practice, we become increasingly aware of the many ways we fall out of attention. We begin to appreciate that we have to support the cultivating of attention by making adjustments in our lives.

Support for practice comes primarily from letting go of those aspects of your life that undermine or counteract the cultivation of attention. In the end, the motivation to make such changes must come from your own experience of attention, not from a person or body of teaching that tells you what to do. For practice to be truly your own, motivation and effort must come from within. Even a small experience of the difference between reactivity and presence goes a long way in generating the confidence and inclination needed to make further efforts.

Refining practice involves understanding the principles of meditation and how to apply them. The key principle is the play between clarity and stability. By relaxing when you are distracted by thinking and by energizing when you are dull, you find the way to a vertical shift in which clarity and stability are both present.

Consistent practice is the answer to most problems that arise in meditation or life. You won't win every battle. Resistance and patterns are tenacious and persistent. With clear intention, consistent effort, confidence, and a clear understanding of the principles of practice, you can and will dismantle the patterns that prevent you from experiencing your life. Don't miss a day of practice. When you do, don't succumb to the reaction that all is lost and you might as well quit. A missed day is like a distracting thought. Once you recognize that you aren't practicing, start again. Remember that the essence of meditation is to return, return, return to the natural awareness that is already there.

With the cultivation of attention, we have the primary tool we need to move into presence. Original mind is covered by many layers of conditioning, including patterns of perception, emotional reactivity, family history, and social and cultural conditioning. All these layers have to be taken apart if we are to open to the mystery of being. Yet all this conditioning constitutes the experience of life as we now know it. To take those patterns apart is to take our lives apart, to die to the life we know. That is the challenge ahead: to die willingly and with complete awareness.

CHAPTER 4

Dismantling Attachment to Conventional Success

*"If someone doesn't say something to entertain me," shouted a tyranni-
cal and effete king, "I'll cut off the heads of everyone at court."*

Mulla Nasrudin immediately stepped forward.

"Majesty, don't cut my head off—I'll do something."

"And what can you?"

"I can—teach a donkey to read and write!"

The king said: "You'd better do it, or I'll flay you alive!"

"I'll do it," said Nasrudin, "but it will take me ten years!"

"Very well," said the king, "you can have ten years."

*When the court was over for the day, the grandees crowded around
Nasrudin.*

*"Mulla," they said, "can you really teach a donkey to read and
write?"*

"No," said Nasrudin.

*"Then," said the wisest courtier, "you have only brought a decade's
tension and anxiety, for you will surely be done to death. Oh, what
folly to prefer ten years' suffering and contemplation of death to a
quick flash of the headsman's axe. . . ."*

*"You have overlooked just one thing," said the Mulla. "The king is
seventy-five years old, and I am eighty. Long before the time is up,
other elements will have entered the story. . . ."*

—IDRIES SHAH,
THE SUBTLETIES OF THE INIMITABLE MULLA NASRUDIN

Death, inevitable and final, forces us to face the mystery of being: "What is this that I now experience, which can end at any moment?"

Death has motivated many great teachers throughout the centuries. The sight of a corpse shattered the illusion of continuous happiness for Siddhartha. Gampopa, a Tibetan master of the twelfth century, turned to the great matter of life and death when he lost his wife shortly after they were married. My own teacher's teacher was the monastery's tailor. One day he realized that he, too, was going to die, so he locked himself in the monastery's toilets for seven years so that he could practice.

Why do we spend time thinking about impermanence and death? Contrary to the views of our culture, death is not the opposite of life; it is the end of life. As such, death is as much a part of life as birth is. When we ignore death, we cannot know what life really is and therefore don't experience it fully. Instead, we take what is transitory— money, fame, power, relationship—to be real and base our lives on achieving what cannot last—happiness, wealth, fame, and respect. When we base life on what can be taken from us, we give power over our lives to anyone who can take it away. We become dependent on others and on society for a sense of well-being. We give our lives away to others and to what others deem to be important.

We will die one day. That much is certain. When and how, no one can tell. If we are vividly aware that death can come at any time, however, our attention goes into the actual experience of life, not into the effort to achieve fame or fortune. When we truly understand that everything is transitory, we see money, fame, power, and even relationships in a different light. The hold of conventional notions of success and failure is broken. Living in the knowledge that every relationship we have is going to end, we take nothing for granted and savor every moment with our spouse, parents, or children. Meditating on death and impermanence frees us from the conditioning of culture, society, and upbringing and brings us closer to life, closer to the mystery of being.

Death is not a popular topic. Shortly after completing my first three-year retreat training, I had dinner with a group of people, one of whom was a psychologist. Curious about my experience, he asked what I had studied in retreat. I replied that 90 percent of the curriculum had to do with learning how to die. All conversation stopped.

Reflecting on specific aspects of impermanence and their implications brings us directly up against habituated views and emotional patterns that distort the experience of life. These meditations dismantle socially conditioned attitudes about the meaning and purpose of life. They will change profoundly how you view life and spiritual practice.

Basic meditation training is a prerequisite for the meditations on death and impermanence. Habituated patterns can be dismantled only when you are able to experience the operation of reactive patterns in attention. These practices bring you face-to-face with long-ignored issues, issues that challenge the way you ordinarily make sense of the world. You will feel uncomfortable, anxious, perhaps, or frightened, regretful, ashamed, angry, giddy, excited, perplexed, worthless, stupid—all the feelings that led you to abandon your life to gain others' approval. You will need to have a consistent practice and know how to rest in attention, how to work with distraction, and how to hold attention in reactive emotions. Losing your way in emotional reactions will only make them stronger, so attention is a prerequisite.

Consequently, I encourage you to have a good foundation in meditation practice and to work with an experienced and knowledgeable teacher or guide.

How to Practice

Three Steps: Study, Reflection, and Cultivation

The five meditations on change and death are significantly different from the basic meditation of cultivating attention. In basic meditation, we let go of the thinking process, returning attention to the breath over and over again. Death and impermanence practices use a three-step process: study, reflection, and cultivation. We use these three steps in all the meditations that follow.

Study
The first step is to learn the meditation guidelines. Study them until you have a clear intellectual understanding and can call them to mind at will.

In the case of death and impermanence, this step is not difficult. A careful reading of the guidelines is usually sufficient. At the intellectual level, you know most of the material already. You know that everything changes. You know you are going to die.

Intellectual knowledge, however, is not sufficient. You may say, "Yes, yes, I know, everybody dies," but still believe certain things will never change—a husband's love, the security of your home, the oak tree in your backyard.

Something deep inside you clings to the belief that you will never die. As William Saroyan once said, "We all know that we are going to die, but I really thought that in my case an exception would be made."

Reflection

Reflection is where the work begins. For example, the theme of the first meditation is "Everything changes, nothing stays the same." Construct a sequence of images (if you work visually) or ideas (if you work verbally) that embody the theme. Use the meditation guidelines, and reflect on each point, holding it in attention, thinking about it, and weighing it for a few minutes. During the first few practice sessions, have the guidelines open in front of you. Read one point and think about it. Then go on to the next. After a few sessions you won't need to read them.

Think actively about the fact that everything changes and nothing stays the same. Initially, you will be distracted by totally unrelated topics. Patiently return to the guidelines and the chosen sequence. You will encounter busyness and dullness, which were described in the preceding chapter. Sometimes, you will fall into a dull stupor or just go to sleep. Both reactions, distraction and going to sleep, are manifestations of the part of us that holds the belief that it will live forever. It operates mechanically, eroding attention and shutting down even the possibility of exploring impermanence. As you move into the meditations on death, similar reactive mechanisms function even more powerfully. Such disturbances are common. Just do the practice, and you will work through them.

The point of reflection is to validate the material in your own understanding. Does a particular idea in the guidelines make sense? Does it resonate with your own experience? As you reflect over and over on each point in the guidelines, you will feel a shift in your perception and understanding. This shift is marked by a decrease in distraction. Now the meditation has a greater emotional impact. The effort made in reflection has dismantled part of the pattern of ignoring. You now acknowledge that everything is impermanent, that nothing stays the same. You feel the truth of change and appreciate how much you have ignored the implications of impermanence in your life.

Cultivation

The third step starts with accepting the validity of the key point—in this case, everything changes; nothing stays the same. Now spend more time with the images and ideas. Like a sponge soaking up water, hold the theme, images, and ideas in attention, and let the message sink in. Rest in attention with each element in the sequence, letting it tell you about change and death.

Understanding moves from the intellectual ("Yes, yes, I know") to the emotional ("Oh, I see, there really is nothing to rely on!"). The energy in attention is now sufficient to enable you to stay present in the face of emotional reactions to impermanence. Emotional understanding is not a state of disturbance and reaction. On the contrary, it's a deeper level of appreciation in which reactive tendencies have subsided and are replaced by understanding and acceptance.

Cultivation is the stage at which emotional understanding really develops and where your experience and view of life change. For instance, when you truly take to heart that you are going to die, you naturally focus energy and attention on the aspects of life in which you feel most alive and present. And when you truly take to heart that you could die at any time, you pay full attention to the important relationships in your life. When you leave for work in the morning, you know that you may never see your children again. Imagine how different your life would be if you never took tomorrow or next week or next year for granted.

In the midst of action, intellectual understanding is much slower and less powerful than emotional understanding. To access intellectual understanding, we have to remember to bring what we know intellectually to bear on the situation. With emotional understanding, the understanding is part of our experience of the situation. We don't have to remember. For this reason, emotional understanding leads to deeper and more extensive changes in our lives.

Practical Matters

For the meditations on death and impermanence, divide a session of formal practice into three sections: first establish a base of attention, then bring attention to the material, and finally let the understanding diffuse through your whole being. Whereas a half-hour session was sufficient to make good progress in basic meditation, you now need to extend formal practice to forty-five minutes or an hour.

The first part of any session of formal practice is used to establish a stable base of attention. For fifteen to twenty minutes sit in basic meditation, resting attention on the breath.

Next, spend twenty to thirty minutes bringing attention to the images and ideas drawn from the meditation guidelines. The time is sufficient to produce good results in consistent daily practice yet not so long that boredom or staleness sets in.

Finally, take another ten to fifteen minutes to let understanding diffuse through your whole being by returning attention to the breath, feeling your whole body breathe, and letting go of the images and ideas that you have been contemplating.

The reflections on change and death work slowly and deeply. You will often be distracted by busyness or fall into a dull state of mind. As in cultivating attention, apply relaxing and energizing techniques, and then return to the sequence of images and ideas. You will frequently become confused and lose track of the meditation. When that happens, return to the guidelines.

When you begin to feel confident in your practice—that is, when you can keep attention in reflection and follow the progression of ideas—a second level of resistance arises: "I don't like this practice and its implications." The discomfort is an encouraging sign. It indicates that attachment to the conventional view of the world is breaking down. Be consistent and keep going, neither ignoring the resistance nor letting it disrupt your efforts. Experience the resistance by returning to the breath and expanding attention to include the sensations that accompany it. Either the resistance will dissipate, or you will become aware of the next layer of resistance. Step by step, attention will penetrate the layers of reaction until understanding at the emotional level arises. At that point, you will be in direct touch with death and impermanence, and your view and approach to life will change.

To practice a set of meditations just to say we have "done" them is pointless. The aim of these practices is to understand death and impermanence at the emotional level. When understanding reaches this level, you feel something break or shift inside you. How long that takes varies widely from person to person. An idea or a belief has been shattered, and you know you can't go back. Ideally, you should practice each of these meditations until you feel that shift. Then have your understanding confirmed by your teacher. An old adage says, "Practice until you get a result. Then practice for three more days, and then three more, and then three more."

Work at these practices intelligently. On some days you will feel supple and easily open to the material. Work hard and deeply at such times. On other days you will feel hard, rigid, and perhaps even brittle.

When that happens, work at the practice consistently, but don't try to break through the rigidity. Pushing directly on resistance only makes it stronger.

Kalu Rinpoche frequently emphasized the importance of keeping the mind supple and workable. "Once the mind becomes stiff and rigid, practice becomes very difficult. Then the mind is like a leather bag that has been used to store butter. When butter penetrates leather, it becomes hard and brittle. The bag is useless and has to be thrown away. No amount of reworking the leather will make it soft and pliable again. Don't let your mind become like that."

Structure and Use of Guidelines and Commentaries

Meditation on death and impermanence is divided into five meditations, which follow in sequence, each building on the previous ones. Each meditation includes a purpose, a key phrase, and a sequence of images and ideas. Each is designed to wake you up to a specific aspect of change or death.

The five key phrases are the original form of a Kadampa meditation that dates back to fourteenth-century Tibet. They function as keys. After you have spent a substantial time contemplating death and impermanence, recalling a key phrase can unlock all the effort you put into the practice, giving you instant access to the understanding that has developed in you. The phrases are concise and easy to memorize. Memorize them.

The sequence of images and ideas is used to focus the attention during meditation practice. The sequence is not sacrosanct. If you find other images or ideas that resonate more deeply for you, use them.

The commentaries on each of the meditations include guided meditations to give you an idea of how to use the guidelines for reflection and cultivation.

A number of quotations from traditional sources are included in the guidelines. Most of them are taken from *The Jewel Ornament of Liberation* by Gampopa. He, in turn, drew on a long tradition of texts and commentaries by Indian and Tibetan masters.

Working with Fear

Death is frightening. Change is frightening. Fear arises frequently as you do these practices. You will feel fear in your body, you will feel fear emotionally, and you will have fearful thoughts. Death will haunt you whenever you step into your car. Some nights you may not be able to sleep; instead, you may lie awake thinking about your inevitable death.

At the level of thought, we react to fear by thinking about other things or slipping into a dull stupor. Boredom and irritation with the practice are common, but stopping does no good. Not meditating on death and impermanence is not going to keep you from dying. The only issue is whether you continue to ignore your own mortality and your own life.

A woman in her forties had been practicing with these meditations for several months. One day she came into my office, sat down, and turned to me. "I hate these meditations! They just get worse and worse. Honestly, Ken, I don't know why anybody studies with you."

After a moment or two I asked, "So, the meditations haven't been helpful?"

She took in the question and then replied, "I didn't say that. I wake up, do the meditations, and they are not fun. And then I go through my day with death walking behind me as you suggested. And I've never felt more alive."

"Very good," I replied.

Then she laughed. "I still don't know why anybody studies with you."

> All men should try to learn before they die what they are running from, and to, and why.
>
> —*James Thurber*

Although physical discomfort is common in this practice, you will not die from doing these meditations. The body, however, does not know that. Intermittently, your heart beats faster, you feel sick in the stomach, you become tense and agitated. Actually, these are all signs of effective practice—you are moving into the fire. When you experience these signs, work with inclusive attention, resting with the breath and including the physical sensations of tension, agitation, and fear.

Open emotionally to the experience of fear itself. Use the breath as a basis for attention, and then open to the feeling. If the fear is too hot, open only a little, experiencing as much as you can while maintaining attention on the breath. When you can stay present with that bit of fear, open a little more, and then a little more.

A higher level of attention is forming. It enables you to feel fear without falling into a reactive pattern. You know, at the emotional level, that everything changes and that we will all die. You won't necessarily overcome the fear, but you will learn to stay present in it.

The ability to experience emotions and not fall into distraction or reaction is one of the most important aspects of practice. After students assimilate an understanding of a particular topic, I suggest that they stop using the guidelines and spend more time feeling the impact of their insight. For instance, in the second meditation, we see that death is inevitable. Sit for another couple of weeks or a month with the question: "I'm going to die. How do I feel about that?" The question acts as a weight, taking us down into the deep waters of our fear and bringing attention and awareness into those areas where there is only fear and confusion.

Nobody likes these meditations, but we cannot be present in life until we stop ignoring death and change. We start with change.

Meditation 1: Everything Changes

Purpose:
To know that everything we experience is impermanent.

Key phrase:
Consider how everything changes; nothing stays the same.

Change in the World

- Galaxies, stars, and planets
- Oceans, continents, mountains, hills, lakes, and rivers
- Plants, trees, shrubs, grasses, meadows, prairies, forests
- Animals, mammals, birds, reptiles, fish, insects
- Human society, empires, countries, nations, governments
- Clothes, fashions, fads
- Philosophies, social and scientific theories, artistic forms
- Weather, long-term cycles, seasons, day by day
- Moment-to-moment change in the world around us

Change in the Body

- External changes: hair, skin, fingernails, and toenails
- Internal changes: muscles, bones, blood, heart, lungs, and other organs

- Abilities: to see, hear, taste, touch, smell, think, remember
- Appetites: food, sex, exercise, sleep
- Changes in height, weight, and shape as we mature and age
- Cellular and metabolic changes

Change in Personality and Belief Systems

- Dominant personality traits
- Likes and dislikes
- Beliefs and ideas about who we are
- Beliefs and ideas about the world
- How we are in relationships
- How we see and experience the world
- How we think and how we interpret experience

Commentary

This meditation wakes us up to the understanding that everything is impermanent. The meditation is divided into three sections. Spend three to four weeks on each section.

Change in the World

Start by envisioning the largest and most stable objects in the universe, and work down to the smallest and most unstable, observing how every one of them forms, endures, and eventually disintegrates. From galaxies to stars and planets, from seas and oceans to ponds and puddles, from continents to islands, everything changes. All living things, from the largest animals and plants down to the smallest bacteria and viruses, are evolving and adapting even as they constantly convert matter to energy and energy to waste matter. Molecules, atoms, and even subatomic particles are created, endure, and disintegrate, some over inconceivably long periods of time, others so quickly that the most sophisticated measuring devices can barely detect them. Nothing stays the same. Mountains erode, seas dry up, and whole species of plants and animals become extinct while others take their place as they evolve over the millennia.

Observe the shifting patterns of shape, color, light, sound, tone, and pitch that you perceive. Sensory experience is an ever changing play of sight, sound, tastes, odors, and textures. Notice how waves change in shape as they come into the shore, how clouds appear and disappear in the sky, and how colors change with the shifting light as day passes into night. The play of sounds—music, a baby's crying, a car alarm, the roar of a jet plane, the wind in the trees—is constantly shifting and changing. Eat a strawberry, and observe how quickly the taste shifts from sweet to tart to sweet again. Then experiment with the other senses— smell, touch, and hearing—and sit in the experience of change.

Extend these reflections to everything, both the world of nature and the world constructed by human beings. See the cycles of change in nature and the cycles of change in societies: buildings, cultural institutions, artistic movements, systems of thought, governments, and countries.

Gradually, the sense that everything around you is constantly changing sinks in deeper and deeper, triggering emotional reactions. You may become confused by the uncertainty of change, obsessed, depressed, tense, agitated, or anxious because of it. Here is where the attention developed in basic meditation pays off.

When emotional reactions distract or disrupt your reflections, return to the breath. Feel it going in and out until you again can rest with the breath. This step reestablishes a base of attention. Then, while continuing to rest attention on the breath, open to the emotional reaction arising in you—irritation, anxiety, uncertainty, raw fear, and so forth. When you can rest calmly in the experience of the reaction, the reaction is merely an object of attention; it's not you. The irritation may remain, but you no longer identify with it. The irritation (or any other emotional reaction) either dissipates or gives way to another layer of reaction. If the reaction subsides, return to the contemplation of impermanence. If another layer of reaction has been revealed, return to the breath once again and repeat this process.

By peeling away layer after layer of habituation, you arrive at the fear at the core of emotional reaction. It arises as a feeling of being in an earthquake, or being swept away by a wave, or being totally alone, or falling from a great height, or being nothing at all. Your immediate impulse will be to move away from the feeling in any way you can. Instead, breathe and stay present, including in your attention as much of the fear as you can experience without falling into confusion or reaction.

Another way to contemplate impermanence is to simply sit with the question "Is there anything that doesn't change?" Rest attention on the breath and pose the question. You will feel a shift in attention, and the question will sit heavily in your body. Let the question act like a weight, and sit holding the weight: is there anything that doesn't change? Uneasiness, sadness, despair, and other feelings will arise. As before, use the breath as a base of attention to stay present in the reactions.

Periods of formal practice are often filled with distractions, uncomfortable feelings, and other challenges. When you go about your day, however, you feel lighter, clearer, and more appreciative of each moment of experience. These are all signs that a real understanding and acceptance of change has begun to form.

Change in the Body

After three or four weeks, begin the next section, on change in the body. Note the changes that take place in your body from the time you are born until the time you die.

As a baby, you are round and soft, very flexible but limited in how you can move. As a child, you learn to walk and talk, and your body grows until the bones and muscles become strong. In adolescence, your body changes again, developing according to your gender. In middle age, the skin begins to roughen, wrinkles develop, and the hair loses its shine and begins to gray. Eventually, your face is creased with wrinkles, your body bent with age, your bones brittle, and your muscles weak and unresponsive.

As you imagine your body aging, you feel uncomfortable; culturally, we are conditioned to value youth and the appearance of youth. One woman, after doing this meditation for a couple of weeks, came to class, looked me squarely in the face, and said, "I hate you."

Our bodies inevitably age. We can keep fit and flexible with proper exercise and diet, but nothing can stop the body from aging.

Reflect also on how the composition of the body constantly changes. With each breath you take in oxygen and expel carbon dioxide. You eat food. The nutritional components are absorbed, and the other parts are eliminated. Hair and nails grow. Skin flakes off and is replaced. Oxygen and food combine in the body to provide heat and energy. Blood, propelled by the regular beating of the heart, constantly circulates. Every cell in the body absorbs nutrients until it divides and becomes two. Nothing remains constant. If you stop breathing, you die.

Change in Personality and Belief Systems

Again, after three or four weeks, move on, to changes in attitudes, worldviews, your personality, the sense of who and what you are, and how you relate to the world.

The first thought is often that these don't change much. We automatically feel that how we think and how we behave remain the same, despite the passage of years. However, a careful examination of your life at, say, five-year intervals will reveal many changes. Picture yourself at five years old, and recall what you liked, what you didn't like, the important relationships in your life, how you felt, how you behaved, how you looked at the world, and what you believed. Then move to age ten, and go through the same reflections, and then to fifteen, and so on, up to your present age and beyond. A question forms: "What about me doesn't change?"

When you go through your life, you see patterns of behavior and connections among events that you never noticed before. An ex-Marine, a person who had seen plenty of death and destruction during the Vietnam War, made a good transition back to civilian life. He felt that he had put his demons to rest by writing three novel-length cathartic accounts of his wartime experience. He now had a thriving consulting business. In this meditation practice, he noted that his father had been absent through most of his childhood, and he realized how much he had missed his father's company. Then he recalled that his father had been a Marine and that he had made the decision to join the Marines shortly after his father died. Up to that point, he had been unaware of any connection between his father and his decision to join the Marines.

By reflecting on how you change as you go through life, you will see how your life is shaped, if not determined, by deep emotional patterns that operate outside awareness.

Eventually, you see that change is part of everything you experience. Emotional understanding is maturing into a different perception of the world. You understand that everything changes, that what seems so constant and permanent can actually vanish or change beyond recognition at any time for reasons that are completely beyond your control. You do what needs to be done, but your anticipation and your expectations of seeing the results of your actions are replaced by more attention to what you are actually doing and to your experience of each moment. You begin to appreciate that the notion of control is an illusion. Circumstances change, and you simply don't know what is going to happen next. The only thing to do is what's in front of you, making the best effort possible. Your approach to life becomes "This is what is meaningful to me right now, so I'll make this effort. What will come of it, I don't know, but this is what needs to be done right now."

A farmer lived with his son on a few acres of land. They were not well off, but they did have one horse, a good horse, with which they were able to plow the fields. One day, while they were repairing its paddock, the horse escaped and ran away. When the neighbors heard about the loss of the horse, they came around to commiserate. The farmer would have none of it. "What makes you think this is a disaster?" he asked, and he sent them away.

A week later, the horse returned with a wild horse accompanying it. The farmer now had two horses! When the neighbors heard the news, they came around to celebrate, but again, the farmer would have none of it. "What makes you think this is a blessing?" he asked.

A few weeks later, the son was thrown from the new horse while breaking it in and badly broke his hip. He healed up to a point, but although he was still able to help his father, his activities were limited. Again the neighbors came to commiserate, and again the farmer asked, "What makes you think this is a disaster?"

The next month, an army came through. Short on troops, the officers conscripted every able young man they could find and forced them at gunpoint to join their war. But the army had no use for anyone with a broken hip.

Whenever my teacher taught impermanence, he invariably began his talk with the four ends:

The end of accumulation is dispersion.
The end of building is ruin.
The end of meeting is parting.
The end of birth is death.

These four lines summarize change and are easy to remember. Use them to bring attention to change during the day.

Meditation 2: Death Is Inevitable

Purpose:
To know that we are going to die.

Key phrase:
Reflect on the many who have died.

Human History

- Prehumans and the early hominid species
- People in different civilizations: Chinese, Greek, Roman, European, Aztec, Inca, etc., from ancient history up to the present day
- The world population of the past few hundred years, people in different countries

> *It is doubtful that you will ever see or hear of*
> *Anyone who was born and will not die.*
>
> —Asvagosha

People with Exceptional Abilities

- Athletes (people with great physical prowess)
- Rulers and politicians (people with great temporal power)
- Military leaders and fighters (people who deal directly with death)
- Scholars, academics, and researchers (people with great intellectual powers)
- Artists (people with great creative abilities)
- Sages (people with great intuitive and miraculous abilities)

> *The great sages with their five kinds of miraculous knowledge,*
> *Though they were able to walk far in the sky,*
> *Could not go to a place*
> *Where they would not die.*
>
> —from *Shokavinodana*

- Saints and religious leaders (people with great spiritual insight and understanding)

Your Family and You

- Ancestors
- Parents and relatives
- People you love and care about
- You

Commentary

The purpose of this meditation is to wake us up to the fact that we are going to die. There are three sections, and you should practice each for about two weeks.

Although each section has a different focus, approach all of them with the single question, "Has there ever been anyone who didn't die?" While the answer is obviously no, understanding at the emotional level only arises when you apply attention to the question again and again.

Then spend an additional two weeks sitting with the certainty of death as explained below.

Human History

Begin with prehistory. Picture the early hominids wandering around the Serengeti, hunting for food and avoiding becoming food. Are any of them still alive? Later, different species of humans evolved, but except for Homo sapiens, all of them are now extinct. Are any of the original Homo sapiens still alive?

Both the Jewish and Chinese calendars date back five thousand years. Where are all the people who lived ten thousand or fifteen thousand years ago?

Continue by considering the great European and Asian civilizations, the African civilizations, and the many Polynesian societies. Did any of them avoid dying? We all know what happened at Pompeii, but what happened to everyone else who lived in Italy at that time?

What about the New World—the Mayan, Aztec, and Inca cultures? If you investigate all the cultures that have come and gone in the world, the answer begins to reverberate: *everyone dies.*

One student doing this meditation came to see humanity as a vast sea. Cultures and societies are like waves, cresting and ebbing, moving through time and space. The crests peak with the full development of empires such as the Egyptian, Roman, or Chinese. The troughs are the intervening periods of chaos such as the Dark Ages in Europe or the Period of Warring States in China when whole cultures are dying and new ones are being born. Everyone, however, whether living during a crest or trough or somewhere in between, dies.

People with Exceptional Abilities

Maybe you think death makes an exception for people with extraordinary abilities. Consider the special qualities and abilities you admire and seek to develop. Consider individuals who have or had those abilities. Did they or will they die? Is there any trait or ability that prevents death?

Sheer physical ability isn't enough. The fastest runners can't outrun death. The strongest weight lifters can't overpower death. The hardiest survivalists can't hold out forever against death. The fittest people can't use their conditioning or their diet to prevent themselves from dying. The most beautiful people can't seduce or charm death. Political power counts for nothing. Politicians can't legislate an end to death. Dictators can't ban their own death. Soldiers can't intimidate, threaten, or kill death. Scholars and researchers may have looked deeply into death, but all their ideas and conclusions don't stop them from dying. Artists may capture reality in verse or on canvas, but, even with all their creative abilities, death still comes. Doctors and nurses can't stop themselves or others from dying; they can only postpone the inevitable. The sages all succumbed. Their knowledge, insight, or miraculous powers could not prevent death. Even the greatest religious figures—Buddha Shakyamuni, Lao Tzu, Jesus, and the masters of all traditions—have died, despite their understanding of truth, divinity, or reality or their realization of God, emptiness, or Atman.

Political power and influence, physical strength, beauty, charm, intellectual brilliance, creativity, resourcefulness, courage, bravery, understanding, insight—none of these qualities will prevent you from dying.

Your Family and You

All your ancestors are dead—your grandparents, your great-grandparents, everyone, as far back as time goes. Your parents have died or will die. Aunts and uncles on both sides of your family are gone. Everyone from whom you have inherited your genetic makeup is now dead or will die. Are you going to be any different? You sit. And now you know, "I'm going to die."

Despair sets in. What's the point? What's the point of making any effort in life? Why try to learn or do anything if I'm just going to die?

Now regret appears. The illusion that you can somehow avoid dying by making the right effort is shattered. You suddenly realize how much of your life has been about avoiding dying. Now what do you do?

Sitting with the Certainty of Death

Once you feel the cold breath of death, spend an additional week or two sitting with the question "I'm going to die; how do I feel about that?" Don't try to analyze or reason. Rest attention on the breath, pose the question, feel the shift, and feel how the question acquires weight. Hold it in attention, and open to what you feel. Understanding penetrates deeper, and you are more aware and present in your life.

A king took great delight in his court jester. After a particularly entertaining evening, the king gave his jester a bag of gold coins and said, "Without doubt, you are the greatest fool in the world!"

The jester bowed his head and said, "Your Majesty is very kind, yet I know of a greater fool."

The king replied, "Well, you must show him to me. Bring him here!"

"Now is not the time, Your Majesty, but in due course, I will show him to you."

Many years passed. The king fell ill, and the doctors failed to heal him. Even he realized he was dying. He was fearful and afraid, so he called for his jester to entertain him.

The jester came and said, "Ah, Your Majesty, I was just coming to see you."

"You were? Why?"

"Do you remember my saying I knew of a greater fool than I?"

"Yes!" said the king, his eyes flashing with a spark of life despite his condition. "I do."

"I can show him to you now, if you wish," said the jester.

"Yes, yes, show him to me right now."

"He is you, Your Majesty. For your whole life you knew that one day you would die, yet you did nothing to prepare for this moment. Now you are fearful and afraid, and you can do nothing because you are ill and weak. Don't you agree that you are a much greater fool than I?"

Death casts a different light on life. The more fully you relate to death, the more fully you relate to life. You are clearer about what is and isn't important, what can and cannot be done, what is and isn't meaningful. Increasingly, you look beneath the surface of things and seek what really matters. Social prescriptions and promises of success and security ring hollow. Conventional definitions of success and failure—happiness and unhappiness, gain and loss, fame and obscurity, respect and disdain—lose their hold. Your relationship with society changes. You stop following convention for convention's sake or tradition for tradition's sake. In the end, you may do many of the same things, but you will do them for different, more personal, reasons. Each action, each meeting, each word you say comes from a personal connection to life, not from what you've been told to believe or do. The more you accept death, the more you embrace life.

Meditation 3: Death Can Come at Any Time

Purpose:
To know that we could die at any time.

Key phrase:
Again and again, reflect on the many causes of death.

Death Can Come in Many Ways

- Walk through a typical day, and observe how many ways you could die.
- Take an inventory of your home and your work, and observe how many objects could cause your death.

Death Can Come at Any Time

- Is there a time when it would be impossible to die?

Death Cannot Be Prevented

- Is there anything in your body that prevents you from dying?

First open this heap of skin with your intellect,
Then separate the flesh from the bones with the
*   scalpel of awareness,*
Open the bones and look into the marrow
And see for yourself
Whether there is anything solid.

—Shantideva

• Can wealth, possessions, friends, or abilities prevent you
  from dying?

There is no one to whom we can turn for help.

—Shantideva

We cannot defeat death, nor outrun it,
Nor argue with it, nor seduce it.

—Kalu Rinpoche

Commentary

The third meditation has two sections: reflecting on the guidelines, and
sitting with the fragility of life. Spend two to four weeks working with
the guidelines until you clearly appreciate that death can come at any
time. Then spend another two weeks sitting with the fragility of life.

A prevailing sentiment in today's world is that we all have a "right"
to live out our "full" life. An unspoken but pervasive myth in many
religious traditions is that if we live "properly," we will be rewarded
with a long life. The platforms of many political parties say that as
human beings, we "deserve" a long and healthy life. Rights, rewards,
and deserving have nothing to do with life and death. Life is fragile.
Good people die unexpectedly, just as bad people do. Anyone who
watches the coming and going of the breath knows that life and breath
are synonymous. When the breath stops, so do you. We can no more
invoke a "right" to life than we can waive a "right" to die.

Death is present everywhere in life despite the elaborate protections
society and people put in place to establish a death-free environment.

See how death lurks around every corner as you walk through a
typical day. You wake up, and as you swing your legs over the side of
the bed, your feet tangle in the sheets. You trip, strike your head
against the dresser, shatter your skull, and lie dying on your bedroom

floor. Maybe you escape that fate and walk to the bathroom. The pipes are old and leaky. Raw sewage has infiltrated the tap water you use to brush your teeth. Death has entered your body. Perhaps you slip in the shower and crack your skull open or are electrocuted by the electric razor or hair dryer. You step into the kitchen, where knives, electricity, gas, and bacteria are all ready to do you in. Having made it through the lethal obstacle course of your own home, you leave for work. The steps are wet and icy, so you slip and fall. Once in your car, your odds of arriving at work go down sharply. Fatal traffic accidents happen every day; you've just been lucky so far.

Continue through your day, noting all the different ways you can die in each moment. You don't have to be especially creative. Look closely, and you will see that death lurks everywhere.

Go through your home, noticing all the cutlery and plates, cooking utensils, electrical and mechanical equipment, cleaning solvents and other chemicals, objets d'art, pictures in heavy frames, and other objects that could be the cause of your death.

Stand on the sidewalk of a busy street. One step, one bump, and you die. Despite the precautions taken against food contamination, you are never completely safe. The canned tuna you have for lunch may be the last thing you will ever eat. Companies often recall large quantities of improperly processed meat. Death can come at any moment.

Can you think of a time and place when you absolutely could not die? A hospital? Think of all the different kinds of bacteria and viruses, not to mention errors in surgery or medication. Your own home? You've already seen that it's a death trap. Out in nature? You could die from lightning, earthquakes, tidal waves, volcanoes, falling rocks, falling branches, or snake or insect bites. Where and when are you completely safe from death? The cartoonist Gahan Wilson once drew a cartoon of a middle-aged woman staring at a man's hat crushed by a meteor. The caption read, "Harry always said that a meteor would get him."

Is there anything in your body that prevents you from dying right now? The body is a complex organism in which even a tiny dysfunction can quickly lead to death.

Can your wealth, friends, or abilities prevent you from dying at any given moment?

Outside formal practice, continue to cultivate awareness of how close death is all the time. Imagine that death walks just behind you as you go through your day. Imagine that you feel death's breath as you talk with people, do your work, drive your car, walk to your home, go to a movie, or make love.

At night, when you go to sleep, imagine that you are actually dying. Your life is over. You are not going to wake up. Anything can happen. It's not certain which will come first, tomorrow or the next world.

When you sit in meditation, imagine that every breath you take is your last.

Sitting with the Fragility of Life

As the possibility of dying at any moment sinks in, the first impulse is to shut it out so that you don't have to face uncertainty, fear, and discomfort. Instead, use the breath as a base of attention, and experience the uncertainty, fear, and discomfort *in attention*. Sit with the question "I could die at any time; how do I feel about that?" As in the previous practice, don't analyze or reason; simply open to the emotional impact of the fragility of life.

An obsession with safety makes people impotent in the face of threatening situations, conflicts, or difficulties. In other words, the fear of death weakens your connection with power. The Stoics valued what could not be taken by another person. Since one's life can be taken by another, they didn't regard life as the highest value and were prepared to give their lives for what did have value. What has value for you?

You can die at any moment. Expending energy to be completely safe is, in the end, a waste. Better to direct energy into being prepared to die at any moment. Are you prepared to die right now? What have you left unsaid or undone in your important relationships? What debts, obligations, or responsibilities have you not fulfilled? What do you need to do to make your life complete in each moment? These are the important questions of life that this practice brings to the fore.

The two central facts of human experience are that we are going to die and that we don't know when. We generally ignore these facts and go about life in a quasi–dream state. If you wish to be present in life, however, to enter into the mystery of life itself, you cannot ignore them. You have to face the question of how to live with the absolute certainty of death and the complete uncertainty of life.

On the one hand, you know that nothing lasts forever, that every relationship will end, and that the time will come when you have to leave everything you know behind. What is important to you? What is worthy of attention? What are you willing to live and die for?

On the other hand, you don't know when you will die. Relationships can end at any moment or last for many years. You may never see the results of current work, but you could just as easily see it through and then have to decide what to do next. Perhaps you will die today, perhaps in fifty years. With such uncertainty, what do you do?

In other words, since you can't count on the future but chances are you won't die this instant, how do you live? Suppose that you are a mother home from work in the evening. Do you prepare tomorrow's dinner or not? Suppose that you are a research doctor and you discover a new treatment for arthritis. Do you go about setting up field trials that may take many years to complete? Imagine that you are a contractor and your client refuses to pay you for your work. What do you do?

Life is what we experience. The inevitability of death is the ever present reminder that life is what we experience—not what we own, not what we leave behind, and not how history views us. The fragility of life reminds us that the present moment of experience is all we have. To be present in life is to experience the present moment. Be present in the moment, and you will know what to do.

> I am in the present. I cannot know what tomorrow will bring forth. I can know only what the truth is for me today. That is what I am called upon to serve, and I serve it in all lucidity.
>
> —*Igor Stravinsky*

Meditation 4: Dying

Purpose:
To know what happens at death.

Key phrase:
What happens when I die?

This meditation has three parts:
1. Approaching death
2. The dying process
3. Life is what you experience

Approaching Death

Dying of Old Age

- What do I experience as I approach death?
- How do I feel about my life: do I have regrets, or does my life feel complete?
- What preparations have I made?
- To whom do I say good-bye and how?
- How do I feel knowing that this room is where I'm going to die?
- Whom do I want to be with me?

Dying from Terminal Illness

- How do I feel now that I am soon going to die?
- What do I need to do to make my life complete?
- What preparations have I made?
- To whom do I say good-bye and how?
- Where do I want to be?
- Whom do I want to be with me?
- What do I regret?
- What am I grateful for?

Dying in a Car Accident

- What do I experience as my life slips away?
- How do I feel, knowing that this car or the pavement is the last thing I will see in this world?
- What preparations have I made?
- What do I now wish I had done or said?

Commentary: Approaching Death

The guidelines for approaching death contain three scenarios: old age, a terminal illness, and a car accident. Spend a week or more on each one. You may, of course, use other scenarios, but take care that they cover three ways of dying: death that is the natural end of life, untimely death, and sudden or unexpected death.

Dying of Old Age

Imagine that you are old. You have lived for seventy, eighty, or ninety years. The gradual decline of your body has forced you to give up many activities that you enjoyed. You know that time is running out and that, like all your friends and companions, you are going to die soon. You are physically frail. You can't drive anymore. You can't see clearly, and your arms and legs don't respond the way they used to. You have lost your vigor and vitality. You need the help of others to do even the simplest things—to put on your clothes, cut up your food, or prepare to sleep at night. You have difficulty communicating what you want or need. You hear people talking to you, but you have difficulty understanding what they mean. You can barely walk or even sit. Food is tasteless. Everything irritates. You become increasingly dependent on others. You can't even eat or wash or go to the toilet without help. Your body struggles to stay alive even though all its systems are breaking down. Death doesn't come easily.

What goes through your mind? Have you come to terms with your life—the successes, failures, dreams, and disappointments? Does the proximity of death make you reexamine your relationships and what you have or have not accomplished? Do you feel that you have lived in an illusion of your own creation and the illusion is now disintegrating? Are you bitter, afraid, sad, confused, relieved, or at peace? Are you concerned about how you are going to meet your death or what will happen after? Do you pretend that you are not dying and tell everyone that you are fine? Are you confident that nothing dies, as some spiritual traditions teach? Does that confidence come from belief or knowing? In the words of one man dying from AIDS, "In the fire of dying, philosophies melt like ice cubes."

Dying from Terminal Illness

In a second scenario, imagine that your doctor calls after a regular checkup and asks you to come to her office. She suggests that you bring a loved one. Sitting in a plush chair opposite her desk, you learn that you have a terminal illness. There are no treatment options. You have six to eight months to live.

As you leave her office, what happens between your loved one and you? Do you talk? What do you say? How do you go about these last months of your life?

Do you focus on practical matters such as your personal affairs and the financial security of those close to you, or do you focus on relationships? Do you pour energy into a pet project or reflect on what life has meant for you? Do you fall into confusion and have no idea which way to turn or what to do?

An unexpected terminal illness cuts short all expectations, plans, and hopes for the future. Hoped-for accomplishments vanish like breath on a mirror. How do you react to the unforgiving reality of your illness and your shortened life?

Are you at peace with how you lived? Yes, you will miss seeing your children grow into adults, but do you regret how you have lived and what you have done with your life?

Do you live in regret over the wasted time and missed opportunities? Do you blame others for your failures and disappointments? In the light of death, do you see things more clearly, seeing how pride and anger, desire and fear shaped what happened or didn't happen in your life?

Sitting with such reflections and insights is like lying on a bed of nails. The pain of our stupidity and blindness is penetrating and unrelenting.

What do you need to be able to let go and die in peace? Do you need to repair your relationships, to understand what life is about, or to know that those close to you will be taken care of? Does your illness leave you enough emotional and physical strength to make this effort, or will you die in regret, knowing what you need to do but unable to do it?

Dying in a Car Accident

In the third scenario, imagine that you are in an accident and are thrown out of your car. Your body is broken and in pain. Perhaps you go into shock and your body is numb. You are immobilized and incapacitated. In complete disbelief, you wonder, "How could this accident happen? How can I be dying? A moment ago I was full of life and ability, and now I am lying here on the ground dying. This pavement or dirt or grass is the last thing I will see. I don't want to die. I'm not ready."

Thoughts and ideas rush into your mind: "I never told her I was sorry," "I'll never see my children again," or "No, I refuse to die." You feel your blood and life energy slipping away. You lie dying in the midst of confusion as paramedics and police officers sort through the chaos.

> Only put off until tomorrow what you are willing to die having left undone.
>
> —*Pablo Picasso*

In a few short moments, you have to say good-bye to everything you know. No one can do anything to help you. Regrets about how you have lived, relationships that are not complete, and dreams you never pursued flood your thoughts. You, alone, have to meet this tide of feelings, thoughts, insights, and realizations. Can you do so with openness, clarity, and acceptance?

> We don't receive wisdom; we must discover it for ourselves after a journey that no one can take for us or spare us.
>
> —*Marcel Proust*

Countless examples can be cited to illustrate how the prospect of impending death forces us to see more clearly what is true, real, and valuable. Ironically, we often make no effort to know what we truly value until we are faced with our own death, the death of someone close to us, or some other crisis. We spend much of our lives pursuing values that we have been conditioned to accept, focusing on what is valued by others, and not living out of our own knowing and awareness.

Lee Atwater, former chairman of the Republican National Committee and one of the more brilliant and ruthless political strategists of recent times, was diagnosed with incurable cancer when he was thirty-nine. The cancer led him to see his life differently, and he didn't like what he saw:

Mostly I am sorry for the way I thought of other people. Like a good general, I had treated everyone who wasn't with me as against me. After the election, when I would run into Ron Brown, my counterpart in the Democratic Party, I would say hello and then pass him off to one of my aides. I actually thought that talking to him would make me appear vulnerable. Since my illness, Ron has been enormously kind and I have learned a lesson: politics and human relationships are separate. I may disagree with Ron Brown's message, but I can love him as a man.

The '80s were about acquiring—acquiring wealth, power, prestige. I know. I acquired more wealth, power and prestige than most. But you can acquire all you want and still feel empty. What power wouldn't I trade for a little more time with my family? What price wouldn't I pay for an evening with friends? It took a deadly illness to put me eye to eye with that truth, but it is a truth that the country, caught up in its ruthless ambitions and moral decay, can learn on my dime.

But we can't learn on someone's else's dime; we must learn it for ourselves.

THE DYING PROCESS

Dissolution of Psychophysical Structures

- Earth (solidity) dissolves
    Unable to move body
    Experience of crushing weight
    Consciousness is like a shimmering mirage

- Water (fluidity) dissolves
    Loss of control of fluids
    Experience of flood
    Consciousness is hazy and smoky

- Fire (warmth) dissolves
    Warmth recedes from limbs
    Experience of intense heat
    Consciousness is like sparks or fireflies

- Air (movement) dissolves
    Breath stops
    Experience of strong wind
    Consciousness is like a glowing ember

- Space (consciousness) dissolves
    Dissolution of sense faculties
    Experience of mirage, smoke, sparks, and ember

- Dissolution of explicit sense of self (anger)
    Experience of white brilliance (moon)

- Dissolution of implicit sense of self (desire)
    Experience of red brilliance (sun)

- Dissolution of ignorance structures
    Experience of black brilliance

- Full dissolution
    Pristine clarity or luminosity

Commentary: The Dying Process

According to Tibetan Buddhism, all experience arises as a combination of five elements: earth, water, fire, air, and void. The body is composed of the five elements: the muscles and bones are earth, the fluids in the body are water, the warmth in the body is fire, the energy and breath are air, and the cavities in the lungs and other organs are void. Earth manifests as solidity and structure, water as flow and adaptability, fire as heat and intensity, air as movement and activity, and void as space and wholeness. The experience of stability is earth, of emotional connection is water, of passion is fire, of ideas and insights is air, and of completeness is void.

The experience we call life is formed from these five elements as well. At death, they dissolve back into emptiness, and the experience of life comes to an end.

The classical texts say that one element dissolves into the next, but according to my teacher, Kalu Rinpoche, the process is a little more complex. As each element dissolves, the stored energy is released, affecting our perception and consciousness. The subjective experience of that element is temporarily intensified. When the energy has dispersed, the next element starts to break down.

By going through the dying process, by imagining we are actually dying, we meet the fears and reactions that keep us from being present in the experience of death. We recognize that the same reactions arise whenever we encounter change: the end of a relationship, the loss of a job, the shattering of a belief. Meditation on the dying process helps us to be present in the many little deaths life deals us.

For this meditation, first rest attention with the breath for ten or fifteen minutes, and then imagine that you are dying. Feel death grip you as you realize that the end has come. Breathe. Stay present in any fear or other reaction that arises.

You slowly realize that you can no longer move your arms and legs. You recognize the change as the sign that the earth element is breaking down. You feel imprisoned in your body as if it's made of rock. A thousand pounds of stone crush your chest. You can't move at all. Your consciousness loses its stability. Everything around you, your room and the people attending you, floats like a mirage. Fear grips you. You are being crushed, and your mind is going! You do your best not to panic and try to stay present in what is happening.

You realize that you are urinating and that spittle is dripping out of your mouth and that tears fill your eyes. You can't control the fluids in your body anymore; the water element is dissolving. As it dissolves, you feel as if you are swept away by a river, churned around by huge waves, engulfed by tons of water. You are drowning! Your perception of the world loses clarity. Everything around you becomes clouded and hazy. You think that something has gone wrong with your eyes. Again, rest in the sensations, staying present with what is happening and what you are feeling. Experience the disorientation and fear.

You hear someone say, "Oh, his (or her) hands are so cold!" You realize that the heat is receding from your limbs, the sign that the fire element is dissolving. Inside, however, you are on fire. You are desperately thirsty but can't tell anyone what you need. The heat is worse than the worst fever. Every cell of your body feels as if it's on fire. Your perception becomes feeble, diminishing to little flashes—a spark now and then.

Breathing becomes increasingly difficult. Your breath rasps as it goes in and rattles as it goes out. Each breath is a struggle, and you dimly realize that the air element is dissolving. Bursts of energy, like gusts of wind, race around in your body. You are lost in all the commotion as if you were carried away and whirled around by powerful winds. Your consciousness becomes very dim, like a weakly glowing ember. You are barely aware of those around you.

Your sense faculties completely disintegrate. Sight, hearing, taste, touch, and smell are gone. You have a rapid series of hallucinations in which everything appears like a mirage, then hazy, then as weak flashes of light, and then like a dim glow. Then everything dissolves into light. You sense a movement of energy downward, and you are in a field of light that has no center or periphery. There is no other, and all sense of aversion has gone.

In this phase, thought consciousness and the explicit conceptual sense of "I" dissolve. The explicit sense of "I" is a sense of being something that is unique, permanent, and independent. It sets us apart from the world and therefore functions as the basis of anger. As this pattern dissolves, the structures that support anger and aversion also dissolve. There is an experience of clarity without dimension. Traditionally, it is called the white brilliance and is likened to moonlight. It is the first of four experiences of sheer clarity that arise as the illusion of ordinary consciousness dissolves.

Then you feel a movement of energy upward and the light intensifies. If the first experience of light was like moonlight, this second experience is like sunlight. The sense of "I" and any sense of attraction are gone. There is just an experience of light.

The second phase is the dissolution of the emotional mind and the implicit sense of "I." The implicit sense of "I" is the one that persists even when the mind is quiet and still. It sees everything as belonging to it and therefore functions as the basis of desire and attraction. As these structures dissolve, attraction ceases to function and a more intense experience of clarity arises. This clarity is called the red brilliance and is likened to the sun. The clarity isn't actually red, however. The color has symbolic significance and indicates a greater intensity than the previous experience.

The two movements of energy then converge. What was infinite light now becomes infinite blackness—no up, no down, no right, no left, no center, no front, no back. There is nothing with which to orient yourself, just blackness.

The dissolution of the base ignorance is next. Base ignorance, or fundamental not-knowing, is the not-knowing on which the misperception of "I" is based. As this fundamental not-knowing dissolves, a corresponding experience of clarity called the black brilliance arises. In this experience, there is no reference, no orientation. There is total blackness. The basis consciousness is dissolving into fundamental pristine awareness.

The dying process is reversible during the first two phases of dissolution. When the third phase, the black brilliance, arises, the process can no longer be reversed. You are dead.

Next, the blackness dissolves and you experience an infinite field of light as if you were at the center of the sun. You experience total and utter emptiness indivisible from brilliant clarity. This is original mind. Rest in this brilliantly clear and empty original mind for a few minutes.

Pristine awareness is experienced as sheer clarity, more brilliant and intense than anything that has arisen before. According to the Tibetan tradition, at this point, if attention operates at a sufficiently high level of energy, full awakening is experienced. If attention is weak and unstable, base ignorance reasserts itself and obscures this clarity, habituated patterns reassert themselves, and the experience of separate existence begins again.

LIFE IS WHAT YOU EXPERIENCE

- Form the intention to be in your life.
- Become who you are ordinarily, and carry the sense of pristine clarity.
- Go about your day as if you are dead and everything you experience is like a dream.

Commentary: Life Is What You Experience

Now, form the intention to experience your life, your home, the people you know, and the routine of the day. Rest for a few more minutes so that you know where you are, but carry the sense of original mind, of infinite light. Then go about your day as if you are dead and everything you experience is simply an arising in your mind. Remind yourself over and over, "I am dead; everything I experience arises out of nothing and subsides back into nothing. It is just an experience."

The practice of going about our day as if we were dead is very powerful. We learn that we can function effectively in the world without depending on the framework of "I" and "other." The power of reactive emotions and social conditioning is greatly reduced. We realize that life consists purely of what we experience in each moment, nothing more and nothing less. We realize that because we are caught up in emotional reaction about what happened in the past or might happen in the future, we habitually pay little attention to what we actually experience.

Meditation 5: After Death

Purpose:
To know what is important in life.

Key phrase:
What happens after I die?

Content of This Life

- The body disintegrates.

    It is consumed by a blazing fire,
    Drowned in water and eaten by worms,
    Or hidden away in the earth where it rots.
                                    —Shantideva

- Everything you owned goes to someone else or is thrown away.
- Your role as parent or grandparent goes to another.

- Your work is done by others or is forgotten.
- Other people move into the positions you held.
- People find new friends.
- All that remains of your achievements is an object, an institution, memories in the minds of others, articles, or pictures.

Relationship with This Life

- You can never change anything you've done.
- You will never again experience this life.

Commentary

The purpose of this meditation is to understand that ultimately we are not the content of our life. To say exactly what we are is very difficult. Ordinarily, we define who and what we are in terms of our body, our wealth and possessions, what we have achieved, and our position in family, work, and society. All of that ends with death. Death shatters the illusion that our body, our possessions, or our relationships define what we really are.

Are you your body? Imagine your body in a funeral parlor. Your body is preserved with formaldehyde and reshaped after the rigors of dying. The undertaker makes it look as attractive and lifelike as possible, using makeup, hair dye, and your best clothes. Is this what you are—a caricature of life? Every effort is made to give the impression that you are merely sleeping, that you are still part of the world.

A short time later, your body is either burned or buried. The body is broken down into its component atoms and molecules, either in the intense flames of a crematorium or in the digestive tracts of worms and insects. Bones last longer, but even they eventually crumble and turn to dust.

What happens to your possessions? Imagine everything you owned at the time of your death being heaped up into a big pile, all the books, clothes, furniture, jewelry, cars, sports equipment, paintings and other art objects, houses, and land. Is this what you are? Everything in that pile is either thrown away or goes to someone else. A lock of hair from your first lover, a photograph of you as a child with your parents, a book, a necklace—such objects hold special significance for you, but to those who are still alive they mean nothing. They are just things to be preserved in a museum if they are historically significant, sold if they are worth anything, given to charity if they are still usable, or thrown away. No, you are not your possessions.

Your wealth meets a similar fate. It goes to your heirs, to organizations, or to the state, depending on what legal documents you have or haven't left behind. Our legal system provides elaborate and complicated procedures for the transferal of property from the name of the deceased to those who are alive. Such terms as "the estate of so-and-so" are used to refer to the property, but nobody is under the illusion that so-and-so still owns the property. The property is now owned by those who inherit the estate. One way or another, the sum total of your wealth is handed over to the control or ownership of others. It's out of your hands.

Your role in your family is finished. If you were the head of the family, the person on whom everyone relied, someone else now fills that function. Perhaps the family falls apart and your relatives go about their lives in a different way. If you die before your parents do, they experience terrible grief and loss. Your life is over. They are still living. You are dead. Their child no longer exists. They may not be the same because of your death, but you are no longer part of their lives.

One student doing this practice was struck by the realization that one hundred years from now there would be no one alive who had ever known her and that, at best, she would be only a name or possibly a picture in a book.

In your job, the situation is even more cruel. You are replaced as soon as possible, or your job disappears. In either case, your work is given to someone else. Clearly, you are not your work.

A producer in Hollywood was overseeing the outdoor shooting of a commercial that involved a full symphony orchestra. The day was hot and the sun beat down on the musicians. Suddenly, the oboe player had a heart attack and died. Before the paramedics arrived, the producer was on the phone to a musicians' union saying, "I need an oboe player, now!"

Your work may never be completed. How many painters, writers, and scientists have died with their work unfinished and forgotten? Even if you made major contributions to the well-being of others, to the advancement of ideas, or to the introduction of new values or perspectives, all your work becomes the work of others. It is changed, confirmed, modified, or developed; forgotten, disproved, dismissed, or neglected. No, you are not your work or your achievements.

How can you know what is going to happen after you die? Look at what happens to other people's lives after they die. Look at the rich and famous, the poor and unknown, the respected and despised, the admired and vilified. Look at those who hoarded everything they could and at those who lived simply and frugally, leaving almost nothing behind. Look at those who devoted their time and energy to others, who gave generously and contributed much to the world. Look and see what happens to the content of their lives, their bodies, their possessions, their wealth, their family, their jobs, their contributions, and their effect on the world.

Once you die, you cannot change anything about your life. You can't apologize to a friend you let down. You can't tell those you loved how much they meant to you. You can't take back words you regret having spoken. You can't repair relationships damaged by your actions. You can't turn over a new leaf.

> Do not fear death so much, but rather the inadequate life.
>
> —*Bertolt Brecht*

Never again will you experience waking up with your spouse beside you. Never again will you experience your children greeting you. Never again will you experience the support and appreciation of your friends and the people with whom you work. Never again will you smell a flower or sip a glass of wine.

This experience we call life comes to an end. How much of it do you really experience? How much of it do you miss because you are lost in confusion and reaction? When you consider deeply what happens after death, you realize more clearly that all we have is our immediate experience. That is life. Everything else—gain, fame, respect, loss, obscurity, disdain, even happiness and unhappiness—is a construction, if not an abstraction. Taking these constructions to be real, we spend our lives pursuing or avoiding them. In the process, we miss the actual experience of life itself. What a waste!

DEATH AND PRESENCE

Each of us is a unique combination of consciousness, perception, environment, family, growth, and development. We die, and who and what we are is gone forever. Does experience continue to arise after death? How can we know? Yet the seeming darkness of not-knowing illuminates the experience of life. Presence is possible only when we are in touch with the totality of experience, both what appears to arise internally and what appears to arise externally. To touch the totality we have to let go of beliefs—that is, what we think we know. Not-knowing becomes a path.

The path is not easy. Our personality is organized on the basis of control. Stepping into not-knowing means stepping out of the illusion of control. Habituated patterns do not go easily. Resistance often arises as fear, fear of the unknown. A gulf opens in front of us, and we don't know what will happen if we step into it. Meeting that gulf is the essence of spiritual practice. It is why meditation on death is so important. To step into that unknowing is to die to the life we think we know and control. To live awake means to face this dying in each moment.

> One doesn't discover new lands without consenting to lose sight of the shore for a very long time.
>
> —*André Gide*

During my seven years of retreat training, one of the genuine surprises was the extent to which the theme of impermanence and death permeated advanced meditation practice, particularly the direct-awareness practices that we will consider later.

Direct awareness is practiced by letting all expectations drop away so that we rest in total awareness. To let all expectations drop is to die in the moment. Therefore, meditation on death and impermanence plays a crucial role in preparing and sustaining awareness practice.

Practice is not about achieving alternative states of consciousness. It is about using the raw material of our lives to deepen our relationship with life itself. The essence of practice is presence. Presence is natural awareness. It is our human heritage. Awareness of death and impermanence cuts through the veils of personal habituation and socially conditioned agendas. It puts us in touch with life itself.

CHAPTER 5

Karma and
Dismantling Belief

"What is Fate?" Nasrudin was asked by a scholar.

"An endless succession of intertwined events, each influencing the other."

"That is hardly a satisfactory answer. I believe in cause and effect."

"Very well," said the Mulla, "look at that." He pointed to a procession passing in the street. "That man is being taken to be hanged. Is that because someone gave him a silver piece and enabled him to buy the knife with which he committed the murder; or because someone saw him do it; or because nobody stopped him?"

—IDRIES SHAH,
THE EXPLOITS OF THE INCOMPARABLE MULLA NASRUDIN

What is this experience called life? That is the great mystery. The life that we think is real and substantial—bodies, families, relationships, achievements, our wealth and possessions—is really just one experience after another. The shared world of communication with its attendant beliefs in order, relationships, and values is only one aspect, albeit an important one, of life. The so-called objective world is an abstraction from what we actually experience. To know what life is we must die to the belief that the objective, shared world of experience is what is.

Ordinarily, we direct our life energy toward gaining power, wealth, respect, and security—values that all depend on shared perception. Neither gold nor a seashell is intrinsically valuable. One culture values gold, so it becomes a measure of wealth. Another values seashells, so they become the measure of wealth. One culture admires and respects those who never show their feelings. Another culture admires and respects those who show their feelings passionately. In the face of death, we see clearly that such culture-based values are not what is real. The shared world disappears when we die. Death brings us face-to-face with the mystery of experience, the mystery of life.

> One must be thrust out of a finished cycle in life, and that leap is the most difficult to make— to part with one's faith, one's love, when one would prefer to renew the faith and recreate the passion.
>
> —*Anaïs Nin*

When confronted with a mystery, we turn to beliefs; we wonder, "Why did that happen?" or "Why is this happening to me?" Beliefs provide a way to interpret what happens in life as part of a larger order, plan, or structure. They tell us what is possible and what is not. Beliefs appear to confirm our place in the scheme of things because the interpretation they offer accords with what is already inside us. Beliefs offer the impression of security and shelter from the mystery of being. Beliefs are a form of sleep.

All of us, at some point in our lives, have looked up at a clear blue sky and asked ourselves, "Why is the sky blue?" There it is, as blue as can be, and we feel the mystery. In that moment, a curiosity, an opening, stirs in us.

Science holds the belief that the sky is blue because the chemical composition of the atmosphere is such that light of certain frequencies is absorbed or scattered and the result is a blue sky. A belief from the culture of Buddhist India circa 500 C.E. holds that the sky is blue because it reflects the blue slopes of the mountain at the center of the universe. Both beliefs seek to explain away the mystery, but neither really does. Science does not tell us why the physics of the universe is such that the atmosphere filters out exactly that frequency or how and why we call the sky "blue." Buddhist cosmology fails to explain why the side of the mountain is blue.

Even if we accept these and other beliefs, they leave us dead inside. When we ask such questions as "Why is the sky blue?" we are not asking for an explanation or the reiteration of a belief. Something else is going on.

Look into the deep blue of the sky and ask, "Why is it so blue? Where does the blue come from?" Feel what happens inside you. Don't analyze the sky or what stirs inside. Just rest there, in the mystery of it all. Something opens inside you, and you feel more present in life. If what stirs inside causes you too much discomfort, however, you turn away—"This is silly!"—and go back to sleep.

KARMA AS BELIEF

Most human activity not directly connected with survival is a response to two questions:

- Why do I experience what I do?
- How do I change what I experience?

The teachings on karma are Buddhism's response to these two questions. As such, they are intended to dismantle belief and help us open to the mystery of experience. Ironically, the opposite often happens. Karma is taken as a belief and used to explain away the mysteries of life.

Differences in Individual Experience

Why is one person tall and another short? Why is one person born into great wealth and another into poverty? The Western belief is that individual differences are based on genetics, developmental psychology, sociology, history, and so forth. Belief in karma attributes the differences to the results of actions in past lives. The ripening of past actions is responsible for the conditions of life now, whether we are rich or poor, enjoy good fortune or bad, are good-looking or ugly, or are strong, weak, healthy, sickly, intelligent, stupid, extroverted, or introverted.

Karma also explains differences in fate. Why does one person emerge from an accident unscathed while everyone else is killed or seriously injured? Why does one person die after a meal while no one else eating the same meal even becomes ill? Why do some people work hard and have nothing to show for it while others work very little and become wealthy? Karmically speaking, untimely death, illness, and disability are all seen as consequences of harming others in previous lives. Individuals who enjoy longevity, vitality, and extraordinary abilities are seen as reaping the results of helping others in previous lives, regardless of their personality, character, or behavior in this life. Is such a perspective moving us closer to the mystery of experience or only allowing us to be more comfortable with the discrepancies that we observe?

Creation and Collective Karma

How was the universe created, and why is the universe the way it is? In Buddhist cosmology, the universe evolves from the karma of the beings who will be born into it. Their karmic energy manifests as a wind that condenses first into clouds, then into rain, which forms an ocean. The ocean is churned by the wind, producing earth, just as the churning of milk produces butter. When the universe and its multiple world systems have formed, beings, whose karma has dictated its particulars, are born into it. What is experienced as the objective world is the manifestation of the karma of the beings that inhabit it. As the karma plays itself out in this particular manifestation, the universe dissolves back into nothing and the karmic energy of the beings forms other universes.

The concept of collective karma naturally emerges from this explanation. The collective karma of a group is the total of the individual karmas of the beings in the group, whether the group is a universe of beings, a country, an institution, or a family. The workings of karma are now applied not only to individuals but also to entities that are the product of the shared world of experience.

In substantiating the objective world, have the cosmological explanations moved us closer to the mystery of being or farther away from it?

Is the Universe Just?

The mystery of experience has consistently provoked people in many different cultures to project human values onto the universe. Several years ago, I began a class on karma by asking everyone what they thought karma was. Over three-quarters of the class replied that karma was the mechanism that made the universe just.

The desire for justice is a human desire. We all want to live in a society that enshrines the rights of individuals in its culture, customs, and laws. Naturally, we would also like to believe that the universe is just. Karma, from this viewpoint, is the mechanism that punishes those who violate the rights of others and rewards those who care for and do good to others.

When the view of karma as the balancing mechanism in a just universe is combined with the view that individual differences are caused by karma, we are forced to project into past and future lives in order to keep these views from conflicting with our own experience. When innocent people are murdered or die in an epidemic, earthquake, or war, their fate is regarded as the fruition of evil or cruelty that they performed in a previous life. Similarly, when we see people profiting from cruelty, tyranny, theft, murder, rape, or duplicity, we must attribute their present good fortune to virtuous activity in previous lives. Such conclusions are forced on us if we are to maintain both our belief in karma and our belief that the universe is inherently just. The time frame may be vast, but the beliefs are set: good actions lead to good experiences in future lives; bad actions lead to bad experiences; and everything balances out in the end. Such conclusions not only are insupportable by experience but also lead to a passive approach to life.

> In the beginning, the universe was created. This made a lot of people very angry, and has been widely regarded as a bad idea.
>
> —Douglas Adams

Political and Social Systems

Political and social institutions reflect and embody the prevailing beliefs and worldview of a society. When the inequities present in a culture are attributed to the good and bad karma of individuals, attention is diverted from the way the political or cultural structure itself may be creating and perpetuating inequities. Belief in the divine right of kings diverts attention from social inequities, just as belief in the efficiency of free-market capitalism diverts attention from economic inequities.

Thus, karma as belief can contribute to maintaining political and social structures. The behaviors that support the system inevitably become part of the moral code of the culture. How can we tell whether moral codes are serving a cultural structure? One sign is that the culture discourages the questioning of established behaviors. The codes have to be observed even when no clear basis, spiritual or otherwise, exists for the behaviors they prescribe.

Rigidity in Moral Position

Belief in karma is regarded as one of the criteria for "right views" in most traditions of Buddhism. Beliefs about the world and about who we are form the basis for our determining what is morally right and wrong. When those beliefs are firmly in place, we rely on the authority of the beliefs instead of our own awareness and experience to determine right from wrong. We have difficulty accepting actions that, however appropriate for the situation, violate the established morality.

> A regime cannot be understood in its essence unless its underlying moral reality is seen for what it is.
>
> —*Michael Ignatieff*

The caste system of India is an example of how rigid and stratified a society can become when karma is taken as an explanation of why the world is the way it is. Another example is the posture that Zen institutions in Japan adopted in World War II, supporting the war effort, celebrating the aggression of the military, and justifying the slaughter of people in the belief that the emperor and the Japanese army were the instruments of karma. In Christianity, similarly specious justifications were used for the Crusades.

We also interpret what happens in terms of our beliefs. Since those beliefs form the structure that underlies who we are and our place in the world, we resist strongly, sometimes violently, any interpretation of events and experiences that would bring them into question.

Faith Vs. Belief

Faith, not belief, is the way to approach the mystery of being. Belief is the effort to eliminate the mystery by interpreting experience to accord with what is already conditioned in us.

Relying on karma as belief inhibits the work of dismantling habituated patterns and waking up to how things really are. Belief in karma works against the effort to enter into the mystery of being. It lulls us to sleep by telling us that the universe has an order and that that order is just. It allows us to project the universe we would like to exist. It is also used to justify social injustice and an inflexible morality that turns its back on obvious suffering.

Faith is the willingness to open to the mystery of life itself—to see and know things as they are, not as we would like them to be.

KARMA AS THE EVOLUTION OF PATTERNS

What is karma? The peripatetic Kagyu teacher Khenpo Tsultrim defines karma as

> Physical, verbal, or mental acts that imprint habituated tendencies in the mind.

Classically, Buddhism assumes that all actions are volitional. Psychoanalysis, behaviorism, and other modern psychological theories assume the opposite, that all actions are conditioned. Neither of these viewpoints is completely true.

All of us have had the experience of acting in ways we did not intend when anger, love, greed, or shame dictated our actions. All of us have had the experience of acting volitionally, when we went against all our impulses and conditioning, somehow knowing what had to be done and just doing it. The meditations presented here have two aims: to expose how habituated patterns rule much of our lives and to show how we can end their tyranny.

Four characteristics are associated with patterns: mechanicality, resonance, crystallization, and habituation. *Mechanicality* captures the automatic, nonvolitional nature of patterns. *Resonance* describes how patterns absorb the energy of attention and cause attention to decay. *Crystallization* refers to the formation of internal structures that propagate the mechanical operation of patterns from moment to moment. *Habituation* is the accumulation of energy in the operation of a pattern. In other words, the more it runs, the stronger it becomes.

By way of an example, a person I know is adept at attracting attention. In every situation, he finds a way to crack a joke, make an astute comment, raise a personal health issue, or offer advice. Outgoing, entertaining, and interesting, he is unable to be part of a group or event without at some point drawing attention expressly to himself.

The pattern had crystallized to such an extent that he consistently justified his behavior as being helpful, raising legitimate concerns, introducing important insights, or providing entertainment. Most of the time, his actions were helpful. He and I discussed this behavior, and he insisted that it was volitional. Not convinced, I suggested he make an explicit effort to refrain from drawing attention to himself at the next social event he attended.

A short time later he went to a dinner party with a group of friends. Everyone else was engaged in a lively conversation, but the subject matter was one he did not know well. The feeling of being left out resonated with the core of the pattern that demanded attention. He forgot our discussion, and the pattern started to run mechanically. He introduced a highly controversial topic, derailing the previous discussion, and became the center of attention, arguing his case passionately even though he ended up taking a position contrary to his own professed values. Later that evening, after he had left the party, he realized that he had no interest in the topic per se and couldn't justify the position he had been espousing. He realized that, at least on this occasion, his behavior was not volitional and that the pattern was more deeply habituated than he had thought.

The meditations in this chapter bring attention to the nature and operation of conditioned patterns. The patterns are revealed as self-organizing and self-perpetuating autonomous structures that function to degrade attention. They form in response to an experience too powerful to face, they develop into conditioning, and they continue to elaborate throughout our lives. Large areas and long periods of our lives are determined not by our volition but by the operation of such patterns. Suffering is inevitable because patterns bring about precisely the experiences that we are trying to avoid. The meditations show how to apply attention in order to dismantle habituated patterns and create the possibility of volitional action. The result is original mind, an unfettered mind that allows us to live in awareness and act volitionally.

Fundamental change does not take place without strong motivation, so teachers through the ages have emphasized motivation over technique. The purpose of the meditations on death and impermanence is to dismantle attachment to conventional success in order to shape a suitable internal environment for spiritual practice. The purpose of the meditations on karma is to dismantle the belief that each of us is an autonomous self that acts rationally and volitionally. When we see clearly to what extent conditioning runs our lives, we are strongly motivated to go further in dismantling the patterns that form and shape our experience.

Practice Guidelines

Spend between forty minutes and an hour every day on these meditations, working for two to four weeks on each. You may need more time on some meditations and less on others. The aim here is not just to do these practices but to change the way you see your life and what runs it. When working with meditation or with patterns, self-deception is always a danger, so at each stage, confirm your understanding with your teacher.

For each meditation, start by reading both the meditation and the associated commentary carefully. Many of the perspectives will be new and possibly challenging. During the meditation period, use specific examples and incidents from your own life in which patterns have caused problems, difficulties, and pain for you. To revisit painful events is unpleasant. Until we see what patterns are operating and dismantle them, however, we are susceptible to the same reactions in the future.

> It is a painful thing
> To look at your own
> trouble and know
> That you yourself and
> no one else made it.
>
> —*Sophocles*

A practice session consists of three parts: forming a base of attention (basic meditation), bringing attention to the material, and letting the understanding diffuse through your whole being.

A good fifteen to twenty minutes should be spent in basic meditation to establish a base of attention.

Next, spend twenty minutes to half an hour on bringing attention to the images or ideas in the meditation guidelines. The time is sufficient to produce good results in consistent daily practice but not so long that resistance sets in as boredom.

At the end of the practice period, take another ten to fifteen minutes to let the understanding spread in you. Return attention to the breath and sit with very open attention, as if you were looking into the sky or over a vast landscape. Let go of all the ideas and reflections from the meditation, and just rest in open awareness. This concluding period reduces the likelihood that the emotional reactions stirred up by the meditation practice will be carried directly into your life.

The meditations on karma, like the meditations on death, use the three-step process of study, reflection, and cultivation. The purpose is the same—to instill understanding at the intellectual and emotional levels.

The key to effective practice is to rely on attention and not to rely too much on the intellect. Constant analysis and reasoning will only create confusion and frustration. The meditation material is intended to illuminate your experience, not establish a new set of beliefs. Learning and study are used to develop a sound understanding of the material in the guidelines. Use reflection to check it against your experience.

Effective cultivation rests on the ability to hold what you are looking at in attention. When you hold a theme, situation, or state of mind in attention, it gradually unfolds and reveals how it functions and of what it is composed. Understanding arises first as feeling and then as seeing. Deduction is not part of the process.

Many of the transitions and states of mind described in the meditations are momentary and fleeting. Their transient nature makes them difficult to identify. Use incidents from your daily life. Play through them again and again until you can identify the shifts described in the meditation guidelines.

As you hold different parts of your life in attention, you will observe a range of reactions—distraction, daydreaming, dullness, sleep, agitation, fear, anxiety, and anger, to name a few. These reactions are also habituated patterns that work to absorb energy from attention so attention cannot penetrate to what lies underneath. Remember, all the distractions and difficulties you experience in meditation are the result of patterns operating. Hold the reactions in attention, too. Let them be there. Do not try to prevent them from arising. Do not get lost in their operation.

For both the meditation material and the reactions, let your attention rest on the breath, and then include as much of the material and the reactions as you can without losing attention. Initially, you will be able to include only a little because the feelings triggered are so strong that you fall either asleep or into distraction. Your ability will increase with consistent practice. When you can hold both the meditation material and the reactions in attention, the meditation begins to unfold.

The operation of the intellect is easily co-opted by habituated patterns. You may end up in a blind alley or with so many different views that you are unable to tell what is what. When that happens, acknowledge that habituated patterns have won a round, and return attention to the breath. Reestablish a base of attention, and then turn to the meditation again. You may lose one battle or many, but no pattern can withstand the consistent and determined application of attention. You will win the war.

When flashes of understanding arise, don't immediately assume that your understanding is complete. Little aha's pop up all the time.

They come and go very quickly. Hold even these flashes in attention. You will first become aware of aspects of behavior and reaction and then see the whole picture. Understanding arises as seeing and experiencing without relying on analysis or reason. You will know that the meditations have penetrated to the level of emotional understanding when you perceive a shift in the way you feel and the way you regard patterned behaviors in your life.

The reflections on karma are difficult. They challenge our beliefs about who and what we are. Beliefs die hard. Don't be surprised if you experience strong physical as well as emotional reactions to these meditations. Accept them as the effects of practice.

In the death meditations, fear is encountered over and over again. Because death involves the end of physical existence, fear is triggered at the level of the body. In karma, however, you are more likely to encounter nervousness and nausea—nervousness about who and what you are and nausea about how much of your life is run by patterns.

When you first suspect that your girlfriend or boyfriend does not love you, you feel nervous and anxious. When you find out that he or she really does not love you, you feel sick and nauseated. Dismantling beliefs about what we are and how we function is not threatening at the level of the body, but it is profoundly threatening to our feeling and conception of what we are and our relations with others. Nervousness arises when we begin to suspect or anticipate that things are not as we had thought. Nausea is a reaction to the realization that we have been emotionally attached to a fiction, the fiction of an autonomous volitional self.

Later you will feel lighter and clearer and emotionally alive. What you once resisted you now accept, often with a tinge of sadness because a cherished illusion has been shattered. Intellectual understanding does not have the same effects. While you may have a feeling of confidence in your comprehension, the emotional vitality is not present.

The intention of formal meditation practice is to develop sufficient attention to see into the operation of patterns and take them apart, but this is only half of the practice. The other half is to exercise attention in your daily life so that your actions arise from presence rather than from reactive patterns.

Be alert to the operation of patterns in your daily life. The graphic and archetypal images in some of the meditations provoke strong reactions and help you identify patterns. When you notice the same reactions in your life, know that a pattern is running. Observe it, and, when you can, cut it with attention.

During the day, you will probably notice your reactions more than you did before. While it is often disconcerting, increased awareness of a reactive pattern is a good development. First, it gives you the opportunity to see how it operates in your life. You may feel like a puppet, being jerked this way and that, but you begin to see your behavior for what it is, the operation of patterns rather than what you intended to do. One woman, when she paid attention to her speech patterns, reported back to the group, saying, "She never shuts up!" referring to herself.

Second, your relationship with a pattern changes as you continue to observe its operation. You will see it clearly as a source of difficulties in your life and are motivated to take it apart and be free of it. During this phase, you will also find that seemingly inconsequential events or situations elicit strong and powerful feelings. You suddenly feel very angry or hurt or needy. These surges of emotion are caused by your being in touch with the pattern and its emotional core. You need to be even more attentive to the practice of mindfulness during the day so as not to be taken over by these surges.

Finally, you will discover new ways of acting in situations, ways that you could not imagine, see, or do before. The first time you act differently you may experience a wide range of feelings—elation, power, anger, confusion—all at the same time. The feelings come from the release of the energy that was locked in the pattern. Mindfulness practice is particularly important at this point to prevent you from being carried away by the released energy.

Meditation 1: The Six Realms

Purpose:
To understand the suffering inherent in the worlds projected by reactive emotions.

MEDITATION METHOD

Begin each session with a period of basic meditation, resting attention on the breath.

For the main part of your practice session, reflect on the imagery of the realm until you find an image that captures your experience of the corresponding emotion. Recall instances in your life that provoked feelings similar to the descriptions of the realm. Observe how, when the reactive emotion is operating, you are effectively living in that realm.

Spend at least another ten minutes resting attention on the breath again. Let the images and feelings fall away and subside. Rest with your mind and heart open, as if you were sitting in the middle of infinite space.

Spend about two weeks on each realm.

Anger and Hatred: The Hell Realm

The hell realm is the realm of anger, which includes both the hot anger that flares up to incinerate any opposition and the enduring cold hatred that freezes you inside and makes any movement excruciatingly painful. The neighboring hells describe what happens when you try to avoid the anger that burns inside you.

Hot Hells

The hot hells are about hot, seething, burning, and explosive anger. The air crackles with aggression. The ground is red hot rock with rivers of molten metal. Trees are towers of flame, and the air you gasp sears your lungs. Everywhere you look, every way you turn, demonic figures are bent on destroying you. They wield sharp, jagged weapons that hack and tear the flesh from your bones. You collapse on the burning ground, only to revive and experience a new flare of anger. Flaming spears pierce your body and char your flesh. A red hot iron rod running through your torso burns you from the inside out. Mountains of white hot rock collapse and bury you. You are caught in a house whose flaming walls relentlessly close in on and crush you. Aggression and confusion have such a grip on you that you can't tell what's inside or outside; all you know is that everything is burning. There is simply no relief. The flames rise up inside and outside. When you cry for respite, all you hear is the roaring of fire, all you feel is the heat of the moment. All you can do is run and fight and fight and run. Whenever you attack what's in front of you, it bursts into flame and destroys you. You lose all sense of time, and this fiery nightmare is all that you know.

Cold Hells

The cold hells are about hatred, the kind of hatred that first freezes your heart and then never moves. Everything is frozen in the cold hells. Ice covers the ground. Only the wind moves, and its cold intensity penetrates the marrow in your bones. Time has no meaning here. Things never change. The unremitting cold is unbearable. You can't tell whether it comes from outside or inside. Cold hatred is agony. You want to cry out, but your mouth is frozen in contorted hate and no words or sounds leave your lips. You hear yourself crying and wailing, but no sound escapes your lips. Your body cracks, and the cold enters the cracks until the pain is unbearable. You try to move but you can't. Your whole body is so stiff, so frozen, that moving an arm or a finger or changing your position even slightly is unthinkable. You are so rigid with cold that the slightest movement will cause your body to crack or break. You sit in the cold, but your body cracks apart anyway.

Neighboring Hells

You tiptoe across a bed of flaming hot coals, trying hard not to disturb the anger that rages deep inside you. You are distracted for a moment, and you fall into a pit filled with the flames of your rage—you are incinerated. You try to walk on water, on the surface of your anger, a foul and noisome swamp. A moment's inattention, and you fall into the foul water, where horrible worms rip holes in your flesh and bore into you. You climb out of the swamp but discover that the grass is made of razor blades, shredding your feet with every step you take. You try to find a safer place by running into a forest, but the leaves of the trees are huge metal blades. Stirred by the wind, they cut you to pieces.

You hear a crying sound from the top of a hill, and you are sure it comes from your child or spouse or loved one. You rush up a hill covered with iron thorns. When you arrive, no one is there, but the cries now come from the base of the hill. You rush down, and the thorns are now pointed against you. In every direction something or someone is blocking you, pushing you back into the cycle of anger and violence. You can't escape.

Greed: The Hungry Ghost Realm

The hungry ghost realm is the realm of greed—hard-edged, all-consuming avarice that can never be satisfied. Imagine a thin, spindly person with long bony limbs, bent forward, with desperate eyes, a face that struggles to mask the desperation within, and long thin fingers reaching to clutch and grasp anything they can.

The hungry ghost realm is described in three ways: external distortion, internal distortion, and general distortion. Each kind of distortion captures an aspect of greed.

External distortion conveys how greed prevents you from finding any satisfaction or enjoyment from the world around you. You see the world as desolate and barren, devoid of food, water, and the necessities for life. Bitter winds whip up dust and sand, which clog your mouth and nose and blind you. You desperately need food and water, but you cannot find even a morsel of food or a drop of water. You wander, aimless and confused, in a futile attempt to find something that you can ingest. You are in a world of poverty: no crops, no food, no jobs, and no money. Everyone hoards everything they have. Everyone wants something but will give nothing to get it. Stealing and deception are rampant. In your poverty-stricken mentality, you see no richness or beauty in the world.

The internal distortion portrays the way in which greed prevents you from enjoying anything you do find. As a hungry ghost, you have a horribly distorted body. Your mouth is so small that not even the tiniest morsel of food or drop of water can pass through it. Your neck and throat are like threads, but your stomach is a huge cavern. You search and search for something to eat. You find a half-rotten banana peel in the garbage. It's pretty disgusting, but it's all you can find. Is this all the world has to give to you? You are so angry, bitter, and resentful, you can't see straight. In your desperation you push it into your tiny mouth. You can't chew it. Your mouth is so dry that you have trouble swallowing. You swallow anyway, and your throat burns and aches from the effort. Painfully, the peel goes down. Now you feel even hungrier, for that little bit of nourishment only makes you more conscious of how deprived and needy you are. Your needs are insatiable, and you have no way to appease them. You feel deprived and depressed. You are crazed by your own neediness.

The general distortion reflects the way greed prevents you from feeling any satisfaction even in the midst of plenty. You live in sumptuous luxury. Everything around you is beautiful, rich, and sensually provocative. You pick up a piece of fruit, but it turns to rotting garbage in your hand. You lift a glass of fragrant wine to your lips, but it bursts into flame. You have the Midas touch in reverse. Your body is huge, and it is infested with thousands of other hungry ghosts living in it. They feed on your body but hate it because it never satisfies them. Your own neediness is devouring you, eating you from the inside out.

Instinct: The Animal Realm

The animal realm represents instinct, which is concerned with only the most basic needs: food, survival, reproduction, and avoiding pain. You are extremely proficient inside the narrow frameworks of your conditioning, but outside them you have no idea how to function.

Imagine that you are a fish in the ocean. Swimming is second nature. You glide through the water effortlessly. You are also in the food chain. Big fish eat small fish, and the chain is completed when the smallest fish (parasites) eat the biggest. Everybody eats and is eaten by somebody. Your whole existence is shaped by two imperatives: find something to eat, and avoid being eaten. You swim in a school of other fish to better your chances of survival. Your neighbor turns one way so you do too. You are constantly searching for food, nosing along the bottom or instinctively following the currents in the ocean. Instinct alone drives you. When, in your life, do you live this way? By some accident, you are thrown onto the shore. Do you know where you are? Do you know what to do? No. All you know is that you can't breathe, and you flip around desperately. You have no idea where the ocean or river is. You flip and flip until you accidentally fall back into water or you die.

Imagine that you are an elk. In addition to food concerns, you must deal with heat and cold. In the summer, you move to higher altitudes; in the winter, you come down to the valleys. You fight for the right to reproduce. You constantly watch for wolves and mountain lions. The rest of the time you spend grazing. No fancy menus for you, just grass and shoots, but you know exactly what's good, where it grows, and when. You follow the herd, being careful never to be separated, and you make sure your children also stay with the herd. Suppose you wander onto a highway. What now? What do you make of these objects that whiz by faster than you or any wolf can run?

Imagine that you are a worm. Your whole existence is burrowing through earth, ingesting and excreting it. You happen upon another earthworm, you mate, and then you go back to the dirt. When it rains and your world is flooded, you head up for air, up where the birds are waiting.

Choose several different animals, and enter into their world fully. See the world as they see it. Do what they do. Imagine how they might react to situations outside their conditioning.

As an animal, you strive to reduce discomfort. You are driven by instinct and cannot imagine other ways of acting or behaving. Your behaviors are specialized and highly effective in their own domain. When you encounter circumstances that don't fit your conditioning, however, you are at first bewildered, and then you fall back on what you know. Whether it works or not, you just keep doing it.

This is the plight of most wild and domestic animals. Why else would domestic animals endure the suffering that humans inflict on them, growing them for food, slaughtering them en masse, making them work, and making them fight or race for human entertainment? Imagine how confused, desperate, and finally defeated you feel when you can't find any way to change things. All you can do is endure as best you can.

Desire: The Human Realm

The human realm is about desire and the busyness that accompanies it. It is about establishing preferences and living according to those preferences. You work to get what you want, but what you want keeps changing. You have your car, your job, and your family, but now you want a bigger car, a better job, and more time with your family, so you work harder. Your work consumes more of your life. You persevere because you know that at the end of the rainbow, there really is a pot of gold.

The difference between greed (the hungry ghost realm) and desire (the human realm) is satisfaction. Greed is never satisfied; desire is temporarily satisfied. You feel good when your desires are sated. You want that feeling and are willing to work hard to have it.

As soon as you have what you want, however, you start worrying about how to keep it. Others try to take it away from you all the time. You invented government, banks, and other institutions to protect your money, your possessions, your loved ones, and your freedom, but these institutions now take away your money in the form of taxes, fees, and other charges. You have to work even harder just to stay in the same place. Where does it end?

All you want is to be with the people who mean something to you, but that's not so easy. You buy a home for your family and then spend most of your time earning money to pay the mortgage. Now you have even less time to spend with the people you love. Your work forces you to interact and associate with people you don't like, and you spend more time with them than you want to. You do so in order to earn enough money to spend time with the people you do like. Things never work out the way you intended.

Consider how much of your life is taken up by these four concerns:

- Being with people you want to be with
- Avoiding people you don't want to be with
- Getting what you want but don't have
- Keeping what you do have

The basic task of government is to make the populace secure. The security of the populace is based on meeting needs. The basis of meeting needs is in not depriving people of their time. The basis of not depriving people of their time is in minimizing government exactions and expenditures. The basis of minimizing government exactions and expenditures is moderation of desire. The basis of moderating desire is in returning to essential nature. The basis of returning to essential nature is in removing the burden of accretions.

Remove the burden of accretions, and there is openness. To be open is to be equanimous. Equanimity is a basic element of the Way; openness is the house of the Way.

—*THE BOOK OF LEADERSHIP AND STRATEGY*

Jealousy: The Titan Realm

The titans are demigods. In the titan realm, you enjoy great wealth, strength, and ability, but you live right next to the gods and you can see that they live even better than you do. You feel that something is wrong with you. You set out to achieve what the gods have to prove you are just as good.

You should have what the gods have! You are determined to have it. You don't care that the gods are more powerful. You don't care that all your previous efforts ended in failure. All that matters is that you are going to have what they have, be what they are, even if the effort kills you—and it usually does.

This is jealousy. It's a war you can never win. You plot, you scheme, you plan, you train, you develop new weapons, you develop new strategies—you do everything you can. When the time comes to go against the gods, however, you always lose. The status, wealth, ability, power, or happiness you do have feels empty. You can't enjoy what you have because others have more. They are smarter, more beautiful, more graceful, stronger, faster, richer, or have more friends.

You feel your lack intensely. You are less than they are. To avoid that feeling, you strive to achieve bigger and bigger goals, tearing others down when necessary, to prove that you aren't less than they are. Yet your striving changes no one's opinion, not even yours. You still feel "less than."

Pride: The God Realm

You are special. You don't suffer the way others suffer. You are a god. Everything you have and enjoy is yours by right. You live in luxury. The hard edges of life don't touch you. Your food is delicious, and someone always does the dishes. Life is a concert today, an opera tomorrow, dinner on the terrace, and a bouquet of flowers. It's a walk in the park, where the view is always beautiful.

If you do work, you enjoy it, and your work confirms that you are superior. Your income allows you to live in a protected environment in which you have no concerns about security. Everything you could want or need is available. You are one of the beautiful people. You dismiss any idea that the way you live isn't what life is all about. You live in a vision of life shared with others who, like you, are definitely superior to those outside your circle. With your fellow gods, you have arrived at a world and a worldview that are unquestionably right and true. You feel separate from those who struggle with the difficulties of life. Your principal concern is to maintain your life, to avoid change, and to keep out anything that threatens your vision and way of life.

Eventually, you see that the good life cannot last forever. Health, happiness, and wealth begin to wane. The baser aspects of life intrude. Change and death cannot be avoided. After avoiding the ups and downs of life for so long, you see that you are like everyone else. You, too, will age and die. The prospect is unimaginable, terrifying. None of your friends will talk to you. Your failure to maintain the good life, to be perpetually young and vibrant, has made you unacceptable to them. You hadn't realized how narrow your life was. The people you thought were your friends will have nothing to do with you. They shun you as you shunned others. They don't want to be reminded of suffering or death. You end up totally alone as you await what you have always secretly dreaded.

Commentary: The Six Realms

The six worlds of projected emotion are known as the six realms of beings: hell beings, hungry ghosts, animals, human beings, titans, and gods. The six corresponding reactive emotional patterns give rise to six different interpretations of experience. In effect, we project the emotional reaction onto the world of experience.

When we experience the world through anger, we see everything as an enemy and fight our way through life. We live in hell.

With greed, we see the world as unable to satisfy our needs and strive to satisfy an insatiable neediness—the eternal hunger of the hungry ghosts.

With blind instinct, we relate to the world through instinct only and strive to limit discomfort. Like an animal, we do only what we are conditioned to do.

Desire leads us to see the world as a place of pleasure. We pour energy into activity in order to gain the means to enjoy life. As human beings, we are always working to obtain what we want and to keep what we have.

Jealousy is based on a perception of personal deficiency. We strive to overcome that perception through achievements and victories in order to demonstrate that we are equal to, or better than, anyone else. We are like titans who wage futile battles against the more powerful gods.

With pride, we feel that the world is our oyster. We feel superior to others and strive to maintain the feeling, materially or emotionally. Like gods, we are convinced of our rightness and superiority.

When we look closely at each of the projected worlds described by the six realms, we notice that each realm precludes the possibility of success in the associated striving. For instance, when we see the world in terms of opposition, no matter how many battles we win, we still see enemies everywhere and continue to live in hell. As long as our view of the world is based on a feeling of not having or being enough, no amount of achievement will change the way we feel. We continue our titanic but futile struggle against the gods.

The six realms form a map of the basic reactive patterns we find in our experience. The imagery and descriptions are useful for identifying those patterns within us.

To help you recognize the six realms in others and in you, try this exercise with a partner. Sit down, facing each other, and just rest attention on the breath for a minute or two. Then look directly at each other. Your partner says, in an even, unemotional voice, "You're against me." You don't reply. Both of you observe what reactions arise. This is the hell realm. Then, after a minute or two, your partner says, "I'm taking everything." Again, observe reactions. This is the hungry ghost realm. The phrase for the animal realm is "I'm just trying to survive"; for the human realm, "I want you"; for the titan realm, "I'm better than you"; and for the god realm, "I'm right, and that's just how it is." Then reverse roles, you saying the six phrases, pausing between each to observe the reactions. Whether you are saying the phrase or just listening, observe the reactions that arise in you.

Speed of Reaction

Is there any significance to the order of the six realms, from the hell realms to the god realms? If we look at the world that each emotional reaction creates, we see that the lower the realm, the faster the basic reactive pattern. Anger is very fast. It wells up in us in an instant. It can be overwhelmingly intense. Injunctions against anger abound in Buddhist literature, including the famous "One moment of anger destroys the good work of ten thousand lifetimes." If we set aside the literal interpretation, this injunction points to anger's power to establish intense reactive patterns quickly. Emotional energy pours into anger faster than it does into any other pattern.

In the hungry ghost realm, the speed of reaction is slower, but we can easily feel how quickly the impulse to grasp arises. Many people become hard and grasping as soon as the matter of money arises. Greed emerges, and they focus only on taking or keeping as much as they can, even when physical or financial survival is clearly not at issue.

In the animal realm, the movement into reactivity is still slower. The primary effort is to avoid pain. When there is no pain, threat, or pressure, we ignore and do nothing. Watch your cat, for instance. Make a noise, and your cat reacts, pricking up its ears and looking in the direction of the noise. Make the noise again, and your cat reacts again, but just enough to check again that no threat materializes. Make the noise again, and your cat ignores it.

The human realm and the titan realm have still more space. We are not driven by anger, greed, or instinct. We have moments when we aren't caught up in reaction, moments of pleasure and peace. We don't stay with them long. In the human realm, we go back to work in order to experience more pleasure. In the titan realm, we work to achieve bigger and better goals in order to compensate for the feeling of deficiency inside.

In the god realm, things really slow down. The basic ignoring of reality that underlies pride means that little effort is made to be present. In this realm we coast along, enjoying the pleasure of luxury and ignoring the fact that it can't last.

Higher and Lower Realms

We move from realm to realm as different reactive emotions move through us. The movement from a higher realm to a lower realm, or vice versa, is based on three different dynamics: habituation, level of energy, and frustration.

Habituation

The three higher realms of gods, titans, and humans are paired with the three lower realms of hell, hungry ghosts, and animals according to the three poisons: aversion, attraction, and indifference. Aversion is expressed directly as anger (hell realm) and secondarily as jealousy (titan realm). Attraction is expressed directly as desire (human realm) and secondarily as greed (hungry ghost realm). Indifference is expressed directly as instinct (ignoring—animal realm) and secondarily as pride (god realm). The longer or more frequently we stay in the higher realm, the more the underlying emotional pattern is habituated. In effect, we inevitably move to the lower realm because of the force of habituation.

Look at the higher realm in each pairing, and observe that the corresponding lower realm describes the world produced by the reactive pattern of the higher realm. The god realm is about pride and maintaining position. Imagine that you are a god. You are superior to the riffraff that plagues the planet. Those poor, misguided souls just don't understand how life works. If they did what you do, they wouldn't be suffering so much, but they won't listen, so why spend time trying to help them? Instead, you shut them out of your world and turn back to your toys and entertainment. You ignore the suffering and distress in the worlds below you. The more you ignore, the more you live automatically, according to the way you were trained to behave. You do everything without thinking, simply because it is the "god" thing to do. Without noticing it, you have begun to function more and more like an animal, doing what you have been conditioned to do to avoid pain, discomfort, or any disturbance in your life.

In the titan realm, you are motivated by jealousy, and you live in a world of aggressive competition. You feel that you are less significant than others, so you decide to show the world who you really are by the force of your achievements. Your drive comes from anger at not being appreciated. No matter what you achieve, you are never appreciated. The anger grows and grows until your life becomes hell.

In the human realm, you start by enjoying life, but your enjoyment fades so you work harder. If you can earn enough money or become powerful enough, you can hang out with the people you like. You won't have to consort with those you don't like. You'll have what you want. The harder you work, however, the more you end up doing what you don't want to do. Enjoyment of life becomes more and more fleeting. You are consumed by your efforts to have more time with your family or a better home to live in, but you never actually spend time with your family or in your home. You begin to feel that you will never get what you want, and you slip into the hungry ghost realm.

We cannot maintain the reactive patterns of the higher realms without creating the lower realms.

Level of Energy

The second pairing is based on the level of energy in the reactive patterns. The human and animal realms are paired because their patterns operate with the least strength. There is more opportunity, particularly in the human realm, for attention and awareness. The titan and hungry ghost realms are based on emotional energy, so the level of reactivity is higher than it is in the human and animal realms. In Buddhist cosmology, all demons (symbols for emotional and mental disturbances) belong to the hungry ghost or titan realm. Their ferocious greed and jealousy stem from feelings of neediness and deficiency. The god and hell realms represent total involvement in reactivity, the former in self-absorption to the exclusion of everything else, the latter in reaction to the environment to the exclusion of any internal awareness.

VLADIMIR: That passed the time.

ESTRAGON: It would have passed in any case.

VLADIMIR: Yes, but not so rapidly.

—*Samuel Beckett,*
Waiting for Godot

The classical descriptions of these realms include details about the life span of beings in each realm. The human and animal realms have relatively short and indefinite life spans. The life spans lengthen in the titan and hungry ghost realms and become longer and longer the lower we go in the hell realm or the higher we go in the god realm. These traditional descriptions point to the subjective nature of time. The more we are bound in reaction, the more slowly time seems to pass. When we are fighting pain, the pain seems to last forever. When we are intoxicated by bliss, the state seems to last forever. The more prominent the sense of "I" in relationship to what we are experiencing, the more conscious we are of time. Recall the last time you were bored. Did time go quickly or slowly?

The perception of time depends on the degree of separation from what we experience. Contrast the experience of intoxicating bliss or all-consuming pain with the experience of presence—an intimate conversation with a friend, for instance. In the latter, we have no sense of time or we seem to have stepped out of time. Time disappears when we are one with what we experience.

Frustration
In the third pairing the higher and lower realms are connected according to what happens when the functioning of one realm can no longer be maintained. For instance, when a highly competitive person is placed in an environment where competition isn't acceptable or effective, she or he doesn't know how to function. The person becomes bewildered and dazed, like an animal whose instincts can't relate to the environment. Conversely, when an animal can no longer ignore pressures from

the environment, it becomes highly competitive—a cornered cat or dog, for example. Titans become animals when competition and jealousy don't work, and animals become titans when their instincts for avoiding discomfort fail.

When a person in the god realm is frustrated, no longer able to avoid the needs, wants, suffering, and death in the world, he or she becomes greedy and reverts to the hungry ghost realm. We often see this shift in people who are used to living in luxury but have lost their wealth and comfort. When hungry ghosts aren't able to exercise greed, they move into the god realm. In other words, when their environment is so rich that greed isn't necessary and doesn't work, they become arrogant and insensitive, willing to ignore the existence of what they experienced before yet insecure since they sense that the luxury isn't going to last forever.

Finally, when the dynamics of wanting, temporary satisfaction, and busyness of the human realm are frustrated, people rebel, become angry and locked in conflict. The hell realm is created. Revolutions take place not when a population is oppressed but when people lose income or freedom they had previously enjoyed. Angry people who aren't able to express or make that anger work in their environment start noticing what they want and move to the human realm. This last shift is crucial in mediation efforts between parties locked in conflict. When the option of conflict is removed, the two parties will shift their attention to what they want. Parents use this principle with their children when they say, "I don't care who starts it; the next fight, you both go to your rooms!" The children stop fighting and focus on what they can enjoy.

Meditation 2: The Five Elements

Purpose
To identify the dynamics of the reaction chains that power emotional reactions.

The five elements describe a spectrum of energy, from form (earth) to emptiness (void). In the previous chapter, we saw how at death the elements that make up our experience of life dissolve one by one until we arrive at original mind, or mind nature. Here, the five elements describe modes of reaction, each mode operating at a different level of energy spanning the spectrum between form and emptiness. Earth is the densest and void the least dense, with the others ranged between.

The earth element reaction is to tense up and become rigid—"This is how it is and that's that." For water, the reaction is to disperse energy—"How can I get out of this?" For fire, the reaction is to take over the situation with your own intensity—"Don't you dare speak to me like that!" or "I want to know everything." For air, the reaction is activity for the sake of activity—"I have to keep busy." For void, the reaction is bewilderment—"This can't be true! I don't know what to do."

MEDITATION METHOD

First, rest attention on the breath for fifteen to twenty minutes.

Next, go through the reaction chain for each element, feeling each component clearly:

1. The initial emotional reaction
2. A second feeling that lies underneath the first
3. A deep-seated fear
4. An experience of open space associated with the fear
5. A reaction to the experience of open space
6. The fully formed reaction

Using the breath as a base of attention, sit and hold the sensations and feelings associated with the reaction in attention.

The fully formed reaction then becomes the initial emotional reaction for another cycle of the reaction chain, this time at a higher level of energy. The cycle repeats itself over and over again, spiraling up to higher levels of energy until the energy of attention has been completely consumed in the reaction process.

The following chart summarizes the reaction chains for each of the five elements. Use both the descriptions in the chart and actual situations from your life. With the chart, you will be able to explore the intensity of the feelings in the reaction chain. Situations or events in your life link the meditation to your daily experience. Recall a situation when the reaction chain for the element operated. Replay it in your mind, observing each component of the reaction chain. In life, the reaction chain often cycles in less than a second, so you will need to go through the situation in slow motion, so to speak. You will need to observe carefully to identify each component.

At the end of each practice session, rest in open attention for another ten to fifteen minutes.

Work in each element for about a week.

The Five Element Reaction Chains

ELEMENT	REACTION	FEELING	FEAR	OPEN SPACE	REFORMING	RESULT
earth	inflexible rigidity	hollowness or uncertainty	instability	earthquake	grasping	imprisonment
water	fluidity	external threat	engulfment	tidal wave or strong current	dispersion	frozen
fire	consuming intensity	aloneness	isolation	featureless desert	devouring experience	burned out
air	busyness	nothing to stand on	destruction	falling	activity	torn apart
void	dullness	overwhelmed	being nothing	blankness	fragmentation	dissolved into nothing

Commentary: The Five Element Reaction Chains

All five reaction chains operate in each of us. Usually one or two reaction chains are more deeply conditioned than the others are, so we resort to them most of the time. Our choice of reaction chain also depends on the situation. In some situations, we are more apt to keep connection and disperse energy (water); in others, we are more apt to hold our position and be inflexible (earth). The following descriptions show how each of the reaction chains might manifest in the same situation.

Because the reaction chains describe internal processes, go through the various reactions slowly, feeling and experiencing what arises at each stage.

Earth

Begin with earth, reacting to a situation with rigidity. Suppose that your teenage daughter asks to stay out later than usual. You say no, and when she asks for a reason you say, "You know the rules. You can't stay out later." She keeps asking, and you become firmer and firmer, determined not to budge. Notice what happens in your body. Are you relaxed or tense? How are you breathing? As you notice the tension in your body and breath, you notice also that you don't feel solid inside. The rigidity covers a little uncertainty, a little doubt or hollowness. Breathe and feel what is underneath the rigidity. As you feel the doubt or uncertainty, you realize that you are also afraid. What will you do if she doesn't obey you? What will you do if you let her stay out and she doesn't come home safely? If you are very strict, will she get angry with you, lose out on her social life, rebel, or leave home? What uncertainties and fears lie underneath your rigidity?

As you feel the fears, you simultaneously realize that everything is open. Anything could happen. The realization hits you like an earthquake. You react immediately by latching on to order, rules, and structure. You reaffirm your position—"No, you can't stay out later and that's it"—but she insists, presenting one argument after another. With each new argument, you go through the same process, each time with increasing intensity. Strangely, your order, rules, and structure feel like a prison. You can't tell her how you really feel, what you are afraid of, or how much you care about her. You can't move. You are locked into your position.

Once you have clearly identified the components of the earth reaction in one situation, recall other situations in which you reacted in the same way. Go through them until you become thoroughly familiar with the components and are able to see them operating in your daily life. Spend a week or two on earth and then turn to the water element.

Water

The reaction chain for water starts with an effort to disperse feelings or energy. Again, your daughter asks to stay out later than usual. Instead of reacting with inflexible rigidity, you try to disperse the energy of her entreaties. "Oh, it's not such a big deal," you say. "Just come home at your usual time. You won't miss anything."

She tells you exactly what she's going to miss, so you take a different tack. "Well, there are other nights, aren't there? Besides, we have a big day planned for the whole family tomorrow. You wouldn't want to be tired for that, would you?"

Notice what you feel underneath the attempts to disperse her arguments and requests. Do the repeated requests feel like attacks or threats? If you give in to one, where will it stop? What will she ask next? Will you lose all control? Will she end up doing anything she wants?

Deep down you are afraid, afraid of being engulfed by her energy, your loss of control, or other unnamable threats. Tidal waves of feeling carry you into areas that you don't know how to navigate. You react to disperse the emotional energy surging inside you, but she counters every deflection and you run out of wiggle room, frozen in your own attempts to disperse and evade. When you feel that you can't move at all, you react to that and go through the cycle again.

Fire

The reaction chain for fire begins with the feeling of intensity as we try to consume what arises in experience. Your daughter asks to stay out late, but this time you are short with her. "Don't bother me. No, absolutely not! " She stands her ground, saying that you are mean and unfair. Anger flares in you and you seethe inside. What is underneath the anger? You can do nothing with her. You are helpless and alone. Your frustration and anger make you feel isolated, and the isolation is terrifying. You intensify your reaction so as not to feel the isolation.

"No, you can't, and if you ask again, you're grounded!" She makes a sarcastic comment, and you've had enough. "That's it. You're grounded. Go to your room." Whether she storms out of the house or goes to her room, you end up alone. Now your isolation is too much for you. You storm around your home, throwing objects, burning yourself up.

The fire reaction chain also manifests in desire. Instead of reacting with aversion, you react to the isolation by intensifying the experience of connection, seducing and consuming the other, and burning up both of you in passion.

Air

Air manifests as busyness. When your daughter asks to stay out late, you start tidying up the room, picking up magazines, or putting books back in the bookcase. When she asks again, you say, "I'm really busy right now. Let's discuss this later." You don't know exactly what to do, so you keep busy doing this, doing that. Notice what is underneath the busyness: you don't know what to say. You haven't thought things out, and you have nothing to stand on. You are anxious and a little panicky. A direct response to your daughter is like jumping off a high cliff, so you come up with long-winded explanations, try to change the topic, or speculate about what might happen to her. In the end, you are all words and activity. You go off in all different directions and accomplish nothing. She leaves anyway, so you start rearranging everything in the room, tearing yourself apart in a whirlwind of activity.

Void

Void arises reactively as a feeling of dullness or bewilderment. When your daughter asks to stay out late, you are dumbfounded. You are unable to move, speak, or think. You are totally overwhelmed. You panic inside because you feel that you are nothing and that you are going to drop out of existence. You go to pieces, refusing to move one moment, pleading the next, raging the next, and theorizing the next, only to collapse a moment later and do nothing.

In addition to observing specific situations such as the one used in these meditations, notice what you do when you encounter profound shocks or disturbing events: you lose your job, your partner tells you that your relationship is over, or you are diagnosed with a terminal illness.

Each of the elements expresses a particular way of relating to the world of experience. In earth, you relate to experience in terms of structure and order. Therefore, when you lose your job, you focus on the basics: money, rent, and food. In water, you relate to the world and to what you are by feeling and emotion. You seek out friends and emotional support. In fire, you relate to the world in terms of experience. A loss or tragedy releases a burst of creative energy, and you paint or write a masterpiece, or you drive your car as fast you as you can, or you engage in other activities that are intensely experiential. In air, you relate to the world according to what you do and what you accomplish. Faced with the end of your job or your life, your energy goes into completing the project you are working on, the new garden, or the new operations manual. In a void reaction, you go to pieces and the different pieces do different things. Your behavior is fragmented and disjointed, shifting randomly as you focus now on order, now on intensity, now on how you are feeling, now on your need to do something.

The last two meditations, the six realms and the five elements, put us in touch with two reactive processes that take place in us. What is the underlying drive? That is the subject of the next meditation.

Meditation 3: What's Running the Show? The Pattern Imperative

Purpose:
To identify the imperative that drives a pattern of behavior.

MEDITATION METHOD

The steps in this meditation are

- Choose a pattern of behavior that causes difficulty in your life.
- Push on the behavior with attention by imagining behaving differently.

- Observe the arising and the operating of reactions.
- Observe how reactions are organized around an imperative:
    "must have this, can't have that" or
    "must be this way, can't be that way."
- Observe how reactions serve the imperative.

As you observe the operation of one pattern, you may become aware of another imperative that is operating at a deeper level. For example, the reason you frequently interrupt people may not be aggression but because you are afraid of not being heard. Shift your observation to the deeper pattern. Gradually you will identify the principal patterns that operate in your life.

Commentary: The Pattern Imperative

A pattern is a process, a sequence of reactions operating to serve a specific imperative. In this meditation you learn how to identify the imperative that drives a pattern. Once the imperative is identified, you recognize the operation of the pattern in daily life more easily.

Take a behavior that you know or suspect is habituated. Any consistent behavior that creates problems for you will serve: deferring to other people's opinions even when you know they are wrong, finishing other people's sentences for them, consistently arriving late for appointments or meetings, blaming others for inconveniences that arise in your life, or eating even when you are not hungry.

Push on the pattern by imagining that you act differently. For instance, if you are habitually late for appointments, imagine leaving in plenty of time to make the appointment. If you tend to finish other people's sentences for them, imagine waiting for them to finish before you say anything, even if they pause or stumble over their words.

Intellectually, you come up with any number of reasons to reject the different behavior and defend the habituated behavior as the one right way of behaving. Your mind may go completely blank, or you may fall asleep. You may consider any alternative unrealistic, a joke, or to be indulged in only for the purposes of the practice. Emotionally, such feelings as anger, anxiety, fear, or shame arise. As you observe your reasons arising, notice which of the six realms you are in: you have to fight something so you fight the clock (hell), you can't waste any time because time is short (hungry ghost), you just do things this way (animal), you enjoy being busy (human), you like the challenge of pushing limits (titan), or the others can wait for you (god). The element reaction chains arise: you become tense and rigid (earth), nervous and evasive (water), intense and energized (fire), distracted and uninterested (air), or confused and bewildered (void). The feelings register directly as sensations in your body. All the rationalizations, justifications, emotions, and sensations are part of the pattern.

> Let's not forget that the little emotions are the great captains of our lives and we obey them without realizing it.
>
> —*Vincent van Gogh*

Observe what arises. Do not try to counteract or suppress the reactions. Observe them in attention. In the case of being late for meetings, when you imagine leaving in plenty of time, one reaction is to think that if you arrive early you will end up wasting time because you have nothing to do. Emotionally, the reaction is a feeling of uncertainty and even fear at the prospect of your having to wait without activity to fill the open time. Physically, you feel compelled to keep moving, to do something useful, even if you are late for the meeting.

As you repeatedly push on the behavior, you gradually discern that the behavior is based on an imperative that can usually be expressed in the form "must have this, can't have that." Underneath the behavior of being late, for instance, you might see the imperative "must be productive, can't waste time."

Once the imperative has been identified, observe how various thoughts, feelings, and bodily reactions serve the imperative. Your body wants to be active. Emotional reactions to open time compel you to fill it with an activity. Thoughts tell you that if you have free time, you are not being productive. Of course, when you start another task, you leave late for the appointment and arrive late once again.

Use your body to identify the reaction of the pattern as you push on it. If the intellectual and emotional reactions are too fleeting or too intense to identify, relax, remaining awake and present. Rest with the breath, bring the reactive behavior clearly to mind, and again imagine acting differently. Observe carefully how your body responds. Does it relax or tense up? Does it try to squirm out of the practice? Does it suddenly feel hot and uncomfortable? Are you distracted by itches or other minor discomforts? As you observe the body, you will become aware of the emotional component of the reaction. Now rest in attention and include the emotional feelings. Don't analyze or judge them as good or bad. Just note them and open to them. You will become aware that you are full of thoughts and concerns about deviating from the pattern. Voices and feelings arise in your mind and point you to what they consider important. Observe carefully and you will become aware that all the feelings, ideas, and voices are saying the same thing: must have this, can't have that.

For instance, if the behavior is always being agreeable whenever conflict arises in a relationship, imagine not agreeing or even disagreeing. Notice how your body suddenly becomes tense, agitated, or energized. At the emotional level, notice rigidity, defensiveness, aggression, anxiety, or fear. Observe the voices and ideas running around in your mind, saying, "I must stop this conflict now; even if I don't like the result, it's more important that everybody appear to get along. If I continue to disagree, somebody is going to get very upset. I will be in danger. I must have peace; I can't have danger." The message might be that if you disagree, you will be rejected and isolated, in which case the pattern imperative might be "must keep connection, can't be alone."

Once you have identified the pattern imperative, you see clearly how your physical, emotional, and intellectual reactions serve that imperative.

We are now in a position to see what a pattern is—a process that operates automatically once it is triggered. The pattern has several components. In the next meditation, we identify the various components and the ways they interact to establish patterned behavior.

Meditation 4: It Keeps Going and Going and Going—The Pattern Process

Purpose:
To identify the components of a pattern.

MEDITATION METHOD

- Select a pattern of behavior for which you have identified the imperative.
- Imagine a situation that triggers the pattern. Observe the sequence of reactions that arise when you think of the triggering situation.
- Play through the pattern process repeatedly until you can identify all components of the pattern:

  1. Perception of situation that triggers imperative
  2. Falling out of awareness
  3. Emergence of duality—"I" and "other"
  4. Emergence of preference—pleasant, unpleasant, and neutral
  5. Three poisons—attraction, aversion, or indifference
  6. Reaction chain—one of the five elements
  7. Projected world—one of the six realms
  8. Reaction to the projected world

To identify the components, imagine that you encounter a situation that triggers the operation of the pattern. The intensity of the pattern reaction in meditation will be less than it is in daily life. The lessened intensity allows you to observe the pattern more easily, but it also makes the process more subtle. If you consistently feel nothing when you recall a situation that did upset you, shift your attention to the sensation of numbness or disconnection. Use numbness and disconnection as the pattern for meditation.

> It has, I believe, been often remarked that a hen is only an egg's way of making another egg.
>
> —*Samuel Butler*

The pattern process runs very quickly, so repeated observation is usually necessary before all components are recognized. Go through the pattern repeatedly until you have recognized each component.

Alternatively, you can identify the pattern at a later stage of its process, when the reaction chain operates or by determining which realm is projected. Start from wherever you identify the pattern, and follow the pattern process through the stage of reaction to the projected world. At this point the pattern loops back to perception and repeats.

Commentary

In the example about avoiding conflict in the last meditation commentary, the perception is conflict and the imperative is "must keep connection, can't be alone." Now imagine a situation that involves conflict: a disagreement with your boss, your spouse, or a friend or other person with whom you need to stay connected. As soon as the perception of conflict arises (component 1), you momentarily go blank and fall out of awareness (component 2). Next, you experience your spouse, boss, or friend as "other," a threat to who and what you are (component 3). The experience is unpleasant (component 4), and aversion arises (component 5). In the next moment, one of the elemental reaction chains runs (component 6). You dig in your heels (earth)—"I'm not going to fight, no matter what it costs me." You placate (water): "It's no big deal; what do you want?" You rage, attacking the part of you that started the conflict (fire): "Obviously, I'm to blame." You change the subject (air): "Let's talk about something else," or you go to pieces (void): "I'm sorry, I don't know what to do."

Take a breath right now and ask, "How am I seeing the world at this moment in this interaction?" Which of the six realms are you projecting (component 7)? If you see the world in terms of opposition (hell), you fight with either what opposes the feeling of connection or the feeling of connection itself. If you see the world as not satisfying your needs (hungry ghost), you feel how hungry you are for connection and know that you will do anything to keep it. If you see the world as a source of discomfort (animal), you instinctively move to limit the discomfort of aloneness. If you see it as limiting your enjoyment (human), you edit your experience of the relationship so that you feel good about the connection. If you see it in terms of competition and achievement (titan), you keep the connection to be in a better position vis-à-vis others. If you see the world as your oyster (god), you insulate to avoid conflict and to maintain your superior position.

Suppose you see the world as your oyster. You strive to stay connected, but your pride prevents you from seeing your part in the conflict. You assume you are in the right (component 8), the conflict inevitably escalates, and your feeling of connection diminishes even further. Now you run through the whole process again with a higher level of reactive energy. The pattern delivers exactly what you are trying to avoid.

A pattern is triggered when an aspect of a situation, as we perceive it, resonates with the emotional core of the pattern and activates the imperative. In the resonance, the pattern absorbs energy, attention goes passive, and we drop out of awareness and go blank. In the next moment, the habituated subject-object framework of "I" and "other" of the pattern is firmly in place. The pattern then scrutinizes everything that arises in experience at lightning speed, determining whether it supports the sense of "I" or threatens it. We experience attraction to what supports or confirms the sense of "I," aversion to what threatens it, and indifference to everything else.

The three basic emotional reactions—attraction, aversion, and indifference (the three poisons introduced in chapter 2)—are reactions to the preferences established by the sense of "I." They poison our whole experience of life and lead to reactions and behaviors that produce suffering, just as drinking a poisoned cup of coffee produces suffering. The shift from bare perception to one of the three poisons takes place very quickly. It is most easily identified by the moment of blankness that signals falling out of awareness. We all experience gaps in the continuity of awareness. To identify the pattern, note the emotional charge that immediately follows the moment of blankness.

The next step in the pattern is a reaction chain based on one of the five elements, as in the second meditation in this chapter. Observe which element or elements the pattern resorts to at this stage.

All five reactive chains operate in everyone. A given pattern, however, will usually rely on the one or two elements in which its operation has developed. For instance, in conflict, you reflexively hold to your position (earth) and, failing that, threaten people if they don't agree (fire). You don't consider negotiating or brainstorming for other possibilities. Which pattern operates depends on many factors, so don't waste effort trying to deduce what caused you to move into one element or another. Just observe what does happen.

As we saw in the meditation on the five elements, the fully formed reaction then becomes the basis for another cycle through the reaction chain. The feedback loop creates a dynamic that invests more and more emotional energy in the reaction chain. The energy accumulated in the reaction chain acts as a lens that distorts what arises in experience. Our distorted interpretation of experience is based on the three poisons—attraction, aversion, and indifference—which, at the level of emotion, arise as six reactive emotional patterns: anger, greed, blind instinct, desire, jealousy, and pride. Distorted experience is habituated by constant repetition until the pattern locks into one of the six realms. Then, whenever the pattern is triggered, we see and experience the world as that realm.

No matter which of the six realms you project, you are doomed to failure. For instance, you will never find what you need as long as you live in the hungry ghost realm because the realm is based on the experience of not finding what you need. You will never find peace in the hell realms, never find lasting enjoyment in the human, and never overcome the feeling of deficiency in the titan realm. The experience of failure again triggers the pattern imperative—"must have this, can't have that"—and the whole process repeats itself.

Habituation is reinforced by two feedback loops, one operating with the five element reaction chains, the other with the six realms.

Take the fire reaction chain, for example. Tom, an intelligent and witty person, likes to stir up trouble. He is a bit of a social outcast. Whenever he joins the conversation in a group, he makes comments that are insightful and accurate yet controversial and disturbing. The conversation quickly becomes more intense, with everyone reacting to his comments. After a short time, however, the people in the group grow uncomfortable with the level of intensity and move to less controversial topics. Tom is ignored, so he makes another insightful and disturbing comment, initiating another cycle of reaction.

The operation of the reaction chain constantly recreates the conditions that trigger the reaction. Each new cycle takes place at a higher level of intensity, spiraling upward in energy. Tom continues to make situations intense as a reaction to the feeling of isolation, and groups react by isolating him.

The crystallization of energy in the fire reaction chain increasingly distorts his perception of others. He sees them as against him because they always reject him. His perception is that even though he makes insightful and helpful comments nobody wants to talk with him, so they must dislike him. He moves into the hell realm, seeing everything and everyone as an enemy. Of course, the more he fights, the more others fight with him, so his perception of the hell realm is consistently reinforced, too.

Together, these two feedback loops lead to the crystallization of energy into the fixed structures that constitute our personality and view of the world. Unfortunately, the patterns always bring us exactly what we are trying to avoid. In Tom's case, he is looking for connection and friendship. Instead, he is isolated and disliked.

At present, our lives are the results of the operating of such patterns. The extent to which these patterns operate is the subject of the next meditation. By now you may be feeling a little dismayed, nervous, anxious, or queasy, if not out-and-out sick. These are signs of effective practice. Don't try to change anything at this point. Focus on observing the patterns in your life and seeing how they operate. In later chapters you will learn how to dismantle the projected world (component 7), how to transform the reaction chain (component 6), how to expose and stay present with the emotional core underlying the imperative (component 1), and how to step out of "I-other" perception (component 3).

Meditation 5: Patterns, Patterns Everywhere and Not a Moment's Peace

Purpose:
To see the extent to which patterns consume your life.

MEDITATION METHOD

The Pattern Imperative

Take a pattern you have already identified. As you rest attention on the breath, keep the pattern imperative in mind and look at different areas of your life:

- How do you learn?
- How do you work?
- How do you have fun?
- How do you interact with your family?

- How do you interact socially, with friends?
- How do you interact at work?
- What does your spiritual practice look like?

The Reaction Chain

Take the same pattern you used in the previous exercise. This time, hold the reactive chain, whether earth, water, fire, air, or void, in mind as you observe the operation of the pattern in different areas of your life.

- Does the pattern always use the same reaction chain?
- Does it use all of them or only one or two?
- Does the pattern manifest in expressive or receptive mode?
- When and where in your life do you experience this reaction chain?

The Projected World

In this exercise, observe which of the six realms the pattern projects. Rest attention on the breath, and let the pattern run in your imagination. Use a specific situation or incident from your life.

- Does the pattern always project the same realm?
- Does it use all of them or only one or two?
- Does the pattern manifest in expressive or receptive mode?

As the pattern runs, observe how the pattern views the world, and then hold the question "When do I view the world in this way?" Examine each area of your life to see how the projected world arises in it.

Pattern Operation over Different Time Scales

Finally, using the same pattern, hold the whole process in mind, from initial perception and pattern imperative to projected world. Although the operation of a pattern may be compressed into a few moments or extended over decades, the process is exactly the same. Look at your life on different time scales to see how the pattern runs through the same process, whether in a few minutes or over years:

- Thoughts and feelings, usually on a scale of minutes or hours
- Social and family interactions, on a scale of hours to days
- Casual and intermittent relationships, on a scale of days to weeks

- Significant and long-term relationships, on a scale of months to years
- Career and marriage, on a scale of years to decades
- Values and beliefs, on a scale of years to decades

Commentary

The purpose of this set of meditations is to reveal how patterns pervade your life. Think of these exercises as putting your life on a dissecting table and taking it apart to see what it is. The scalpel is attention. It separates out the pattern imperative, the reaction chain, and the projected world from the activity of your life.

One of the central problems in spiritual practice is the tendency to protect parts of our life from the practice. The protected parts are always formed from patterns. The patterns continue to run, and the protected parts eventually take over our life, in spite of all our efforts in practice. Therefore, do not spare the knife. Cut deeply with your attention. Don't protect anything, for what you protect will consume you. Remember, what you don't work through, you become.

The Pattern Imperative

Suppose that the behavior is being busy all the time. By going through the previous meditation exercises, you have (for the purposes of this example) identified the pattern imperative as "can't depend on others, must do everything myself."

Now, rest attention on the breath, and bring the pattern imperative clearly to mind. Go through your life using the meditation guidelines.

What do you do for fun? Do you get together with other people, or do you prefer to read or listen to music alone—activities that don't depend on others? If you do get together with friends, do you make the arrangements, or do you let other people make them? Do you enjoy team sports or individual sports?

When you want to learn a new skill, do you read a book on your own, enroll in a course, form a study group, find an expert in the area and learn from him or her, or rely on trial and error until you figure it out yourself? How does the imperative operate here?

Do you prefer to work with others or to work on your own? How do you feel when you are responsible for the task? How do you feel when someone else is responsible? How do you feel when you depend on the cooperation of others over whom you have no direct authority? Do you ever permit that situation to arise?

In your home life, do you delegate some of the tasks and responsibilities to others, or do you do everything? If your spouse doesn't do what was agreed on, how do you react?

Spiritually, do you practice on your own, or do you attend a center and practice with a group? Do you study with a teacher or try to understand how to practice, pray, or meditate on your own? Under what circumstances, if any, would you join a group or study with a teacher? What do you do when difficulties arise in practice or you don't know how to proceed?

Observe how the imperative operates in relationship to values. Do you rely on others to decide what is right and wrong? How do you decide what is right or wrong? Which values and beliefs are only reflections of the imperative?

Notice when and how the pattern imperative operates in each of these areas. What situations trigger the pattern? What are the common characteristics of those situations? How does the pattern play out? What happens around you and to you as the pattern runs? How and when does the operation of the pattern end?

Go through every area of your life, investigating how the pattern operates. How has your life been shaped by its operation?

The Reaction Chain

After a few days, turn to the next exercise, in which you use the reaction chain to identify the operation of the pattern in your life.

Suppose that you are busy and burdened with a long list of things to do. How do you react? Do you become tense and rigid, ordering your day precisely, following the schedule and never departing from it? Do you figure out what trade-offs you can make or what items you can postpone without causing too much disruption? Do you blast people around you for not helping more and leaving everything up to you? Do you become a whirlwind of activity, just doing, doing, and doing, until everything is done—and then finding something else to do? Do you fall into confusion, wonder what on earth you are doing and why, and somehow muddle through? Which of the reactive chains do you go to: earth, water, fire, air, or void? Do you always go to the same one? If not, which ones do you go to most often?

The reaction chains can run in either of two modes, expressive or receptive. Expressive earth is being a bulldozer, crushing others, while receptive earth is letting others break themselves on you. Both behaviors are earth reactions. If the pattern can't crush the other person, it flips to the receptive mode. Now the other person runs into your fixed position and ends up coming to grief on the rocks of your rigidity. Expressive water is engulfing others with your agenda. Receptive water is letting others engulf you. In either case, no real connection or relationship forms. In the former, others feel that you have taken over. In the latter, others feel that you are just going along with them. Expressive fire is consuming others with your desire or anger, while receptive fire is being consumed by others. Expressive air is engaging in activity for the sake of activity, while receptive air is letting yourself be caught up in the busyness of others. Expressive void is going to pieces, while receptive void is withdrawing into confusion.

Look at other areas of your life to see where and how the same dynamic operates. Suppose you see that you consistently become angry when you feel overworked. You feel the aloneness and see that the anger is a way of intensifying experience so that you feel less lonely. Where else do you feel lonely—at work, in your family, with friends? How often do you say or do something disruptive just to stir things up?

The Projected World

After a few days, turn to looking at the projected world. Continuing with the same example, you see that you consistently become angry. Everyone is the enemy. Why? Because they aren't helping you with all your work! Recall how you felt when you were the only one at the office working on an important project due the next day. Recall that you stayed up late at the beginning of your vacation because you had to prepare lunch for everyone for the long drive. When you recall these incidents, perhaps you also recall that a co-worker had offered to stay but that you were already angry and brushed him off. Perhaps one of your children asked if she could help you prepare the lunch, but you didn't want her to be tired the next day, so you sent her to bed. When you are angry, the whole world is against you. You can't accept help from anyone, so you end up all alone and angry, and the pattern runs. As you become clearer and clearer about the pattern and the world it projects, you will recall more and more times and places when you felt the same way.

Like the element reaction chains, the six realms have their expressive and receptive manifestations. For instance, do you fight, or do you feel people fight with you? Do you actively look for what you need and become frustrated when you can't find it, or do you wait for others to give you what you need and become frustrated and angry when they don't? The same polarities operate in the other realms.

Patterns Over Different Time Scales

As I traveled overland to India, I met a lot of people. Sometimes the connection lasted for a few hours over dinner, sometimes for a few days. While I was staying at my teacher's monastery, the connections lasted for weeks or months as people came and went. I observed that, regardless of the length of time, the process always followed the same pattern: introduction, formation of impression, interaction, revision of impression, more interaction, and eventual parting. The longer the period of connection, the deeper the relationship, but the process, whether over an evening or a year, was exactly the same.

Consider the pattern "can't depend on others, must do everything myself." In the very short term, as soon as someone suggests that he or she help you, the imperative is triggered and you decline the offer. You choose activities that don't involve other people so that you never have to depend on them. Perhaps you are always the person who makes the reservations when you get together with a group of friends. You choose work activities that one person can do and avoid team projects. You never learn to delegate effectively, but you become a superstar in your particular area. You have little patience for people who can't work as hard as you can. In your marriage, you are the active person, while your spouse becomes increasingly dependent on your initiative. You carry all the responsibility, and you feel resentful toward your spouse for not doing more.

Do you see how the same dynamic operates, regardless of the time scale? The only difference is the length of time the pattern takes to unfold.

Artificial Life

Karma is a process of evolution: behaviors evolve into experienced results. Even though evolution is usually reserved for living entities, recent research into the behavior of complex adaptive systems, including computer programs, has shed much light on the subject. Totally mechanical systems can and do exhibit extraordinarily lifelike behavior when the system includes a feedback mechanism that accumulates and stores energy. Within these systems, minor interactions and chance behaviors (the seeds of karma) start to store energy because of the feedback loop.

They develop into complex, self-maintaining entities. Sometimes the entities behave erratically, and no stability develops. In the right conditions, or sometimes by chance, the entities create a stable environment in which they grow. Sometimes the whole system stagnates. At other times an entity evolves to the point that it upsets the stability. Then new entities develop and a new stable environment may or may not develop. Such systems have been dubbed "artificial life," though awareness, volition, and intention are meaningless concepts in this context.

The purpose of these meditations is to see that much of our lives consists of "artificial life"—essentially mechanical systems of patterns interacting and elaborating to produce the complex experience we call life. What looks like awareness and volition is often just a pattern imperative running mechanically. The feedback loops of the reaction chain and the projected world store energy in the pattern. The pattern becomes habituated, and the energy crystallizes into a definite structure—personality.

The structure of personality, like the structure of complex adaptive systems, is self-similar; that is, it looks the same on any scale. Erosion, for instance, looks the same whether it is on the scale of the Grand Canyon or a little gully in our backyard. A water drop runs downhill and in doing so digs a little channel. The next drop of water, instead of finding a new way down the slope, follows the same channel so that the channel becomes a little deeper and wider. Eventually, the slope is cut by a few deep gullies. The sides of each of these deep gullies have smaller gullies, and the sides of the smaller gullies have still smaller gullies. In other words, the feedback mechanism that concentrates the flow of water and the action of erosion into gullies gives rise to similarly shaped structures at every level.

We do not need to look for one mechanism that causes small gullies, a second mechanism that causes medium-sized gullies, and other mechanisms that cause still larger gullies. The mechanism is exactly the same in each case. The only difference is the scale on which it manifests. Like the gullies formed by erosion, the same pattern structure recurs over and over in many areas of our lives, on different time scales and to varying depths of conditioning. We do not have to look for a cognitive explanation to explain our thinking, a psychological explanation for our feelings, a moral explanation to explain our values, and a philosophical explanation for our beliefs and worldview. All these different dimensions can arise from the operation of one pattern mechanism. Cognitive, psychological, moral, and philosophical explanations may, in fact, obscure the deeper perception that one pattern is at work.

When we try to change any aspect of our lives, whether at the physical, behavioral, emotional, or intellectual level, we often experience frustration. Despite our efforts, we revert to the same old ways of thinking, feeling, or behaving. Often, we fail to change because we are directing our efforts at the manifestation of the pattern, not at the pattern itself. The pattern is a process, just as erosion is a process. If we change our behavior without taking the pattern apart, the pattern continues to function and the old behavior is soon restored. We might as well try to stop erosion by changing the shape of one of the gullies by shoveling earth. When the next rain comes, the process of erosion continues and our work is quickly undone. One way to stop erosion is to plant trees and shrubs. They hold the soil, and less water runs down the slope. More is absorbed, and the trees and shrubs flourish. In other words, the energy inherent in the water is transformed into trees and shrubs. Plant your life with mindfulness and attention, and it will change, too.

Use these meditations to *see and experience in attention* the mechanisms that erode your life. One glimpse into a pattern's operation is a big step but not enough to dismantle its operation. A pattern falls apart only when you experience both its operation and the imperative in attention.

When I was teaching these meditations to a group, one woman had difficulty following the details of the pattern process. She also suffered from a pattern whose imperative was "can't look bad, must look good." The classes were very hard for her because she thought she would never understand patterns. Then, in one class, she deliberately violated the imperative to look good by refusing to participate in the discussion. The pattern exploded into operation, and in the middle of the class she *saw* the pattern as a mechanism and almost vomited from the shock. She experienced the fear of isolation, the anger, the feelings of failure, and the feeling that I and everyone in the class were her enemies. Because of her meditation practice, however, she also saw that everything she was experiencing had nothing to do with the actual class. It was all the operation of the pattern, distorting her experience to conform to the beliefs, self-image, and projected world of her pattern. The experience shattered her beliefs in her own limitations and her anger at the world and opened up a new dimension of freedom in her life.

Once a pattern has been dismantled, every aspect of life that depends on the pattern also falls apart. Friendships, relationships, work, and beliefs that were expressions of the pattern change or disappear. The projected world of the pattern no longer operates. As we die to the pattern, the world of the pattern dies and we experience the loss of everything in it. Why would we take apart our lives in this way? Before we turn to that question, we need one more piece—how patterns formed in the first place.

Meditation 6: Shock—
The Moment I Couldn't Face

Purpose:
To understand how a pattern forms and develops around an unreleased core of experience.

INTRODUCTION

The formation of patterns is a subtle process and difficult to explain. How does an eddy form in your bathtub when you let the water out? How does a pattern of cracks form in mud when a puddle dries up?

Patterns form because a very small action is repeated many times. A feedback loop causes a structure to form from the constant repetition of the action. The example of erosion mentioned earlier illustrates the process. The action is a stream of water running down a smooth slope of loose earth. The first drop of water flows anywhere. Its path is completely unpredictable. As the water flows down, however, it carves a very small trough. Because of gravity, a second drop of water tends to follow the trough carved by the first and makes the trough a little deeper. When the trough is deep enough, earth falls into it and is carried down the slope by the water, and the trough widens. If enough rain falls, the smooth slope is transformed into deep gullies with smaller side gullies, which in turn have still smaller side gullies. Even though rain falls evenly over the whole slope, water flows only in the gullies. The whole structure is created by little drops of water running down the slope. Gravity is responsible for the feedback loop that forms the gullies.

In this meditation, we are trying to observe the subtle shift that transforms the smooth slope of being present in experience to the gully-riven "I-other" experience. The drop of water is movement or action. The trough is the disruption in experience that arises as a feeling of not being. The earth's falling into the gully is the reaction that compensates for the feeling of not being.

Imagine an infant interacting with her mother. As long as the infant experiences her mother's emotional presence, her experience of being consists of a flow of movement and response. When the mother withdraws, the emotional connection is broken and the infant experiences no response. Movement—the drops of water in the erosion example—still arises, but without the response, the flow of energy is disrupted and experience is not released. The unreleased experience is the core of the pattern. In our analogy, it is the small trough carved in the experience of being. The infant reacts by trying to elicit response, by smiling, laughing, or crying. The reaction that elicits response eventually becomes the pattern imperative—"can't be alone, must smile" or "can't be alone, must cry"—albeit at a preverbal level. Whenever the experience of being is disrupted, the infant again tries to elicit response. As the gullies deepen, a sense of "other" emerges first, then a sense of "I." The three poisons—attraction, aversion, and indifference—now arise. Fears about not existing and about dying emerge in connection with the felt sense of "I," and the elemental reaction chains form. As the gullies deepen still further, the pattern develops a projected world, one of the six realms.

The pattern includes the unreleased core, fear, pattern imperative, compensating behaviors, elemental reaction chain, and projected world. Together, these constitute a self-image that we take to be what we are.

MEDITATION METHOD

Rest attention on the breath. Recall a moment when you experienced a shock and were unable to act. For this meditation, a shock is any experience for which you have no frame of reference—an unexpected comment or reaction from a friend that stuns you temporarily, for instance.

Sit in the experience of the shock, and feel the absence of any frame of reference. Everything is open.

Now, feel how energy moves toward an action, but with no frame of reference, the energy cannot be expressed in action, so you experience

- The shock of emotional energy
- Open space and four reactions:

    1. Nonrecognition of what open space is
    2. A reaction to clarity—the illusion of other
    3. A reaction to emptiness—the illusion of self
    4. A reaction to the unceasing arising of experience— confusion

- A reaction to open space—fear of nonexistence of the sense of self generated by confusion
- Setting of the I-other framework

The Formation of "I" and "Other"

The guidelines for this meditation follow the formation process up to the I-other framework. You are already familiar with the subsequent development of the three poisons, the elemental reaction chain, and the projected worlds from Meditation 4.

Imagine or recall a situation in which you are or were completely disoriented, were unable to take anything in, or had no idea what to do. A person asks you an unexpected question, and you don't know how to reply. You are told that you will lose your job, and your mind goes blank. Your child has an accident, and you can't take in the news.

Make the experience of the shock as vivid as you possibly can. Perhaps you remember an incident in school or when you were growing up. One student remembered being asked by her teacher to go into the hall to see what the time was. She remembers standing in the hall, looking at the clock, and being in complete shock because she didn't know how to tell time. She stood there so long that the teacher came out to see what had happened to her.

Sit and breathe. In the experience of shock, you have no frame of reference. There is just an experience of disruption, of not being. You feel the impulse to act, but without a frame of reference you don't know what to do, so you go blank. In meditation practice, the blankness initially lasts for only a moment before an emotional reaction takes over.

Go back to the original shock and sit in it again until you can observe the shift into blankness. As you do this again and again, you see that the blankness is a state of no reference, and you stay longer and longer in the experience of no reference.

Gradually, you see that three reactions take place very quickly. The first is a reaction to the clarity of original mind. This reaction generates the illusion of "other." The young girl in the hall experienced the teacher, the clock, the hall, everything, in vivid clarity as something that was "other."

The experience of "other" triggers the second reaction, which is to look for an internal referent. You find nothing because original mind is not a "thing"—it is empty. The reaction to the emptiness of original mind generates the illusion of "I." You can't be just pure experience; you have to exist, so a sense of "I" forms. The sense of "I" is shaped by the situation. In the case of the young girl in the hall, the sense of "I" was associated with feelings of being wrong, bad, and stupid. You can imagine the pattern imperative that formed!

The third reaction is to the unceasing arising of experience. With "I" and "other" in place, your experience of thoughts, feelings, and sensations is confused. You struggle to make sense of them in terms of "I" and "other."

Commentary: The Forming of Patterns

A pattern forms when a situation pulls together energy but the energy is not released. The situation may be a single traumatic event that elicits a high level of emotional energy or repeated related stresses that lead to a buildup of emotional energy.

Energy can be discharged in three ways. First, energy can be released in awareness. When we have a sufficiently high level of attention so that the situation can be experienced in awareness, the energy releases itself in the field of awareness, and we experience an arising and subsiding in presence.

Second, the energy can flow into action. The action is appropriate and effective because it arises directly from presence. In effect, the situation manifests what is appropriate. We are present in what is happening. The movement of energy in action is a response to what is arising in experience.

Third, without a frame of reference for action and without enough energy in attention to release the experience, the energy is neither released in awareness nor released as an expression of presence. The unreleased experience evokes the possibility of not existing. Fear of nonexistence is the fundamental fear of the human condition, deeper even than the fear of death. The unreleased experience freezes, initiating the formation of a pattern, just as a grain of sand in an oyster initiates the formation of a pearl. Layers of nacre form to reduce the sensations caused by the grain of sand. In the same way, mechanisms form around the emotional core to smother the threatening feelings of the undischarged emotional core.

The nonreferential space connected with the blankness in the meditation practice is a disruption in experience. In early childhood, experience is associated with the body, so the shock of disconnection feels like a threat to physical survival. The shock, which arises as a feeling of not being, is not released in awareness. The emotional core of a pattern is the unreleased experience. Fear of the experience is one of the first layers. The pattern imperative is a reaction to that fear.

When experience arises and is released in awareness, no patterns form. When you encounter situations that can't be released in awareness, however, you experience no response, either internally or externally. With no response, you don't know whether you exist or not. Unable to remain in the nonreferential state, you react to elicit a response by any means possible. The pattern is essentially a continuous performance for others (including the "others" stored inside you), a performance intended to confirm what cannot be confirmed—that you exist apart from what you experience. As the pattern consumes your life, your whole life becomes a performance.

The shock is not the same as the open space of original mind— awareness-emptiness, the way things are, what is ultimately true, pure being, mind itself, or any other of the countless names that Buddhism uses to refer to it.

Yet the open space of original mind is a powerful challenge to the self-images developed in the process of growing up, which rely on patterned reaction to function. According to the mahamudra tradition, mind is empty, clear, and unceasing. That is to say, while mind is not a thing, there is a clarity that arises as awareness, which is unceasing and ever present. When we experience open space or mind and our attention is passive, we do not recognize it for what it is. The reaction to the clarity of the mind generates the illusion that something else exists. The reaction to the emptiness generates the illusion of being something, and that something is a sense of self. At that point, the reaction to unceasing awareness and experience generates confusion.

Once the sense of self has arisen, the experience of open space is experienced as a threat to the self, even though the self only appears to exist. The self-other framework is now set, and all experience is appraised as pleasant, unpleasant, or neutral based on the extent to which it supports or undermines the sense of self. Pleasant, unpleasant, and neutral form the basis of the three emotional patterns of attraction, aversion, and indifference.

The reaction chain develops in order to erode attention, transforming the experience of open space to conform to the I-other framework. When we experience open space as the shaking of the ground we stand on, we grab, hold on, and become rigid (earth). When we experience open space as a wave engulfing us, we try to disperse the energy (water). When we experience open space as open nothingness, we seek to experience sensations as intensely as possible (fire). When we experience open space as being without ground, we try to do something to stop the feeling of falling (air). When we are overwhelmed by the experience of open space, we either fall into confusion or we fragment (void).

Which reaction chain arises in a given situation depends on many different factors. Once one or two have been established, however, they become the default settings, so to speak, and tend to operate even in new situations. While all five elemental reactions operate in all of us, most of us have a primary relationship with one reaction chain, a secondary relationship with another, and only slight tendencies to go to the others.

> It's déjà vu all over again.
>
> —Yogi Berra

Whenever we encounter a situation that is similar to the unreleased experience at the core of the pattern or any other part of the pattern, resonance takes place. As with two tuning forks, the core of the pattern resonates with the situation. The pattern is triggered and degrades attention. Direct awareness is obscured, and emotional energy cannot be released in awareness or into action that arises from presence. Therefore, we move into the projected world of the pattern and react accordingly.

For the formation of the patterns that constitute our personality, the reaction dynamic is far more significant than the content of the actual situation that precipitated the shock. The dynamic is repeated whenever we encounter different situations that resonate with the core emotion, and the pattern often results in exaggerated reactions to ordinary situations.

Reaction to the projected world sets up another feedback loop. The pattern evolves, and its operation becomes more elaborate, complex, and multileveled so that it can maintain its function of eroding attention in more and more situations. The accumulation and storing of energy in habituated feelings and behaviors is what forms the structure of the personality. Fear that waking up means losing your personality is another example of how the pattern of "I" maintains itself.

Meditation 7: How Can I Live Like This?

Purpose:
To understand how pattern-based living produces the three forms of suffering.

MEDITATION METHOD

Take a pattern that you have already identified. As you rest attention on the breath, let the pattern process unfold in your imagination. Go through the pattern three times. During the first cycle through the pattern, use your attention to observe the body. During the second cycle, observe emotional shifts. Finally, observe the quality of attention and presence when the pattern is running.

Body

- How does the pattern manifest in the body?
- Notice the ways in which you hold your body and any habituated movements and gestures you make as the pattern operates.
- Does the body feel responsive or mechanical?
- How does repetition of the pattern affect the body's capabilities?
- How do such movements affect the body over time?
- Do the physical manifestations of the pattern help or hinder your ability to satisfy desires or avoid what is undesirable?

Emotion

- As the pattern unfolds, observe the shifts in feelings of fulfillment and disappointment.
- How do you feel after the pattern has run?
- What is the predominant emotion that is operating as the pattern runs?
- How does the predominant emotion affect the way you interpret what is happening around you?
- How are other people viewed through the lens of the pattern?
- What emotional reactions arise when your experience diverges from the expectations of the projected world of the pattern?
- How does the pattern attempt to reestablish itself?

Awareness

- How stable is attention when the pattern is running?
- What causes the pattern to stop running?
- How present are you when the pattern is running?

- What, if anything, is missing when the pattern is running?
- What are you not seeing?

Commentary: The Three Sufferings

Pattern-based living can be described in terms of the three forms of suffering discussed in chapter 2: the suffering of pain, the suffering of change, and the suffering of existence. The three sufferings correspond to three minds: the mind of the body, the mind of emotion, and the mind of awareness. In the following explanations, I refer to the five aspects of pristine awareness. These are more fully explained in the next chapter, which deals with dismantling the elemental reaction chains.

The mind of the body is concerned with balance. In terms of the five pristine awarenesses, the mind of the body is *effective pristine awareness*. It is always present and knows what needs to be done. However, the mind of the body takes on habituations formed in the mind of emotion. The habituations distort the functioning of the mind of the body into reactions based on the projected world of the pattern, not on what is happening. The suffering of pain is the reaction to sensory experience. Pain is a sensation, but emotionally we react to it as a threat to survival. If we bring attention to pain, letting go of the emotional reaction, pain can be experienced as pure sensation, and suffering does not arise.

The mind of emotion responds (or reacts) to change. It is *sameness pristine awareness* and *distinguishing pristine awareness*. Most patterns, and the emotional cores of the patterns, operate in the mind of emotion. The early patterns from childhood develop here. The mind of emotion, when functioning in a pattern, gives rise to the projected world of the pattern. Since it operates at a higher level of energy than the mind of the body, it can override the mind of the body, giving rise to habituated physical behaviors and distortions in the functioning of the sensory faculties. As change takes place in and around us, what is happening diverges from the projected world of the pattern. The corresponding emotional reactions to change constitute the suffering of change.

The mind of awareness includes. It knows what we are and what arises in experience. In terms of the five pristine awarenesses, the mind of awareness is *totality pristine awareness* and *mirrorlike pristine aware-ness*. Because it functions at a higher level of energy, the mind of aware-ness can refine the mind of emotion and dismantle habituated patterns. When our level of attention is insufficient to function at the level of the mind of awareness, habituated patterns at the level of emotion take over. We feel not quite present, even when everything is going right with our lives. The subtle sense of not being completely present is the suffering of existence. It may also arise as a feeling of incompleteness or separation from what is happening around us.

Suffering of Pain: That Hurts!

The suffering of pain consists of reactions to what is experienced, whether what is experienced is explicitly painful or not. The mind of the body naturally knows what needs to be done and how to do it. When the presence of emotional patterns impedes the action of the body, physical blocks develop that impede the flow of energy and cause sickness and disease to develop. As fixed ways of acting develop, a set of routines and rituals that maintain and reinforce the operation of patterns is established. The demand of the fixed rou-tines takes its toll on the body. The reaction to the body's decline is suffering. Suffering also arises from the inability to satisfy desires or avoid what is undesirable. Our actions and behaviors become increasingly out of balance with what is going on around us. Physical pain also arises from external conditions, such as a brick falling on a foot. The suffering of pain is a reaction to the sensations of pain.

Suffering of Change:
Can't Everything Just Stay Like This?

The mind of emotion rides change. Patterns, on the other hand, make minimal adjustments to change. The constant effort to control what arises in experience manifests externally and internally. When circum-stances line up with the projected world, we experience fulfillment. When circumstances are contrary to the projected world, we experi-ence disappointment. The emotional swings of hope and fear, attrac-tion and aversion, anger and desire, grief and triumph, loss and gain characterize the suffering of change. Whenever the divergence opens up space between the world as it is and the world of our projections, the five elemental reactions arise as attempts to control what is being experienced: rigidity, evasiveness, devouring, busyness, and confusion. Over time, our range of experience and feeling shrinks to conform to the dictates of the pattern. We defend against change in every way possible. The following story illustrates how the mind of emotion makes minimal adjustments to the experiences of life.

> A duck walks into a bar, climbs onto a bar stool, and waits.
> The bartender comes over and asks, "What can I give you?"
> "Got any grapes?" asks the duck.
> "No, I don't have any grapes."
> "Got any grapes?"
> "No. This is a bar. We don't carry grapes."
> "Got any grapes?" asks the duck yet again.
> "Listen, duck," growls the bartender, "I don't have any grapes, but I'll tell you what I do have—a gun. You ask about grapes one more time, and I'll blow your head off. Got it?"
> The duck smiles, climbs down from the bar stool, goes out the door and up the street. He goes into the next bar, climbs up on a bar stool. The bartender comes over.
> "Got any guns?" the duck asks.
> "No. This is a bar. No guns here," says the bartender.
> "Got any grapes?"

Suffering of Existence: This Is a Life?

The suffering of existence is the most subtle effect of living a pattern-based existence. At the same time, it is the basis for the suffering of change and the suffering of pain. When we are living in a pattern, attention is passive. The pattern distorts experience to conform to the projected world. When another pattern is triggered, we switch from one projected world to another, unaware that the projected worlds and the corresponding reaction patterns have changed. Because all patterns are based on a sense of separation, a sense of separation permeates this way of experiencing the world.

Existential philosophers were acutely sensitive to the sense of separation and took it as fact, not false perception.

The suffering of existence also arises as a feeling of incompleteness. The incompleteness is not in what we are but in what happens when we are unable to maintain awareness. Patterns are based on incomplete experiences. Part of the manifestation of the pattern is the projection of incompleteness onto our sense of what we are, so we feel lifeless inside, internally empty or separate from the world. Instead of opening to these feelings and moving into the mystery of being, we shut down to it and look for something that will make us feel complete. That something may be an order or structure, a feeling of connection, intense sensations, or an activity. Whatever it is, it defines what is meaningful to us. Because we are looking away from what we are for completion, we never experience the completeness of being itself. Therefore we suffer.

A central tenet of Buddhism is that we are already complete in being what we are. The sense of incompleteness is a projection and persists as long as the pattern operation degrades attention and prevents the emotional core from being experienced. When the core is released in awareness, experience is no longer incomplete and the sense of incompleteness associated with the pattern disappears.

> Man is abandoned on earth in the midst of his infinite responsibilities, without help, with no aim but what he sets himself.
>
> —*Jean-Paul Sartre*

In previous meditations, we have seen that patterns operate mechanically, that they are present in every area of our lives, that they form around an unreleased core of experience, and that their operation creates suffering in our lives. Patterns develop through four mechanisms: crystallization, habituation, webbing, and layering.

Meditation 8: Merlin's Crystal Cave— Imprisonment

Purpose:
To understand the process of crystallization.

MEDITATION METHOD

Using the five steps below, observe how such structures as beliefs, positions, and fixed behaviors form from crystallizing energy.

- A space opens.
- Ideas and ideals arise as interpretations of sensations.
- Some ideas attract more energy or interest; attachments and preferences form.
- Preferences condense into feelings and tacit understandings.
- Feelings and tacit understandings develop into fixed reactions, behaviors, positions, and beliefs.

Alternatively, take a reactive behavior, a position, or a belief. Hold it in attention until you become aware of the feelings and tacit understandings implicit in the position or belief. Hold the feelings and understandings until you see the attachments and the ideas on which the pattern is based, thereby dissolving the reactive behavior back to open space with the use of attention.

Commentary: Crystallization

How do structures form? They don't spring into being fully formed. The beliefs, worldviews, and behaviors that govern our lives developed from emptiness, from nothing.

In the 1960s, during a period of social and political upheaval, the feminist movement generated new ideas and possibilities for relationships between men and women (air arising from void).

In the mid-1970s, a law professor at Yale wrote a series of articles arguing that there should be protection against sexual harassment in the workplace, since women often suffered serious setbacks in their careers if they refused sexual advances from men, particularly supervisors. Other law articles further reviewed existing law and synthesized the current thinking and changing mores. These articles were used in arguing lawsuits filed to stop sexual harassment (fire).

Gradually, through the 1980s and with a lot of confusion, tacit understandings emerged for both men and women about what was and was not appropriate (water).

Eventually, with judicial decisions and company policies beginning to reflect the changing ideas and mores, laws forbidding sexual harassment were enacted to codify the new social consensus (earth).

The same process takes place inside each of us. Instead of developing a legal structure, we develop a structure of beliefs about the world, codes of behavior, and ways we do things. Both structures, legal and internal—indeed, all structures—form in the same way.

First, from emptiness (void) energy arises as movement (air) in mind, which is first experienced as ideas. The ideas represent interpretations of sensations. One or more ideas, selected by emotional dynamics and previously established patterns, gather energy, and attachments form (fire). The attachments are often experienced as preferences or points around which we feel passion (attraction or aversion). The attachments condense further into feelings and tacit understandings (water) that come and go, like waves, but arise whenever similar situations are encountered. The feelings and tacit understandings then give rise to increasingly fixed reactions consisting of behaviors, positions, and beliefs (earth). The reactions may arise as thoughts and feelings, as verbal expressions, or as physical actions.

The reverse process, in which we start with a fixed reaction or belief, reveals how it formed. We use the reverse process to transform the energy at each stage to a higher level, dissolving the solidity of fixed reactions and beliefs back to the ideals from which they formed. As they become less solid, our emotional investment in them decreases and we will be able to change them, or at least consider alternatives, more easily. The reverse process is particularly useful when we encounter conflict. Usually the parties have fallen into a fixed set of reactions. If the parties trace the formation process in reverse, they may discover a solution to a seemingly intractable difficulty based on different interpretations of a common experience.

For instance, take the case of a company that produces a toxic effluent. Environmentalists take the company to court to stop the emission of toxic wastes. Management fights the case and the workers at the factory side with management. The judge orders the parties into mediation. In the course of negotiation, the feelings behind their respective positions begin to come out. The environmentalists are not against the company but are concerned about the health of their children. The management doesn't like producing toxic waste but sees no competitive alternative. The workers have their own concerns about working with toxic materials but want to protect their jobs. As talks progress and trust grows, all three begin to appreciate that they are passionately attached to certain ideas: the environmentalists to the idea of a safe and healthy place to live, the management to building a business that produces a good profit, and the workers to secure jobs. Increasingly, they exchange ideas. The environmentalists, realizing that they can't deprive people of their livelihood, research and develop a different industrial process. The workers embrace the new idea because they are concerned about their own children. Management, seeing the increasing unease of their own workers and the erosion of their public image, agrees to clean up the toxins already emitted. Because the process saves money, management also agrees to invest in training the workers. In short, by dissolving fixed positions back to open space, all three parties are able to generate the trust and creativity necessary to find an acceptable resolution of their differences.

The diagram below illustrates the energy transformations associated with the five elements. It corresponds to both the process of dying and the process of attention dissolving the structures of pattern-based experience, as well as negotiation, conflict, and other forms of human interaction. The diagonal arrows indicate the upward transformation of energy, and the dashed downward arrows indicate attention directed at what is in parentheses at each level. If mindfulness is lost, the energy decays in the same direction as the dashed arrows so that in negotiation, say, a discussion about the key points of attachment may suddenly decay back into fixed positions.

ENERGY TRANSFORMATION CHART
FOR THE FIVE ELEMENTS

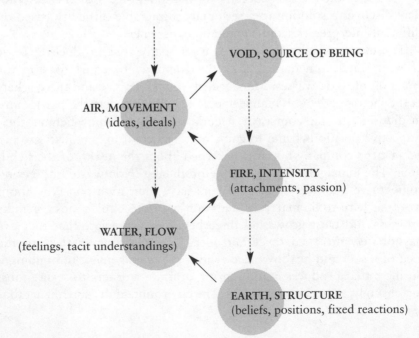

VOID, SOURCE OF BEING

AIR, MOVEMENT
(ideas, ideals)

FIRE, INTENSITY
(attachments, passion)

WATER, FLOW
(feelings, tacit understandings)

EARTH, STRUCTURE
(beliefs, positions, fixed reactions)

Meditation 9: Habituation—Enslavement

Purpose:
To understand how repeated behaviors evolve into self-perpetuating results.

Meditation Method

Doing Harm

Pick an action that causes harm to another person, such as stealing. Imagine that you are in charge of cash deposits for an organization. In that capacity, you discover that you can put a bit of cash in your pocket without anyone noticing.

Imagine that you do steal some money. Notice what happens in you to enable you to steal.

- What shuts down inside you?
- What do you ignore (for example, the effects of your action on the owner, the business, your co-workers)?
- How do you feel during the act of stealing?

Notice what happens after you have stolen money successfully.

- What was your motivation to steal?
- Are you more or less inclined to steal again after you have stolen successfully?
- How is your perception of others affected by having stolen?
- Is your perception of the cash that comes in different after you have stolen? How?

Now, imagine that stealing has become habituated. You steal on a regular basis. Reflect on the same four questions:

- What is your motivation to steal?
- Are you more or less inclined to steal again?
- How is your perception of others affected by stealing?
- How do you regard the cash that comes into the organization?

Repeat the exercise using other actions that harm others: killing, lying, slandering, or speaking offensively.

Helping Others

Go through the same steps using actions that are helpful to others, such as being generous, being courteous, complimenting a person, helping a person in need, speaking truthfully, or healing.

Commentary: The Four Results

Habituation is the simple principle that patterns become stronger the more they run. The reaction chain associated with the pattern is used more frequently. We live more and more in the projected world of the pattern. Karma is primarily habituation, after all, and the end process is described by the four results: full ripening, a predisposition to reproduce the behavior, a predisposition to reproduce the experience, and perceptual distortion.

Full Ripening

The fully ripened result is the projected world of the pattern—whichever of the six realms corresponds with the emotional basis of the pattern. The pattern is so deeply established that everything is interpreted in terms of the projected world.

Greed is the usual motivation for stealing. You see the world as not providing what you need. Your need is insatiable, so your only recourse is to take what you need. This is the realm of the hungry ghosts. In the case of killing, anger is the most common motivation. You experience the world as opposition, the hell realm.

The way you experience even the simplest things depends on how you are feeling at the time. Take water, for example. On a hot day, a glass of plain water is refreshing and restoring. Offer it to a proud person who expects a fine wine, however, and he will take it as an insult. For a person suffering from dehydration, a glass of water is life-saving medicine.

You are already familiar with the six realms. In this meditation, pay attention to the way in which the emotion that motivates a specific action projects a world that conforms to the pattern. A friend of mine is very talented at languages. He learns languages quickly and easily. He is unable to understand why other people have difficulty and tends to regard them as lazy or stupid. As far as language is concerned, he lives in the god realm.

Another person I know is a very caring individual. She helps people in every way she can. Within a few minutes of meeting you, she uncovers an area of your life in which you can use some help and is already putting the assistance into place—and you appreciate her care! But her behavior is all pattern. She can't ever be with you and just enjoy your company. She has to be helpful, caring, and doing something for you. She lives in the hungry ghost realm, driven by an insatiable need to be helpful.

You move from one realm to another in a moment, so don't think of the realms as enduring states. When one emotion, say desire, arises, you look for enjoyment. Then you become greedy and move to the hungry ghost realm. Luck favors you, you win the lottery, and you are suddenly in the god realm.

Once, a samurai went to a Zen master and asked about the difference between heaven and hell. The Zen master turned away, pointing his nose in the air, saying, "I don't have time to teach fools."

The samurai was enraged and reached for his sword, but before he could draw it, the Zen master turned back and said, "That's hell." The samurai then relaxed and the Zen master continued, "And that's heaven."

> All beings do not see mountains and waters in the same way. Hungry ghosts see water as raging fire or pus and blood. Dragons see water as a palace or a pavilion. Some beings see water as the seven treasures or a wish-granting jewel. Some beings see water as a forest or a wall. Human beings see water as water. Water is seen as dead or alive depending on causes and conditions.
>
> —*Dogen*

Predisposition to Reproduce the Behavior

Having stolen once successfully, you now know that, whatever you believed before, stealing is a viable way to procure something that you don't have. The act of stealing confirms the way you feel inside: the world doesn't provide you with what you need, so you have to take it. When you encounter new situations that trigger that feeling, stealing is the action you select.

The more we reenact the pattern process, the more habituated our actions and reactions become. The more we act in a given way, the greater our predisposition to act in that way again. The pattern is enslaving us.

Predisposition to Reproduce the Experience

The third result is a little more subtle. When you steal, for example, you take what is not yours and make it yours. Knowing that the usurpation of property is possible because of your own action, you are less trusting of others. The more you steal, the more you behave as if other people are going to steal from you. The pattern of stealing creates a predisposition for feeling that you are the victim of theft, even when you are not. In the same way, when you give, you naturally feel open and generous. In other words, you feel as if you have been the recipient of generosity even when you are the agent.

These two results, the predisposition to reproduce the action and the predisposition to reproduce the experience, are the basis for the expressive and receptive modes of reactive patterns. In the case of stealing, the expressive mode is stealing, while the receptive mode is being stolen from. When a pattern forms, both poles are present, though we usually identify with one more than the other. When enough energy, pressure, or tension arises, however, the pattern flips from one to the other. A thief, when caught, will often claim to be a victim of injustice.

Perceptual Distortion

The fourth result is the way the pattern affects sensory perception. Sensations arise that conform to the structure of the pattern. For instance, when you are in love, you tend to see your beloved as having large, radiant eyes that flood you with attention. In the example of stealing, your perception of the incoming cash changes: you regard it as yours. It just isn't in your pocket yet. If a colleague asks what you are doing just after you have hidden the cash, you see him as a prying, intrusive busybody. If the cash coming in that day is less than usual so that you had to steal less to avoid detection, you think that the world is being unjust. You may even see colors as less vivid and objects as sharper and more angular. In other words, your sensory perceptions conform to the pattern and the projected world of the pattern.

We have already seen how patterns form and how they create suffering. We have seen how the projected worlds, the six realms of the reactive emotions, are also suffering. We now see how patterns enslave us in their operation by determining what we experience and how we are predisposed to react. Karma does not determine what we actually do in each moment. That is a function of attention. Without a practice of attention, we cannot possibly recognize the projected world or the way we are predisposed to act. We just accept the projected world as the real world and our predispositions as our personality. We have no hope of dismantling the patterns that run our lives. With a practice of attention, however, we have a chance. Realistically, we have about as much room to shift as a violin has in its case, but it's enough.

RED RIDING HOOD: What big eyes you have, grandma!

WOLF: All the better to see you, my dear.

RED RIDING HOOD: What big ears you have!

WOLF: All the better to hear you.

RED RIDING HOOD: And what big teeth you have!

WOLF: All the better to eat you.

In addition to crystallization and habituation, webbing and layering are two other mechanisms by which patterns consume our lives. Webbing refers to the way patterns interact to form a web of interactive mechanisms. One part of the operation of one pattern resonates with the emotional core of another pattern, so it starts to run. The corresponding pattern imperatives or projected worlds may contradict each other, in which case we experience internal conflict. They may reinforce each other, in which case both patterns are reinforced.

Personality is like a shattered mirror. Beliefs and set positions form when energy crystallizes into structures by means of the operation of habituated patterns. Different patterns generate different beliefs. Each pattern functions like a piece of the mirror, reflecting and refracting experience in a unique way. Patterns are activated by resonance with what is arising, but we are so convinced of our existence as an independent entity that we rarely notice the transition from one resonated pattern to another. We move from one belief to another and never notice the contradiction. When we encounter situations that simultaneously resonate with the patterns of contradictory belief structures, we experience internal conflict. Such moments are potentially valuable from the perspective of internal transformative work because they provide a chance to see the structure of the web.

> You must not count overmuch on your reality as you feel it today, since, like that of yesterday, it may prove an illusion for you tomorrow.
>
> —*Luigi Pirandello*

The other mechanism is layering. As we have seen, patterns generate structures as they operate repeatedly. The structures become components of other patterns, which generate structures that become components of still other patterns. The result is highly complex and seemingly intelligent aware behavior. How can we tell whether we or another person is acting out of presence or pattern? The key is to look at intention and result: what is being served?

Presence serves the intention of the situation, not conditioned agendas of individuals, groups, or institutions. The results of patterned operation are the reinforcing of patterns; the deepening of conditioning; and the decay of attention, presence, and awareness. Whenever a situation resonates with the emotional core and triggers the pattern, the pattern runs, regardless of its appropriateness in the given situation. Over time, the operation of the pattern becomes more elaborate, but the function remains the same: transforming the experience of open space and awareness into reaction so that the emotional core never arises in awareness. The results of presence, on the other hand, are new dimensions of freedom, transformation of behavior, and increased attention and awareness.

Meditation 10: How Are Patterns Dismantled?

Purpose:
To understand how attention dismantles a pattern.

In your meditation sessions, begin by resting attention with the breath for ten to fifteen minutes.

MEDITATION METHOD

Take a pattern you have observed and work through the four steps to freedom: recognize, disidentify, develop a practice, and cut. For this contemplation, a weak pattern will be more useful than a strong one, because you need to be able to imagine acting differently from the tendencies set up by the pattern.

Recognize

No pattern can be dismantled until it is recognized as a process that runs mechanically. How did you recognize this pattern? Sit in attention, and let the pattern play out in your imagination. Any or all of the following points can be used to identify it:

- Shifts in your body, emotional state, or perception of things
- A repeated chain of reactive emotions
- The way the pattern projects a world
- Familiar automatic behaviors—physical, verbal, or mental
- Familiar results, such as how your relationship with others is affected
- A divergence between your intention and what actually happens

Disidentify

As long as you take the pattern to be a part of what you are, the pattern cannot be dismantled. See the pattern as a process that operates independently of your intention. It is triggered by resonance with a situation, it runs until attention has been degraded, and then it collapses, leaving you wondering what happened. Whenever the pattern you are working on arises, hold one of its components that you can recognize in attention, whether it is the pattern imperative, the reaction chain, or the projected world. The pattern manifestation will appear to disappear. You then feel a release of energy, see a deeper pattern underneath, or both. When you see the pattern as a process, your relationship with it changes. You no longer identify with it, and you can take it as an object of attention. Observe the pattern in attention:

- Is it in line with your intention in situations when it is triggered?
- Does it serve your well-being?
- Does it use behaviors and motivations that reflect the way you want to be?
- In what way is it part of you?

Develop a Practice

Develop a practice that interrupts the erosion of attention. In other words, think of something you can do to remind you to return to attention as the pattern is running. Patterns have no internal mechanisms that limit their operation or evolution. They are limited only by the amount of energy available to them. To dismantle a pattern, you have to disrupt the operation of the pattern by systematically bringing attention to its operation. Energy then flows into attention, not into the pattern.

Cut with Practice

Once you have developed a practice, the fourth step is to cut the pattern again and again with the practice. Whenever the pattern arises, cut it with attention. Step by step, you identify all the components of the pattern, all the associations, and you are able to experience them in attention. The unreleased experience is released in awareness, and the pattern falls apart.

Commentary: Dismantling Patterns

Each of the four steps is essential, and each presents its own difficulty.

Recognize

You cannot even start the process until you recognize that a pattern is operating. When you are completely identified with a pattern, the projected world of the pattern is taken to be the way things are, and habituated reactions are taken to be appropriate responses.

Friends, teachers, spouses, or significant others can be very helpful in your effort to recognize patterned behavior. Even more helpful, though more difficult to appreciate, are the contributions that come from people with whom you do not get along and from adverse and difficult situations. Reactive patterns always operate more strongly in adversity. You say things you regret saying and do things you regret doing. In other words, patterns take over and dictate your behaviors. By paying attention to how you react under stress or adversity, you can see patterned behavior clearly.

One sign of pattern-based reaction is that the results of your actions are consistently contrary to your intentions or expectations. Another sign is consistently unfulfilled expectations. The usual tendency is to attribute bad results to external factors, a form of projection in line with the projected world. Pay attention to the things you attribute to external factors, and then look inside to see what sees things that way and what you do to allow those external factors to affect you.

For instance, you notice that whenever you ask friends for help, they say, "Sure," but never follow through. You conclude that your friends are unreliable and you stop asking for help. Then one day you are struggling with a project. "Why didn't you ask for help?" a friend asks. Surprised, you accept the help. He works with you late into the night and you finish the project together.

You now look at how you asked for help in the past and you notice that you expected your friends to turn you down, so you asked in a way that suggested you didn't want their help. Then you look at what in you expects people not to help you and you see that you are afraid of not being able to reciprocate.

Careful observation of actions and their results eventually leads you to recognize patterns. For instance, suppose you notice that whenever you do x, sometime later y happens. You see no reason why x causes y, so you attribute the connection to coincidence, but y keeps happening whenever you do x. It makes no sense to you because the pattern blinds you to the actual connection. If you temporarily suspend your reliance on logic and observe carefully, however, you eventually see that x and y are connected. Observation means bringing attention again and again to the pattern. The repeated effort results in a higher level of attention that penetrates what the pattern obscures. An additional method is to follow, with the attention, exactly what happens after you do x. Follow the gesture initiated by x and see how it produces y. Then you recognize the pattern.

In the example above, you can also observe what happens when you ask a friend for help, what tone of voice you use, how you stand, what you say, whether you follow up on the assent, whether you set a date or time to get together. By observing precisely what you do, you uncover the pattern in you that transmits the message "I don't want help" even when you are asking for it.

Disidentify

Disidentification is the process through which a pattern becomes an object of attention. Observation is the first step. You see more and more clearly that the pattern has a program that is different from or contrary to your own intention. You begin to feel, perhaps, that the pattern is a machine that is following its own mechanical functioning. It's not part of what you are. Initially, you feel helpless and unable to do anything about the pattern. Actually, you have started to separate from it.

The big fear in disidentification is that you won't be able to function without the pattern. Artists and hard-driving businesspeople are particularly likely to have difficulty on this point. They fear that they will lose their creativity or their edge and that their work will suffer. Remember, the pattern operates mechanically to erode attention. In the world of the pattern, the pattern reaction is the only logical way to function, and, as far as the pattern is concerned, you will die if you don't react according to the pattern.

> A student asked Dingo Khyenste Rinpoche, "Why do we practice?"
>
> He replied, "To make the best of a bad situation."

You have to die to the pattern's world. You have to die to the belief that your ability to survive rests on those patterned behaviors. You have to trust that what you are—open, clear awareness—can function effectively. The irony is that open, clear awareness functions much better than patterned reactions. Artists see how their reactivity limited their ability to see things as they are. Businesspeople are often surprised that even a little meditation allows them to relax, see more clearly, and be more effective in their work.

In disidentification, you really see how you can be more present in your life, but the attachment to patterns is so strong that many people abandon their practice at precisely this point. They are unwilling to pay the price, which is to die to the life that these patterns have created.

How do we develop the willingness to die? By clearly facing the predicament we are in; by opening to how things are; by questioning the nature of things; by caring about what is.

Develop a Practice

The third step is to develop a practice. The practice can be very simple. For instance, if you observe that you are upset by stop-and-go traffic, rest attention on the breath whenever the traffic comes to a stop. The practice can also be complex. Deity practices in the Tibetan tradition involve elaborate visualizations, rituals, and codes of behavior that work together to sever identification with the habituated perception of experience.

The principal challenge in developing a practice is that you have to deliberately change your behavior. You can recognize a pattern and even have a degree of disidentification from it but still let it run what you do. The purpose of a practice is to change how you actually do things. At first a pattern seems so solid that you can't imagine doing anything differently. Constant observation inevitably reveals other possibilities. Take one of the possibilities as the practice.

Suppose you notice that you have difficulty giving to others. As a practice, you decide to give an actual object, no matter how insignificant, to another person once a day. This practice changes behavior in the mind of the body. You come in touch with the pattern conditioning in the mind of emotion. Even when all you are giving is a paper clip to a colleague, you bring attention to the contraction or resistance in you. You see that the resistance runs whether the object is valuable or insignificant, so you begin to appreciate that the difficulty in giving has little to do with the object. The difficulty is a manifestation of a pattern. At the same time, you experience actual giving, so that you know that you are not the pattern.

Disidentification and developing a practice interact with each other. As you separate from the pattern, you come up with more and more ways to practice. As you implement different ways to practice, identification with the pattern becomes weaker and weaker.

Cut with a Practice

The fourth step is using the practice to cut into the pattern. The key effort is consistency. Cut again and again and again. Most patterns have been in place for a long time. They consist of solid structures of beliefs, personality traits, and behaviors. They use every available resource to degrade attention—exaggerated fears, distorted perceptions, depression, elaborate rationalizations, or physical illness. Consistent cutting is the key to freedom. To cut more deeply into the pattern, note when the pattern operates more strongly. In the case of giving, for instance, note the people to whom you avoid giving and observe what takes place in your mind and body. Deliberately give a flower or a piece of candy to a person you consistently avoid and watch what comes up. You will soon learn what is going on in you internally, but only if you make the effort in your chosen practice.

The power of patterns to degrade attention is impressive. Even in the exercise of giving insignificant objects to others, you may suddenly notice that you haven't given anything to anyone for three or four days. What happened to your intention? Did you forget? When you look over the past few days, you may recall thinking that the practice of giving was stupid and pointless. So, you reinstate the practice and the same thing happens! This time when you look back you notice feelings of anger and resentment connected with your idea that the practice is stupid and pointless. Your practice is beginning to cut into the pattern and reveal what drives it. Remember, difficulty in practice, whatever form it takes, is a sign that your practice is effective. Your practice has activated patterns that resist the development of attention, patterns whose operation you can now observe.

As you cut deeper and deeper into a pattern's structure, the energy stored in the pattern is released. The energy of the pattern, which is transformed into attention, increases your ability to cut deeper into the pattern. If you do not maintain attention when the energy is released, the energy flows back into the pattern or other patterns and reinforces them. After retreats, many people are surprised at how reactive they are when they return to their homes. They thought that they would be calmer, more relaxed, and less reactive, but they let their efforts in mindfulness slip, and the energy of attention accumulated in retreat now decays and powers the patterns triggered by the return to their home environment. Mindfulness is even more important after a period of intensive practice.

The more success you have in cutting into the pattern, the more pronounced are the pattern's efforts to maintain its operation. Consistency in the form of patient endurance is the only way to get through. You may feel that you are at war, and in a certain sense you are. The pattern is a mechanical process that functions to degrade attention. It has no interest in your well-being, much less your waking up. It has no interest in anything, yet it runs whenever it is triggered and shapes your life accordingly. In the end, the work of dismantling patterns comes down to a single question: who is going to live your life—you or your patterns?

Whenever a pattern arises, don't hesitate. Cut right into it. Negotiation is not an option. Cut whenever you can. As Thich Nhat Hanh says, "Practice every day. It will save your life."

The four steps to dismantle patterns appear in different forms in many spiritual traditions. Recall that the first noble truth is the truth of suffering. It is about the *recognition* that suffering exists. The second noble truth is the origin of suffering, the truth that suffering arises from reactive emotions. It is about *disidentification*—knowing that suffering is a reaction and that you are not the reaction. The third noble truth is the truth of cessation, which holds that an end to suffering is possible. It opens up a new possibility, the end of suffering, and it is an invitation to *develop a practice*. The fourth noble truth is the truth of the path, that there is a way to live that brings an end to suffering. It is about using attention to *cut* through the process of suffering in every area of your life.

Another instance of the four steps is the four forces, a traditional method for stopping the evolution of actions into experienced results. The four forces are regret, reliance, remedy, and resolution. Since we are usually interested in limiting the effects of negative actions, the four forces are discussed in terms of actions that harm others.

The first force, *regret,* corresponds to recognize. Regret means that you admit what you did and acknowledge the harmful consequences, in terms of the four results discussed in Meditation 9. The intention of regret is to remove any defense or justification of the action in your mind. In Buddhism, nonvirtuous actions are regarded as negative because they grow into unpleasant and painful experiences, not because they violate an authority or law. Therefore, regret does not involve guilt. Suppose you unwittingly drink a glass of poison and learn right afterward that what you drank is poisonous. You haven't violated a law. You don't feel guilt, but you do feel regret because you will suffer from the poison.

The second force, *reliance,* corresponds to disidentify. Reliance means that you renew your connection with spiritual practice, whether it be through devotion, compassion, awareness, or presence. You act negatively when you fall away from attention and mindfulness. Reliance means that you deliberately reestablish your practice so that the conditions for negative action are no longer present in you. By reconnecting with your spiritual practice, you disidentify with the pattern.

The third force, *remedy,* corresponds to developing a practice. Remedy means that you act in a way that disrupts the operation of the pattern behind the negative action. If you can, correct the negative action: apologize, make restitution, make amends. If you cannot remedy the action itself, then undertake a positive action with the explicit intention to remedy the negative: make a donation to charity, do some community service, help a friend, or, better, help someone you don't like. Remedying does not by itself remove the patterns of negativity established by the negative action, but the introduction of positive behavior does change the way the action develops into experienced results.

The fourth force, *resolution,* corresponds to cutting with practice. Resolution means that you form the intention not to act that way again. As long as you retain the slightest sense that you might repeat the action, the patterns associated with that action have a place to grow and develop. To stop the karmic process from evolving further, renounce completely any defense of the action and any intention to act that way again. The resolution you make irrevocably commits you to cutting through the pattern whenever it arises.

Experience of Pattern Dissolution

When you first bring attention to a pattern, you run into a rain of thoughts and ideas that undermine your efforts. What are you doing? Why are you doing it? Wouldn't you prefer to see a movie, read a book, or clean all the junk out of your garage?

Next, you begin to feel resistance in your body. Resistance in the body may arise as discomfort, agitation, aches, pains, or even illness. The discomfort is evidence that attention is penetrating the structures of the pattern stored in the body. Rest attention on the breath or in awareness, and include the sensations of the physical discomfort in your attention. If you focus attention only on the physical discomfort, you increase the level of energy in the resistance itself and make matters worse. For this reason, work with inclusive attention, which holds the sensations in a broad field of awareness.

You also encounter emotional resistance. You will gradually notice emotional sensations that are connected to the physical discomfort. The emotional sensations destabilize your attention initially, but as attention grows stronger, you can hold the emotional sensations in attention. The emotional sensations often seem to subside as the physical sensations increase, and vice versa. The alternation may continue for some time.

Gradually, attention develops sufficiently so that you can hold the physical and emotional sensations in attention simultaneously. Attention penetrates the structure of the pattern, which begins to disintegrate. The energy released from the pattern arises as emotionally charged thoughts. These thoughts are much more powerful and intense than the thoughts encountered at the beginning of the process. The emotionally charged thoughts are often connected with your sense of who and what you are, and you may feel quite threatened.

At this point, experience takes on a dreamlike quality. You wonder what the point of everything is. You feel as if you are losing something vitally important, so you try to strike a bargain, saying that you are willing to let go of this as long as you can hold on to that. You are experiencing the acceleration or intensification of the pattern's operation to undermine attention, which occurs because your identification with the pattern is beginning to break up.

As the pattern breaks up, you experience waves of raw emotion. Often you cannot name these feelings. They seem to come from nowhere, pervade your entire being, and then subside. When they come, you feel giddily ecstatic or depressed beyond despair. Energy surges run through your body. In this chaos, you reexperience the core emotional dynamic of the pattern and may reexperience the situation in which that core dynamic was set up. In either case, the core dynamic is released in awareness. You may feel more complete and whole, or you may feel that a chunk of you has broken off and disappeared. The upshot is that you are less reactive. Even when you encounter a situation that triggers the core dynamic, the pattern no longer takes you over. You are just aware of it running inside, as a sequence of thoughts and feelings. As the pattern collapses, you experience the situation for what it is, without projection.

Patterns build up in layers. When you penetrate one layer of a pattern, you will experience an increase in energy and freedom. A short time later, however, you become aware that another layer of patterned behavior, feelings, and perceptions was operating underneath. Turn attention to that pattern. Often, you will feel that you are making no progress or that you have taken a step back, whereas, in fact, you have cut deeper into the web that separates you from your life.

The Middle Way

The middle way—not falling into extreme positions—is one of the great teachings of Buddhism. Too often, the middle way is interpreted as a balance point between two extremes. Finding such a balance point is often very difficult, but that difficulty is nothing compared to the difficulty of trying to maintain the balance from moment to moment. What is the balance point between being too strict or too loose in how you discipline your children? If you could find the perfect balance point, could you maintain it? This way of thinking is highly problematical.

The middle way is traditionally described as not falling into an extreme position. You don't need to find the ideal balance point. Travel the middle way by keeping *both* extremes in attention at all times. You fall into one extreme only when the other falls out of attention. By keeping both extremes in attention, you never fall into either one. Buddha's life illustrates the middle way. He grew up in the extreme of luxury and never gave any consideration to restraint or even simplicity. He then followed the extreme of asceticism and ignored his physical and mental health. Neither lifestyle led to an understanding of suffering or the end of suffering. Then he followed the middle way. He ate when he was hungry and didn't eat when he wasn't hungry. With his health restored, he was able to bring attention to the question of suffering and come to full awakening. In his teachings, he consistently discouraged asceticism for asceticism's sake and indulgence for indulgence's sake.

In terms of working to dismantle patterns, apply the middle way to the extremes of the pattern imperative and associated behaviors. The expressive and receptive modes define two extremes, for example. Hold both extremes in attention. A higher level of attention forms. You can now experience the pattern and the feelings associated with it as objects of attention. Hold the feelings in attention, and direct awareness into activity. You will shift into an undefined state that is not part of the projected world of the pattern. The undefined state or open space again triggers the pattern, so continue to hold the reactive process in attention, following its unfolding.

Initially, you only perceive different ways of acting; later you will be able to act differently. You then experience an increase in awareness, and the pattern is more clearly defined as an object instead of as what you are. The more the pattern is seen as an object, the more you are able to cut into its operation. When the pattern is cut, either the pattern releases itself in the field of awareness or the pattern is opened more deeply and you can see into the next layer.

KARMA AND FREEDOM

We started with two questions:

- Why are we the way we arc?
- How do we change?

We are the way we are because complex patterns of reactions have developed into the structures of our personality. Patterns are completely mechanical processes that interact and evolve on their own, elaborating themselves on the basis of emotional imperatives that have formed around unreleased feelings or experiences. The results of pattern-based living are the three forms of suffering: the suffering of pain, the suffering of change, and the suffering of existence.

We change the way we are by bringing attention to bear on the operation of a pattern. The pattern is disturbed by the energy of attention, just as the crystalline structure of ice is disturbed by the energy of heat. When attention penetrates deeply enough, the pattern cannot hold together and falls apart. The process of bringing attention to a pattern is summarized in the four steps: recognition, disidentification, developing a practice, and cutting with the practice. To dismantle patterns we need determination, guidance, methods of practice, and a willingness to die to the life that is based on patterns.

The teachings of karma are central to the practice of Buddhism. While karma developed into a belief system in many Buddhist cultures, the essential import of the teaching of karma is that we are responsible for the way we experience what arises in our lives. All too easily, the teaching of karma can be misunderstood to mean that we are responsible for what happens to us. We are not—neither in the traditional belief that we reap the painful results of actions done in past lives nor in the naive modern belief that we choose what we experience. Both interpretations rest on the belief that all our actions are volitional. They ignore that much of what we do is not volitional but based on set patterns of perception and reaction. Karma teaches that these patterns are reinforced by our actions. If we don't pay attention to the way we live and act, our lives are consumed by the "artificial life" of patterns.

This approach to karma rests not on belief but on our own experience of the way patterns operate in us. The meditations in this section direct attention toward the operation of patterns so that we can see and know without relying on belief.

There is a Tibetan saying that summarizes karma.

To see what you've done, look at what you experience now.
To see what you will experience, look at what you are doing now.

Here is an American version of the same idea.

When you do what you always did, you get what you always got.

Moral codes exist for various reasons—to provide simple formulas to meet life's challenges or to regulate or control the masses—but ultimately we have to rely on direct experience. The more we practice, the less dogmatic we become. All we can do is bring our attention to bear on situations that we encounter in life, using attention to cut through the operation of habituated patterns. We show up in each situation, open to what is happening, see what is, and serve what is true to the limit of our perception. We act and receive the result. If the situation blows up in our face, we have to pay. We will see our part in it if, and only if, we have brought all our attention to our action. We do not blame anyone for the result because we know we did our best. Instead, we learn about where we were weak, blind, stupid, or out of touch. There is no other way to learn. Any lesson is cheap if it doesn't cost us our ability to make further efforts in waking up.

In effect, we approach each situation as a mystery and know that all we can do is be present, to the best of our ability, in that mystery. We don't need beliefs, we don't need comforting, and we don't need explanations. We can be open and awake, staying present with all that arises in our experience.

This is the real teaching of karma. It directs attention to our actions, bringing us in touch with the habituated patterns that dictate much of our lives. It alerts us to the self-reinforcing nature of those habituations and the importance of attention in dismantling them. It also leads to a compelling appreciation of the blind suffering that is present in a life when attention and presence are not cultivated.

Thus, karma provides a powerful motivation to become free. It also tells us how to become free—by dismantling patterns. All Buddhist practices are directed toward one end, the freedom that comes from dismantling conditioned patterns. The practices vary considerably from culture to culture, from tradition to tradition, yet Buddhism is remarkable for the degree of common purpose and common understanding it exhibits across cultures and across traditions.

What does living free of patterns mean? To live free of patterns is to live in awareness. In the course of our growing up, many patterns developed as ways to meet new situations, but the patterns continued to evolve on their own. Our personality is made up of patterns of reaction that are based on past experiences and that prevent us from responding appropriately in the present. The patterns have evolved to exclude the unknown, the mystery, from our lives as much as possible.

When we start dismantling patterns, we are, in effect, shifting the basis of the organization of our personality away from conditioned patterns and the constructed identities they maintain to awareness itself. The shift is radical. We move from believing we are something to knowing that we are not anything. We are stepping directly into the mystery of our being.

To live in the mystery of being requires faith. We must be willing to open to the mystery itself. We cannot expect to know what will unfold in the future. We must live without the false reassurances of explanations, order, and structure. In embracing the mystery by living in awareness, we are free from the sense of incompleteness, separation, or internal hollowness that pervades pattern-based existence.

CHAPTER 6

Dismantling
Reactive Emotions

When the Mulla was a judge in his village, a dishevelled figure ran into his court-room, demanding justice.

"I have been ambushed and robbed," he cried, "just outside this village. Someone from here must have done it. I demand that you find the culprit. He took my robe, sword, even my boots."

"Let me see," said the Mulla, "did he not take your undershirt, which I see you are still wearing?"

"No he did not."

"In that case, he was not from this village. Things are done thoroughly here. I cannot investigate your case."

—IDRIES SHAH,
THE EXPLOITS OF THE INCOMPARABLE MULLA NASRUDIN

The work of dismantling patterns must be taken very seriously. An old Tibetan saying advises, "Perhaps better not to start, but, once started, better to finish." If you start dismantling patterns and don't finish the job, problems arise.

Zemyne is a snake with a single eye. Whoever she bites will die immediately. She may be seen only in summer, and then only at either noon or midnight. The blood of Zemyne is black, but it can cure every illness, and whoever bathes in the blood is protected against all magic.

God has granted Zemyne dominion in the realm beneath the ground. The metals belong to her. "If I had two eyes instead of one,"

Zemyne once said, "I would kill enough people to cover the walls of my home with their skulls."

Zemyne was once a lovely young girl, who refused the advances of a wicked magician. He cursed her, and she assumed her present form. Whoever wishes to rescue her must beat her until her skin falls off. Then he must burn the skin immediately, to prevent her from resuming her present shape.

A young peasant habitually killed all the snakes he found in the garden, forest, and field. One day when he was cutting grass in a meadow, he suddenly heard a loud hiss. He became aware of a movement in the grass behind him. Looking around, he recognized Zemyne. To kill her and take her blood would have given him great power, but he had dreamed of rescuing the maiden.

Seeing his chance, the peasant pinned Zemyne's head firmly against the earth with the blade of his sickle. Then he grabbed a knotted branch with his free hand and pounded the snake furiously, until her skin broke open. All of a sudden, a beautiful maiden was standing before him. Beside her sparkled the skin, now a many-colored dress.

The maiden reached for the dress, but the peasant was faster. He grabbed the garment, placed it beneath his arm, and led the maiden to his home. There he gave her new clothes and food. She smiled charmingly, but said nothing of her past.

They were married and lived happily together for years. The wife gave her husband many children, and their joy increased still more. But one day the wife found a chest containing the many-colored dress, for the peasant, instead of burning it, had hidden it away. She put it on and changed immediately back into a snake. Then she killed her husband and children with her poisonous bite, and, leaving the farmstead, took up her old residence in the meadow by the forest.

—THE PEASANT AND ZEMYNE
(LITHUANIAN FOLK TALE RETOLD BY BORIA SAK)

Like all folk tales, this story has multiple levels of meaning and can be read in many ways. One reading is to take Zemyne as a distorted expression of the energy of original mind, distorted by the unwanted advance and the subsequent curse. The potency of the locked-up energy is vividly conveyed by the remarkable powers of her blood. Zemyne is also an appropriate metaphor for habituated patterns. She is limited in vision and embodies an anger that knows no limit, for she would line the walls of her room with skulls.

Many of the patterns that shape our lives were instilled in or even beaten into us. Like the maiden, we probably didn't ask for the unjust, harsh, or insensitive treatment, but it happened, and the patterns that developed now run our lives.

The peasant, in this interpretation, is attention. He notices Zemyne and dismantles the pattern, freeing the maiden inside. The pattern now is just a piece of cloth, beautiful and fascinating perhaps, but just a covering. Unfortunately, the peasant doesn't complete his job. Attention goes passive. Something about the dress entrances him, so he holds on to it. Now it is only a matter of time.

By chance, the dress is discovered, and the pattern is reactivated. Zemyne, the snake, strikes. Love, affection, joy, relationship, and caring, even for one's own children, are gone. Everyone dies, and the pattern goes on. Patterns that aren't completely dismantled come back to bite.

All spiritual work is essentially destructive in nature. The great spiritual traditions universally hold that the essence of our being—in Buddhist terms, original mind—is clear, empty awareness. The purpose of spiritual work is to return to original mind, to reclaim our lives from the confusion and distortions of conditioning and wake up to what we are and what this experience we call life is. No matter what or how we think of the sources of conditioning—karma, environment, family background, genetic structure, evolutionary inheritances, cultural values—we are deeply conditioned. Habituated patterns of reaction and behavior run much of our lives. They create suffering for us, create suffering for others, and cut all of us off from the mystery of being.

The last chapter described the structure and components of habituated patterns: the projected world, the reaction chain, and the emotional core with its attendant sense of "I." To uncover original mind, we must direct attention to these components and demolish them.

A rough analogy to this process is the demolishing of large buildings such as high-rise apartment buildings or large hotels. A few charges placed strategically on the structural supports bring the whole building down. It collapses on itself. Only twenty to forty pounds of explosive are needed to level a large apartment building. The rest of this book describes where to place and how to set off those charges—how to demolish specific components of the conditioned patterns that constitute your personality.

The first question you must ask is "Do you want to do this?" Well, clearly you do, or you wouldn't have read this far. Still, your intention to travel this path must be strong and stable. You can't go halfway and stop. You might as well decide that you don't want to demolish your home after you've knocked out the main structural supports.

To dismantle habituated patterns one by one is an impossible task. Instead, we direct our efforts to dismantling key structural components of habituated patterns: the reactive chains, the projected worlds, the undischarged emotional cores, and the sense of "I." Once these are dismantled, all patterns that use them collapse.

The determination to leave behind the life of reactive patterns is called renunciation. The decision comes from the recognition that you are doomed to suffering as long as you cycle through the realms projected by reactive emotions and habituated patterns. Your life is broken and cannot be fixed. You are done with patterned existence. You become a refugee, leaving behind what has become intolerable and journeying into the unknown—another perspective on the theme of refuge described at the end of chapter 2.

We also need an outlook that shows us a way out of the confusion of patterned existence. The outlook provides us with a map. It shows us how things are and how to change them. Both elements are important. Just as a map must reflect the terrain accurately to be useful, the outlook must correspond with experience sufficiently so that it makes sense to us. It must also show us a way out of confusion. Otherwise it is useless.

An outlook is not a belief. An outlook points to the mystery of being and shows how to open to it and live in it. In the practice of presence, the outlook is that we are open awareness, the open awareness of original mind, and all experience consists of arising and subsiding in open awareness. Often, we fall into the error of mistaking the map for the territory. While an outlook provides us with a map that shows us where we can go and how to get there, having the map is not the same thing as making the journey. We still have to tread the path.

We need a practice, a way of proceeding, a way of treading the path. A practice has three components: a way of cultivating attention and coming into presence, a way of generating higher levels of energy to power attention, and a set of methods that bring attention to habituated patterns. In the journey metaphor, attention is the ability to walk, energy is food, and bringing attention to habituated patterns corresponds to navigating obstacles in the landscape.

We also need a way of living that brings the attention cultivated in practice to the activity of life itself. Life becomes an ongoing effort in attention, an ongoing journey into the mystery. You would probably prefer not to look at some parts of your life, but to ignore the areas of life that are uncomfortable to look at is not a good idea. If we protect any aspect of our life from the practice of attention, the habituated patterns connected with that part of our life absorb the energy of practice and gradually take over our lives. We become what we don't dismantle.

Formal meditation sessions are only half the practice. The other half is to employ the methods during the day. For instance, in the meditations on death, you think of death following you around all day, just behind your left shoulder.

We also need a teacher or other source of guidance to teach us how to cultivate attention, what presence means and how to move into it, how to generate energy, and how to bring attention to the operation of habituated patterns.

It is virtually impossible to do this work without a daily practice and a teacher to spot the operation of patterns that you don't pick up. Regular and consistent practice over time will lead to greater abilities in attention. Without someone to guide you and help you through difficulties, however, there is a very good chance that you will fall into one or more of the many reactive patterns that undermine attention. Remember that patterns function to degrade attention to prevent the core of the pattern from being experienced. All resistance in practice comes from the operation of patterns. Patterns are mechanisms. They have no awareness of the consequences of their operation. Like parasites that inadvertently kill their host, patterns can and do cause insanity, paralysis, and even death.

Once in Tibet, a student informed his teacher of his decision to practice in a secluded retreat until his experience of original mind was stable. His teacher nodded and expressed his approval. The student then added that he would leave retreat for only one reason, if his parents became ill. His teacher looked at him carefully and said, "Hmmm. This is not so good. Here, take this scroll. If, for any reason, you leave your retreat, open this scroll and read it."

The student departed, journeyed into the mountains to an unpopulated valley, found a suitable cave on the slopes of a mountain, and practiced alone for many years. One day as he sat looking over the valley, he noticed a man on horseback. Slowly, the horse and its rider climbed the long path and arrived at his cave. The man said, "I've come with a message for you. Your parents are very ill, and they would like to see you."

He had allowed for this one condition, so he gathered up his few belongings and climbed on the back of the horse with the messenger. As they rode down the mountain, he remembered his teacher's words. He took out the scroll and opened it.

The next moment, he found himself sliding and rolling down the hillside. He flung his arms out to stop his slide and came to rest at the edge of a cliff. He looked around and saw no horse or messenger, just his belongings scattered around him. The hallucination had arisen because of a small chink in his armor of resolution and only his connection with his teacher had saved him from death.

In a sense, you are in combat, and the conflict is over who or what is going to live your life—you or patterns. As in combat, one or the other has to die.

A pattern dies when you die to its operation, when you can hold attention in the emotional reactions at the core of the pattern and not fall into the pattern of reaction. So the last requirement is the willingness to die to the life generated by patterns of reaction. When you die to the operation of a pattern, you feel as if you are dying. You are not dying. The pattern is. You experience the five stages of dying that Elisabeth Kübler-Ross has described: denial, anger, bargaining, depression, and acceptance.

The pattern, usually in the form of voices or phrases, initially denies the problem or any connection with it. You see no problem, or, if you do, you see the problem as coming from outside, not from anything you are doing. You then experience anger, even rage, at whatever is bringing the problem to your attention. You may try to kill the messenger because you don't want the message. The rage is the pattern's projection of aversion onto what threatens the sense of self associated with the pattern. Next, the pattern engages relentlessly in bargaining, again in the form of voices, phrases, or behaviors: "I'll stop doing this if I can do that instead." You sink into depression, which is the pattern's way of shutting down attention. Then, you go through a dying process (as described in the meditations on death and impermanence) and a corresponding dissolution of the elements in greater or lesser intensity. You see those parts of your life that were based on the pattern as an extended illusion, and grief arises as the associated relationships and activities fall apart. With disillusionment you arrive at acceptance and the emotional core of the pattern is released. You experience it in attention. Freedom comes when you know, through your own experience, that you are not the pattern or any of its components.

The practices that follow are like the dynamite charges used to level a building. They have been carefully refined through centuries of practice and experience. They are directed at specific components of habituated patterns. The five dakinis practice transforms the five-element reaction chain into presence and pristine awareness. Emptying the six realms takes apart the projected worlds so that you see things as they are. The practice of the four immeasurables brings attention to the passive relationship with undischarged core emotions so you become an active agent in your own life. Taking and sending undermines self-cherishing, so you can serve what is true. Insight removes the fundamental misperception that takes the content of experience to be something "other" and ignores the mystery of being.

THE FIVE DAKINIS

The five dakinis meditation is directed at the five-element reaction chains. It employs a method we have not used up to this point: symbolic enactment of the transformation of reaction into presence. Symbols speak directly to the mind of emotion, avoiding the distractions and rationalizations of the intellect. Enactment takes us through the dismantling process, familiarizing us with reactions, fears, experiences, and transformations so that we can recognize the reactions and fears in daily life and transform the reactive pattern into presence and awareness.

Dakini is a Sanskrit word that means "sky-traveler" or "she who moves in space." The space here is the totality of experience, the mystery of being. To live in the mystery of being, you must move in the sky of awareness. A dakini, in Tibetan Buddhism, represents the energy of pristine awareness in the totality of experience. She moves and functions in this space freely and is, at the same time, one with it. She embodies the power and dynamism of pristine awareness. The female generally represents original mind, which can be known only through direct experience. Any attempt to ignore, possess, manipulate, or control the energy of original mind is an expression of habituated patterns. Such attempts backfire viciously, entangling you in patterned behavior. Working at the level of energy that the dakinis embody is a bit dangerous. If you aren't present with the energy, it flows into habituated patterns.

Khyungpo Naljor, a twelfth-century teacher in Tibet, once had a visionary experience in which a lion-headed dakini appeared to him and sang this song about working with dakini energy:

> *Crystal dakini guards against interruptions.*
> *Jewel dakini increases wealth.*
> *Lotus dakini gathers energy.*
> *Action dakini gets everything done.*
>
> *When wanting and grasping hold sway*
> *The dakini has you in her power.*
> *Wanting nothing from outside, taking things as they come,*
> *Know the dakini to be your own mind.*
>
> *The essence of mind is knowing.*
>
> *Know that the crystal is the non-thought of mind itself*
> *And the crystal dakini guards against interruptions.*
>
> *Know that the source of wealth is contentment*
> *And the jewel dakini fulfills all wants and needs.*
>
> *Know that the lotus is the non-thought of freedom from attachment*
> *And the lotus dakini gathers energy.*
>
> *Know that action has no origination or cessation*
> *And the action dakini gets everything done.*
>
> *Those who do not understand these points*
> *Can practice for eons and know nothing.*
>
> *So, the heart of the matter is*
> *To know that the dakini is your own mind.*

Pristine awareness has five aspects or functions: to know clearly, to know without judgment, to know the particulars, to know what to do, and to know the totality. These five functions, freed from the limitations of reaction and confusion, are known as the five pristine

awarenesses: mirrorlike pristine awareness, sameness pristine awareness, distinguishing pristine awareness, effective pristine awareness,
and the pristine awareness of totality. The distorted manifestations of
the basic functions produce conceptually based knowing and emotional reactivity.

The five pristine awarenesses are the pure undistorted manifestations of the five elements. The chart below summarizes the relationships between the five elements, the five functions, and the five pristine
awarenesses.

ELEMENT	PRISTINE AWARENESS	FUNCTION
earth	sameness pristine awareness	know without judgment
water	mirrorlike pristine awareness	know clearly
fire	distinguishing pristine awareness	know the particulars
air	effective pristine awareness	know what to do
void	totality pristine awareness	know the totality

Practice Guidelines

The five dakinis meditation is a visualization practice, though a better
term might be active-imagination practice. Instead of trying to see the
dakini or the symbols, vividly imagine that the dakini and other symbols are present. Because of the visual content, most people practice
more effectively with their eyes closed. When you do this practice, you
are, in essence, acting out a drama, so you should use all your senses.
Make the drama as real as possible.

You already have experience with the reaction chains from the
meditation on the five elements in the previous chapter. The five dakinis practice builds on that experience, transforming the reactive
process into presence and pristine awareness.

Bodily and emotional sensations will arise in the course of doing
these practices. You may feel energy flooding your body, notice areas of
tension or physical pain that you haven't noticed before, or hear ringing
in your ears or other sounds. All such phenomena are indications that

attention is penetrating the reaction chains. Don't get lost in the movement of energy or other sensations. Work through the visualization practice, doing it as ritual. All distraction, resistance, or images that arise other than what you intend come from the operation of habituated patterns. Do not be distracted by them, but don't ignore or suppress them, either.

In each meditation session, go through the visualizations for all five elements. When you start, spend most of your time on the earth reaction chain and the earth dakini. Do the other four dakinis quickly. Then, after a couple of weeks, do the earth dakini quickly and spend most of your time on the water dakini. Then do the other three dakinis quickly. Work through all five dakinis in the same way, spending a week to two weeks on each.

Be sure to spend time on the dissolution of the visualizations and the conclusion part of the practice. The dissolution disperses the energy from the practice evenly through your body and your world so that it doesn't flow into reactive patterns or build up behind blocks and cause physical or emotional disturbances. As you progress through these practices, the conclusion section becomes more and more important. At the least, the pure light from the visualization functions as a similitude of original mind, preparing you for the practice of presence, which will be introduced in the chapter on insight. The energy from the visualization of the dakinis and the enactment of transformation can also open the door to the direct experience of original mind itself.

The Five Dakinis: Transforming Reactive Emotions

Purpose:
To transform the five-element reaction chains into pristine awareness and presence.

The five elements—earth, water, fire, air, and void—are energies that, when free, arise as the five aspects of pristine awareness and, when locked, arise as the five reactive qualities: rigidity, fluidity, consuming, busyness, and dullness. In this practice, the free energy of pristine awareness, symbolized by an elixir, transforms the reaction chains associated with the five elements into the respective aspects of pristine awareness.

FOUNDATION

Base of Attention

As before, start by resting attention with the breath for fifteen to twenty minutes. Be aware of your whole body. Your attention may move from the breath to contract and focus on physical sensations in different parts of your body. As soon as you notice the contraction, expand attention to include the whole body again, and continue resting in the breath.

Removing the Basis of Habituated Patterns

Imagine that your body is made of light and that you are completely relaxed. Your body is like a rainbow or hologram, no substance, just appearing. It radiates light. You are in a spacious, open place in which you feel completely at ease. If you are familiar with deity meditation as practiced in the Tibetan Buddhist tradition, you can imagine that you are Tara, Avalokiteshvara, Vajrayogini, or any other peaceful or semi-wrathful deity and that the setting is their domain of awakening or their mandala.

The purpose of this step is to remove the basis of habituated patterns. The physical body carries emotional conditioning. By imagining that your body is a body of light, you remove the support for habituated patterns. Imagining that your body is made of pure radiant light and you are in a beautiful and spacious setting also undermines negative self-images and such beliefs as "I can't do this" or "I'm not like this."

MAIN PRACTICE

Earth Dakini and Sameness Pristine Awareness

Light shines from your heart and invites the earth dakini. She is yellow and is dressed in flowing robes of gold and the colors of autumn. All the richness of earth surrounds her. Her presence is so strong that you are in awe. The feeling of awe goes beyond conditioned reactions. It is an intuition that you are in the presence of a being who sees things exactly as they are, from whom there are no secrets, and who can see right through all your patterns and know you completely. You are intimidated, perhaps, but not afraid. In her left hand she holds a gold flask or pitcher filled with liquid light, the elixir of pristine awareness.

You look into her eyes, she looks into yours, and you connect. You know that she sees right into you and knows you completely. She stands in front of you until you make a gesture to her expressing your willingness to enter the process of transformation. She steps forward and pours the elixir over your head. The fluid pours into you, through the crown of your head, flowing down through your body to the earth center, which is located about two inches below your navel in the center of your body, just in front of the spine.

In the earth center, you notice that you feel inflexible, rigid, and resistant to change. As the elixir pours into it, you first observe the whole reaction chain associated with earth. You feel uncertainty or vulnerability behind the rigidity and then fear, as if the ground you stand on is shaking or has split open or you have walked into quicksand. Everything suddenly opens up and becomes empty. You react by grasping or holding onto anything you can get your hands on. You tense up, hardening to protect yourself from the open space and the fear. The reaction of rigidity has a whiff of pride—you assume that your position is superior to others. But the hardening and the tension confine you. You are so rigid that you can't move. The rigidity grows stronger, crushing you as it imprisons you. You feel the uncertainty or hollowness inside and cycle through the reaction chain again.

Elixir fills the earth center. The light of the elixir mixes with the reaction chain, and you realize that all the components of the reaction chain have become pure energy. The light of the elixir radiates from the earth center and fills your whole being. The light is so intense that the rigidity, vulnerability, fear, and reaction all dissolve into light. Sitting in a field of light, you relax deeply, all rigidity and tension falling away, and you become aware of a stability that depends on nothing but presence. The light in the earth center becomes a jewel, a deep, rich yellow jewel. It represents stability, which is the ability to stay present and be with what arises in experience.

The stability brings with it a new sense of energy. The light intensifies, and sameness pristine awareness, the aspect of pristine awareness associated with earth, arises: the understanding that all experience ultimately is just experience and that true stability is internal and doesn't depend on external factors or conditions.

Light shines from your heart and from the earth dakini in front of you. Hundreds of thousands of earth dakinis and their male counterparts appear around you. Some come out of the ground, some from the space around you, and some from the sky. They are all holding flasks, and they pour their elixir of pristine awareness into you. Your body and being are completely filled with pure awareness. You are filled with the energy of earth, which is fertile, rich in resources, stable, and present. All the dakinis, including the one in front of you, dissolve into you. You are so filled with light that you feel like you have swallowed the sun. Rest for a few minutes.

Water Dakini and Mirrorlike Pristine Awareness

Again, light shines from your heart and invites the water dakini. She is white and is dressed in white. The water element is associated with winter and clarity, the crystal clarity of a winter day with a blue sky and newly fallen snow. Her presence, like that of the earth dakini, inspires awe in you. She holds a crystal flask or pitcher filled with elixir. You look into her eyes, and she looks into yours, knowing you completely. You indicate your willingness to begin the transformation process. She approaches and pours the contents of the pitcher over your head.

The elixir of pristine awareness flows through your body down to the water center, which is located in the center of your body at the level halfway between the navel and the solar plexus.

In the water center, you notice the reactive quality of water, dispersing energy so that any experience of presence is dissipated. As the elixir penetrates the water center, you become aware that underneath that dispersion reaction is a feeling of being threatened. If you were really present, being who you really are, you would be dangerously exposed, so you evade, mask, blend, or envelop—all of which are ways to disperse the energy of presence. The feeling of being threatened grows stronger and stronger. It is like a huge wave that will wash over you and carry you away. Stay in the fear, sitting with it, opening to it as best you can. If necessary, use your breath as a rope. Go down into the fear, bit by bit, experiencing it in attention. The fear of engulfment is associated with an experience of emptiness, that flash of openness you experience just when a wave or powerful current picks you up and carries you away. You react, irritated that things aren't going your way, and try to disperse the energy of the wave. Despite your efforts, you can't escape, and your anger grows. You've run out of wiggle room. You freeze. You can't move. Now, when you feel the wave of energy, you react even more strongly and cycle through the reaction chain again.

As the elixir fills the water center, mix attention with each component of the water reaction. The light of the elixir fills the water center. It radiates light, filling your whole being. In this light, you experience all the components of the reaction chain. The light grows in intensity until the dispersion, the threat, the fear of engulfment, and the other components all become light. Sitting in a field of light, you see everything without judgment or reaction. You become aware of a clarity in which everything you experience arises like a reflection in a mirror, brilliant, vivid, and clear. The light at the water center coalesces into a mirror, the symbol of mirrorlike pristine awareness.

Light shines from your heart and from the water dakini in front of you. Hundreds of thousands of water dakinis and their male counterparts appear around you, holding their flasks, and they pour the elixir of pristine awareness into you. Your body and being are completely filled with elixir. You are filled with the energy of water, clear and brilliant. All the dakinis, including the one in front of you, dissolve into you. You become one with the light and energy. Again, rest in this state for a few minutes.

Fire Dakini and Distinguishing Pristine Awareness

Light shines from your heart and invites the fire dakini. She is brilliant red in color and is clothed in robes that flicker and swirl like flames around her. She is connected with the energy of spring, of growth and creativity. Her presence is vivid and intense, and you are awed and perhaps a little intimidated. You look into her eyes, and she looks into yours. You can feel her passionate intensity, and you know that she knows you completely. In her left hand, she holds a ruby flask filled with elixir, the elixir of distinguishing pristine awareness.

You make your gesture, and she approaches, pouring the contents of her flask into you. At the fire center, located in the center of your body at the level of the heart, you feel that you want to consume experience. Merely having an experience is not enough. You need more intensity, so you have to consume or be consumed by what you experience. Rage, drama, and passion are what count. The elixir enters the fire center, and you become aware that underneath all that intensity is a feeling of being alone. And then you feel the fear of isolation. It hits you as if you were in a desert or some other featureless landscape. Nothing moves; nothing lives. In every direction, all you see is the flat line of the horizon. You react to the fear and emptiness from a desire to feel or experience something to counteract the isolation. You make everything you experience as intense as possible, devouring it completely. Your own intensity consumes you. The forest fire inside you burns everything up, leaving behind a desolate and lifeless world. Alone in a lifeless world, you react and again cycle through the reaction chain.

As the elixir fills the fire center, mix attention with each component of the reaction chain. Light from the elixir grows brighter and brighter until the whole reaction chain—the consuming, the loneliness, and the fear of isolation or rejection—dissolves into light. As you sit in the field of light, the need to consume, the need for intensity, dissolves into light, and you become aware of how knowing arises when you connect completely with what you are experiencing. A red flower, a lotus or a rose, forms at the fire center. It represents comprehending what arises in experience. Distinguishing pristine awareness, the ability to differentiate what arises in experience and know it for what it is, arises.

As before, light shines from your heart, inviting hundreds of thousands of fire dakinis and their male counterparts. They pour the contents of their pitchers into you, and you are filled with the energy of fire and distinguishing pristine awareness. All the dakinis dissolve into you, and you rest in a field of light for a few minutes.

Air Dakini and Effective Pristine Awareness

Light shines from your heart, inviting the air dakini. She is green in color and is clothed in the colors of summer, the green of grass and trees. When you look into her eyes, you know that she does whatever she sets out to do. She looks into your eyes, and you know that she knows you utterly. You motion to her, and she pours the contents of her emerald flask over your head.

The elixir pours through your body to the air center, which is located in the center of your body at the level of the throat. You become aware of activity, busyness, doing things for the sake of doing just to keep moving.

As the elixir pours into the air center, you become aware that without all that doing, you have nothing to stand on, nothing that defines who or what you are. You realize that you are afraid that you will no longer exist. To stop doing feels like falling from a high cliff. Everyone else has something to do and seems to know how to do it. You react, feeling a bit jealous and a little paranoid. You start doing anything you can find to do, anything that might provide ground. It doesn't matter what, just as long as you are busy. You pick up one activity after another until you are so busy that the busyness becomes a whirling hurricane or a tornado that tears you apart. At this point, you again become aware of the feeling of groundlessness and go through the reaction chain again.

The elixir fills the air center, which radiates light. The light fills your being, growing so bright that the reaction chain dissolves into it.

Sitting in the field of light, you realize that you don't need to be constantly in motion. You are suddenly aware that you know what to do and can do precisely what is required, neither more nor less. Out of the light a sword forms, the symbol of effective action. You now know effective pristine awareness, the ability to do what needs to be done.

Light shines from your heart and invites hundreds of thousands of air dakinis and their male counterparts. They fill you with the elixir of effective pristine awareness, and your body is filled with light and energy. All the dakinis dissolve into you, and you sit in a field of light.

Void Dakini and Totality Pristine Awareness

Light shines from your heart and invites the void dakini. She is blue in color and is clothed in the deep blue of the sky at high altitudes. She holds a flask made from sapphire and filled with elixir in her left hand. When you look into her eyes, you feel as if you are looking into the vastness of the sky. She looks into you and knows you completely. You motion to her, and she approaches, pouring the elixir of totality pristine awareness into you.

The elixir comes down to the void center, which is located in the center of your head at the level of the eyebrows. You feel dullness, heaviness, and the fogginess of sleep. Underneath the heaviness, you discover bewilderment and confusion. You don't know the way things are, you don't know how you are connected with others, you don't know what you like, and you don't know what to do, so you go to sleep. As you feel the bewilderment and confusion, you realize that you are overwhelmed and disoriented. You are afraid that you are nothing. Everything goes blank inside, and in that blankness you react. Your reactions are like all the other elements rushing at you from every direction, rocks crashing out of the sky, huge waves rising threateningly above you, volcanoes erupting below you, and violent winds whirling around you. You fall to pieces, fragmenting into the different elements. Your body turns to dust, and you feel that you are nothing. Dull and heavy again, you recycle through the reaction chain even more intensely.

The elixir fills the void center with light, and the light grows so bright that all the components of the void reaction chain dissolve into it. You realize that you can just be present with everything that is arising. You don't have to react at all. A circle of light appears, the symbol for void. You experience the pristine awareness of totality, the totality of all that arises in experience, with no reference point; no sense of inside or outside; and no notion of existing or not existing, coming or going, one or many, arising or subsiding.

Light shines from your heart and the heart of the dakini in front of you, inviting hundreds of thousands of void dakinis and their male counterparts. They appear spontaneously from everywhere and pour the elixir of totality pristine awareness into you. You are filled with light, and all the dakinis dissolve into you. Rest in the light for a few minutes.

CONCLUSION

Feel the connection of all five transformed elements—the jewel, the mirror, the flower, the sword, and the circle of light—lined up in the center of your body. Light blazes from all of them simultaneously, and you, your body, and everything you experience dissolve into light.

Rest with your mind and heart open, clear, awake, undistracted, and present.

The Indian master Tilopa taught:

Let go of what has passed. Let go of what may come. Let go of what is happening now. Don't try to figure anything out. Don't try to make anything happen. Relax, right now, and rest.

At the end of your meditation session, go about your day, taking note of the element you are using in your meditation and how it manifests in your life.

Commentary: Transforming Reactive Emotions

The five dakinis meditation uses symbols and visualizations to bring a higher level of attention to the reactive chains and to transform their operation from reaction into presence. In Buddhism, as in many other traditions, the feminine represents natural, unconditioned knowing, the mystery of life and being. By imagining the dakini in front of you, you are invoking the mystery of being and the possibility of direct awareness that doesn't depend on reason, logic, or inference. The elixir is pristine awareness in liquid form. As it pours into you, you shift to a higher level of attention and experience the reactive cycle more vividly than in the meditation on the reactive chains in the previous chapter.

When the reactive quality and the underlying feeling are held in attention, they go empty. They seem to disappear. At this point, you touch the basic fear that drives the reaction chain. That fear is directly connected to a loss of the reference that the reaction chain uses. The loss is experienced as open space. For earth, the reference is order and structure, so the loss feels like an earthquake or like stepping into quicksand. For water, the reference is the flow of energy back and forth in relationship and interaction, so the loss feels like a tidal wave that you can't escape. For fire, the reference consists of feeling, experience, and sensation, so the loss of reference is like a desolate landscape. For air, the reference is activity, so the loss is a loss of definition, as if the ground had disappeared and you are falling. For void, the reference is your whole experience, so open space is totally disorienting and you fall apart.

> Use the power of attention to transform reactions in daily life. When you notice a person reacting, identify which reaction chain is operating: earth (rigid), water (difficult to pin down or understand his or her agenda), fire (intense, explosive, or seductive), air (distracted, intellectual, busy), or void (spaced out, bewildered, or confused).
>
> Next, explicitly address the underlying fear. To address an earth reaction, say, "Your position is solid; you are on solid ground."
>
> For water, say, "You are safe. No one is going to hurt you. I will make sure of that."
>
> For fire, say, "You are not alone. This is a difficult situation, but you and I are going to get through it together."
>
> For air, say, "You know what has to be done, and I know you can do it."
>
> For void, reorient the other by saying, "Where are we right now? Here, in this room. This is where we are."

Ordinarily, the space feels like a threat, and the reaction chain reforms. By imagining that your body is made of light, you loosen the hold of the reaction chain in the mind of the body so that you have a greater capacity to observe its operation. The elixir that pours into you again raises the level of energy in your attention so that you can observe the reaction chain and stay present in it. In particular, you stay present in the fear and the experience of loss of reference or open space. The fear and open space ordinarily flash by very quickly, so you may have to go through the reaction chain two or three times before you identify them clearly enough to rest in them.

Up to this point, you have been observing the movement from form (the reaction) to emptiness (loss of reference and open space). With the reforming of the reaction, the movement from emptiness to form begins. The movement into form is experienced as a reassertion of the original reactive quality. The reaction intensifies until the movement into form can go no further. In daily life, we experience the fully formed reaction as intense agitation colored by the reactive quality. We feel that we can't go any further. If the reactive process is driven further, the state of agitation shatters and we experience the underlying feeling again. Form has become empty and the cycle repeats. The reactive chain runs again and again, spiraling up to higher levels of energy and greater reactivity.

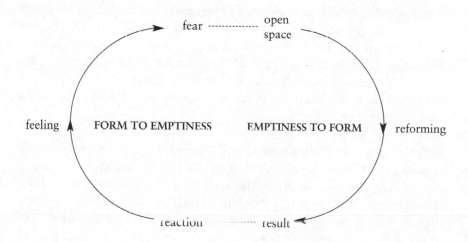

In the meditation practice, you hold the experience of the five components of the reactive chain in attention simultaneously. The elixir and the light represent the operation of attention. The whole reactive process dissolves into energy, which then powers attention. The higher level of attention opens up the nonreactive or present quality of each element: stability (earth), clarity (water), knowing (fire), effective action (air), and union (void).

The quality of presence takes the form of a symbol that appears at the body center associated with the element. Feel the quality of presence as strongly as you can without contrivance, and view the world as if you have that quality in abundance. In other words, shift to the worldview of the dakini associated with that element.

At the same time, the operation of attention uncovers the corresponding aspect of pristine awareness. Understanding arises in you, an understanding that has no beginning in time, is completely natural, and is available to you all the time.

The chart of the reactive chain for each of the elements is reproduced on page 227 with the addition of the location of the centers, the symbols, and the corresponding pristine awarenesses.

The thousands of dakinis dissolving into you symbolize your connecting with the present or awake quality in every aspect of your experience. When you bring attention to what you experience, the present quality of the element arises instead of the reactive process. Pristine awareness becomes active in your life, and the energy of the elements is available to you.

The five dakinis practice is principally about opening to experience. The patterns associated with the five elements limit what you see and how you act. As the energy of pristine awareness fills your being, you open to your life. During formal practice sessions or during the day, you may have strong feelings of warmth or bliss. You may also develop a tender and loving connection with one or more of the dakinis. The warm or blissful feelings are the result of higher levels of energy generated by the practice. The tender feelings come from energy flowing into patterns of projection and relationship. The only caution is not to attach to the feelings. Don't suppress the feelings, or you will obstruct the flow of energy and run the risk of unbalancing your body and mind. Instead, open to them, letting warmth and bliss flow through you. In particular, at the end of formal sessions, let the energy disperse evenly through body and mind by imagining that you are sitting in a field of energy that extends outside your body to a distance of three or four inches. As for the tender and loving feelings, let them power your practice, opening you more fully to the energy of the dakinis. Regard everything that arises in practice as feelings and apparitions that arise in a dream, vivid and clear but not objectively real.

OBSERVING THE ELEMENTS

To deepen your understanding of the five elements, pay attention to the way each element arises in your life during the one or two weeks you are doing the meditation on the corresponding dakini and reaction chain.

Observing Earth

When you are meditating on the earth dakini, explore the earth element in your life. Look at mountains, hills, trees, rocks, buildings, concrete,

Transformation of Element Reaction Chains into Pristine Awareness

ELEMENT	LOCATION	REACTION	FEELING	FEAR	OPEN SPACE	REFORMING	RESULT	SYMBOL	QUALITY	PRISTINE AWARENESS
earth	in the center of the body two inches below the navel	inflexible rigidity	hollowness or uncertainty	instability	earthquake	grasping	imprisonment	jewel	stability	sameness pristine awareness
water	in the center of the body between the navel and the solar plexus	fluidity	external threat	engulfment	tidal wave or strong current	dispersion	frozen	mirror	clarity	mirrorlike pristine awareness
fire	in the center of the body at the level of the heart	consuming intensity	aloneness	isolation	featureless desert	devouring experience	burned out	rose or lotus	knowing	distinguishing pristine awareness
air	at the level of the throat	busyness	nothing to stand on	destruction	falling	activity	torn apart	sword	effective action	effective pristine awareness
void	in the center of the head at the level of the eyebrows	dullness	overwhelmed	being nothing	blankness	fragmentation	dissolving into nothing	circle of light	union	totality pristine awareness

sand, fields, parking lots, and valleys. In your body, the earth element consists of the muscles, tendons, and bones, which provide form and structure. Notice the way the bones support you when you move and how the muscles extend and contract. When you sit, feel how the skeletal framework supports your body. How much weight is carried by the shoulders? How much is carried by the spine?

Notice what supports you in your life. Your house or apartment supports you by providing you with a place to live, a place where you can rest and relax or pursue what interests you. Your car provides you with the means to move. Notice what brings order to your life: daily routines, rules, laws, and regulations.

Notice what is solid or grounded: the earth in your backyard, rocks, trees, hills, mountains, sand, pavement, concrete, wood, and metal.

Notice what you are walking on: carpet, wood, concrete, dirt, grass, or rock.

How does earth manifest in relationships? When are you supportive, protective, and nourishing? When are you rigid or controlling?

Where do you spend most of your time? What places do you go to frequently? What routes do you take?

Do you take care of matters in an orderly way? Do you fulfill your responsibilities? Do you have a snow shovel or flares for emergencies in your car? Where is the first aid kit or fire extinguisher in your home?

Everything that provides form, structure, or support is an expression of the earth element. Where is earth balanced in your life? Where is earth out of balance, either not providing enough form or providing so much that you are imprisoned?

Observing Water

When you work with the water dakini, pay attention to the water element in your life. Look at oceans, lakes, rivers, rain, and dew. In your body, the water element consists of blood, water, and other fluids that move through your system. Your body depends on water. Without the circulation of blood, cells quickly die. If you don't drink, you die. What goes in must come out, so notice how fluids flow out of your body, as urine, sweat, or tears.

Notice things that flow: emotions, money, the stream of cars and people in rush hour, water in a river or stream near your home. What happens when the flow is obstructed? What happens when it dwindles?

Notice what comes in waves: waves of grief and joy, waves in the ocean, waves in styles and fashions.

How does water manifest in relationships? When are you empathetic and understanding? When are you unguarded and intimate? When do you mask or evade, giving only the appearance of friendship or intimacy?

What flows in your life, and what doesn't flow? Does money pour out of your life as fast as it goes in? Do your feelings leak out everywhere, or do you dam them up, channeling them into narrow forms of expression?

What is your relationship with objects? What are you attached to? How do you become attached to objects or people?

What do you do compulsively or addictively? What sweeps you up or carries you away? What do you experience freely and openly?

Observing Fire

For the fire element, focus on warmth, vitality, passion, and intensity in your life. Observe the heat from the sun, from a candle or fire, from a warm rock, or the absence of heat on a cold night or when your furnace goes out. In your body, the fire element takes the form of heat and warmth, the heat of digestion, metabolism, the slow burning of food and oxygen in the cells of your body. When you are ill, you experience a fever, the body increasing its heat to kill and consume the invading bacteria. When you are cold, your body contracts, preserving heat in every way possible.

Notice what energizes your life, what you experience vividly, where you feel creative, what you feel passionate about: your home, your family, your job, a project you are working on, working out, running, playing basketball, racing downhill on a mountain bike, painting a picture, or playing a piece of music.

Notice what generates or radiates heat: the sun, a fire in your fireplace, a nuclear reactor, a candle, arguments, or conflict. Sit and watch a fire or a candle, and watch how fire burns and consumes. Rub your hand on a rough piece of cloth, and notice the heat of friction.

How does fire manifest in relationships? When are you really engaged with another person? With whom do you connect by sharing experience? Who burns you up? Who do you feel consumes you or uses you?

What do you like to experience? What do you consume? What can you not get enough of? What experiences and sensations do you try to avoid? What do you want to explore or learn more about? Where do you feel starved or depleted?

Everything that generates warmth, vitality, passion, and creativity is an expression of fire. Where is fire in balance, generating energy but not burning you or anyone else up? Where is it lacking, leaving you feeling desolate and alone? And where is it too strong—where do you feel fried or burned out?

Observing Air

While working with the air dakini, observe movement and activity. Feel the air that you breathe, the winds and breezes, gusts and hurricanes. In the body, the primary manifestation of air is the breath. Notice your breath during the day. Notice how it changes according to what you are doing and what you are feeling. Listen to your own voice when you speak. Your voice depends on the movement of air. It carries the vibrations of your larynx to the ears of the person you are speaking to. Does the tone of the voice match what you are saying?

Notice the activity of your life. What do you spend most of your time doing: physical activity (working out, moving things, gardening, building), emotional activity (artistic expression, working with people), or mental activity (reading, thinking, planning, studying)?

Notice what moves: breezes, gusts of wind, the breath. Movement and air are closely connected. Air cannot be experienced unless there is movement. Hold up your hand. Can you feel the air around it? No. Move your hand. Now you can feel the air.

How does air manifest in relationships? With whom do you like to brainstorm? Who likes to explore new things with you? Air connects through understanding, leading to growth and the expansion of possibilities. Who plays intellectual games with you so that you never feel connected or know where they are coming from? Who disappears into ideas or finds something to do whenever you ask a direct question?

The air element manifests as activity and movement. Where is air balanced in your life? Where do you act effectively, knowing what to do and how to do it? Where is air out of balance? Perhaps you wonder who you are and try one thing after another to give meaning or definition to your life. Perhaps you are caught up in a whirlwind of activity and never have time to smell the roses.

Observing Void

While working with the void dakini, pay attention to space and emptiness. Look at the sky. Think about the infinite space in the universe.

Look at space in ordinary objects. The study of void directs your attention toward what is usually ignored. Without space, you could not pour coffee into your mug in the morning. You also could not drink without space in your stomach. In the body, void is present in the hollow organs, the heart, stomach, lungs, and bladder. In each joint, there is a little extra space. Without it, you could not bend your finger, walk, or sit down.

Pay attention to the space in rooms when you walk into them. Look at the sky, open vistas, the still point at the center of a wheel.

Pay attention to emotional space, conceptual space, or creative space. Without void, nothing could take form. None of the other elements could arise. Look at the space between things instead of at the things themselves.

Void manifests in relationships as presence. You have the feeling that the other is really there. He or she gives you room to be who you are, without judgment. In its reactive form, void takes over everything, so you feel you have no room, no place, or no relevance. In fragmentation, the other person is all over the place—a bit of this, a bit of that, but no one you can really relate to.

Notice when and where in your life you are present. Where is there open space? How much space in your life do you have for internal or spiritual work, for what you need to do, for what you care about, for relationships, for what supports and provides you with life? All the other elements arise and subside into void.

The purpose of observing how the five elements arise in your daily life is to move you away from identifying with the content of experience and toward understanding that life is a series of experiences. The mystery of life is in the arising and subsiding of what we experience, just as the mystery of dreams is in the arising and subsiding of the dream. What we dream about is largely meaningless. We don't define who and what we are by what we dream.

Yet in life we rely on the content of life—whether we are happy or sad, whether we are rich or poor, whether we are famous or obscure, whether we are respected or disdained—to define who and what we are. In the end, life is just what we experience, and these exercises on the five elements direct your attention to just that.

Outside a village, a monk lived simply, devoting his time to practice and meditation. The villagers respected him for his way of life and brought him food and other necessities. One day, a young woman was discovered to be pregnant. Her parents demanded to know who the father was. Frightened and ashamed, the woman said that the monk had fathered the child. The parents were outraged. They confronted the monk, who, when he heard the charges, only replied, "Is that so?" They demanded that he take care of their daughter and provide for the child, and they left her with the monk.

Needless to say, he had to change his lifestyle. The villagers no longer respected him. They stopped supporting him. He had to take up a craft to support the young woman and himself. He had to journey to the next village to sell the small items that he made. The young woman soon grew tired of living with the monk. She went to her parents and told them that she had lied about the monk being the father. The real father was a young man who had briefly visited the village and had long since departed. She had lied out of shame and embarrassment. The parents were very upset by the revelations. They went to the monk to apologize for their hasty accusations. They asked his forgiveness for doubting his devotion to his way of life and impugning his honor. When they finished their entreaties, the monk looked at them, said only, "Is that so?" and returned to his simple life.

The Five Dakinis: Form and Emptiness

Purpose:
To return the reaction chains to their original nature.

MEDITATION METHOD

This next meditation directs attention toward the two points in the reaction chain where attention decays: the movement from form to emptiness and the movement from emptiness to form (see the diagram on page 225). First use the metaphors in your meditation to become familiar with the reactions and shifts in awareness. Then use actual life situations that trigger the same reaction chain, and adapt the meditation to the situation.

Work first with the movement from form to emptiness. As in the previous practice, start with the earth element. Think of a dangerous— a lethal—situation or event, and let the earth reaction chain run in you.

Imagine you are in an earthquake, for instance. You feel very vulnerable; the ground is shaking under you. You escape. How you escape is up to you. Be creative. Be realistic. Don't invoke magic or fantasy elements, but be creative. Escape. Or imagine you are sinking into quicksand and you escape.

Now, go back into the situation and feel the vulnerability again, but this time you die in the earthquake. How you die is up to you, but you die.

Go back a third time. Put your attention into the experience of the earthquake and your fears and reactions. Everything, including all your internal reactions, becomes brighter and brighter until both the earthquake and you become pure light. Rest in the light for a few minutes, then let the jewel form at the earth center.

Now, do the other elements and dakinis as in the previous meditation.

When you are clear about the images and can stay present in your reactions, take a situation from life and go through the same process. For instance, your boss accuses you of not doing your work properly. You insist that you are, but you are uncertain inside because you are not sure what criteria are being applied. He pulls out reams of data that reveal that your work isn't up to par. First you escape, perhaps by showing how the data is in error. Then bring up the situation again, and this time you die—you lose your job. Then bring it up a third time, and let everything turn to light.

After three to five days, work with another lethal situation, and focus on the movement from emptiness to form, the reforming of the reaction. For earth, the metaphor is imprisonment. Imagine that you have built a fortress around you, but the fortress has become a prison and you are trapped. The walls are slowly closing in on you. You can't move. The walls continue to close in. Then you escape. The way you escape is up to you. Again, be realistic but creative.

Go back to the situation a second time. Now the walls close in and crush you. You die.

Go back a third time, bringing attention to the situation until everything, including you, turns into light. Rest there for a few minutes.

Then, again, pick a situation in your life in which you were imprisoned by your rigidity, and go through the same three scenarios—escape, die, and turn to light.

After three to five days, turn to the water element. Now, do the earth dakini as in the transformation meditation, and then go through the same process described above: three to five days of working with the movement from form to emptiness in water, then three to five days working with the movement from emptiness to form. Do the remaining elements and dakinis as in the transformation meditation without the additions. The following chart gives the imagery for each of the elements.

FORM AND EMPTINESS IN THE FIVE ELEMENTS

ELEMENT	FORM TO EMPTINESS	EMPTINESS TO FORM
earth	instability, earthquake or quicksand	grasping, holding that imprisons, crushes, or stifles
water	engulfment, drowning, swept away by a wave	frozen, by efforts to disperse energy
fire	isolation, abandoned in a desert or empty landscape	inferno, explosion of energy, such as a volcano or forest fire
air	falling, from a cliff or high building	activity, torn to pieces in a hurricane or tornado
void	become nothing, all elements converge and dissolve	fragmentation, body is reduced to dust and disintegrates

Work through all five elements over the course of about five weeks. In each meditation session, you will likely do all three scenarios only one or two times. As with all these practices, the more vivid you make the experience, the more the practices cut into the operation of the patterns.

For each of these ten points, imagine lethal situations, and then go through them, first finding a way to escape, then dying in them, and then turning them into light. As in the first meditation on the five dakinis, this practice uses reenactment to undermine the operation of the reaction chain. By coming up with a way of escape, we undermine the tendency to accept the situation as the pattern sees it. We reach in for a creative response and step outside the confines of the pattern. By dying in the situation, we undermine the tendency to perpetuate the pattern by resisting it. For instance, when faced with rigidity in another person, we react the same way, perpetuating the pattern of rigidity in the interaction. Dying by holding on to the patterned reaction reveals that the pattern functions blindly, to the detriment of our welfare, even our life. Finally, by imagining that everything in the situation becomes light, we return the experience of the situation to its original nature and undermine the tendency to take the content of experience as what is real. Remember that the intention of spiritual practice is to be present in the mystery of being, the arising and subsiding of experience.

This last set of practices is quite difficult. Once again, you come in touch with one of the most powerful fears in human experience, the fear of death. Your experience with the meditations on death in chapter 4 will help you here. We are enslaved by habituated patterns because we are unable to stay present in the fear of death and nonexistence. The more you come to terms with the possibility of death and your fear of it, the more awake you will be in your life.

Emptying the Six Realms:
Dismantling Emotional Projections

Purpose:
To dismantle the worlds projected by reactive emotions.

Just as the meditations on the five dakinis work to dismantle the reaction chains associated with the five elements, the practice of emptying the six realms works to dismantle the worldviews projected by habituated patterns. In the grip of anger, we experience the world as the hell realm and strive against opposition. When greed is active, we project a poverty-stricken attitude and see the world in terms of neediness. The animal realm represents automatic functioning to limit pain and discomfort, while the human realm represents the operation of preferences and the constant effort to satisfy desires. When jealousy colors our worldview, we act from a sense of deficiency and strive to prove through achievements that we are better than others. With pride, we view everyone else as inferior and strive to maintain our position of superiority.

This practice builds on the meditations on the six realms in chapter 5. Reread the descriptions of the six realms before starting this meditation.

FOUNDATION

Base of Attention

Rest with the breath for fifteen to twenty minutes to establish a base of attention.

Removing the Basis of Habituated Projections

As in the dakini meditations, imagine that you have a white body, radiant with light. In addition, imagine that you are the embodiment of awakened compassion and that you have an infinite ability to let go of emotional reactivity, stay present, open to what is happening, do what needs to be done, and accept the results, whatever they may be.

MAIN PRACTICE: EMPTYING THE SIX REALMS

The practice consists of emptying the six realms one at a time by going through five steps:

1. Enter and open to the experience of the realm.
2. Observe how the realm triggers a reactive pattern in you.
3. Bring attention to the reaction and let it go.
4. Open again to the experience of the realm.
5. Dissolve the realm into light.

Anger: The Hell Realm

Imagining that you are the embodiment of awakened compassion, form the intention to enter the hell realms. The way you enter the hell realms is up to you. You can descend from above, walk through a portal, or suddenly appear in the center of hell.

Around you is a world of unspeakable violence and pain. The searing heat, noxious fumes, and intense aggression are suffocating. Horrifically disfigured figures wielding strangely shaped swords, knives, spears, and hatchets cut and slice at one another, hacking without mercy until they fall down dead. Nobody stays dead for long here. As soon as they revive, they rush at the nearest assailants, lusting for revenge, and strike them down.

Your first impulse is to grab anything you can find as a weapon and strike down the figures around you before they kill you. Like a spear of red-hot iron, the urge to destroy burns inside you. Feel the anger and aggression, but remember that you have infinite resources of attention, patience, and clarity to call upon. Bring attention to the anger that is rising inside you. Open to it, and you will feel a shift. The anger becomes an object of attention and dissipates.

Now, again open to the hell realm about you. Look at all the beings who are suffering in their anger, aggression, and pain. If you feel another impulse to anger, bring attention to it. Repeat this process until you can open to the hell realm and just observe the anger and aggression that surround you. Notice what arises in your heart at this point.

Now, imagine light shining from your heart. Your whole body is filled with light. Your heart radiates with such intense light that the light fills the whole hell realm. The realm and all the beings in it dissolve into the light. All the light is absorbed into your heart. You now know the hell realms. You know everything about anger and aggression, about hate and revenge, about how anger generates suffering, and about what the suffering is. Everything, including your body, becomes light.

Rest in the light for a few minutes.

Greed: The Hungry Ghost Realm

Form the intention to enter the hungry ghost realm and go there. All around you, thin, grasping figures with swollen bellies and tiny mouths search desperately for food and water. Vicious squabbles break out constantly over nothing. These are hard, merciless beings, their eyes glazed by greed. You know that their only interest is in satisfying their needs, and their poverty-stricken view of things begins to affect you. You feel a similar hardness in you. Your hands reach out to grasp anything you can find, and you feel distrust infecting your heart. Observe the pattern of greed that is arising in you: the grasping, the neediness, the unremitting gnawing that is never satisfied. Open to the feeling, knowing the neediness and knowing that it can never be satisfied. Just let it be there.

You feel a shift, and the greed in you dissolves in your attention. Now, open again to the hungry ghost realm around you. If you feel greed arising, bring attention to it. When you can open to the hungry ghost realm and remain in attention, observe what arises in your heart.

Then, as in the hell realms, imagine light shining from your heart, dissolving the whole hungry ghost realm into light. The light comes into your heart, and you know all the suffering of greed and the suffering of the hungry ghosts. You know the distortions that greed causes and the way greed tries to discharge its energy through harsh, intolerant, and selfish grasping. Everything, including your body, becomes light.

Rest in the light for a few minutes.

Instinct: The Animal Realm

Form the intention to enter the animal realm and go there. Here, the sense of limitation is almost numbing. Everything is instinct. Animals just react. The highly refined specialization of other animals pushes you to rely on instinct. It's eat or be eaten. Animals are so highly specialized, so good at what they are conditioned to do, that you are reduced to a blind survival instinct. You start to lose all sense of presence and understanding. As you experience the numbing effect of instinctual drive, bring attention to it. You become aware that the numb unknowing is part of all reactive patterns, and it dissolves in your attention.

Now again open to the animal realm. Look at each animal, and observe how it lives, relying on conditioned behaviors almost completely, and see that it has a limited capacity to learn or adapt to new situations. Observe what arises in your heart.

Light shines from your heart and fills your body and the whole animal realm. The realm dissolves in the intensity of that light, and the light returns and is absorbed into your heart. You now know the animal realm, that dullness and limitation of instinct, completely. Everything becomes light. Rest in the light for a few minutes.

Desire: The Human Realm

Form the intention to enter the human realm and go there. All around you, people are busy, meeting with friends, avoiding people they don't like, working to have what they want, and trying to keep what they have. Everybody is busy doing something. All the busyness comes from wanting. They know enjoyment and pleasure and are working to have more enjoyment and more pleasure in their lives. You join in. You'd like to have a bit of fun, too. Bring attention to the arising of desire in you. It dissolves.

Open again to the people bustling around you. They are bent on fulfilling their desires. Notice how they let their lives be completely consumed by wanting and desire. Notice what arises in your heart.

Light shines from your heart, and the human realm with all its wanting and busyness dissolves into light. As the light is reabsorbed into your heart, you know what it is to be caught up in unquestioned striving and a constant sense of incompleteness. Everything, including you, becomes light, and you rest for a few minutes.

Jealousy: The Titan Realm

Form the intention to enter the titan realm. Go there. The titan realm is like a nation at war with a more powerful opponent. Jealousy, paranoia, and competition drive every aspect of life. A sense of injustice and injury colors everyone's actions. Wealth and the pleasures of life are ignored. A titan's only concern is to fight to get what should be his. Yet inside, the titans know that their struggles are almost certainly futile. You feel this logic at work inside you, sensing how it twists your interpretations of events and how it acts to reinforce your fears. Bring attention to the jealousy that is rising in you. Open to it. You feel a shift as the jealousy dissolves.

Now, open to the titan realm again. See how the titans function. With the enemy clearly in place outside, they can avoid facing any feeling of lack inside. See that all their efforts are about overcoming or avoiding feeling deficient. See the way that they are all bent on showing the world that they count.

Light shines from your heart. It fills the titan realm, dissolving it into intense radiance. The light returns to fill your heart, and you see how jealousy creates a world of competition and violence, how it distorts perceptions, and how it covers the feeling of deficiency. Everything becomes light. Rest in the light for a few minutes.

Pride: The God Realm

Form the intention to enter the god realm. Go there. Your first impression of the god realm is one of such unlimited and exquisite luxury that unhappiness is inconceivable. You gradually become aware, however, that everyone is living in his or her own world. The atmosphere of overwhelming superiority affects you, so that you, too, feel that you are superior and have a right to the best that life can offer. The air drips with refinement and ease. Still, a sense of ignoring lingers like the aroma of onion even after you've washed your hands.

Bring attention to the pride that is moving in you. Open to it. It shifts and dissipates. Open again to the god realm. You understand how pride protects against the harsh reality that this luxury and ease can't and won't last. You understand why people in the god realm view their position of health, wealth, and happiness as what is right and true. You understand their pseudo-pitying contempt for those who have not risen to their levels or don't appreciate their way of life. You understand why they ignore the suffering outside their realm. You are aware of the attitude of superiority, pride, and entitlement without being drawn into it. Notice what arises in your heart.

Light shines from your heart and fills the god realm. The intensity of the light dissolves the god realm, and the light is absorbed into your heart. Your knowledge is complete. You know pride and the illusory world it creates to cover the truth of change and suffering. Everything dissolves into light.

CONCLUSION

Continue to rest in light. If thoughts arise, don't lose attention. Relax and return to a feeling of infinite space. Rest without distraction. Don't try to make anything happen. At the end of the meditation session, form the intention to be present in your life, and go about your day.

Commentary: Emptying the Six Realms

In this practice, you enter each realm of your own volition. Ordinarily, when reactive patterns operate, we move in and out of the six realms without knowing it. One moment you are in hell, arguing with your spouse over the arrangements for a dinner party; the next you are in the titan realm, taking out a bottle of fine wine to impress your guests. A moment later, you plunge into the animal realm, struggling to find a corkscrew, instinctively ransacking drawers looking for it, forgetting completely that you put it in the living room so that you would know where it is.

The six realms can be seen as six forms of striving to overcome a world projected by reactive emotions.

When you are stuck in one of the six realms, use the following three questions to step out of the realm. Pick one pattern and identify either the dominant emotion or the particular realm the pattern projects. In the case of anger and the hell realm, the three questions are:

1. What am I trying to *oppose* in this situation?
2. Do I have to *oppose* it?
3. Is *opposing* called for at all?

For greed and the hungry ghost realm substitute *take,* for instinct and the animal realm *survive,* for desire and the human realm *enjoy,* for jealousy and the titan realm *achieve,* and for pride and the god realm *maintain.*

You can also use these questions to invite another person to drop their emotional projections.

In the hell realm, the world is seen in terms of anger, and you react to anger with anger. The experience is a constant striving against opposition. To empty the hell realm, you have to die to opposing. "To die to" means that you stop trying to avoid or put an end to the experience of opposition. You can avoid opposition by giving up, by losing whenever conflict arises, but giving up doesn't free you from the anger inside. Often, it just intensifies it. You become increasingly resentful. Putting an end to conflict doesn't end the anger either. You can win the battle, but acting in anger reinforces it, and the war against opposition goes on. You die to opposing when you can stay present in opposition and conflict. You stop trying to end the conflict by either winning or losing. You stay present in the experience of opposition, meeting all the internal reactions with attention and not falling into the projected world of opposition, the hell realm. When you can stay in conflict and opposition without moving to anger, you have begun to die to the hell realm. Attention now goes deeper inside you, and you shift your attention to what you need, so you move to the hungry ghost realm.

In the hungry ghost realm, you see the world as a place where your needs cannot be satisfied, and you react accordingly. You are constantly striving against your own neediness. Habitually, you try to end neediness by grasping for what you think will satisfy it or by denying that you need anything. In the former case, you are never satisfied. In the latter, the neediness gnaws deeper and deeper into you. Your denial of it makes it operate more strongly. When you can stay present in the experience of neediness, you die to the hungry ghost realm. In your daily life, you experience an increased capacity to let the feelings of needing this or that come and go. The actual feeling of neediness carries less charge, and you don't feel the compulsion to act on it. Attention has penetrated the hungry ghost realm of experience. Your attention shifts to matters of survival and avoiding pain.

You enter the animal realm, where you are driven by instinct. While you struggle to meet immediate physical needs, the more fundamental striving is to limit discomfort and pain. You do what comes automatically, ignoring other possibilities. The animal realm is emptied when you no longer reactively try to control pain. Attention then turns to what you want, and you move to the human realm.

In the human realm, you see the world through the eyes of desire. You want this and don't want that. Your whole life is based on preferences. You strive not to feel desire, either by losing yourself in enjoyment or by ignoring what you want. In the former instance, you end up working to get what you enjoy, and you lose your life in busyness.

In the latter, you push the feelings of desire down, but they come out in other, more twisted, ways. You die to desire and empty the human realm of experience when you no longer strive to fulfill desire. When enjoyment and pleasure are no longer sufficient to give your life structure and meaning, you feel that you are missing something. You feel deficient inside and begin to notice what others have done. Achievements become important, and you move into the titan realm.

In the titan realm, you are constantly comparing your achievements with the achievements of others. The titan realm is driven by the feeling that if you can build a bigger business, a better mousetrap, have more friends, be more famous, or have more money, then you will have a place in the world. The titan realm is based on the belief that you don't really belong and you have to prove that you do. You are jealous of those who seem to belong and are accepted or appreciated for what they've achieved or contributed. You try to validate your existence by achieving more and more. To empty the titan realm, you die to achieving, the effort to do more and more to justify your existence. When you stop trying to achieve, a little space opens in your life, and you turn attention to maintaining what you have and your position in the world.

You have entered the god realm. You experience the world in terms of pride and superiority. Your way of life is the way life should be lived. You strive to maintain your perfection and position. This effort puts you at odds with the impermanence of all things. You see the world as opposing you. You have returned to the hell realm. If, instead, you die to striving to prolong pleasure and you stay present with whatever experience arises, you empty the god realm.

As long as reactive patterns are in place, we cycle from one realm to another, moving from realm to realm as different patterns are triggered and play themselves out. In emptying the six realms, we disengage from the reactive emotions of anger, greed, instinct, desire, jealousy, and pride. We also disengage from the characteristic striving of each realm, striving to overcome opposition, neediness, and discomfort and striving based on enjoyment, achievement, and maintaining position.

The meditations on the five dakinis and emptying the six realms fundamentally change our relationship with reactive emotions, the former by transforming the reaction chains into presence, the latter by dismantling the way patterns distort how we experience what arises and view our lives. The next step is to move from reactive emotions based on conditioned agendas to the higher emotions: love, compassion, joy, and equanimity.

CHAPTER 7

The Four Immeasurables

Nasrudin saw a man sitting disconsolately at the wayside, and asked what ailed him.

"There is nothing of interest in life, brother," said the man; "I have sufficient capital not to have to work, and I am on this trip only in order to seek something more interesting than the life I have at home. So far I haven't found it."

Without another word, Nasrudin seized the traveller's knapsack and made off down the road with it, running like a hare. Since he knew the area, he was able to out-distance him.

The road curved, and Nasrudin cut across several loops, with the result that he was soon back on the road ahead of the man he had robbed. He put the bag by the side of the road and waited in conceal-ment for the other to catch up.

Presently the miserable traveller appeared, following the tortuous road, more unhappy than ever because of his loss. As soon as he saw his property lying there, he ran towards it, shouting with joy.

"That's one way of producing happiness," said Nasrudin.

—IDRIES SHAH,
THE EXPLOITS OF THE INCOMPARABLE MULLA NASRUDIN

In Shakespeare's *The Merchant of Venice*, Portia, disguised as a judge, appeals for mercy in the face of Shylock's insistence on cutting a pound of flesh from Antonio's chest:

The quality of mercy is not strain'd,
It droppeth as the gentle rain from heaven
Upon the place beneath: it is twice blest;
It blesseth him that gives and him that takes.

These lines express a kind of emotion quite different from the reactive emotions associated with habituated patterns. Mercy is neither strained nor reactive. It flows from the heart, transforming the anger of the persecutor and the fear of the victim and uniting them both in a moment of presence. How different from anger, jealousy, or greed!

In Buddhism, four emotions have the same transformative quality as mercy: equanimity, loving-kindness, compassion, and joy. They are called the four immeasurables because there is no limitation to their depth or scope. Unlike reactive emotions, the four immeasurables do not function in the service of any habituated pattern, sense of self, or personal agenda. While they are impersonal in that they are not based on personal agendas, in their expression and experience, they are intensely intimate. Their power comes from their ability to open up a moment of presence. In his introduction to *One Robe, One Bowl,* John Stevens relates the following incident about the Zen master Ryokan:

> Once his brother asked Ryokan to visit his house and speak to his delinquent son. Ryokan came but did not say a word of admonition to the boy. He stayed overnight and prepared to leave the next morning. As the wayward nephew was lacing Ryokan's straw sandals, he felt a drop of warm water. Glancing up, he saw Ryokan looking down at him, his eyes full of tears. Ryokan then returned home, and the nephew changed for the better.

Clearly, as long as our actions and feelings operate in the service of personal agendas, we will not be capable of such presence. The four immeasurables operate at a higher level of attention, a level that opens the door to profound, natural emotional responses to the exigencies of life. Equanimity dismantles our reactive judgments and prejudices about other people so that we understand and appreciate them as they are. Loving-kindness is a radiant warmth, independent of personal likes or dislikes, that stops us from shutting down to others. Compassion counteracts discomfort, withdrawal, or contraction in the face of others' pain so that we are truly present with them. And joy—unapologetic joy in being and passion for life—eliminates any envy or criticism of other people's success or happiness.

Ordinarily, we think of emotions as positive or negative. In Buddhism, the more important differentiation is between reaction and response. Reactions are always based on agendas associated with the sense of "I" and, consequently, do not serve the reality of the situation. The four immeasurables are emotional responses, not reactions. They dissolve subject-object duality and so transform giver and receiver. Both experience a moment of presence, a moment outside ordinary reaction.

The four immeasurables also serve as an important bridge to the practice of insight, in which we see directly into the nature of experience and penetrate the three deepest habituated patterns: subject-object perception, taking subjective experience as reality, and the fear that makes us turn away from open, direct awareness.

INTENTION AND ORDER IN THE IMMEASURABLES

The sequence in which the four immeasurables are cultivated varies from tradition to tradition. Many people mistakenly feel that there can be only one "right" way. They fail to appreciate that differences in the order of the immeasurables reflect differences in their purposes and in the roles they play in each system.

Historically, the original sequence is loving kindness, compassion, joy, and equanimity. The Theravadan traditions of Southeast Asia use this sequence, explaining it in terms of stages of child rearing. We first pay attention to the child's welfare (loving-kindness), protect and remove her from suffering (compassion), celebrate her success as she grows (joy), and let her go about her business when she knows what she is doing (equanimity). The intention of this approach is disengagement, to reduce reactive emotions and create an environment that facilitates the cultivation of attention and insight. The intention in the Theravadan traditions is to use the four immeasurables to generate high levels of energy to power attention for insight practice.

In several of the Tibetan traditions, the practice of the immeasurables begins with equanimity and then proceeds to loving-kindness, compassion, and joy. The order emphasizes eliminating prejudice before cultivating loving-kindness and the other immeasurables. The emphasis reflects the Mahayana teachings on totality and presence. Equanimity serves as a basis for loving-kindness because equanimity removes prejudice. Loving-kindness serves as a basis for compassion because loving-kindness counteracts shutting down. Compassion serves as a basis for joy because compassion removes self-centeredness. And joy serves as a basis for presence because joy removes the need for external validation.

The Mahayana intention is to be awake, both in the understanding of what life is and in the way we relate to what arises in experience. When we know directly that everything that arises in our experience is our life, we can embrace conflict yet not regard any element of experience as an enemy. We can open to others without owning or fusing with them. We can know how things are yet not fall into discrimination or criticism. We can lead and not be out of touch with those we serve.

A third sequence comes from the four ways of spiritual work: power, ecstasy, insight, and compassion. Power is the ability to stay present in action. Ecstasy is the ability to open to experience. Insight is the ability to see into what is happening. Compassion is the ability to let go of personal agendas. Each of these spiritual paths has an associated emotional energy—one of the immeasurables. When we exercise power, joy arises. When we open ecstatically, loving-kindness arises. When we exercise insight, equanimity arises. When we practice compassion, compassion arises.

In Buddhism, power is cultivated in the practice of basic meditation and in meditations on death and impermanence; ecstasy through meditation on suffering (meditation on suffering involves opening to the experience of suffering) and through devotional practices; insight through meditations on what is ultimately true; and compassion through such practices as taking and sending and awakening mind, which are presented in the next chapter.

The order of the four ways of spiritual work follows a different logic from that of either the Theravadan or Mahayana approach. In the four ways, we begin with joy, the feeling "I am here." The emphasis is not on the sense of "I" or "am" but on "here." Joy moves us into presence. Loving-kindness takes presence as its starting point and radiates awareness into the environment. In the field of awareness, we come to know that all representations of experience, internal and external, are empty (not absolute) through the practice of equanimity. In open empty space, movement arises in response to the destructiveness of suffering. That movement is compassion, the expression of direct awareness. The intention behind the sequence of the four ways is to move directly into presence and live from there.

All these sequences work in practice. Each uses the energy of one of the three poisons: attraction, aversion, and indifference. The Theravadan tradition starts with loving-kindness, transforming the energy of attraction into opening. The four ways approach starts with joy, using the energy of aversion to be present. The Mahayana traditions start with equanimity, using the energy of ignoring to see. Which sequence you use depends on the tradition you follow, the training of your teacher, and your own intention.

None of the three sequences starts with compassion. True compassion comes from a clear understanding and experience of all the other immeasurables. In the absence of joy, conditioned values dominate and distort the expression of compassion. In the absence of loving-kindness, personal needs dominate. In the absence of equanimity, prejudices dominate. In all three cases, compassion degenerates into attempts to control others.

TRANSMISSION

Where does the capacity to cultivate the four immeasurables come from? In the meditation on loving-kindness, you use your own experience of kindness, the experience of warmth and love freely given by another person. If you have never experienced kindness, you might have difficulty in this practice, but such people are very rare. Work with what you have, even if the only experience you can recall is a shopkeeper giving you a piece of candy or a teacher not embarrassing you in front of a class.

Just as the experience of kindness is needed to cultivate loving-kindness, other key experiences are needed for the other immeasurables. For compassion, you need to have experienced another person who was willing to be with you when you were in pain. A friend of mine recalls an incident from his adolescence. He was having a very difficult time with his parents and was seriously considering running away. Somehow, an uncle was aware of his difficulties and wrote to him. The uncle didn't offer him any advice. He just acknowledged that life was sometimes difficult and painful. To this day, my friend tears up when he recalls that letter.

In order to cultivate joy, you need to have experienced your success or happiness being celebrated by another person. An aspiring writer submitted stories, articles, and scripts to publisher after publisher, receiving no acknowledgment, not even rejections. Then, finally, a check arrived from a publisher who had accepted a piece of her work. She showed the check to her mother, who was delighted with her daughter's success. Despite subsequent difficulties with her mother, the daughter always remembers how her mother's celebration united them in a moment of joy.

To develop equanimity, we need to have been seen without judgment by another person. Another friend recalls an English teacher whom she hated. He was a very good teacher, but because of difficulties in her own life, she hated him with a vengeance. Finally, her hatred compelled her to put her feelings in a vitriolic letter that she actually gave to the teacher. He took the letter and did nothing—no comment on the letter, no reprimand, no judgment about her whatsoever. He continued to treat her like every other student in the class. While his attitude didn't change, hers did. Her anger and hatred subsided, and she started to appreciate him and what he had to teach.

The immeasurables transform relationship by cutting through subject-object dualism to unite the giver and receiver in a moment of presence, a moment that carries the energy of the immeasurable and plants it in the heart of the receiver. Whenever we see someone without judgment, accepting that person as he or she is, a seed of equanimity is planted. Whenever we express warmth to another freely, through generosity or love, a seed of loving-kindness is planted. Whenever we stay present with another person who is in pain, a seed of compassion is planted. Whenever we celebrate or delight in another person's success or happiness, a seed of joy is planted. Every interaction has the potential of transmission, of planting a seed of presence in both of you.

PURPOSE, METHOD, EFFECTS, AND RESULTS

The more we learn about a tradition of practice, the more susceptible we are to losing our way. Suzuki Roshi discusses this apparent paradox in *Zen Mind, Beginner's Mind,* summing it up with the observation, "In the beginner's mind there are many possibilities, but in the expert's there are few." As we learn more about practice, experience heightens expectations. A taste of presence whets the appetite, and we want more. Understanding how the techniques work, we try harder. A gradual and subtle shift takes place: we begin to overlook the actual method of practice and try to practice the way we want to be or the way we think we should be, or we try to make happen what we think should be happening. Little by little, we move away from the actual method of practice. Instead of being present, we begin to live in the idea of being present.

> Think of all sentient beings as buddha, but keep your hand on your wallet.
>
> —*Tibetan saying*

The work on the four immeasurables is particularly susceptible to such confusion. Traditional texts contain extensive descriptions of the results of practicing the four immeasurables. Who does not want to be equanimous, loving, compassionate, and joyful? Who does not want to meet the world with peace, openness, caring, and energy? Our expectations are raised. The expectations of others (friends, colleagues, our tradition or meditation group) are equally problematic. These subtle and often unexpressed expectations develop into fixed notions of what we deem to be acceptable feelings and behavior. We suppress what we really feel, thinking, "I shouldn't be angry. I should greet this with equanimity." We reject common sense, again thinking that, because we are loving or compassionate, we should let others take advantage of us.

In the chapter on cultivating attention, I described how many problems in practice come from not differentiating the purpose, method, effects, and results of basic meditation practice. Just as expectations about being free of thoughts impede the cultivation of attention, expectations about being compassionate or loving impede the development of the immeasurables. Because the practices of the immeasurables take us deep into difficult and painful feelings, feelings that appear to be the very opposite of the immeasurables, we need to be very clear about purpose, method, effects, and results.

To try to live the four immeasurables without first dismantling what prevents them from arising is ineffective and dangerous. Papering over the cracks in a wall solves nothing. The wall looks good for a while, but the cracks soon reappear and the wall looks even shabbier. Worse, the structural problems that generate the cracks remain unaddressed. The best-case scenario is that you become a caricature of the four immeasurables; the worst-case scenario is that you develop serious emotional problems and become mentally imbalanced. The intention of the practice of the four immeasurables is not to look good but to transform the deeply conditioned passivity associated with the sense of "I." Once this structural problem is addressed, the result, the four immeasurables, manifests naturally.

Purpose

The fundamental purpose of the four immeasurables is to dismantle the reactive patterns that prevent us from experiencing free emotional energy. Because we are largely unaware of these patterns, nothing inhibits their operation and our lives lurch from one pattern to another, like Mr. Toad and his wild ride in *The Wind in the Willows*. We are, in effect, passive passengers in our lives, and the patterns are at the wheel.

The four immeasurables end this passivity. Recall the example of erosion in the chapter on karma. You can't stop erosion by filling in the gullies with more earth. You have to plant grass, trees, and shrubs to hold the soil, or build drainage ditches that divert the water and let it flow away without carrying the soil with it. Similarly, changes in behavior will not be enough if you haven't changed your interior landscape. The old patterns just reassert themselves in time. To change, you have to become an active participant in your own life. You can do so only when you experience free emotional energy, energy that is not consumed by the operation of habituated patterns. That energy comes from uncovering the four immeasurables. As you develop free energy, you feel more alive and more awake in your life. Now, you do act differently, but the changes in behavior are not forced or contrived. They emerge naturally as the realization of the purpose of the practice.

Method

A meditation method is a way of bringing attention to the operation of habituated patterns. Practice is effective only when attention and conditioned patterns actually meet and the conditioned patterns are experienced in attention. If you merely reexperience conditioned patterns without attention, the patterns are reinforced. On the other hand, if you cultivate attention and do not bring attention to bear on conditioned patterns, the energy in attention inevitably flows into the habit-uated patterns *and* the inhibiting patterns. Both sets of patterns become stronger.

When attention and conditioning meet, the reactive process of the conditioning is stopped. The reactive process can't function in the presence of attention because the energy it runs on is going into attention.

The method used here for the four immeasurables is a power method. It consists of three steps—observation, reorganization, and consistency—which are described in the practice guidelines. The intention of this method is to cut through the operation of habituated patterns and move you directly into presence.

A good approach for power methods is to regard practice as ritual. Form the intention to do each step as described in the instructions. Everything that arises in the practice that is not connected with your intention is the operation of a habituated pattern. By observing such departures from the form of the practice, you can see how patterns operate and thus bring the patterns into attention. On some days, strong feelings, reactions, insights, or experiences arise. On other days, you feel that nothing is happening and you are only going through the steps. In either case, stick to the form, and bring attention to everything that arises.

The sections on extending the immeasurables use an ecstatic method. The intention of this method is to open the immeasurable that has been uncovered and extend its operation into all areas of your life.

Effects

Effects vary greatly from one person to another. For instance, if you are engaged in physical training, the effects can include a sense of heightened energy, exhilaration, stiffness or clumsiness, or a pulled muscle. In practicing the four immeasurables, effects include surges of energy, waves of universal love or compassion, depression, fear, loneli-ness, regret, boredom, or numbness.

When intention is unclear or weak, effects undermine practice in three ways. When you experience pleasant effects such as waves of universal love, your practice subtly shifts from doing the method to generating the pleasant experiences. Gaining ideas—notions that the conditioned image of who you are will benefit from the practice—have crept in, and your practice suffers. Unpleasant effects such as fear or regret cause you to avoid areas where you encounter painful emotional material. Neutral effects such as boredom and numbness make you feel that practice is pointless, fruitless, and a waste of time.

Monitor your practice, and don't fall under the spell of effects. Practitioners often attach to pleasant effects as an indication that the practice is going well and take unpleasant effects as an indication that the practice is not going well. In my experience, pleasant and unpleasant effects are very unreliable indicators of effectiveness or progress in practice.

Take note when a particular effect recurs with increasing frequency or intensity. Intensification usually indicates that a pattern is beginning to break up or that your practice is unbalanced or misdirected. In physical training, repeatedly pulling a muscle points to a problem in your training routine. Consult with a teacher who has a sound technical knowledge of the practice, has had personal experience with it, knows you, and is genuinely interested in your well-being.

The tendency is to attach too much significance on effects. Most of them are fluid and transitory, arising one day and gone the next.

Results

Discussions of results can help or hinder. Some teachers never discuss results so as to avoid raising students' expectations or reinforcing patterns of competition, achievement, pride, or inferiority. Other teachers talk about them at length to inspire students or to confirm their understanding.

The key point is to remember that results are not practices. When you practice the four immeasurables, you will probably feel that you should change your behavior to emulate the results of practice: be composed and even-minded, be open and loving, be compassionate and caring to everyone you encounter, and be joyful and full of energy all the time. Such efforts to act "properly" inevitably cause you to suppress what you are really feeling. You develop an artificial personality, a "spiritual" personality that papers over the cracks in your psyche. More and more energy goes into maintaining an idea of how you should be. Less and less energy goes into actual practice. By trying to be a "good" student, you undermine your own practice. Instead, focus your energy on the method—bringing attention to the operation of patterns—and let the results arise on their own.

If you take the purpose as the method, you will quickly encounter frustration and confusion. The purpose is to dismantle passivity. Passivity doesn't evaporate immediately any more than a lake dries up as soon as the sun comes out. The method creates the space for the four immeasurables to grow. As they grow, passivity falls apart and you become more present, awake, and active in your life. Equanimity, loving-kindness, compassion, and joy manifest naturally.

If you take the effects as the method, you become fixated on states and experiences. You avoid "bad" states and seek out "good" experiences. Notions of good and bad are defined by habituated patterns, so you end up reinforcing patterns that are already in place. Instead, take what practice brings you. Exercise equanimity—not good, not bad, just experience—and keep going.

If you take results as the method, you create the artificial personality I mentioned above. Instead of engaging in a process of fundamental internal change, you adopt prescriptions for the behaviors, attitudes, and ways of thinking that you think you should have. You become increasingly rigid as you try to conform to the prescribed way of being and increasingly frustrated with your inability to meet the impossible standards you have set.

Four Efforts

For practice to be effective, you must make four efforts: know the purpose, trust the method, understand what happens in practice, and accept the results.

First, does the intention of practice align with your motivation for practicing? Many people never ask this crucial question. They passively assume that any method of practice will serve their purpose. If your intention is to relax and release stress, then meditation on compassion is not a good place to start. The first question is "What do I want to get from my spiritual practice?" The second is "Does this method of practice take me in that direction?" To ask this second question, you must know what the purpose or intention of the practice is.

Second, you must understand and have confidence in the method. Confidence comes from your own understanding or from your trust in your teacher. Whatever the source, confidence is essential if you are to maintain practice in the face of the difficulties that inevitably arise. You cannot manufacture or fake confidence. If you do not trust your teacher, talk with him or her or find another teacher. If you do not have confidence in your ability to practice, look inside at the pattern that says, "I can't do this." If you do not have confidence in the method, study it more deeply until it makes sense to you, or work with another method that you do understand.

Third, you must know and be able to recognize the variety of effects that practice can produce and avoid being seduced by the pleasant, put off by the unpleasant, or put to sleep by the neutral. Pleasant, unpleasant, and neutral responses trigger the emotional reactions of the three poisons: attraction, aversion, and indifference. The three poisons form around and maintain the sense of "I." All effects in meditation practice are expressions of patterned mechanisms that function to degrade attention and return you to pattern-based functioning. You need to have the determination to serve what is true, original mind, and not to serve what is false, pattern-based imperatives.

> The chains of habit are too weak to be felt until they are too strong to be broken.
>
> —*Samuel Johnson*

Finally, you have to accept the results of your practice. Effective practice reveals the patterns that run your life. You may not like what you see. If you turn away from them, they win and continue to operate. They grow and take over your life completely as you grow older. Remember, what you don't work through you become. You cannot control what happens in practice, because practice initiates a growth process and growth, by its nature, is unpredictable. All you can do is maintain your intention.

The real results of practice often come as a surprise. You encounter a difficult situation, do what seems to come naturally, and then, after the fact, realize that you handled the situation very differently from the way you used to. The natural, effortless expression of awareness, equanimity, loving-kindness, compassion, and joy is the true result. At the time, what you do seems perfectly natural. "It's no big deal," you might say to a friend who asks how you were able to stay present and do what needed to be done. But it is a big deal because the natural expression of these qualities changes your life and the lives of everyone you encounter.

PRACTICE GUIDELINES

The meditations on the four immeasurables share a similar structure:

Foundation
  • Establishing a base of attention

Practice
- Uncovering the immeasurable

    observation
    reorganization
    consistency

- Extending the immeasurable to all areas of life

Conclusion
- Mixing the immeasurable with awareness
- Letting go of effort

Foundation

Begin each meditation with a period of resting attention on the breath to establish a base of attention. Ordinary mental activity, tension, and dullness usually take fifteen to twenty minutes to dissipate, regardless of how long you have been practicing. Rest attention on the breath for at least this period of time to let things settle.

Practice

Spend twenty to thirty minutes on the main practice.

Because these practices involve a lot of imagery, you may find them easier to do with your eyes closed.

For each immeasurable, go through all three steps: observation, reorganization, and consistency. Initially, most of your time will be taken up with observation. As you see the shape and structure of the reactive patterns, spend more time on reorganization. Consistency becomes the main effort when you can hold attention in the emotional core of the pattern. When attention penetrates the emotional core, the core breaks up, and the experience of the immeasurable arises naturally.

Once you have a clear experience of the immeasurable, spend most of your practice time extending the immeasurable to all parts of your life. Extend in stages, beginning with aspects of life that arouse weak or moderate reactions and working up to areas that are difficult and painful to face. You will need to return to observation and reorganization again and again, since each new area of extension will unearth different variations of the basic reactive pattern.

Portions of the material in the meditation will resonate strongly with your own experience. Others will open new doors for you. When you start, learn all the material and reflect on it until it makes sense to you. Start using it in your practice. You may not be able to cover all the material in one session, so break it up and work through it over several sessions if necessary. But do go through the three steps—observation, reorganization, and consistency—in every session.

Spend at least one month, preferably two, on each of the immeasurables. This length of time is usually sufficient for you to have a clear experience of each. The immeasurables are cumulative, however, so quite often, when people are working on compassion, say, they spontaneously have a deeper experience of loving-kindness or equanimity.

Uncovering the Immeasurable

The immeasurables are expressions of original mind. They are not created in meditation practice but are uncovered by means of a process in which you face and move through the habituated patterns that stand in the way. This process consists of three steps: observation, reorganization, and consistency.

A twelfth-century Tibetan teacher, Chekawa Yeshe Dorje, described three challenges in spiritual practice. The first challenge is to recognize a reactive emotional pattern. The second is to develop a way of working on it. The third is to work on the pattern until it collapses. Chekawa's three challenges correspond with the three steps. Observation reveals the reactive pattern, reorganization develops a way of working on it, and consistency cuts into the pattern until it no longer operates.

Observation The first step is to observe how you react to a specific aspect of your experience of others. For equanimity, observe your reaction to the presence of others. For loving-kindness, look at your reaction to opening to others. For compassion, observe your reaction to the suffering of others. And for joy, look at your reaction to the happiness of others.

The task in this step is to see the reactive processes that prevent the immeasurable from manifesting: prejudice blocks equanimity, shutting down blocks loving-kindness, fear of suffering blocks compassion, and feeling deficient blocks joy. You will experience a lot of discomfort in this step as you see how the patterns operate. The discomfort is part of the reaction process operating to erode attention. As in previous meditations, don't avoid the feelings of discomfort. Hold both the pattern and all the reactions in attention.

Observation means observing how patterns operate. Don't try to change anything at this stage. Observe. Another name for observation is *follow the gesture:* use attention to follow the way that the pattern functions. The act of observation changes your relationship with the reactive patterns. You see them as patterns, not as what you are or as what is real. As you continue to observe, you will see other ways of working with what arises in experience.

> You can see a lot just by looking.
>
> —*Yogi Berra*

Reorganization The next step begins when you can observe the reactive process clearly. Your relationship with the pattern changes. The pattern is now an object of attention. You see how the same reaction operates externally, in your relationship with others, and internally, in your relationship with thoughts, feelings, memories, associations, and other aspects of experience. You see the reaction for what it is—a reaction that arises, plays itself out, and subsides. You see it as an experience rather than as a fixed element of your personality. In other words, your identification with it breaks down.

You begin to realize that you don't have to go with the pattern. You can sit and let the pattern arise, play itself out, and subside during your meditation practice. You then discover that you can do the same thing in your life. You can watch it arise, play itself out, and subside. You don't need to express it or suppress it in everyday situations. You have free energy, energy that is not consumed by pattern operation, so you see and act differently in your life. Reorganization is also called *going another way* because new avenues of action and behavior open up and you are able to take them.

Consistency In consistency, you use attention to cut into the pattern again and again until it falls apart, so another name for consistency is *cut*. One of two things arises at this point. Either the pattern dissolves and you are free from its constraints, or you become aware of a deeper level of conditioning. In the latter case, repeat the process, going back to observing the deeper pattern until the possibility of reorganization arises.

Once you see a pattern as a process, you can hold it in attention more easily. You experience the undischarged emotional core that triggers the pattern imperative as well as associated memories and bodily sensations, the reaction chain, and the projected world. Your effort now is to hold the whole reactive process in attention. At some point, the reaction becomes empty and you experience a shift. The shift can come quite suddenly, as if you have broken through a wall, or the shift can come gradually, in which case you realize that all the turmoil has vanished and you are in a very different state of mind. In either case, the shift has a quality of opening, relaxing, and knowing, and it marks the arising of the immeasurable. For equanimity, the shift is marked by clarity; for loving-kindness, by openness; for compassion, by fearlessness; and for joy, by presence. Sit in the openness and understanding. Your relationship with the immeasurable is not yet stable, so when the opening fades, return to the practice, hold the reactive process in attention until it empties, and then rest again. Consistency consists of repeating these steps, cutting again and again until the underlying core falls apart and the immeasurable becomes stable in experience.

Extending the Immeasurable to All Areas of Life

The first phase of the practice puts you in touch with the underlying feeling that blocks the development of the immeasurable. Once that feeling has been exposed to attention and you have experienced the immeasurable, the next step is to extend the immeasurable to all areas of life. Do so in steps. Each of the immeasurables follows a slightly different sequence of steps. To extend equanimity, for instance, you begin with people who don't arouse strong feelings of attraction or aversion and then gradually progress to those who do. To extend compassion, you begin with people and situations that arouse sympathy in you and progress to ones that you don't want to face. The goal is to extend the immeasurables to all beings and all situations, in other words, to the totality of experience.

Conclusion

At the end of the practice session, open your eyes and rest in attention. The conclusion stage of practice has two functions. First, resting in open attention allows emotional energy brought up in the course of practice to disperse evenly through body and mind. Dispersion of energy is an important component of practice. If energy builds up behind emotional or physical blocks, it causes imbalance, disturbance, reinforcement of habituated patterns, and even illness.

Second, resting in attention in the field of emotional energy transforms the emotional energy into a higher level of attention and creates the conditions necessary for the four immeasurables to arise at the level of awareness.

The conclusion of practice involves two steps: mixing the immeasurable with awareness, and letting go of effort. Spend about ten minutes on them.

Mixing the Immeasurable with Awareness

Look directly at the experience of the immeasurable, whether it is equanimity, loving-kindness, compassion, or joy. One of the easiest ways to look directly at the immeasurable is to pose the question "What is this experience of loving-kindness?" Don't look for an intellectual answer. Instead, let the question direct your attention to the immeasurable, and just look. You will see nothing, but the effort in attention raises the level of energy in the immeasurable and begins the mixing of the immeasurable with awareness.

Letting Go of Effort

Rest right in the looking. Initially, you will be able to look only for very short periods. When the looking fades, return attention to the breath and rest with the sensation of breathing for the rest of the period of meditation. Gradually, you will be able to rest longer in the looking. You will experience the quality of the immeasurable as a knowing or a radiance while simultaneously being aware that the immeasurable is not a thing. As the immeasurable and awareness mix, just rest in the awareness, doing nothing.

Meditation 1: Equanimity

Rest attention on the breath for fifteen to twenty minutes to establish a base of attention.

Move now to uncovering equanimity. Imagine three people in front of you. On the left is a person you like, a friend. On the right is a person you dislike. In between is a person for whom you have no strong feelings, positive or negative. Choose people for whom your feelings are clear but not overwhelmingly strong.

OBSERVATION

Identifying Attraction, Aversion, and Indifference

Start with the person you dislike, and observe how you experience him or her physically, emotionally, and mentally. Go through the following reflections with this person. Then do the same thing for the person that you like and then for the person toward whom you are indifferent.

Physical
- Are they present in their bodies?
- How do they look—are they physically appealing, do they have distinctive physical features?
- How do they stand or sit—relaxed, tense, receptive, distancing?
- Are their movements clumsy, graceful, aloof, furtive, vigilant?
- How do they dress—for appearance, for comfort, for effectiveness, to conform, to make a statement?
- What animal does each person evoke in your imagination?

Emotional
- Are they present emotionally?
- How do they talk—aggressively, patiently, authoritatively, hesitantly?
- Does the emotional tone of expression match the emotional energy?
- How do they interact—give and take, rigidly, intellectually, passionately, or energetically?
- How do they form connections and relationships?

Mental
- Are they awake and present?
- How do they look at the world—what are their political, social, religious, or philosophical views?
- Where do they put their energy—into career, relationships, causes, or entertainment?
- What are their interests? What do they talk about or do?
- How do they relate to the world—as a place to fight, satisfy needs, fulfill social responsibilities, explore interests, prove themselves, or maintain their position?

Notice what you like, dislike, and don't care about in each person. Don't edit what you feel. Just note it. Spend enough time on this section so that your feelings of attraction, aversion, and indifference are clear to you.

Understanding That Reactions Are Based on Internal Representations

Turn your attention to the person you dislike. Recall how that aversion developed.

- Are your feelings based on personal experience or on what you have learned about the person from others?
- Are your feelings based on how you met this person, a particular incident in your relationship, or a feeling that has grown clearer over time?
- Does one physical trait, emotional trait, or mental trait dominate your feelings?
- Do you dislike everything about the person?

Seeing the Fluid Nature of Representations

When you are clear about the factors that shape your feelings for this person, change a factor you dislike to one that you like. For example, if the person ignored you the first time you met, imagine that he or she greeted you warmly on that first occasion. If you don't like the way he dresses, imagine that he dresses differently. Your imagined changes don't have to correspond directly to factors that you dislike. Perhaps you dislike the person because he speaks loudly and you feel he does not care about others. Now imagine that the first time you met him, he returned your child to you when your child was lost in a shopping mall.

Change factors one by one. After each change, check internally on how you feel about this person.

A point will come when you notice that your feeling of aversion shifts first to indifference and then to attraction. Often, the shift through indifference is very fast, so you may suddenly realize that you like the person you are considering.

Next, turn your attention to the person that you like and go through the same reflections, but use changes that arouse aversion in you. Keep making changes until you feel aversion.

Finally, turn your attention to the person for whom you feel indifference, and imagine first changes that make you dislike the person and then changes that make you like the person.

How often have you formed an opinion of a person, only to have it change when you learn about a side of that person you weren't aware of? The point of this step is to become aware of the difference between the person and your internal representation of the person. Once you make this distinction, you see how your feelings about other people are based on what is stored inside you.

REORGANIZATION: BRINGING ATTENTION TO INDIFFERENCE

Attraction, aversion, and indifference are different manifestations of the same level of emotional energy, the level of the three poisons. In the reorganization step, you reorganize your relationship to this spectrum of energy.

Reduce Reactions to Indifference

Imagine the same three people in front of you. Your internal representations of these people cause you to like one, to dislike the second, and to be indifferent to the third. Go through the process as before until you feel indifference toward all three people. Change factors in the person that you like until you feel indifferent to him or her. Change factors in the one you dislike until you feel indifferent to him or her.

Bring Attention to Indifference

You now have a "clear" experience of indifference. Indifference is a passive, dull state of mind. Bring attention to the experience of indifference itself as you hold the images of the three people in front of you. Note the dullness, passivity, unresponsiveness, and flatness of indifference. If you are distracted or go blank, return attention to the breath, and then recall the three people and the feeling of indifference.

CONSISTENCY: MAINTAINING ATTENTION

Indifference Becomes Empty

Experience the indifference as clearly as you can. Don't try to change it or get rid of it. Stay awake so that it doesn't take you over. At some point, you feel a shift. The indifference appears to crumble, dissolve, or vanish. In its place, you experience a clear knowing that feels totally natural. The knowing is open, spacious, relaxed. This shift is the result of indifference going empty.

Don't try to make the indifference go away by thinking it is empty. You will only end up thinking that you have experienced equanimity when all you have done is construct an idea or notion of equanimity. Instead, go right into this dull, bland, lifeless state of mind, and experience indifference in attention.

When indifference collapses, attraction and aversion also collapse.

Equanimity: Open Clarity Free from Attraction, Aversion, and Indifference

Clear knowing is free of the reactive confusion of attraction, aversion, and indifference. You see the three people in front of you, but you now see them free from the distortion of internal representations. They are just people. You see that, like you and everybody else, they just want to be happy and not suffer. They are the same as you and everybody else in this respect. You understand how they are. Equanimity is uncovered when the spectrum of emotional reaction based on attraction, aversion, and indifference collapses. You see people without the filter of your own reactions.

EXTENDING EQUANIMITY TO ALL AREAS OF LIFE

Start the practice of extending the immeasurable when you have a clear experience of equanimity. Consultation with your teacher is important at this stage. Some people do not recognize the clear open knowing as equanimity and keep trying to have a "transcendent" experience. Others play an intellectual trick on themselves, imagining a clear empty knowing and taking what they are imagining as equanimity. A capable teacher can help you avoid these traps.

Once you have experienced equanimity clearly with one set of three people, pick another set of three and go through the same process. After four or five sets, equanimity comes more easily. Now, you can work with people for whom you have stronger feelings, both positive and negative. Work also with various groups of people, groups you like, groups you dislike, and groups you feel indifferent about. As you extend the practice to more and more people, you will uncover new areas where judgment and preference operate in you. Again and again, return to the process of reducing attraction and aversion to indifference and bringing attention to the indifference until it goes empty. Extend the practice of equanimity to all people everywhere.

CONCLUSION: EQUANIMITY AT THE LEVEL OF AWARENESS

At the end of each session, let go of all the images and feelings you have been working with. Rest in whatever sense of equanimity you have uncovered with the mind open and clear. Pay attention to the experience of equanimity. What is it? Where is it? Where does it come from? Do not try to reason, analyze, or think about these questions. Use the questions to direct the attention. Just rest, looking at the experience of equanimity.

Commentary: Equanimity

At every stage of practice, a price has to be paid for clarity. The price is the loss of an illusion. In equanimity, you lose the illusion that your preferences and prejudices accurately reflect what is real.

Equanimity practice is tough. It first exposes prejudices and then works to pry you loose from them. Not everyone lets go easily.

One difficulty you may encounter is admitting that you don't like a particular person. Such an admission pushes against what may be a carefully constructed view of yourself as an open, tolerant, and accepting person.

One person stated flatly that she couldn't do the meditation because she no longer used categories of "like" and "dislike." Her attitude reflected two relatively common problems: an attachment to a self-image of being a person who has gone beyond likes and dislikes, and a tendency to relate to emotions through the intellect in order to maintain the self-image. After a lengthy discussion, she grudgingly admitted that she felt warmer toward some people than others and used "warm" and "less warm" as the basis for the first part of equanimity practice.

Another mechanism by which people avoid admitting the operation of personal prejudice is an insistence on "truth." The logic of this mechanism is interesting. If you can discover what is "true," what "actually happened," then you don't have to admit exercising any judgment. Your actions are justified by "the truth," and you are absolved of any responsibility for your views. The logic is faulty, of course, because it ignores the criteria by which "the truth" is determined. Personal prejudice determines the criteria, a process that is all too evident in political debate, for instance, when a politician focuses only on one aspect of a situation to make his or her point, ignoring all other factors or criteria.

Dissociation is another common problem. You consistently disconnect from the experience of the practice by falling into distraction, spacing out, or going to sleep. To counteract this tendency, try to bring attention to the experience of dissociating. This approach is difficult, but close observation will eventually lead you to the emotional patterns that trigger dissociation.

> Our friends show us what we can do, our enemies teach us what we must do.
>
> —*Goethe*

You cannot practice equanimity or any of the other immeasurables with the intellect. More often than not, the intellect is in the service of habituated patterns. Even when it isn't, it does not have enough energy to penetrate reactive emotions, let alone dismantle them. Thinking your way through these practices is not enough. You will develop only a veneer of equanimity or one of the other immeasurables, a veneer that will shatter as soon as you encounter a really difficult situation. As the Dalai Lama once said, patience with friends is easy; patience with those you dislike is what counts.

If you have difficulty deciding whether you like someone or dislike someone, go to your body. Imagine the person in front of you, and notice what your body feels. If you rest with the breath for a few minutes, thus effectively stilling the intellect, you will feel emotional reactions operating in your body, telling you whether the person is liked or disliked. Don't judge the reactions. Just observe them and acknowledge that they operate in you. That's the first step.

A second difficulty in understanding internal representations is distinguishing between the person and your view of the person. As you come to know a person, you accumulate information from meetings and conversations, from observing behavior, and from hearing what other people have to say. A picture of the person forms inside you. How all that information is organized inside you may have little or nothing to do with who that person is. You like a woman because her hair or a mannerism reminds you of an old friend. You have had bad experiences with people who speak loudly, so you automatically regard a loud speaker with distrust. You may not even make the connection yourself, but the connection affects how you view the other.

The internal representation is the picture of the other person inside you. Your reactions, particularly your feelings of like and dislike, are largely based on your picture, not the person. When you have difficulty imagining a person you dislike doing something positive, the difficulty indicates your attachment to the internal representation. Start by changing small things in the internal picture, such as the way the person dresses or talks. Notice the resistance in you to viewing the person differently. By studying where the resistance is active, you will see clearly how the internal representation is organized inside you.

> The origin of human violence is that we hold other peoples' past against them.
>
> —*Michael Conklin*

Imagining a person you don't like doing something positive is one thing. Imagining a friend doing something negative is another. You immediately think, "He would never do anything like that." There, right there, is the internal representation. Most people are more invested in their view of their friends than in their view of people they don't like. When you do this meditation, you may feel that you are betraying your friends or tearing apart your network of relationships. Again, such feelings are instances of reactive patterns being triggered by your effort in the practice. You are not betraying anyone. You are not hurting anyone.

You will see your friends and those close to you more clearly as a result of this practice. You will notice aspects of their personalities or behaviors that you hadn't seen before. Equally, you will see people you dislike in a different light. Isn't that precisely the point of the practice, to dismantle your prejudices?

Another common area of difficulty is bringing attention to indifference. Indifference is an inherently dull state of mind. It's based on ignoring, not paying attention. Ignoring, however, is exactly what makes prejudices possible: we ignore what we are actually experiencing and rely instead on internal representations. In this step, you are bringing attention into the mechanism of ignoring. This step is like entering a dark room. You can't see anything. You lose all reference and fall back, time and again, into the old patterns of like and dislike. Keep coming back to the indifference and sitting in it, letting go of all notion of like and dislike.

This step feels a bit like dying. It is, in a way. You may well feel angry because you can't control the process. You may try to figure out a way to develop equanimity another way, usually with the intellect. You may feel that the meditation is stupid, that you've understood the point, or that you can't do it. All such notions are side steps away from the practice. Keep coming back to the indifference and sitting with the feelings of frustration, anger, and helplessness, letting them just be there.

Indifference is like a black wall made of a material that you can't even feel. Sit and go into the wall. At some point, it crumbles and disappears. You can't make it crumble, but you will know when it does. A screen or veil is gone, and you see the three people free from the operation of your internal representations. For some people, the experience is disorienting. The usual points of reference are gone. At the same time, you realize how narrow and restricted your view of others has been and what a burden those prejudices and preferences were.

In the extension phase, the greatest danger is to lapse back into the intellect. Because you now know what equanimity is, you may feel that recalling the feeling is enough. It's not. With every person and every group, you must work until you experience the veil drop, the space open, and your prejudices disintegrate. Clearly, when considering repugnant people, perpetrators of hate crimes or mass violence, for instance, equanimity is more than a little challenging. You will know when a measure of equanimity is present when you can know—directly, not intellectually—that, just like you or me, even such people as mass murderers are trying to be happy, trying not to suffer, though their actions are horribly distorted expressions of these basic human yearnings.

When you work at equanimity, you discover how you defend and maintain your sense of being different from others. You may see your struggles in life as being superior and

> To go in the dark with
> a light is to know
> the light.
> To know the dark, go
> dark. Go without
> sight,
> and find that the dark,
> too, blooms and
> sings,
> and is traveled by dark
> feet and dark wings.
>
> —*Wendell Berry*

more meaningful than the struggles of others. You may see them as being inferior and less meaningful. In either case, the sense of difference is the basis of pride. Judgments and prejudices are like a razor-wire fence, separating you from the rest of humanity. The central point in equanimity is that *everyone* is trying to be happy and trying to avoid suffering. Understanding this point cuts through the fence and puts you in touch with the essential humanity of all people.

Meditation 2: Loving-Kindness

At the beginning of each session, rest attention on the breath for fifteen to twenty minutes to establish a base of attention.

Begin by noting how you react to even a small act of kindness, such as a friend's opening a door for you. You naturally feel respected and appreciated, and even if you dislike the person, you feel a little more open toward him or her. But note also how you move away from opening to the other by ignoring the kindness, dismissing it, or not acknowledging it. Strange, isn't it?

OBSERVATION:
REACTING TO THE KINDNESS OF OTHERS

For the meditations on loving-kindness, choose a person who has been kind to you. If possible, choose a person whose kindness to you is clear and unambiguous: a parent, a teacher, an uncle or aunt, or a camp counselor. Do not use a child, your own or anyone else's.

Recognizing Kindness

Imagine the person in front of you. Recall explicit occasions when he or she was kind to you. Observe how you react to these images. Do you open and relax? Do you tense up? Are you distracted? Do you space out? If you observe that your reaction is not to let the kindness in, observe how you try to keep it out. Do you take the position that he didn't have any choice? Do you suspect that he had his own selfish motives? Do you consider that her kindness was only natural and appropriate? Maybe her action just made no sense to you, so you forgot about it as quickly as possible. Perhaps you thought, "Yes, that was nice, but it was no big deal." Or maybe you feel that you are special and everyone should be kind and nice to you because of who you are.

Acknowledging Kindness

The second step is to acknowledge that kindness is *always* a gift. Recall specific occasions when the person you have chosen for this meditation was kind to you. Consider what that person gave up to be kind to you. Perhaps the person is a teacher you had in high school or college. How often did you talk with him? How much time did he give you when he could have been doing something else?

Perhaps you are thinking of a co-worker who helped you with a difficult assignment. She canceled her own plans so that you could complete the project on time. Perhaps a friend backed you up in a confrontation and put herself at risk. Perhaps you recall that your uncle came over to take you out one day, after you had had a bad disagreement with your parents and you didn't know what to do. You never talked about your troubles, but you remember the day gratefully, and you have never, until now, given any thought to what he gave up to spend that day with you.

Every instance of kindness involves people giving you their time, their care, their support, or their help. Kindness means that they gave freely, they chose to give, and they chose to give to you.

Did you deserve their kindness? Are you grateful? Are you obligated to them? Are you puzzled by why they were kind to you? Do you resent the kindness even as you are grateful? Do you dismiss it or try to deny it?

Observe what arises in you as you acknowledge the kindness that this person showed you.

Appreciating Kindness

Consider what effect that kindness had on you. How did it help you at the time? How did you feel when the person was kind to you? What did you take or learn from the experience? What difference has it made in your life?

Because of kindness others have shown you, you have been able to live, to grow, to learn, and to enjoy new opportunities. Observe your reactions to appreciating how kindness has affected your life. If you feel that kindness hasn't affected you in any way, hold exactly that feeling in attention, noting how it manifests physically, emotionally, and mentally. In time, it will collapse and you will see how kindness has contributed to your life.

REORGANIZATION: BRINGING ATTENTION TO SHUTTING DOWN

Observation reveals how you shut down to others by not recognizing, acknowledging, or appreciating their kindness. How do you shut down? Do you let only a part of the kindness in and shut out the rest? Do you quickly acknowledge it and then move on, not letting it touch you? Are you surprised or shocked by kindness?

As you practice, you see what was kindness and what wasn't. You may come to a painful realization of how much of what you thought was kindness was not freely given. When such pain arises, sit and breathe, bringing your attention to how this pain also causes you to shut down. Bit by bit, open to the experience of pain. As you recall other incidents when love and warmth were freely given, you recognize and appreciate how important those experiences were for you and how they helped you open to what life is.

Each instance of kindness is a recognition of the validity of your being by another person. All of us open when we are recognized and treated kindly, but different fears may be triggered by opening. What fears arise for you? When someone is kind to you, does it unsettle your view of the world so that you don't know where you stand? Are you afraid that the kindness comes with strings attached and that you are going to be engulfed by the person's agenda? Does the kindness bring out how alone and isolated you feel most of the time? When you feel kindness, do you not know who you are? Do you just go blank or fall to pieces? These are the fears associated with the reaction chains of the five elements. Use your experience with the five elements to experience the fear in attention. The fear is, in the end, just a feeling. Let it be there, using your breath as a base of attention and letting all the physical, emotional, and mental reactions to the fear arise and subside in awareness.

CONSISTENCY: MAINTAINING ATTENTION

Shutting Down Becomes Empty

At some point both the fear and the associated reaction go empty. They seem to disappear. Their power or force evaporates, and you relax and open. Each time you relax, you experience the shutting-down mechanism more clearly. The process of relaxing may take place in jerky steps: opening, relaxing, shutting down, then opening, relaxing, and shutting down.

Opening to Kindness

When the resistance to opening goes empty, you open fully to the experience of receiving kindness. You may recall other instances when this person was kind to you. You open and experience what he or she gave to you freely. Appreciation and gratitude well up from deep inside you, and you see clearly what his or her kindness contributed to your life. A natural feeling of warmth and appreciation arises, free from any sense of obligation, duty, or other conditioned influences.

Loving-Kindness

Loving-kindness is radiant warmth and openness, an unattached appreciation with no sense of duty or obligation. It arises naturally when your attention penetrates the layers of conditioning that shut you down to others. Loving-kindness is the natural and heartfelt wish that this person be happy. You realize that your own wants, needs, or preferences are reactions at a lower level of energy. They pale in the radiant energy of warmth that flows from your heart and wants this person to be happy, to be safe, well, secure, and at peace.

Once you have clearly experienced loving-kindness for the person you originally chose as the focus for your practice, work on loving-kindness for another person who has been kind to you. After a short time, you will feel loving-kindness for anyone who has been kind to you.

EXTENDING LOVING-KINDNESS TO ALL AREAS OF LIFE

Start extending the feeling of loving-kindness to all people. Again, consult with your teacher to confirm your experiential understanding of loving-kindness before extending the practice to others.

When you practice extending loving-kindness, take a person or group as your focus. Begin with equanimity, briefly going through the equanimity meditation to eliminate prejudice and judgment. Connect with the person or group's basic humanity: they, like everyone else, want to be happy and free of suffering. Feel in your heart the warmth and opening you know from your practice, and include these people in the warmth. You will naturally feel the wish that they be happy, too. Gradually extend the feelings of loving-kindness to all beings. Whenever you encounter resistance or difficulty, bring attention to the experience of the resistance until the resistance becomes empty.

Extend loving-kindness in stages, beginning with people for whom your feelings are predominantly positive, then to people who are neutral to you, and finally to people with whom you have difficulty.

CONCLUSION: LOVING-KINDNESS AT THE LEVEL OF AWARENESS

At the end of each session, let go of all the images and feelings you have been working with. Rest in loving-kindness with your mind open and clear. Turn attention to the experience of loving-kindness itself. What is it? Where is it? Where does it come from? Do not try to reason, analyze, or think about these questions. Use the questions to direct the attention. Just rest, looking at the experience of loving-kindness.

Commentary: Loving-Kindness

Where equanimity takes down the razor-wire fence of prejudices and preferences, loving-kindness is more like the spring sun that warms the ground so that grass and flowers can grow. Human kindness is like sunshine, and loving-kindness practice is letting that sunshine warm your heart so that you, too, radiate warmth to the world around you.

One of the first challenges is to admit that you have experienced kindness. Many people don't want to recall or remember kindnesses they have received. You can keep an act of kindness from touching you in any number of ways—by regarding it as common courtesy, as what was due to you, as a fair exchange, or as creating an obligation. How do you regard kindness? What does your view of kindness serve—opening or staying closed?

A person holds a door open for you. He didn't have to. Holding a door open for someone is not much, but it is an act of kindness. Even if the person works for you, he or she may be expressing appreciation and respect, not only deference or servitude. Can you tell the difference?

During the loving-kindness meditation, make a special point of noting the common courtesies of social interaction. Notice when such courtesies are extended freely and when they are required by social convention. Notice the difference in emotional energy.

You may feel that true kindness is a fiction and that any act of kindness comes out of an expectation of something in return. Feel how such an attitude operates inside you, how closed and restricted it is. What does this attitude serve?

When you recall acts of kindness, you may, strangely, feel a bit guilty, as if the kindness were an accident and you really shouldn't have received any. The feeling reflects an internal view that something is fundamentally wrong with you, that you are not worthy of kindness, or that a fundamental law of the universe has been violated, probably by you. When you follow the emotional logic, you see that the feelings of guilt are actually a form of pride, an attachment to a self-image of being fundamentally special and different from others—"I am so bad that kindness to me violates the order of the universe." In this case, the difference is negative, but the dynamic is the same. Push on the pattern of guilt by posing such questions as "What am I guilty of?" or "What fundamental law did I violate?" or "What about me makes me unworthy to receive kindness?" Don't try to analyze or figure out an answer. You will only end up spinning in thoughts, ideas, and speculations. Instead, hold the question in attention as if it were a heavy stone, and let it take you down into the deep waters of guilt and beliefs about being unworthy or fundamentally flawed. This technique will soon expose the self-images that underlie the sense of guilt.

In a similar way, feelings of obligation connected with receiving kindness cause internal contractions that you may experience physically. A feeling of obligation in this context is based on fear and is quite different from the free-flowing warmth and appreciation that is the basis of loving-kindness. The fear may be fear of retaliation if you do not respond to the kindness in the "right" way or fear of being overwhelmed by demands. In either case, note how the feeling of obligation causes you to stay separate and cling to your illusion of independence.

When you recall instances of kindness, don't be surprised if the memories have painful associations. You recall the kindness of an aunt, say, and then wonder why you never thanked her or why you took her kindness for granted. You recall the kindness of a friend and realize that you have completely lost touch as the years have passed, the person is no longer part of your life, and you don't know why. Far from being a negative, the pains associated with these memories are like the creaking of trees in the spring as the sun warms their trunks and the sap begins to flow.

Gradually and naturally, as you do this practice you are able to acknowledge acts of kindness more easily. Sometimes, your heart will overflow with gratitude and appreciation as you remember a teacher taking an extra hour with you after school to explain a problem or help you through a difficulty in your life. Bit by bit, you see how each act of kindness opened something in you and helped you to feel more a part of the world around you.

As you feel the kindness you have experienced in your life, you may react in a number of different ways. Typically, the reactions follow the reaction chains of the five elements. You recall how your mother cared for you when you were ill. Many years have passed and you don't feel particularly close to her now, so the meditation leaves you feeling a little shaky inside (earth), wondering what you may have done to contribute to the separation. On the other hand, you may recall that same instance of kindness and then be seized by the fear of engulfment (water) as you recall how she fussed over you so much that you could hardly breathe. Perhaps you grew up in an environment with little love and affection, and the recollection of kindness brings back the fear of rejection (fire) and the feeling that you would do anything to feel loved. Perhaps you learned to function without kindness, filling your life with events and activities. Now, when you recall acts of kindness, you wonder who you are or what you are doing (air). Perhaps you run into a thick fog of dullness when you try to think of kindness shown to you. After meditation, however, you are a mess. In rapid succession you talk to your siblings about old times, buy flowers for your mother but refuse to return her phone call, take on new work even though you have no time, and decide that now is the time to check on your emergency supplies (void).

Use your understanding of the elemental reaction chains to bring attention to the fears you have associated with opening to kindness. These are the fears that keep you shut down and your heart closed.

The first hit of a closed heart is like a lump of infinitely cold black ice. Bring attention to the feeling, breathing with it, holding it gently in attention, and letting all the fears and other emotional reactions come and go.

At some point, the black ice breaks open and melts away. In its place is a radiant warmth. You feel that your heart is the sun, and you are surprised that you can feel so open and warm to everyone and everything without reservation. All the worn clichés about universal love and understanding now make sense. You can't believe that you feel this way.

The feeling fades. Don't try to recover it. The opening comes from your efforts in practice, but the patterns reset and close over your open heart. Go back to recalling instances of loving-kindness, and go through the practice step by step until you hit the lump of black ice again. Then, rest attention with it until it breaks up. Do this again and again until loving-kindness is easily accessible. Then, turn to extending loving-kindness to all areas of life.

Loving-kindness operates at a higher level of energy than prejudice and preference. The practice of equanimity has dismantled the passive acceptance of preferences, but they still operate. At first, you feel strange and confused, experiencing loving-kindness for someone that you usually avoid. Then you realize that loving-kindness has nothing to do with liking or disliking. The warmth of loving-kindness radiates to everyone simply because they are here in the world. As your experience of loving-kindness deepens, it extends beyond people to everything you experience. You are filled with love for all that arises in experience, regardless of your personal preferences.

A close connection exists between loving-kindness and addictive behaviors. Both involve opening, but in addiction, there are no boundaries. The whole world and everything in it belong to the addict, to be used as he or she wishes. Addictive tendencies show up in meditation practice in many areas. In devotion practices, for instance, you can be obsessively attached to the object of your devotion, whom you come to regard as the sole source of love, meaning, and understanding in your life. You are unable to recognize and accept these qualities in you and become totally dependent on the object of your devotion for your well-being.

You can also become addicted to the high levels of energy in bliss experiences. Traditional instructions include very clear warnings about the danger of attaching to the bliss experiences themselves instead of using them to power attention. Yet, in every generation, many practitioners end up doing just that, taking the intensity of bliss as the goal of spiritual practice.

Most of the problems that arise in loving-kindness practice come from holding to feelings of rejection. You feel disconnected and alienated from the world and grasp at experience to compensate for the feeling of rejection. Loving-kindness dismantles this conception by putting you in touch with your connection with the world—that is, the kindness that others have shown you.

Meditation 3: Compassion

At the beginning of each session of meditation, rest attention on the breath for fifteen to twenty minutes to establish a base of attention.

Begin the compassion meditation with the same person you used for the loving-kindness practice. Do not use a child for this practice.

OBSERVATION: REACTING TO THE SUFFERING OF OTHERS

Seeing Others Suffer

First, imagine your chosen person to be in the hell realms. He screams in pain as he is boiled in a vat of molten metal. His feet are charred as he walks on ground that consists of burning coals. He is buried under flaming boulders, impaled on red-hot spears, or hacked to bits by demonic figures that know no mercy. Observe how you react, contracting, squirming, or going numb in the face of these images.

Imagine your person in the cold hells, too, sitting without shelter or clothing in an icy wasteland where a cold, cruel wind blows incessantly. She cannot move because she is frozen stiff. The cold causes her skin to crack, and fluids ooze out of her body, only to congeal, freeze, crack, and ooze again. You watch her as she tries to move, but each movement is excruciatingly painful. Her body cracks open, and you can feel how the cold pierces her body right to the bone. But you can do nothing to help her.

In the hungry ghost realm, your person experiences intense hunger and thirst. Imagine him crawling for years across a blazing desert, mouth and lips like concrete, craving water but never finding any. Perhaps he finds a drop, but the instant it touches his lips, it bursts into flame and he howls with pain. His face is distorted by insatiable cravings. His eyes reflect such desperation that anything he does ingest only increases his suffering. As you look more closely, you see that he is being devoured by hundreds of thousands of similar creatures that crawl all over and through his body, eating him from the inside out.

In the animal realm, he functions purely out of instinct and is helpless in situations in which instinct does not work. He lives with only two concerns: how to eat and how to avoid being eaten. He is like a fish in the sea, a beast of burden, or a worm in the ground. Like a rabbit, he glances about fearfully, running for shelter, fearful of being caught and killed. Every movement attracts his intense interest. He is a cat playing with a mouse, finally tearing off the head and eating the internal organs. He is a beast of burden, plodding along forever under a heavy weight, feeling the sting of his owner's whip, with no comprehension of how to free himself.

In the human realm, you see her experiencing birth, old age, illness, and death. She comes into the world, hopelessly confused and disoriented, crying and helpless. As she grows, her life is totally consumed by four efforts: being with people she likes, avoiding people she doesn't like, working for what she wants, and guarding what she has. As she grows older, you watch the flower and bloom of youth fade and old age set in. You watch her succumb to one disease after another until her health fails completely and she dies.

In the titan realm, you watch him struggle to prove himself to others. No matter what he achieves, he is soon on the next project. In the end, they all fail. He tries again and again to make an impression on the "right" people, but they never notice him. He goes to war with them, but they swat him away as if he were a fly.

In the god realm, she floats above it all, basking in luxury and utterly complacent to the sufferings of the masses. She makes every effort to avoid even the mention of pain and death. With a shock, she realizes that she, too, will die. Her friends and companions desert her, and she is totally alone to face the horror of her declining health and death.

Imagine that your person is blind. He staggers around at the edge of a terrifyingly high cliff where powerful gusts of wind blow him closer and closer to an edge he cannot see. In this image, the blindness represents basic ignorance, the cliff represents the fall into states of suffering, and the wind represents the powerful forces of habituation that blow us around.

Observing Your Reactions

As you reflect on these images, note your reactions. The first wave of reactions is usually to the practice itself. Do you want to stop because you cannot understand how such painful images can be helpful? Are you afraid that you will hurt the person you have chosen if you imagine that he or she is in pain? Do you avoid practice because you have no energy for it? Are you constantly agitated and distracted and unable to hold the images in mind for even a moment? Do you go blank or forget what you are doing?

Bring attention to your reaction and note its operation. Patiently, return attention to the images. Gradually, attention penetrates the resistance, and you are able to hold the images in mind and be present with the suffering they depict.

Now, a different set of reactions arises to disconnect you from suffering. Some of the images fill you with disgust or revulsion. Other images leave you feeling helpless. Still others make you numb. Disgust arises because you don't want to feel your own discomfort, so you push the practice and images away. Helplessness arises because you want to do something but you can't. You are drawn to the person who is suffering, but the feeling of helplessness keeps you at a distance so that you never actually become present to the suffering. Numbness arises as an expression of ignoring. You go numb so that you won't feel what is in front of you.

REORGANIZATION: BRINGING ATTENTION TO WAYS OF AVOIDING BEING PRESENT

All these reactions are ways to stop your own discomfort. In the reorganization step, each time the disgust, helplessness, or numbness fades, step back into the images of suffering. Every time you reconnect with the images, you feel another jolt of reaction. Stay in attention, let the reaction dissipate, and open again to the pain in the image.

Bringing an End to the Suffering

Now, you come up with all kinds of ways to change or modify the image to make it less painful. You take the person out of the hell realms, reassure her in the god realms, tell him he doesn't have to prove himself in the titan realms, but all these reactions are also ways you avoid being present with the suffering. Recognize them as reactions, hold them in attention until they dissipate, and then return to the images of suffering.

All Resistance Reduces to Contraction

Let attention penetrate deeper. Feel the resistance to being present with the person when he or she is in pain. When the resistance begins to go empty, you will feel how you contract physically and emotionally in the presence of the suffering. Use the physical sensations of your body to identify the contraction. You will gradually notice the emotional contraction as well.

CONSISTENCY: MAINTAINING ATTENTION

Contraction Becomes Empty

Bring attention to the physical contraction first. Let the body relax. As it relaxes, you will feel the presence of pain and suffering more intensely, and the reaction will be triggered again. Keep letting the body relax so that you move more deeply into the experience step by step. At a certain point you will clearly identify the emotional contraction. You feel afraid of what will happen to you if you really open to the pain and suffering of others. Images, associations, and memories from various parts of your life may arise. Do not block these associations or let them distract you. Continue to bring attention to the fear and emotional contraction.

At some point, the contraction goes completely empty. You recognize that all your own agendas have fallen away. You are simply present with the person who is experiencing pain. Your heart is completely open, and you are naked and raw, as if you had no skin.

Compassion: Letting Go of Self-Concern

Yet you are totally present. You are intensely aware that the other person is in pain, but you feel no need to avoid, close down, or distance. You let go of all self-concern and are there, even though being there is intense, even painful. This is compassion.

EXTENDING COMPASSION TO ALL AREAS OF LIFE

To extend compassion, work in stages. Begin with people for whom you have a definite feeling of warmth and affection. Then, work with people with whom you interact regularly on friendly or neutral terms (family, friends, relatives, colleagues). Next, turn to people whose suffering moves you—war refugees, people with chronic, painful illnesses, the poor, the homeless—and then to people who, though difficult for you, obviously create their own pain and difficulties in life. Finally, work with people with whom you do not like to associate and people who have caused or are causing you pain, difficulty, or injury. Work with each group until you have a clear experience of compassion for the people in that category.

Train compassion further by varying the situations as well as the people. Begin with people you care about and train compassion in situations that you can face. Gradually extend your practice until you are working with situations that are difficult for you to face. Then work through the same sequence of situations with people that are more difficult for you. One possible sequence of situations is

- Illness and injury
- Loss of ability (through illness, accident, or aging)
- Difficulty in social relationships
- Compulsive/obsessive behaviors
- Addiction in all its various forms
- Loss of spouse, partner, parent, or child
- Loss of work, money, or social status
- Natural catastrophes
- Physical or emotional violence
- War, imprisonment, rape, or torture

Again and again, you will encounter areas in which personal issues prevent you from either knowing the suffering or experiencing compassion. In each instance, let attention penetrate the resistance until compassion arises. Step by step, let go of areas in you that you protect, and let compassion open you up.

CONCLUSION:
COMPASSION AT THE LEVEL OF AWARENESS

At the end of each session, let all the images and feelings go, and bring your attention to the experience of compassion. By posing such questions as "What is it?" direct attention to compassion itself. Do not try to figure out an answer to the question. Simply use the question to direct the attention, and then rest in the looking. If thoughts, ideas, or feelings arise, do not be distracted. Continue to rest in the looking.

Commentary: Compassion

A Tibetan master had three principal students who were important teachers themselves. One day, he asked an attendant what each of them was doing. The attendant replied that one of them was supervising the building of a temple.

"Good," said the master, "and what about the second?"

"He's teaching a group of students," was the reply.

"Good," said the master, "and what about the third?"

"I'm not sure what he's doing. He's sitting in the corner of his room, facing the wall with a cloth wrapped around his head, crying his eyes out," said the attendant.

The master turned in the direction the attendant indicated and put his hands together in a gesture of respect. "I pay homage to those who cultivate compassion," he said as he bowed deeply.

Compassion practice is difficult, and you will almost certainly shed tears in the process. Tears mean that you are taking the practice to heart. More than a few teachers have said that a compassion practice without tears is not much of a practice.

The principal blocking points in compassion meditations involve fear, and they manifest as control or helplessness. After the radiant warmth of loving kindness, the meditation on compassion delivers a painful shock. The graphic images of suffering in the six realms trigger your own powerful reactions to pain and suffering in others. When you see a person in pain, you feel an immediate impulse to do something about the pain. When the impulse to help comes from your own discomfort, you are reacting, not responding, to the pain of the person. You tend to override the needs or wishes of the person in pain, take control, and become something of a tyrant. If you are unable to do anything, you collapse into helplessness, withdraw from the situation physically or emotionally, and see yourself as a victim of the other person's misfortune and pain.

This practice doesn't allow any of those exits. As you imagine people you care about suffering greatly, you encounter directly the impulse to do something about their pain. Because the pain is imagined, you can do nothing, and you see how much of your urge to help comes from your own fear and discomfort. Because you engage in this practice from your own volition, the helpless-victim exit is also closed. You have no option but to remain in the presence of the pain and observe how you contract to get away from it.

Relaxing into the contraction is hard. Again and again, you will encounter raw fear. One of my teachers, when asked for a definition of compassion, replied, "Fearlessness." Many people misunderstand such a response to mean that you shouldn't feel any fear. That's very difficult, if not impossible. The aim of practice is not to eliminate fear but to stand in the fear—feel it yet not fall into confusion or reaction.

Fear causes the body to contract. As you notice the contraction and bring attention to it, the body begins to relax. Then you feel the impact of the suffering even more, and you contract again. As this process is repeated again and again, you move from a physical reaction to suffering to an emotional reaction. This is where the tears start to flow in earnest. You cry for the person you imagine in front of you. You cry for all the different kinds of pain that people experience. You cry because pain exists. In the middle of all this confusion, you notice that you are no longer contracted. Your heart is open, and you have no skin. Infinite sadness penetrates your whole being. While the sadness is painful beyond measure, you realize that you have somehow become one with it and one with the pain of the world. Through compassion, you have entered into presence and the mystery of being.

Many people think that they will harm a person if they imagine that person suffering. Such notions are a form of magical thinking, the tendency in a child to feel that whatever he or she thinks will really happen. These meditations have been done for centuries. No one has been harmed. Indeed, countless individuals have cultivated compassion using exactly this practice.

Once you have tasted compassion, extend it by working with different people and different situations. Many people try to extend their range of compassion (or the other immeasurables) too quickly. Session by session, work systematically at extending compassion to different groups of people and different situations. As you uncover areas that are frozen or locked, return to the three steps of observation, reorganization, and consistency, or go back, when necessary, to equanimity or loving-kindness. A moment's heartfelt compassion will change you more profoundly than a lifetime spent in feeling that you are compassionate.

Extend the practice of compassion to your daily life. Observe how you switch back and forth between controlling behavior and helplessness when someone else is in pain. Bring your attention to your reaction to the pain, note the fear and contraction, stand in the fear, relax into the contraction, and move, as in the formal practice, into presence.

The "ah" breath is a powerful and useful exercise to train you in compassion, the ability to be present with another person in pain. Have a friend lie down and sit so that his (or her) hand can rest lightly on yours. Observe your partner's breath. Let your breath follow his. Breathe in as he breathes in. Breathe out as he breathes out. After a few minutes, as you breathe out, say "Ah" gently, breathing the syllable out with each exhalation. At any point, your partner can indicate whether he is uncomfortable or wants to stop by squeezing or pressing on your hand. If he does, you gradually, over the course of a few breaths, let the "ah" fade into silence and just breathe with your partner.

This exercise is particularly helpful with ill or dying people who are having trouble letting go of their resistance. You can find fuller accounts in Stephen Levine's *Who Dies* and *Healing into Life and Death*.

The control-helplessness switch also arises in a common dynamic in many relationships: the persecutor-rescuer-victim triad. The pattern begins when Joan attacks Dave, berating or ignoring him, for instance. Joan is in the persecutor role, and Dave is in the victim role. When Joan sees that Dave is in pain, she may or may not apologize, but she does move into the rescuer role, taking control of the situation and trying to make Dave feel better. As Dave moves out of pain, his anger at Joan comes out, and Dave now attacks Joan. The roles are now reversed, with Dave in the persecutor role and Joan as the victim. Both Joan and Dave continue to spin through the roles, with Dave rescuing Joan, who then becomes angry with Dave and moves back into the persecutor role. Both people are unable to stay present with pain, either their own (which they take out on the other person by persecuting) or the other's (which they remove by rescuing).

You can end the cycle at any time by stepping out of all three roles, not persecuting, not rescuing, and not being a victim. To do so, however, you must touch the pain in the relationship, both the pain in you and the pain in the other. When the other person is in the persecutor role, stay out of the victim role: don't take the accusations or abusive comments personally. Know them to be an expression of pain. When the other is in the rescuer role, don't accept the help and don't move to the persecutor role by expressing your own anger and irritation about the relationship. Know that you are okay, just as you are, and that you don't need to be helped and you don't need to attack. When he or she moves into the victim role, don't do anything to reduce his or her pain. Know that you are not the cause of it and you cannot end it.

The term *idiot compassion* effectively captures another common pitfall—allowing boundaries to be violated because you cannot stay present in the face of another person's pain. Idiot compassion, because it subverts what is healthy, can have disastrous consequences, and not just in human beings. Observers of a troop of chimpanzees in Africa noted that an aging mother could not face the frustration of her most recent offspring when she started to wean him. The young chimp learned that he could continue to receive milk from his mother by breaking down her will with aggressive behavior. When she gave birth to her next baby, she tried again to wean the older chimp. He reacted aggressively, and she still gave in, but not as frequently as before because she had to care for the new baby as well. A week later the new baby mysteriously disappeared, and the observers suspected the older chimp had murdered it. The mother died soon after, and the remaining chimp was left on his own. Unable to take care of himself, he, too, soon died.

A father had difficulty disciplining his teenage son. The son was doing badly in school, staying up late, and getting into more and more trouble. The father came to a colleague of mine for advice. When she advised him to set clear limits, he replied that when he did, his son reacted strongly, one moment sobbing and crying about how he was no good and how he could never measure up, the next moment angry and belligerent and accusatory. He said, "I can't bear to see him suffering, so I don't do anything." My friend explained that, as a father, he had the responsibility of maintaining limits *and* staying present with his son in his pain.

Compassion especially applies in situations where no good solution exists. A mother learned that her twenty-year-old son was dealing to support his drug habit. All her attempts to help her son had failed. She had paid for rehabilitation treatments and had made herself available for family counseling, but the son had just moved to another town. She knew that he would likely be caught because he wasn't good at hiding his activities, and she was fully aware that drug dealing carried much heavier jail terms than possession. A friend advised her to arrange to have her son arrested for possession. An added irony was that her son was more likely to receive treatment for his drug problem in prison than outside.

What should she do? If she did nothing, her son would probably spend serious time in jail. If she arranged to have him arrested for possession, even if he got over his drug problem, he would likely never forgive her. The situation tormented her, and she couldn't decide what to do.

At one point, the mother said, "I'm just looking for a good solution." Her friend replied, "There are no good solutions here." The blunt statement of fact broke through her confusion, and the mother recognized that pain was present in every direction. As long as she tried to avoid pain, she could never decide what to do. Compassion, in this case, involved accepting pain—which included the pain of accepting the results of her decision. Once she saw that whatever she did, she and her son were both going to experience pain, she was able to decide what to do.

Meditation 4: Joy

At the beginning of each session of meditation, rest attention on the breath for fifteen to twenty minutes to establish a base of attention.

For the practice of joy, take a person with whom you feel competitive. Do not pick a child or someone significantly younger than you. Suitable people are your colleagues, co-workers, friends, and rivals.

OBSERVATION: REACTING TO HAPPINESS IN OTHERS

Seeing Another Person Happy

Imagine this person being happy with the happiness that comes from doing what he or she loves, doing it well, and succeeding in it.

Observing Reactions

Notice any tendencies you have for judgment, criticism, or any other reactions that prevent you from being present with his or her success and fulfillment. Do you idolize him? Are you unable to imagine rising to his level?

Do you worship her, taking her as your definition of life and feeling that, by knowing her, you are somehow a better or more worthwhile person?

Are you envious of her, jealous of her achievements, unable to comprehend how she accomplished so much while you are stuck where you are? You are sure that you are just as good as she is, but somehow she made it and you didn't.

Do you want to emulate her? Do you note what she likes and dislikes, how she behaves, and what she does? Do you adopt the same likes and dislikes and work hard at being her so that you can enjoy the same kind of success and fulfillment?

Do you want to rebel, be different from him, and go your own way to show everyone that you can make it on your own? Are you angry at his success? Do you feel that the world is unfair? Do you feel that, no matter how hard you try, you will never be as happy?

All these reactions serve the same function: they separate us from being with the other person in his or her happiness.

Seeing How Those Mechanisms Operate Inwardly

Observe how the same reactive patterns operate internally. Recall a time or circumstance in your life when everything was going well but you felt no joy or happiness. What prevents you from feeling happiness, joy, or fulfillment in your life? What patterns prevent you from pursuing what you want to do or what you know to be right or true? What patterns prevent you from knowing what you really want to do or knowing what is right or true?

For each of these questions, don't analyze your life or try to figure it out. Recall specific instances when, for instance, you knew what you wanted to do but didn't do it. When you were in college, you knew what you wanted to study but you took another course instead. Yes, your parents or a professor influenced you, but what in you didn't trust what you knew? What went passive inside? Do the same feelings steer you away from what you makes you feel awake and alive? *Feel* what stopped or stops you. Emotional logic is more important than rational logic. Follow the feelings, and let them speak to you. The feelings will lead you to the pattern imperatives and agendas more reliably than analysis or deduction. You will uncover a set of conditioned imperatives that describe what you should have achieved or should be achieving, what you should not have achieved or tried to achieve, what abilities and qualities you should have, and what abilities and qualities you should not have.

REORGANIZATION: BRINGING ATTENTION TO MECHANISMS THAT CREATE UNCERTAINTY

As you identify the internal representation of who and what you are "meant" to be, you will notice a critical and judgmental voice or feeling that lets you know when you are deviating from "the plan."

Mechanisms Are Based on Criticism

Bring attention to this critical voice, and observe your relationship to it. You feel passive and helpless, as if the learned values, the values this critical quality espouses, are absolute. Turn attention to the critical attitude. What is this critical attitude trying to gain? What drives it? What function does this critical attitude serve? Don't analyze. Hold the critical attitude and these questions in attention simultaneously.

Bringing Attention to the Critical Attitude

Whatever drives the critical attitude, whatever it serves, it has nothing to do with who and what you really are. See the critical attitude as a pattern. It is based on beliefs and does not embody an absolute set of values. You realize with some discomfort that you have accepted these values without question. Stay with the feeling of passivity and helplessness and any other feelings that arise.

At this point, one or more of the five element reaction chains will arise: hollowness, threat, loneliness, anxiety, or confusion. Use the methods from chapter 6 to hold these feelings in attention. In particular, feel the underlying fear—instability, engulfment, isolation, destruction, or being nothing, respectively—and hold it in attention, transforming the reaction into presence.

Exposing the Feeling of Not Being Enough

As attention penetrates the critical attitude, you feel more and more clearly how you are deficient, how you don't meet the harsh and unforgiving criteria you carry inside you. As long as you can criticize others, you don't have to pay attention to the feeling of not measuring up. You aren't actually deficient, but the feeling is powerful and deeply conditioned. The critical attitude has nothing to do with who and what you are. It was trained into you, and you have passively accepted it. No wonder you go through life feeling uncertain or lacking passion. You have been following a conditioned agenda that tells you that you are never enough.

Consistency: Maintaining Attention

Sense of Not Being Enough Becomes Empty

Bring attention to the feeling of deficiency or lack. Experience it completely. Consider the breath as a rope, and, holding on to the rope, lower yourself into the feeling of deficiency. At first the deficiency feels absolute, but gradually you will experience it as a feeling. Then it becomes an object of attention, not who or what you are.

Open to Being Present

At this point, you experience a shift in understanding. You understand that all the values associated with the criticism and deficiency are learned values. They are not absolutes. Paralyzing waves of fear often accompany this realization. Stay with them, and let them be. As the fear dissipates, the critical attitude falls apart. You are present. You know that you are not incomplete or lacking in any way.

The Freedom of Joy

You are released from the learned values. Everything opens up. You are free. You do not need to look to externals for validation of your being. The critical attitude and underlying feeling of deficiency are gone, and you are present in your life. You are free to be without apology to anyone or anything. What joy!

Taking Joy in the Other Person's Effort and Successes

Any tendency to criticize or undermine the happiness, success, or conviction of others now vanishes. Free in your own being, you are also free to celebrate and take joy in the happiness and success of others.

EXTENDING JOY TO ALL AREAS OF LIFE

Once you see through the fundamental sense of deficiency, you begin to find fulfillment in the very activities of life itself. By extending the practice of joy to other people, you uncover additional areas where a sense of deficiency is present in you. Dismantle them as you uncover them. You become more and more present in your life. As with the other immeasurables, start extending joy by turning attention to areas in which you feel critical or competitive with people with whom you have good relations. Extend your practice to people who trigger a harshly critical attitude in you. Finally, extend your practice to include the critical attitudes generated by your family and culture.

CONCLUSION: JOY AT THE LEVEL OF AWARENESS

At the end of each session, let go of all the images and feelings you have been working with. Rest in the joy and presence you have uncovered with your mind open and clear. Then turn attention to the experience of joy. What is it? Where is it? Where does it come from? Do not try to reason, analyze, or think about these questions. Use the questions to direct the attention. Just rest, looking at the experience of joy itself.

Commentary: Joy

Just as loving-kindness and anger cannot coexist, neither can jealousy and joy.

In his great poetic work *Entering the Way of Awakening* (Sanskrit: Bodhicharyavatara), Shantideva, an Indian master of the eighth century, captures both the way jealousy kills joy and the absurdity of jealousy:

> *When others take delight*
> *In giving praise to those endowed with talents,*
> *Why, O mind, do you not find*
> *A joy, likewise, in praising them?*

and

> *"But they're the ones who'll have the happiness," you say.*
> *If this then is a joy you would resent,*
> *Abandon paying wages and returning favors:*
> *You will be the loser—both in this life and the next!*

> *When praise is heaped upon your merits,*
> *You're keen that others should rejoice in them.*
> *But when the compliment is paid to others,*
> *Your joy is oh so slow and grudging.*

By observing your reactions to the success or happiness of others, you can learn about the expectations you have about who and what you *should* be. We *should* be successful, and we feel a pang of envy when we hear of a person's success in any field. When the other's success is in an area that we are working in, the envy hits even closer to home, saying, in effect, "That's how I should be."

One of my students, a journalist, said that she just couldn't connect with this meditation. She couldn't find any area of her life where she felt jealousy or competition. I asked her how she would feel if she completed a good story and, in the editorial meeting, her colleague at the next desk was given three column inches for her piece while she received only two. "Yes," she said, "I might feel something then, and it wouldn't be joy."

A harshly critical attitude lurks beneath jealousy. It is triggered when another person's success or happiness stirs up a feeling of not being enough in you. The critical attitude is actually directed at you, but to avoid the stabbing pain of self-criticism, you redirect it to others. You may even take a perverse, somewhat sadistic, pleasure in diminishing their accomplishments.

The critical attitude is based on internalized expectations about who and what you should be. It often takes the form of a voice, telling you what you should or shouldn't be doing. The voice is not always consistent, yet it still stops you from doing what you know to be true and right. Your relationship with that voice is basically passive. Why? Because that critical attitude was trained into you.

For many people, the critical attitude is so much a part of their worldview and view of themselves that they are unable to identify it. Recall a situation that worked out very badly, and replay it in attention. When did things go wrong? When did you first suspect things were going wrong? What prevented you from taking a different course of action at that point? Little by little, you will tease out instances when something told you, "This is what you are meant to do," and you obeyed even though another part of you said, "This is not right, and you know it."

The meditation on joy brings into question everything that was trained into you by any system, including your family, education, profession, and culture. You feel that your way of life, your values, your beliefs, and your sense of purpose in life are being threatened. They are. The fierce resistance you encounter in seeing the values and beliefs as patterns and not absolutes indicates how thoroughly various systems have instilled their values and beliefs in you.

A system uses shame and the withdrawal of attention to instill a fear of not surviving. It also presents the view that power resides in the system, not in you. The combination trains you to be dependent on the system for survival. As the system is internalized and you identify with it, you adopt the system's view of who and what you are. We see this tendency very clearly in the professions—"I'm a doctor, so I do *x, y,* and *z,*" or "I'm an attorney, so I do *x, y,* and *z.*"

> Take a trivial task, such as arranging toothpicks in a straight line. Have a partner take the role of the critical attitude. Your partner tells you what you are doing wrong, how the toothpicks should be arranged, what doesn't match, what is out of line, and so forth. Your partner's criticisms don't have to be consistent or logical. Whatever your partner says, you try to comply, rearranging the toothpicks, replacing one with another, adjusting the alignment, and so on. Observe how you feel and what goes on inside you. Two or three minutes is usually enough. Reverse roles so that both of you have the experiences of being the critical attitude and of obeying it.
>
> Do the exercise again. This time, arrange the toothpicks any way you want to, regardless of what the critical attitude tells you. Is it difficult to do what you want in the face of your partner's demands? Why? What happens in you? What happens to your partner when you don't do what he or she says? Reverse roles so that you can experience the other side.

Many people feel a distinct lack of joy in the middle of their lives as they realize that they have followed the dictates of the critical attitude and have not trusted what they knew and felt from their direct experience.

One student, a stockbroker, was surprised at how hollow he felt when he achieved a record level of sales. Despite an award and a handsome bonus, he realized that what he had always been told and had come to believe—"Do this and you will be happy"—was just not true.

When you question the critical attitude, you will discover a similar feeling of hollowness or uncertainty. The open space triggers one or more of the five element reaction chains. Use what you have learned from the five dakinis practice to take the reaction chain apart.

After the elemental reaction, you hit a deadness inside. This deadness is the passivity you feel with respect to the critical attitude that was trained into you. When it was trained into you, something in you gave up. You couldn't meet the excessive and inconsistent demands of the system. You weren't enough. Losing your relationship with power, you lost your vitality and passion in being.

Bring your attention to the feeling of not being enough. As with the other immeasurables, at some point it breaks up and you see the learned values for what they are, learned values and not absolutes. You feel free and alive; in the words of one student, "Like running in an open meadow with birds and butterflies joyfully dancing in the sky, light and summery, and the breeze like a spring bouquet."

Commentary: The Four Immeasurables

THE THREE MINDS

In the chapter on karma, I talked about the three minds: the mind of the body, the mind of emotion, and the mind of awareness. The meditation practices of the four immeasurables are directed primarily at the level of emotion. Because the mind of emotion is at a higher energy level than that of the mind of the body, these practices naturally manifest in the mind of the body. The higher level of energy in the four immeasurables frees the body from chronic tensions and distortions imposed by emotional patterns. For instance, the next time you attend a social function, notice how quickly you judge people. Which people do you try to avoid? Which groups do you try to join? Take a moment and observe what is going on in your body. Is it tense around those you are trying to avoid? Does it also become tense when you are trying to join a group? When does it relax? When you observe carefully, you will see that your body relaxes when you are no longer judging. Usually, you only stop judging when you are with the "right" group of people. Now suppose that you could let go of judgment completely and experience all the people at the gathering for who they are, without prejudice. Would you be more or less relaxed, physically? That is how equanimity manifests in the mind of the body.

How do the immeasurables arise in each of the three minds?

Equanimity counteracts judgment or prejudice. In the mind of the body, judgment arises as the physical reaction to sensory experience. In the mind of emotion, it arises as prejudice. In the mind of awareness, it arises as disturbance. For example, your phone rings and the person at the other end asks for you by name but stumbles over it. Your body reacts to the sensory impression, tensing up. Emotionally, you are already prejudiced. You sense that something isn't right. The next words from the caller are, "Would you like a vacation for two . . ."

and you realize that this is another telemarketer and that your prejudices are confirmed. Yet the next words could have been, "I need some advice, and so and so (a good friend of yours) said you would be a good person to talk to."

As the emotional patterns of prejudice are undermined, you relax physically and are less reactive to pleasant (positive) or unpleasant (negative) physical sensations. Whether the other person is a telemarketer or a person seeking advice, you respond appropriately, releasing emotions as they come instead of letting them determine your reaction. At the awareness level, no matter what arises in experience, you rest in composure, free from disturbance or confusion.

Loving-kindness counteracts shutting down to what arises in experience. Shutting down takes place in all three minds. In the mind of the body, we shut down by collapsing down to what arises, whether it is a kind word from a friend or a foul smell in the kitchen. In the mind of emotion, we shut down by collapsing down to the other so that the other becomes our whole world. In the mind of awareness, we shut down by selecting one aspect of experience and rejecting others. Look at a tree. Next, look at one leaf. What happened to the tree? When we look at one leaf, we stop seeing the whole tree, but if we look at the tree, we see every leaf.

Loving-kindness dismantles the reactive patterns associated with shutting down. Instead, we open to all that we experience. The foul smell in the kitchen doesn't stop us from noticing the sunlight streaming through the window. The open warmth we feel for all people means that we treat everyone with respect, courtesy, and consideration.

Compassion counteracts fear of pain and discomfort. In the mind of the body, fear of discomfort arises as physical longing. When we feel hungry, we want food. When we are physically threatened, we long for safety and security. In the mind of emotion, we contract from pain and discomfort. In the mind of awareness, reaction arises as attempts to control. When you pass a homeless person in the street, observe what happens inside you. Instinctively, you are afraid that you might end up in the same situation, so you turn away or give the person a trifling amount of change and quickly move on. You feel

> One can only face in others what one can face in oneself.
>
> —*James Baldwin*

angry at a social system that reduces people to such straits or angry at the city council for allowing homeless people to impinge on you, angry that you can't control everything in your world.

In the mind of the body, compassion manifests as the ability to experience the wants and the longings of the body but not be ruled by them. In the mind of emotion, compassion is the ability to stand in our fear and be present with another's suffering. At the level of awareness, compassion dismantles our need to control; we are free to attend to what needs attending and to let go of what cannot be done.

Joy dismantles the pattern of grasping at experience to validate our sense of who we are. In the mind of the body, grasping arises as a physical reaction for self-preservation. In the mind of emotion, it arises as envy that drives a need for validation through achievement. In the mind of awareness, it is a sense of internal lack that causes us to look externally for validation or meaning. In a competitive environment, you look for a position that gives you an advantage over others. You are intent on winning to show everyone who you are. You feel that winning somehow validates your existence. With joy, however, we are free from the need for external validation and can pour our energies into the activity of life itself.

DECAY IN THE FOUR IMMEASURABLES

Two dynamics undermine the practice of the four immeasurables: decay and corruption. Just as moss, fungi, and moisture break down a fallen tree, habituated patterns consume attention, causing the immeasurables to decay into reactive emotions.

Sooner or later, your practice of the four immeasurables shows up in your life. What a relief to be able to accept the ups and downs of the day without judging or reacting to them! How much more open you are, even to people you have difficulty with, when you genuinely feel the warmth of loving-kindness. A friend comes to you with a painful personal problem, and you can just be with her, neither telling her what to do nor shrinking away from her pain and unhappiness. Now that you have shed some of the conditioned values, you are clearer about what is important to you and can really celebrate the successes of others.

How much you have changed! You are convinced that the old ways are gone forever, and you pat yourself on the back, congratulating yourself on your achievement.

Then you notice that, instead of being equanimous, you are a bit more distant from people than you were before. You aren't reacting the way you used to. In fact, you're not only not reacting; you aren't even responding. You are disengaged, detached, and distant. Nothing touches you. You are above reaction, but the vital awake quality of equanimity has gone. What happened? Equanimity decayed into detachment. Your work in equanimity was effective. It put you more in touch with the world, and being more in touch with the world triggered a pattern of detachment.

Detachment is a form of shutting down. To remedy the decay of equanimity, use loving-kindness to take apart the pattern of shutting down.

Loving-kindness decays into a cloying possessiveness. You regard the other person as an object that exists for your own pleasure. You react strongly when he or she is in pain, resenting the intrusion into your idealized world of peace and love.

Compassion remedies the decay of loving-kindness. By bringing attention to the pain and suffering of the other person, you again see the person as he or she is, not as an object in your world. Compassion uncovers in you the ability to stay present in the face of the other's pain.

Compassion, too, decays. It decays into despair. Compassion puts you in touch with the pain of the world, but you see that you can only do so much. The feeling of not doing enough, of not being enough, in the face of pain triggers despair. In extreme cases, it causes depression.

Joy is the remedy for despair. Through joy, you see that part of the reason for despair is the set of expectations you have about who and what you are meant to be and what you should be able to do. These expectations are seen as absolutes, and you try to ignore the realities of present circumstances. How often have you said, "I should be able to do more"? Joy frees you from conditioned expectations so that you are once again present and know what can be done and how to do it.

According to the Tibetan tradition, Avalokiteshvara, the bodhisattva of awakened compassion, received the awakening being vow from Buddha Amitabha. Avalokiteshvara vowed that he would work for the benefit of beings without limit, and, to convey the depth of his aspiration, he resolved that should he ever succumb to despair his head would burst into a thousand pieces.

For time beyond reckoning, Avalokiteshvara worked to free beings from the cycle of existence. He worked for eons and eons and finally took a break to see how he was doing. To his dismay, he saw more beings suffering in cyclic existence than when he had begun. "What's the point," he groaned, and his head burst into a thousand pieces.

Buddha Amitabha appeared before him and reminded him of his vow. Avalokiteshvara resolved to work again to help beings but this time without any expectation or idea of accomplishing anything. Through the power of Amitabha's inspiration, the thousand pieces of Avalokiteshvara's head became a thousand arms, each with an eye in the palm.

To formulate a new vow of awakening mind, Avalokiteshvara looked over the world of beings and saw three things: beings were suffering from poverty, reactive emotions had grown stronger, and beings needed help fast. Now truly present, Avalokiteshvara experienced the suffering of the world for what it was. Direct awareness took the form of a syllable in his heart, a blue-black *hung,* the syllable of pristine awareness. The syllable *hung* transformed into the Fast Acting Protector, the six-armed form of Mahakala, the embodiment of the wrathful energy of compassion. The Protector represents how the clarity of compassion, free from subject-object dualism, cuts through all confusion and works for the welfare of all.

One way to interpret this story is that compassion becomes true compassion only when you go through despair. Concerns and ideas about what you should be, who you should be, and what you should do all drop away. You just do what is before you, and you do it directly.

Finally, joy decays into elation. You are so full of energy and ability that you forget where you are and who you are. Recall the story of Icarus from Greek mythology. Icarus's father fashioned wings from feathers and wax. Icarus was so elated with his ability to fly that he decided to fly to the sun, despite warnings from his father. The heat from the sun melted the wax, the wings fell apart, and Icarus plunged into the sea.

Equanimity remedies the decay of joy into elation. Equanimity brings attention to the tendency to react to whatever arises in experience—and in the case of joy, what arises is elation in your newly found freedom and power. With equanimity, you remain present in what is happening and are not carried away by your own elation.

The following diagram, adapted from Herbert Guenther's comments in *Kindly Bent to Ease Us,* shows how the immeasurables interact with one another to remedy decay.

REMEDYING DECAY IN THE FOUR IMMEASURABLES

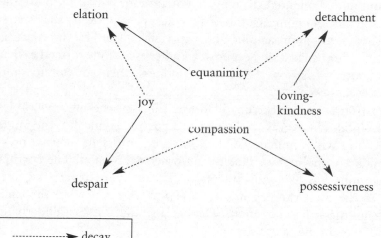

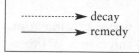

CORRUPTION IN THE FOUR IMMEASURABLES

Corruption is the work of patterns that distort the experience and expression of the immeasurables even before you begin to uncover them. In the practice of the immeasurables, you will usually have the greatest difficulty with the immeasurable that is closest to your patterned way of functioning. People who are detached and distant have difficulty with equanimity because they don't know the difference between manipulating people and connecting with them. Highly competitive individuals, on the other hand, have difficulty with joy. They are used to feeling a sense of power and ability but are unable to bring attention to how those abilities are in the service of conditioned expectations about who they are meant to be and what they are meant to achieve. Loving-kindness is difficult for people with addictive tendencies, and compassion is difficult for people who compulsively take care of others.

In other words, we hide in what is familiar. The operation of patterns prevents us from penetrating to the heart of one or more of the immeasurables. Worse, the patterns now use the practice to justify their operation. Whereas decay comes from lack of sustained attention, corruption comes from patterns that are already in place.

Never compromise with corruption. It has to be systematically rooted out and eliminated. To remove corruption, you have to use the practice of the four immeasurables to take apart patterns that shape the basic way you approach life and experience. The best approach is found in the sequence based on power and presence mentioned earlier in this chapter—first joy, then loving-kindness, then equanimity, and finally compassion.

The patterns of the corrupt manifestations of the immeasurables have two modes of expression: active and passive. Typically, one mode of expression will dominate. When, however, sufficient internal pressure builds up, the pattern flips to the other expression. The corrupt manifestations are like railway tracks. The active expression corresponds to the train running in one direction, the passive to the train running in the other direction. The tracks, that is, the underlying dynamic, remain the same.

The underlying dynamic of corrupt equanimity is manipulation. In its active expression, it manifests as the overt manipulation of others. You keep people at a distance, withholding information or using hidden powers and resources. Prospero, in Shakespeare's *The Tempest,* is the archetypal manipulator, using his sorcery to bring his enemies to him and place them under his power. You keep people guessing about what you are up to; you keep them off balance and never form close relationships. You spend a lot of time in your head, strategizing and speculating about this and that, and you rarely touch the fabric of life.

In its passive expression, manipulation manifests as a seeming innocence. You maintain a facade of naïveté, but you know how to get what you want. When anyone challenges you, you say, "I don't know what you're talking about—I was lucky," or "Isn't it wonderful how things work out just the way you want them to?"

To remedy corrupt equanimity, work at loving-kindness practice. When you open to how other people have touched your life, the warmth of memories of kindness dispels the cold detachment of the manipulator. The patterns that see others as mere objects can't hold, and you move into true equanimity: understanding what makes others do what they do without disconnecting or distancing from them.

Corrupt loving-kindness is envelopment. In its active form, it manifests as addiction. You see no reason to put any limit on your pursuit of pleasure and wind up being enslaved by the very things you would envelop. You become addicted to affection, to emotional intensity, to work, to rage, to entertainment, food, chemicals, or sex. Loving-kindness is about opening to the world. In its corrupt form, you are so open that you are lost in sensory and emotional experience. You can't tell what is yours and what isn't, so you have no boundaries.

In its passive form, envelopment manifests as impotence. Over-whelmed by input, you shut down and close out the world. Nothing brings any pleasure. You have no energy. You can't do anything. Initially, your impotence attracts the care and attention of others. You take and take, never giving anything back. They feel that they are pouring energy into a black hole or are being enveloped by you and your problems, so they withdraw, and your belief in your own impotence is confirmed.

Use joy to undo corrupt loving-kindness. Joy brings a sense of power. You set boundaries, externally and internally. Envelopment is based on a feeling of lack and leads you to take over everything you can in order to fill the hole inside you. In the joy meditation, you see the feeling of lack for what it is—a feeling, a belief perhaps, but not an absolute that defines who and what you are. You can then move into true loving-kindness, the radiant warmth that opens to the world but doesn't seek to take it over.

Corrupt compassion is control. In its active expression, control manifests as tyranny. You fear the worst and you can't let it happen, so you seize control no matter what the cost. You become oblivious to the fear that drives you. Convinced that your actions are justified because you have everyone's welfare in mind, you ride roughshod over people. You become a tyrant, a dictator. For you, the end justifies the means, and anybody who questions your intention or your methods becomes an enemy to be destroyed.

In its passive expression, control manifests as helplessness. Overwhelmed by fear, you don't know what to do. You can't think straight, and everything is confusing. You abdicate responsibility and let other people decide what should be done. Inevitably, somebody usurps your authority, confirming your view that you are helpless, weak, and ineffectual. Angrily, you assert yourself with extreme and unpredictable actions.

To remedy corrupt compassion, use equanimity practice. Fear is the driving force behind control. You are ruled by fear, which distorts your perception of things. Through equanimity, you develop composure, an internal calm that allows you to see into the working of things, to understand the situation, and to know what can or cannot be done.

When you see things clearly, fear doesn't take you over. You move into true compassion: you accept things as they are, do what is possible, and let go of the rest.

Corrupt joy is domination. In its active expression, domination manifests as sadism, the perverted joy that comes from imposing your power on another. You are giddy with power. You are very capable of acting, of getting things done, and of cutting through obstacles. You give no thought to the effects of your actions on others, or, if you do, you derive pleasure from seeing how your power causes pain in others. For you, the exercise of power over another is what gives your life meaning.

The passive expression is masochism. You feel so powerless that the only way you can connect with others is to let them do to you whatever they want. You are powerless. You want to be dominated so that you can feel powerless. You seek out situations and relationships that confirm your view of yourself.

To remedy corrupt joy, use compassion practice. Compassion requires that you open to the pain of the other. It puts you directly in touch with the consequences of your actions. If you can, you act in a way that doesn't cause pain. If you have to cut through obstacles, you do so in such a way as to cause the least amount of pain. Now you can move into true joy: you are present in the vitality of being, effective in action, but doing only what is appropriate, nothing more and nothing less.

I only ever cared about the man. I never gave a fig for the ideologies, unless they were mad or evil. I never saw institutions as being worthy of their parts, or policies as much other than excuses for not feeling. I believe that almost any political system operated with humanity can work. And the most benign of systems without humanity is vile. The trick I suppose is to find the system that gives the least leeway to the rogues. The guarantee of our virtue is our compassion. And if you allow this institution, or any other, to steal your compassion away, wait and see what you become. The man is everything. And if your calling is anything, you will always prefer him to the collective because the collective is humanity's lowest and the collective is most often spoken for by people who are nothing without it.

—John le Carré
(on the British Secret Service)

SHREDDING PATTERN-BASED EXISTENCE

Ostensibly, practicing the four immeasurables cultivates what are generally regarded as wholesome, virtuous, and admirable qualities: equanimity, loving-kindness, compassion, and joy. In reality, they tear up pattern-based existence, shredding patterns at every level, whether they are derived from early childhood struggles to survive, from adolescent strivings for a place in the world, from adult styles of interaction to solidify an identity and worldview, or from spiritual longings for transcendence and peace. The chart below relates the immeasurables to behaviors at different stages of life.

IMMEASURABLES AND BEHAVIORS

IMMEASURABLE	CHILD SURVIVAL	ADOLESCENT COMPETENCE	ADULT INTERACTION	SPIRITUAL LONGINGS
equanimity	ignoring	gain/loss	manipulate	permanence
loving-kindness	attachment to self-image	happiness/ unhappiness	envelop	bliss
compassion	self-centeredness	respect/ disdain	control	universal selfhood
joy	ownership	fame/ obscurity	dominate	purity

Childhood Struggles to Survive

In early childhood, all a child needs to be present is a level of trust in the world around him or her. Sooner or later, the child's trust is betrayed. Whatever the child's parents do, the child will, at some point, experience the parents as absent, needy, controlling, or abusive and feel that his or her survival is threatened. The struggle to survive becomes the core of a sense of self, and the associated pattern may well run for the rest of the child's life.

When, in the practice of the immeasurables, you run into a level of resistance in which you feel your survival is at stake, you are likely running into material that formed very early in your life. Emotions are so raw and powerful that you can't give words to them, and you feel that you will die if you let them in. Don't try to open them up quickly. Instead, rest in attention, opening to them as much as you can while still holding attention. Let attention open them gradually, as the warmth of the sun opens a flower.

Four emotional reactions are associated with the formation of a sense of self, whether in early childhood or later in life: ignoring, attachment, self-centeredness, and ownership. When these reactions come up, you are likely tapping into reactions that first arose as your sense of self was forming.

Recall the analogy of erosion in chapter 5. A sense of self begins to form when the flow of movement and response is interrupted. The open space of no response is perceived as threatening, and we react by ignoring it. A feedback loop forms immediately: when I ignore, the flow of movement and response is interrupted and I experience the open space of no response. I move to ignore it and again interrupt the flow. A sense of self is quickly set in place. The three poisons, attraction, aversion, and indifference, now start to screen experience for what supports, threatens, or is neutral to the sense of self.

The sense of self becomes a home of a sort. Behaviors (including ways of interpreting experience) you use to ignore or overcome the open space of no response are linked to the sense of who and what you are. The sense of self gives you a way to hold on to a sense of existence even when there is no response from the environment. As you identify with the sense of self, you perceive it as essential to your survival. Attachment has more to do with dependency than with desire or liking. You are attached to the sense of self because you feel your survival depends on it. In later life, you continue to hold on to it even though you may not like what you feel you are.

Increasingly, everything in your experience is organized around the sense of self. It becomes the center of your world. Everything and everyone is seen in terms of how they serve your sense of self. People are things to support and confirm who you think you are.

Faced with a world of experience, the self feels powerless, so it starts to appropriate values, beliefs, and ways of doing things, defining itself more and more explicitly in terms of these attributes. The self develops a sense of ownership.

The four immeasurables undermine all four of these primitive emotional reactions. Through equanimity, you discover the possibility of not reacting and thus not turning away from open space. Loving-kindness teaches you how to open, and you then discover that you don't have to be dependent on a sense of self to be present. Compassion puts an end to the illusion that the world revolves around you. Joy frees you from feelings of powerlessness and passivity.

Adolescent Strivings for a Place in the World

How do you remember your teenage years—as a time of peace and order or as a period of confusion and uncertainty? In adolescence, the big issue is competence. As you learn new skills and explore new ways of interacting with others, a whole new world of possibilities opens. Because the earlier sense of self doesn't know how to function in this new world, you run into the classical identity crisis of adolescence. You pour energy into forging a more solid identity, and you rely on social measures to gauge your worth and competence. Concerns about success and failure form in adolescence, but the patterns that develop may run for the rest of your life. How many business executives are driven by the need to prove themselves competent in the eyes of a father or a brother? How many teachers teach their students what they have never learned themselves?

In the meditations on death and change, you saw how death cuts through the eight worldly concerns: gain and loss, happiness and unhappiness, fame and obscurity, and respect and disdain. The four immeasurables dismantle these obsessions in a different way.

Money is now the primary measure of gain and loss. Money was originally invented as a way of exchanging energy. Most people now take money as an absolute, as a measure of competence as well as a measure of worth. In effect, money has become a collective enchantment, distorting everyone's view of what is and is not important. Equanimity breaks the spell. You see people as they are rather than in terms of what they have gained or lost. You see that all people are the same, wanting to be happy and wanting not to suffer, regardless of how rich or poor they may be.

Happiness and unhappiness are subjective feelings. The "I" is happy when it feels that the world supports it, so its focus is always on what is outside. In loving-kindness, you experience warmth and connection with everything that arises in experience. Instead of looking outside for happiness, you radiate warmth into the world.

Similarly, the need for respect from others arises from the early pattern of self-centeredness. In teenage gangs, respect is everything.

How you appear to others and how they relate to you are topmost in your mind. The question "Will they respect me?" haunts you. Compassion cuts right through this self-concern. You connect directly with what is happening. You are there to address the pain and difficulty in the situation. What others think of your actions is beside the point.

In seeking or accepting fame, you take on the identity that others project onto you. You have to cooperate with the forces that propel you to fame, and in the process you sell your soul for the recognition you need. With joy, you cut through the need for recognition. Gone are the values, beliefs, and behaviors that were trained into you, the training that determines who you should be in the eyes of others. You know who and what you are. You are present, and you turn your attention to what needs to be done, not what it will do for your reputation. At a press conference, a journalist asked Archibald Cox why he accepted the job of investigating the Watergate scandal. He replied, "I thought I could do something for my country, and if it didn't work out—then what the hell? I did what I could."

Adult Styles of Interaction to Solidify an Identity and Worldview

In adulthood, patterns continue to crystallize into an increasing investment and belief in the projected world. Maintaining the "I," your notion of who and what you are, is your primary concern. You rely on four ways of interacting with the world: manipulation, envelopment, control, and domination. You rarely experience real connection or presence. You go through the motions of life. Inside, if you ever go inside, you feel separate from what you experience. You know that what you present to the world is a shell, a facade. Life has lost its meaning and its vitality, and you don't know how to recover it.

In the discussion of corruption, you learned how to use the four immeasurables to dismantle these four corrupt ways of interacting with experience. Now, when these patterns fall apart, totally different qualities arise: creativity, inclusion, service, and the ability to stand up.

In equanimity, no manipulation is present. The insight implicitly present in manipulation now becomes a source of creativity. Because you are in touch with people's basic desire to be happy and not to suffer, you appreciate their humanity and are less judgmental of their foibles and mistakes. You connect with others by understanding them.

In loving-kindness, you don't envelop others. The openness implicit in envelopment allows what is good to come together, so you and others around you experience prosperity. Openness and warmth naturally take expression in courtesy and consideration. You connect with others by including them.

In compassion, you let go of control. You do what you can to foster presence, and then you give things a chance to take their natural course. When things take their natural course, everyone benefits.

An attorney was working to reclaim millions of dollars in a trust account that had been mishandled. The accountant in charge of the trust had funneled the funds to a friend, who had basically spent the money on himself. To recover the money, the attorney needed information from the accountant. The attorney met with the accountant and his lawyer. Instead of making demands or threats, he said, "You know what you've done. You know that your firm will be paying for your mistake for the next ten years. You know that there is a substantial amount of money still to be recovered. You know that I need your help to recover it and that I can really do nothing to force your cooperation. The only question is how you want to look back on this matter ten years from now. You can either do nothing to remedy the wrong you did, or you can help me recover what remains of the money. I'm going to leave the room. You decide. I'll come back in fifteen minutes." He let go of control, and the accountant gave him more help than he expected.

From this example, you can see that the result of compassion, of moving into presence and letting things take their natural course, is justice. You must be willing to serve what is true and accept the results. So, in compassion, you connect with people by serving them.

Finally, joy uncovers an internal stability that does not depend on external validation. You can do what is correct, but not in a trivial moral sense; you do what is appropriate and true for the situation. Through joy, you know what to do, and you do it. You connect with people by standing up for them.

At the adult level, then, the four immeasurables give rise to four qualities connected with leadership, four social values, and four ways of connecting with others, as summarized in the following chart:

QUALITIES ARISING FROM THE FOUR IMMEASURABLES

IMMEASURABLE	LEADERSHIP	SOCIAL VALUE	CONNECTION
equanimity	creativity	humanity	understand
loving-kindness	success	courtesy	include
compassion	benefit	justice	serve
joy	correctness	knowledge	stand up for

Spiritual Longings

How do patterns manifest in spiritual practice? At the spiritual level, patterns degrade attention by diverting energy into idealized spiritual longings for permanence, bliss, universal selfhood, and purity.

The promise of eternal life has drawn people to spiritual practice for centuries. You long for permanence only when you are afraid of dying. You are obsessed by the thought of dying and are determined to transcend death. In equanimity, you see that all experience, even the experience of life, has the same nature—arising and subsiding. You meet death with composure because you understand that life, too, is the same as all other experience: it arises at birth and subsides at death.

The promise of bliss also draws people to spiritual practice. You long for bliss because you want don't want to deal with the nitty-gritty aspects of life. You are looking for something special, something that takes you away from the ordinariness of life. You are looking for the perfect high. You are obsessed with experience and want your experience to be the best, the highest, and the most meaningful. You regard everything else in life as drab and lifeless by comparison. In loving-kindness, you discover the possibility of openness without limit. From equanimity, you know that your life is exactly what you experience, neither more nor less. Through loving-kindness, you stop trying to escape your life. You open to whatever your life brings you, whether it be pleasant, unpleasant, or neutral. You savor it because you know, from both equanimity and the contemplations on death and impermanence, that whatever you are experiencing right now will pass.

The third spiritual longing is for universal selfhood. This longing arises as an attempt to transcend the pain of attachment to a limited sense of "I." You are obsessed with yourself. You want to be the most embracing, the most caring, the most powerful, and the most understanding. You will free everyone from pain. When you merge with the cosmic self, you will have all those qualities, and, best of all, you will escape the pain and tribulations associated with being plain old you. Unfortunately, there is no cosmic self to merge with, any more than there is an individual self to transcend. Experience is all there is. Through compassion, you discover the possibility of being present with pain. Compassion cuts through the suffering, which is the emotional reaction to pain, and brings you in touch with what is. Pain is part of life, just as much as pleasure is. Compassion frees you from the confusion of suffering and from the urge to control what arises in experience. Through compassion, you are able to be present with what arises in experience.

The fourth spiritual longing is for purity. You are obsessed with the dirt and grime of life, and you want to be free of it completely. You can't be clean enough. You eat pure food, you live a pure life, but the dirt and the grime keep sneaking in. Every speck of dust, whether on your table or in your personality, is an affront. You become increasingly aggressive in your pursuit of purity, taking harsher and harsher measures to keep the dirt away from you. Joy cuts through all that. Through joy, you discover the vitality of life itself, with all its dirt and grime. You pour your energy into the activities of your life, free from concerns for external validation and artificial conceptions of pure and impure.

Chatrul Rinpoche is a Tibetan teacher who lives a few miles outside Darjeeling, India. Whenever people come to see him, he serves them tea and pastries. A Westerner came to see him, apparently to confirm his spiritual realization. He told Chatrul Rinpoche how he consistently experienced being one with everything that exists. When the tea and pastries were set before him, he declined, saying that he observed a very pure diet and he didn't eat that kind of food anymore. He then returned to his lengthy description of his experiences. Chatrul Rinpoche listened quietly. When the visitor had finished, Chatrul Rinpoche still said nothing, and eventually the visitor stood up to leave. "If you are one with everything that exists," asked Chatrul Rinpoche, "why didn't you have the tea and pastries?"

TRANSFORMATION

Your life has been torn apart. What now? At the same time that the immeasurables are shredding the patterns that run your life, they are transforming locked-up energy into attention. Recall a situation that made you very angry—your vacation reservations didn't hold, you are in a strange city with no place to stay, and your travel agent says she isn't responsible. Let the anger grow. Let it grow until it is vivid, alive, and consuming, until you feel rage coursing all through your body. Then say to yourself, "I'm angry—and I'm glad!"

What happens?

Your anger vanishes in a flash. You are open and present. Your whole view of the situation shifts in a moment. You see the whole situation, but you are no longer identified with the anger. You see it as if it were a reflection in a mirror. You may even laugh at it. Congratulations! You've just transformed anger into mirrorlike pristine awareness by opening to it with loving-kindness.

All the energy locked up in the anger is freed and powers your attention. You see the situation differently. In particular, you see your anger for what it really is, a reaction that limits you unnecessarily. You laugh because you see its absurdity.

The example illustrates how transformation works. Transformation is a spontaneous process that takes place when attention at a higher level of energy is brought to bear on a reactive process at a lower level of energy. The reactive process can't hold, and the energy in the reactive process is transformed to a higher level, roughly halfway between the level of energy in the attention and the level of energy in the reaction. The transformation process can be depicted as follows:

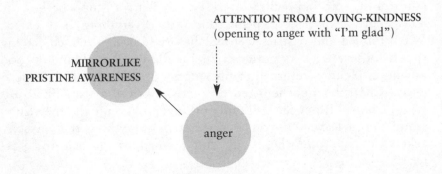

ATTENTION FROM LOVING-KINDNESS
(opening to anger with "I'm glad")

MIRRORLIKE
PRISTINE AWARENESS

anger

Transformation is closely related to the three steps of observation, reorganization, and consistency that you used in the practice of the four immeasurables. Observation begins when you bring attention to the reactive process—in this case, anger. Observation leads to forming a higher level of attention that is not limited to the projected world of the reactive process and can envision other courses of action. When this new level of attention is sufficiently stable, you can act on it—and in a way that was not previously possible. This stage in the transformation process is reorganization. In the example, the reorganization takes place when you say, "I'm angry—and I'm glad." The statement takes you out of the world projected by anger. Now, the energy that ordinarily flowed into the anger is freed: the habituation has been cut. Consistency consists of cutting the habituation again and again until the pattern falls apart. In the example, you keep cutting into anger until the level of energy in your attention is such that, whenever anger arises, it is spontaneously transformed into mirrorlike pristine awareness.

Each of the immeasurables transforms a reactive emotion into a corresponding aspect of pristine awareness. Recall the example of the transformation of anger at the beginning of this section.

When aversion arises in the presence of loving-kindness, the subject-object division on which aversion rests is disrupted by the experience of opening characteristic of loving-kindness. The energy of aversion now arises as *mirrorlike pristine awareness:* what was previously taken as an object that existed in its own right now arises like a reflection in a mirror—an appearance dependent on conditions and empty of any existence separate from those conditions.

When attraction arises in the presence of compassion, the sense of possessing the object of attraction is disrupted by the sensitivity to the other person's feelings. The energy of attraction now arises as *distinguishing pristine awareness:* what previously elicited attraction is now clearly distinguished.

When envy arises in the presence of joy, the critical attitude of envy is disrupted because in joy there is no sense of being deficient. The energy of envy now arises as *effective pristine awareness:* when you are not concerned with who receives the credit, the job simply gets done.

When pride arises in the presence of equanimity, the sense of specialness is disrupted. The energy of pride now arises as *sameness pristine awareness:* all experience is the same in that it is just experience.

Whenever you are confused or feel that you have lost your way in your practice, use the transformation diagram above and ask these questions:

- What is being transformed?
- What is doing the transformation?
- What is the result of the transformation?

The first question points you to what you are working on in your practice. The second points you to what effort you need to make. The third points you to the intention, so you have an idea where you are going. Let's apply these questions to the immeasurables and how they operate at the level of the mind of emotion.

In equanimity meditation, the reactive pattern of attraction, aversion, and indifference is taken as the object of attention. The meditation method reduces attraction and aversion to indifference. Attention is then brought to bear on indifference until it collapses. The result is a higher level of attention that is not limited to attraction, aversion, and indifference. This higher level of attention is equanimity. It sees through the patterns of prejudice.

Loving-kindness practice takes the reactive pattern of shutting down as the object of attention. It brings out the reactive pattern of shutting down by bringing attention to the experience of receiving kindness. Attention is then directed at shutting down until it collapses. The result is loving-kindness—a higher level of attention that does not need to possess or take over when you open to experience. It radiates warmth and does not depend on conditioned personal agendas.

Compassion practice places attention on the contraction and fear triggered by another's pain. The meditation method evokes fear through images in which people close to you suffer intensely. Attention is directed to the contraction until it collapses. The result is compassion, a higher level of attention that enables you to stay present with the pain. It radiates presence and is characterized by fearlessness.

Joy practice takes your internal sense of not being enough as the object of attention. The meditation method brings out the critical attitude responsible for this feeling and shows how that critical attitude comes from the passive acceptance of conditioned values. Attention is directed at the feeling of not being enough until it collapses. The result is joy—an experience of release or freedom that is a higher level of attention with the ability to see that the learned values are not absolutes. It brings you into presence so that you can do what needs to be done instead of what you have been conditioned to do.

ENERGY TRANSFORMATION IN THE FOUR IMMEASURABLES

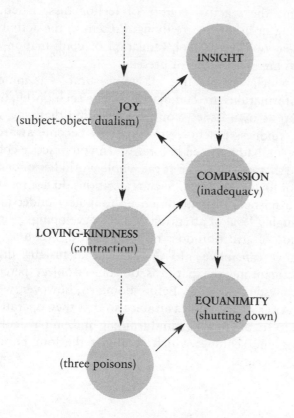

As your practice of the immeasurables matures, the level of energy generated by the practice transforms patterns at the level of awareness. In equanimity practice, the object of attention becomes the reactive process associated with the arising of experience itself. The ordinary reactions to perception—attraction, aversion, or indifference—are transformed, and you rest in composure.

Loving-kindness practice brings attention to how you select objects of perception to avoid opening to what is arising. It transforms the energy of reactive selection into open, inclusive attention, the magnanimous mind that can include everything.

Compassion practice brings attention to the tendency to control what arises in experience. It transforms the reactive energy of control into taking care of or tending to whatever arises. You do what needs to be done with complete attention. You let go of control and receive the results of your actions, whatever they are.

Joy practice brings attention to how you seek meaning from outside. It transforms the reactive energy of feeling dissatisfied with what you are doing or how you are living. Present in the activities of life, you no longer look outside for validation or confirmation. Your actions themselves are expressions of presence.

The order in which you practice the immeasurables is important because the transformations are cumulative. While each of the immeasurables brings up its own issues, you may well find that, say, in the middle of loving-kindness practice, you suddenly become aware of a wall of prejudice you had not seen before. When you practice compassion, you may see that a deep anger at the whole world lies underneath your experience of loving-kindness. Such realizations do not mean that you have made a mistake in your practice. Your new understanding comes from the higher level of attention you are developing.

The progression of attention does not stop at joy, of course. From the level of joy, we can move into the practice of insight, bringing attention and dismantling the patterns of subject-object perception that obscure the mystery of being. Before doing so, however, we need to deepen the practice of the immeasurables so that they operate in all areas of life. To do so, we turn to mind training and, in particular, the practice of taking and sending, which combines the four immeasurables into one practice.

CHAPTER 8

Mind Training

Nasrudin and a friend were thirsty, and stopped at a café for a drink. They decided to share a glass of milk.

"You drink your half first," said the friend, "because I have some sugar here, just enough for one. I shall add this to my share of the milk and drink it."

"Add it now," said the Mulla, "and I will drink only my half."

"Certainly not. There is only enough sugar to sweeten half a glass of milk."

Nasrudin went to the owner to the café, and came back with a large packet of salt.

"Good news, friend," he said, "I am drinking first, as agreed, and I want my milk with salt."

—IDRIES SHAH,
THE PLEASANTRIES OF THE INCREDIBLE MULLA NASRUDIN

With a solid basis in the four immeasurables, we are now in a position to take the bull by the horns, so to speak, and engage in a practice that uses everything that life has to throw at us. The practice is mind training (Tibetan: *lojong*). Mind training is like rubbing two sticks together to make a fire. One stick consists of the perspectives and discipline of the practice; the other is made from the projections and dynamics of habituated patterns. The intention is to burn up both sticks so we experience the world as it is.

Mind training differs from cultivating attention in that it implants a set of ideas, perspectives, and experiences that work to dismantle habituated patterns. Attention aims at resting in the direct experience of what is. As attention grows, we can work more deeply in mind training, generating more friction with the patterns. As the patterns are burned up, the training in attention enables us to rest more fully in the direct experience of what is.

Mind training is not a beginner's practice. We undertake mind training when our commitment to wake up is so strong that we are prepared to use every situation in life to undermine reactive patterns. The intention is to burn up self-cherishing, the emotional attachment to a sense of "I." Whatever the situation, whenever self-cherishing arises, we apply mind training.

> Geshé Ben was famous for the way he used mind training to cut through self-cherishing. On one occasion, he was waiting, along with other monks, to be served the evening soup. The cook ladled the soup from a deep pot. Geshé Ben suddenly yelled, "Thief, thief!" The startled monks looked around but could not see any likely thief. When asked why he had cried out, Geshé Ben pointed to himself, "He's here. I was hoping that the cook would dip the ladle deep into the soup pot so I would get thicker soup than the rest of you."

Taking and Sending

Taking and sending (Tibetan: *tonglen*) is probably the simplest and most powerful mind-training practice. Taking and sending means *exchange*. We exchange our happiness for other people's suffering. To practice taking and sending, we reverse the habituated way we relate to the world. We put others first, in everything, and experience the friction that is generated inside as a result.

FOUNDATION

As in the previous meditations, begin with a fifteen- or twenty-minute period of basic meditation in order to establish a base of attention.

Once the activity of mind has settled and attention is present, review briefly the meditations on the four immeasurables. Take between five and ten minutes to recall and connect with the clarity of equanimity, the radiant warmth of loving-kindness, the understanding and sympathy of compassion, and the radiant presence of joy.

As you open to each of the immeasurables, one or more recent incidents will cause internal material to resonate. Take note of such areas, as they will be useful in the taking and sending practice itself.

PRACTICE

Opening to What Is

In traditional teachings, the practice of opening to what is is called ultimate awakening mind—you are waking up to the ultimate nature of experience.

The practice consists of letting the I-other framework drop and opening to pure experience for a moment. Consider that you are dreaming and you know that you are dreaming. People, buildings, trees, noises, even thoughts and feelings arise, but you know that everything you experience is the content of a dream. It is all your own mind.

You will feel a shift in your body, a temporary suspension of the hold of consensus reality. Although opening to what is takes only a moment or two, it still cuts through the habituation of I-other. Now, turn to the practice of taking and sending.

Or take another step. Ask the question: "If everything is a dream, then what experiences the dream?" You will feel a quick shift, a sudden opening. Again, you can turn to taking and sending at this point.

Or take a third step. As the openness fills up with thoughts and ideas about the question or possible answers, turn attention to the thoughts themselves. Regard them as dreams, too. You will again feel a shift to openness.

For the purposes of taking and sending, you don't have to be able to sustain the openness. Experience the shift in any of these three ways and then turn to taking and sending, but keep in mind that everything—thoughts, feelings, and sensations—is a dream.

Preparation for Taking and Sending

Think of a small group of people who are suffering, a group of homeless people on a cold night, say, or a family in which one person is dying. Recalling the meditation on compassion, allow the feeling of sadness at the thought of pain to become very strong. This feeling is the basis of taking and sending practice.

Let the feeling grow until you would rather experience the pain than have these people experience it.

Imagine that their pain leaves them and comes into you—your experiencing the pain frees them from it. As you experience the pain, simultaneously you experience a deep feeling of joy that other people are free from pain.

Next, imagine giving all your own happiness and good fortune to them, so that they know the same kind of happiness and well-being that you experience. Take joy in their experience of your happiness and good fortune.

Imagine this exchange over and over again, feeling the resistance you have to taking in their suffering and the resistance you have to giving away your own good fortune. Don't suppress or ignore the resistance, but make the exchange anyway. Take the resistance as part of the experience of the practice. When you can rest a little bit in the idea of taking in suffering and sending out happiness, move to the main practice.

Once you are familiar with taking and sending practice, this preparatory step can be omitted.

Taking and Sending: The Main Practice

Now, instead of the small group, take all beings everywhere as your frame of reference. Turn your attention to the breath and imagine that, with each inhalation, you breathe in the pain of the world and with each exhalation you breathe out your happiness to everyone. To make the exchange clearer, imagine that the incoming breath is dark, heavy, almost like tar, carrying the pain of others through your nostrils and into your heart. As the pain comes into your heart, your heart grows heavier and you feel the pain fully.

Breathe out. As the breath goes out, imagine that all *your* happiness, good fortune, abilities, and good qualities take the form of clear radiant light, like moonlight. The light carrying your happiness and good fortune comes out of your heart, goes out through the nostrils with the breath, and radiates to all beings everywhere.

Breathe naturally, synchronizing the imagined exchange with the breath. Don't try to make the breath fit the visualization. If you do, you will quickly grow tired and you will not feel any sense of resting.

Rest in breathing. As you rest, imagine the dark smoke of the suffering of all beings coming into you, into your heart, where you experience that suffering. In the beginning, you will be able to breathe in only one or two kinds of suffering. Start with anything, breathing in the pangs of hunger, the discomforts of illness, the sadness over the loss of a loved one, the stab of rejection, the feeling of failure and disappointment, or the shock of betrayal.

When you breathe out, let the radiant light of your own good fortune pour out of your heart. In the beginning, start with your health, your intelligence, the food on your table, the care and affection of your spouse, the vigor of your body, or your enjoyment in your clothes. No happiness is too small or insignificant to give away. Whatever you enjoy, give it to others so that they experience it, too.

Gradually, extend the practice to take in more and more suffering and to send out more and more happiness.

Rest on the visualization of dark, thick smoke coming in and bright, radiant moonlight going out. After every five or ten breaths, explicitly remind yourself that you are taking in the suffering of others and sending out happiness to them.

Call to mind specific instances of suffering and happiness and use them. For instance, you remember seeing a homeless person. Breathe in, taking in the suffering of hunger, cold, rejection by society, or having no place to call home. Breathe out, sending your good health, intelligence, or satisfaction in your work. Don't think only of this homeless person, however. Take in the suffering of all homeless people everywhere and send your happiness to all of them, too.

Use the archetypal imagery of the six realms. Imagine breathing in the pain of violence and hate of the hell realms, the hunger and greed of the ghost realms, or the pride and arrogance of the god realms. Breathe out whatever happiness, goodness, joy, peace, confidence, security, or well-being you know in your own experience, giving it away to all beings.

You don't have to balance precisely what you send out with what you take in. Take from others what is painful, unhealthy, unpleasant, negative, immoral, malevolent, or stupid. Breathe out what you experience as joyful, healthy, pleasant, positive, moral, beneficial, or intelligent. The important point is to feel that you are taking in what is negative and breathing out what is positive.

CONCLUSION

Dissolution

The way you end a meditation session is as important as the way you begin it. In the last five or ten minutes, let go of the visualization and the exchange. Rest in awareness, completely awake, present, and relaxed at the same time. Rest without distraction, not trying to do anything with what arises, nor trying to make something happen. When thoughts, feelings, or sensations arise, look at them, not to see what they are about, but to see what they are. When you look right at them, they appear to disappear. Rest again.

If you fall into distraction and confusion, return attention to the breath, just sensing it come and go. You will see that the nature and rhythm of the breath when resting differs from the nature and rhythm of the breath when doing taking and sending.

Intention

The second point in ending a practice session is to set intention: take the spirit of taking and sending into your daily life. Choose a phrase that resonates with your own experience of taking and sending. Here are a couple of examples:

> *Give gain and victory to others.*
> *Take loss and defeat for yourself.*

> *Gain is illusion.*
> *Loss is enlightenment.*

You can also use one of the phrases for cutting through obsessions:

> *Everything is a dream.*

> *The trouble is that I believe my feelings.*

> *May all their suffering come into me.*
> *May all my happiness go to them.*

> *This is what you wanted.*
> *This is what you live for.*

Keep the chosen phrase in mind during the day and use it whenever you lose attention or fall into distraction.

Commentary

An often-quoted mind-training instruction is a verse from Langri Thangpa's *Eight Verses of Mind Training*:

> *Give gain and victory to others.*
> *Take loss and defeat for yourself.*

The intention of this and similar instructions is to undermine the habituated tendency of putting "me" first in everything. We habitually take the view that we are the center of our world, a misperception that prevents us from knowing directly that we are just what we experience, neither more nor less.

In the Soto Zen tradition, Uchiyama Roshi writes:

> *Gain is illusion.*
> *Loss is enlightenment.*

These lines bring out the deeper implications of mind training.

Whenever we feel that we are adding something or gaining something, we move deeper into illusion. You may feel that you have a car, a house, a partner, children, friends, or a job, but these people and things are, in the end, only experiences that arise in your life. They are not yours. They may die, fall apart, disappear, or cease to exist in spite of your best efforts to hold on to them. You will eventually cease to have any connection with them, if for no other reason than your own death. To feel that they are *ours* is illusion.

Whenever we feel we have lost something, however, we move closer to knowing how things are. You never really have a car or a house, or a child, a relationship, a point of view, or even a body. All these are experiences that arise in life. Therefore, when you experience loss, you experience the returning of what arises in experience to what it arose from. Loss puts us in touch with the original nature of being. Loss is enlightenment.

Every reactive pattern includes a sense of self, an idea of who and what we are. Part of the pattern dynamic is an emotional attachment to that sense of self, an attachment that generates attraction to experiences that support and reinforce the sense of self and aversion to experiences that undermine or threaten it. The emotional attachment to the sense of "I" is called "self-cherishing," and it takes the view "*I* am the most important thing in the world." Much suffering arises from the profound imbalance generated by self-cherishing.

Self-cherishing is different from holding on to a felt sense of self. The latter is a pattern of misperception—regarding "I" as referring to something that actually exists. The former is the emotional pattern of actively putting the sense of self first in everything we do.

The way we interpret experience is seriously out of balance. We afford too privileged a role to the sense of who and what we are. We seek to maintain our identity, our self-image, often at great cost. Every aspect of experience is immediately judged according to whether it supports, threatens, or is inconsequential to our sense of who we are—these are the three poisons—and everything we do flows out of those initial reactive assessments.

In other words, we are organized around a sense of self.

Taking and sending makes us relinquish the sense of self as the organizing principle of our lives. Initially, we understand that others experience pain and happiness just as we do—they are no different from us. We progress to the direct understanding that pain and happiness are sensations that inevitably arise in experience and that we can, in fact, experience them without disturbance. With this understanding, we are less prone to appropriate only for ourselves what is enjoyable and leave only what is not enjoyable to others. In other words, we begin to relate to the world of experience more as it is than as we would have it be. Finally, we come to know that everything we experience—people, events, sensations, thoughts, and feelings—is simply experience, neither good nor bad in itself.

Taking and sending requires us to relate directly to what we experience, not to what we think we experience. If we have a view of ourselves as superior, taking on the suffering of others opens our hearts to their difficulties. We see that we are not better than anyone else and that others seek to be happy and seek to avoid suffering just as we do. On the other hand, if we see ourselves as inferior and having a life predominantly of pain, the sending part of the practice forces us to acknowledge the happiness, qualities, and abilities that we do have. We cannot maintain a negative self-image, so our view of the world and ourselves moves into balance. The balancing effects of this practice also have the potential to heal the emotional wounds associated with a negative self-image.

WORKING WITH REACTIONS

At first, your reactions to the suffering of others will constrict your efforts to take in the suffering. A common mistake is to ignore your own reactions and concentrate on taking and sending with the other. This is just another form of suppression.

The traditional instruction is

Begin the sequence of exchange with yourself.

Work directly with what is arising in you. When you think of a person who is dying of cancer, your own reactions to having a terminal disease are triggered. Rest in breathing, opening to your own fears, uncertainties, withdrawal, or resistance.

Similarly, when you imagine giving your own vitality to others, you will immediately be aware of your attachment to your vitality and good health. Rest with the breath, open-ing to your attachment and your unwill-ingness to send it to others, to give it away.

To open to reactions means to hold them in attention. Don't ignore them. Don't indulge them. Don't try to get rid of them. Don't try to resolve them. Just experience them in attention as you con-tinue the practice of taking and sending.

Hold them tenderly in attention. Keep attention on the breath, breathing in and out, while you feel the reaction operating in you. When you breathe in suffering, for instance, feel how you want to shrink away from it, avoid it, or let someone else experience it. Open to that feeling and imagine taking in the same feeling of shrinking away or avoidance from all beings. When you breathe out happiness, feel your attachment to it, or, possibly, your discomfort in acknowledging that you feel happy or good. Use taking and sending to open to your own reactions.

Initially, you will only be able to hold your reactions in attention for a short time. Continue with taking and sending, imagining breathing in the dark, thick smoke of suffering, pain, and evil and breathing out the radiant moonlight of happiness, comfort, and goodness. From time to time, touch the reaction. As your ability to hold it in attention increases, you feel its operation more deeply. The breath acts as a base of attention, allowing you to rest calmly and at ease with the reactive process as you open to it more and more fully. Eventually, you experience the reaction without disturbance, and an

In the desert
I saw a creature,
    naked, bestial,
Who, squatting
    upon the
    ground,
Held his heart in his
    hands,
And ate of it.
I said: "Is it good,
    friend?"
"It is bitter—bitter,"
    he answered,
"But I like it
Because it is bitter
And because it is
    my heart."

—*Stephen Crane*

understanding of its basis and its role in your life often arises spontaneously. The understanding does not come from intellectual analysis or reasoning but from the direct experience of the reactive pattern itself as it is released in awareness.

Your practice broadens and deepens, moving from the level of personal reactions to the level of the immeasurables. You can now take in the suffering of others and send your own good fortune to them.

As you embrace a progressively wider range of human experience, you inevitably run into other personal issues. As you move deeper in attention, you open more fully to the whole range of human experience. Again and again, you run into areas where personal experience prevents you from embracing what arises. Use taking and sending to hold the reactive process in attention until it releases.

When you practice taking and sending, you must be willing to go into every area of life. You need courage, faith, acceptance, and care. *Courage* is the willingness to endure what arises, to stand in the face of the reactive patterns provoked by taking and sending. *Faith* is the willingness to open to the mystery of experience, to open to what arises even though you have no idea what lies ahead. *Acceptance* is the willingness to hold what arises in attention without trying to label, define, analyze, or explain it. *Care* is the willingness to assume the responsibilities of presence and to act on what you perceive when you are free from the confusion and distortion of reactive patterns.

> If you could really take away the suffering of everyone in the world, taking all of it into you with a single breath, would you hesitate?
>
> —*Kalu Rinpoche*

One commonly held misinterpretation undermines the true transformative dynamic of taking and sending. The practice of taking and sending does not mean transforming the suffering of others into happiness and then sending that happiness out to them. To do so would remove the friction between your habituated patterns of self-cherishing and the practice. With this interpretation, you would end up "working" with suffering without ever being touched by it.

The correct approach in taking and sending is to take in the pain of others and imagine experiencing it in place of them. You send your own happiness to them and imagine that they experience it. Done this way, the practice dismantles the way you habitually react to suffering. Taking and sending does not transform the pain itself.

THE FOUR IMMEASURABLES IN TAKING AND SENDING

The four immeasurables lay the foundation for taking and sending. Equanimity shifts us out of the immediate reactions of attraction, aversion, and indifference. Loving-kindness counteracts the tendency to close down to others. With compassion, we stand in the discomfort caused by other people's pain and suffering. With joy, we freely celebrate their joy and happiness.

In taking and sending practice, each breath is the practice of the four immeasurables. Equanimity is practiced by embracing all sentient beings without prejudice or bias. Loving-kindness, the wish that others be happy, is practiced by sending what is good in your life to others. Compassion is practiced by taking in the suffering that others experience. Joy is practiced by taking joy in the process of the exchange.

Taking and sending means *exchange*. The suffering of others is being exchanged for your happiness. No matter how you imagine the suffering of others coming into you, you experience it. Typical reactions are disgust, helplessness, and numbness. The compassion component of the practice is the willingness to be with the suffering. Do not try to keep your distance or guard against it. When you imagine taking in the internal pain of a murderer or a rapist, you will cringe, contract, and shut down. Sit and breathe, using the methods in the compassion meditation to relax the contraction until you can stay present with the pain.

If, for instance, your reaction to the suffering of others is disgust, then shift your attention to taking in disgust, taking in all the disgust, revulsion, and antipathy that others experience. This shift puts you more in touch with the reaction. You feel the underlying contraction more fully. As you bring attention to the contraction, then, just as in the compassion meditation, the contraction gradually releases and you are able to take in the suffering of others more completely.

If the reaction is helplessness or numbness, proceed in the same way.

Similarly, send your own happiness and good fortune to others. Initially you may have difficulty in figuring out what to send to others, particularly if you have a negative self-image. Begin with the simplest of things: good health, feeling good about something you did yesterday, intelligence, kindness to others, having enough to eat, having a job. There's always a little bit of happiness in your life, even if you habitually ignore it and cling to a self-image as someone who suffers and never experiences any happiness. The sending part of taking and sending effectively uproots this conception by putting you in touch with the happiness and good fortune you do experience.

In sending happiness and good fortune to others, you will become aware of your attachment to "your" good fortune and your reluctance even to share it with others, much less give it away. The reluctance is a manifestation of closing down to others. Use the methods for loving-kindness practice to release the pattern of closing down. Indeed, the sending of your own good fortune to others is the loving-kindness aspect of taking and sending.

Another potential issue is partiality. You may be willing to practice taking and sending with friends but not with people who irritate you or cause you difficulty. Use the methods for equanimity to break down partiality so that you can practice taking and sending with everyone. You may also discover that you are willing to take on certain forms of suffering, ill fortune, and unpleasantness, but not others. For instance, you can imagine taking in illness and disease, but you resist taking in anger or lying and deception. Cut through judgment and take in everything.

Similarly, you are willing to send out good health, wealth, and even your career but are unwilling to part with intelligence, honesty, or integrity. Everything you are attached to is a component of a self-image. Give it away, no matter how valuable, noble, or essential it appears to be.

The practice of taking and sending turns your habituated way of relating to experience upside down. Why train to welcome defeat and loss and relinquish victory and gain? The answer lies in the experience of presence. Gain and victory tend to reinforce the sense of who and what we are, increasing our separation from the world. With loss and defeat, everything collapses: the sense of who we are, what the world is, how we see and understand things. When we open to the loss fully, the habituated sense of self falls apart but awareness is still present.

This discovery is accompanied by a deep sense of joy, not the joy of excitement or titillation, but a deeper, quieter joy—the joy of being. Now, we welcome others' pain and suffering because they help to break down our own conditioning. We give our good fortune to others joyfully, too, for we know we do not need it to define who or what we are. In other words, when we fully take in the pain of others and send out our own happiness, we discover that we lack nothing and we open to immeasurable joy.

TRANSFORMATION

The teachings of mind training were brought to Tibet in the eleventh century by the Indian master Atisha. Numerous teachers compiled practice summaries of mind-training methods. Taking and sending stands out among these practices because it combines the techniques of cultivation and transformation in a single practice. In cultivation, one nurtures the seeds of understanding and behavior. In transformation, one transforms the experience of what arises from reaction to presence.

Taking and sending uses both approaches simultaneously. By resting attention on the breath, taking in the suffering of others, and giving away our own happiness, we nurture the four immeasurables. The guidelines for mind training include numerous instructions that direct our effort at cultivation. A few examples from *The Seven Points of Mind Training* are

Don't let your practice depend on external conditions.

Be patient, whether things are good or bad.

Work on the stronger reactive patterns first.

At the same time, mind training works to change the way we experience thoughts, emotions, and sensations, transforming the reactive patterns of aversion, attraction, and indifference into the experience of presence. Sample instructions are

Be grateful to everyone.

Adverse conditions are spiritual teachers.
Illness sweeps away evil and obscurations.

Taking and sending is fundamentally a method for cultivating compassion. Nevertheless, one of the special features of this practice is that it transforms ordinary habituated experience into presence and clarity.

Transformation methods operate differently from cultivation methods. In the latter, you create the conditions for the growth of such qualities as attention, compassion, devotion, or awareness of impermanence. You work to maintain the conditions for growth by watering and fertilizing the growing qualities. As the level of energy in these qualities increases, they manifest more in your life.

In transformation methods, you direct attention to the habituated patterns set in motion by what arises in experience. In taking and sending, transformation takes place naturally when you use the practice to open to your own reactions and experience. The level of energy in attention needs to be higher than the energy in the habituated reactions in order to penetrate and dismantle the habituated reactions as they arise. The energy locked up in the habituated patterns then fuels attention and opens up deeper awareness, insight, compassion, or devotion.

Transformation methods are intended to be used in both formal practice and daily life. Even more than cultivation methods, they use what arises in experience as fuel for practice. During the day, practice taking and sending by taking in, for a moment, the pain or suffering of others and sending, for a moment, your own happiness and joy.

Transformation techniques, by their nature, are more dangerous than cultivation techniques. If you cannot generate attention at a level of energy higher than the reactive patterns, no transformation takes place and the reactive patterns run the show. If you are unable to maintain attention during the transformation, the energy in attention decays into habituated reactions and makes them operate more powerfully. If you are unable to hold the released energy in attention, the energy again flows into reactive patterns and they operate more powerfully than before.

Transformation methods in taking and sending operate at three levels, in the mind of awareness, the mind of emotion, and the mind of the body. These are also discussed in the chapters on karma and the four immeasurables.

Mind of Awareness

Transformation at the level of awareness means to know what arises for what it is, an arising in the field of experience, free from emotional and psychological projections, and free from the projections of subject and object. Transformation at this level requires a high level of attention.

The essence of this transformation is to move into direct knowing when you encounter a situation that triggers reactive patterns. When a pattern is triggered, enter into the reaction with attention, take the reaction into you, and then go empty: stop breathing for a moment, or open and rest in awareness. Go empty and experience no separation from what arises in experience.

See confusion as the four dimensions of presence.

Take anger, for example. When you look at anger to see what it is, you see nothing (the dimension of what is). On the other hand, you experience anger vividly (the dimension of what appears). Hold both of these experiences in mind simultaneously and your experience of anger shifts, its reactiveness replaced by a heightened awareness (the dimension of quality). All three of these make up the totality of the experience of anger (the dimension of being).

In classical terms, know what arises to be an arising in experience, not a thing that exists independently. In other words, know what arises to be empty as it arises (the dimension of what is). The arising is, nevertheless, vivid; it is experienced (the dimension of what appears). The vividness and the emptiness are not two different things (the dimension of quality); they occur together and cannot be separated. The totality, the emptiness, the vividness, and the occurrence of the two together are simultaneous (the dimension of being).

When you experience things this way, reactive patterns have no opportunity to operate. Energy at the level of the mind of awareness flows into the mind of emotion and the mind of the body. You know what is and what to do, immediately and directly. You attend to it with complete attention, appropriately, naturally, and spontaneously. In other words, you move into pristine awareness.

Mind of Emotion

At the level of emotion, transform your emotional reactions to what arises into presence. When we encounter negativity, we usually seek to blame the problem on something external to us and we resent the person or persons we hold responsible for the problem. The relevant instruction here is

Drive all blame into one.

To transform negativity at the level of emotion, take responsibility for whatever arises. To be more precise, blame habituated patterns for precipitating the problem. When a colleague expresses disappointment or displeasure in you, don't blame him or her for making you feel ashamed. Direct blame at your attachment to being a highly competent or decent person. You will step out of reaction and be more able to address the problem he or she is having with you.

Blame your habituated patterns for everything that goes wrong in your life. The shift in perspective creates a lot of emotional friction. Hold the friction in attention to transform the energy of negativity into attention. With this method you stop being a passive participant in your life. When you see all problems as being generated by habituated patterns, you change your relationship with the patterns. You see them as unthinking mechanisms and you become the active agent, bringing attention and awareness to bear on the mechanisms until they fall apart. Now your life is no longer a product of mechanisms. You start to live intentionally, taking responsibility for your part in everything you experience.

The transformation will put us in touch with what we can actually do in the situation. Even if the only course of action is to bear the unpleasantness, we are able to do so with presence and clarity instead of anger and resentment.

Be grateful to everyone.

When unpleasantness arises, take the experience of unpleasantness from others. If people evoke dislike, take dislike from others. If they evoke affection and joy, send the experience of affection and joy to them. In short, be grateful to everyone because they provide you with opportunities to bring attention to your own reactions.

Needless to say, transformation at the level of emotion requires a dedicated commitment to dismantling the habituated patterns of self-importance and self-centeredness. In particular, you have to be able to maintain attention in the heat of the friction generated when this practice rubs against habituated patterns—and it can get pretty hot.

Mind of the Body

At the level of the body, transform the experience of action. When you engage in an activity, let go of any idea of achieving a goal or deriving

a benefit from the activity. Be in the doing. Whether the task is pleasant or unpleasant, make it an offering to awareness. If you jog, be in
the jogging. Don't think about how you will do in an upcoming
marathon. The effort to be present in the activity disrupts the way
habituated emotional patterns take over the body. By staying present
in the doing, you stop reinforcing projection and self-interest and
move to the pure experience of the activity itself.

In the mind-training tradition, one prayer is

If it's better for me to be ill,
I pray for the blessing of illness.
If it's better for me to recover,
I pray for the blessing of recovery.
If it's better for me to die,
I pray for the blessing of death.

A woman with terminal cancer found this prayer deeply disturbing
when she first heard it. "What kind of prayer is that?" she demanded.
Yet, she couldn't keep the prayer out of her head. She came back to it
again and again. Then she found that her relationship with her body
and her illness changed. Yes, she was sick and probably dying, but her
body relaxed. She stopped fighting being ill. She didn't stop her investigation of new treatments and approaches, but she did stop driving her
body beyond what it could handle.

EXTENSIONS OF TAKING AND SENDING

Taking and sending can be practiced in three different ways. The first
is the traditional practice of taking in suffering and sending out happiness, coordinating the taking and sending with the breath.

The second is to do the same practice while imagining that you are
an expression of full awakening. For instance, you could identify with
Avalokiteshvara, the embodiment of awakened compassion. This form
of practice puts you deeply in touch with emotional resistance while at
the same time reducing the identification with emotional patterns.

The third way is to practice taking and sending knowing that you
are not separate from what you experience. In this approach, you
practice presence as a flow of energy, suffering coming in and happiness going out. All experience, whether it is suffering or happiness, is
released in awareness.

Up to this point, we have focused on the first, the basic practice of taking and sending. The other two methods develop naturally from the first; they are extensions of taking and sending into the domains of deity practice and the practice of direct awareness.

Deity practice is one of the principal methods used in the Tibetan tradition to transform your experience of the world. Deity practice involves imagining that you are an expression of awakened mind, a deity or, in Tibetan, a *yidam*. Avalokiteshvara, the embodiment of awakened compassion, is one such yidam, as are such deities as Vajrayogini (awakened passion), Hevajra (awakened anger), and Green Tara (awakened activity).

Deities are highly symbolic representations of aspects of awakened mind that have appeared to past teachers in visions. These visions became the basis for meditation practices using that deity. When you imagine being the deity, the habituated patterns associated with your ordinary sense of self have no place to function. Because deities are all expressions of awakened mind you, as the deity, have infinite resources to call upon in taking in the suffering of others and sending out happiness. You know that all suffering is empty, so you open fearlessly to the experience of the pain and the problems of others. Similarly, as the deity, you experience the bliss, clarity, and emptiness of mind; have infinite and inexhaustible capabilities; and embody compassion. Therefore, you can send infinite good fortune freely to all beings without the slightest sense of concern, regret, attachment, or fear. By embedding the practice of taking and sending in deity practice, you can do the practice more freely and more powerfully than when you are identified with your usual sense of who and what you are.

Why, then, isn't taking and sending always practiced in the context of deity practice? Deity practice requires a willingness to allow your habituated sense of self to be replaced by a more subtle, open, and free way of relating to the world. Most people are not able to take that step without suitable preparation. Guidance by a qualified teacher is essential. In fact, taking and sending is often used as preparation for the transition to deity practice. Once a student is trained in deity practice, however, he or she can use the deity as a basis for taking and sending.

The third way to practice taking and sending is in the context of direct awareness. First, you must know direct awareness through your own experience. Then you do taking and sending to enhance your experience and understanding of emptiness and compassion.

In presence, you know all that arises in experience as just that, an arising in experience. Thoughts are known to be thoughts, feelings to be feelings, sensations to be sensations. The level of energy in attention is such that direct awareness is not disrupted by the content of thought, feeling, or sensation. As associations are triggered, the arising of the associations is seen for what it is. Remain present, and perceive the myriad threads of interdependent arising.

Thoughts, feelings, and sensations release themselves as they arise because they are experienced completely in direct awareness. You experience taking and sending as a flow of energy. When energy arises as pain and suffering, take it in. When energy arises as pleasure and good fortune, send it out. Subject (the meditator), object (suffering and happiness), and practice (taking and sending) drop away and taking and sending just flows.

WARNINGS

To practice mind training, you must have a fearless determination to undermine habituated patterns, the ability to know and acknowledge what you are feeling, and the ability to maintain attention in the face of reactivity. Otherwise, mind-training instructions are recipes for emotional problems.

If you are not ruthless in your intention to dismantle habituated patterns, you will not have the courage and determination to embrace the approach to life that mind training requires. In mind training, you deliberately lose arguments in order to dismantle your reactions to losing. You have to not only let go of your attachment to winning, but also let go of showing how clever you are and the rightness of your position. You have to endure the triumph of your opponent and any comments he or she makes about winning. When you sit through all the internal turmoil, you realize that what you are does not depend on winning or losing. What you are depends on nothing! Attachment to winning and losing is reduced to ashes and you are freed from the tyranny of victory and defeat.

You will experience a wide range of emotional reactions in the course of taking and sending practice—everything from oceanlike equanimity to crushing despair, from deep bitterness and anger to unrestricted warmth and caring, from acute shame and embarrassment to inexpressible joy and freedom.

Patterns are not burned up if you suppress your reactions. You must experience them in attention. In one instance, a psychiatrist attempted to apply the mind-training instruction "Be grateful to everyone" to a person who had filed a legal action against her. Misunderstanding the technique, she pushed away her feelings of anger and resentment and tried harder and harder to feel gratitude to the person who was suing her. However, because she felt that the lawsuit was baseless and unjust, she couldn't bring herself to feel gratitude. She couldn't capitulate to the other party's demands. To compound her confusion, she genuinely believed that her inability to let go of her anger and resentment and her resistance to capitulation meant that she had failed in her practice of mind training.

Eventually, she just sat in the whole mess—anger, resentment, failure, confusion—and discovered that she could experience all of those feelings as feelings. She uncovered a clarity that she had never known before and that showed her exactly what to do. Then she really did feel gratitude for the whole mess because it had led her to discover this clarity. She consulted an attorney and defended the lawsuit successfully, free from anger and resentment at the other party.

At first glance, the instructions of mind training seem to be excessively negative. We are instructed to give away everything we regard as good and take on what we regard as bad, even evil.

Evil takes many forms, but, for our purposes, two different but related views will serve. The first is that evil is the incapacity to experience one's own pain. Evil is the opposite of dismantling patterns. Instead of experiencing the pain at the core of a pattern, an evil person lets the pattern run, externalizing his or her own pain by creating pain and suffering in the world.

The second view is that evil is deliberate ignoring. By deliberately ignoring what is painful or unresolved inside, a person acts out of habituated patterns, creating pain and suffering for others.

Taking and sending directly counteracts our potential for evil by forcing us to face precisely what we so often ignore or try to ignore. Suffering, loss, shame, embarrassment, and defeat are not evil in themselves, but what results, when they are ignored, often is. By taking in what is negative, we come to know directly that suffering, loss, shame, and embarrassment are just experiences that have, in the end, nothing to do with what we are.

Taking and sending rubs the habituated patterns of self-importance and self-cherishing the wrong way. It violates the way we have come to regard who and what we are, what we value and deem important in life, and even what we ordinarily regard as fair or just. Taking and sending, however, is not about justice or fairness. We practice taking and sending to root out habitual patterns, so we must be careful that misconceptions about the practice—misconceptions that arise from habituated patterns—don't trip us up.

Perhaps the most common pitfall is magical thinking, the tendency to think that imagining something happening will make it happen. In taking and sending practice, one form of magical thinking is "If I take in other people's illness, I will become sick" or "If I take in their anger, it will pollute me."

Magical thinking is a way of thinking left over from childhood, when you could not clearly differentiate between internal mental processes and events in the world. You take what arises in your mind as concrete and substantial, as what is actually happening. The problem with magical thinking is that it is false. You do not become ill because you imagine taking in the illness of another person. Another person does not become wealthy because you imagine sending your own wealth and prosperity to her.

Counteract magical thinking by remembering that everything that arises is only an experience. Undermine it with the more radical attitude: "If I can really take on someone else's pain, then let me have it so that he or she will be free from it."

A student once asked Kalu Rinpoche, "What if all that suffering really came into me?" He replied, "That would be very good." The student was totally taken aback but then realized that what Rinpoche had said was right—how wonderful to be able to free another person from suffering! That realization cut right through the fear and hesitation based on magical thinking.

A second pitfall is the notion that you are being noble by taking on the suffering of others. Nonsense! You are practicing taking and sending in order to be free from the imprisonment of your own habituated patterns. Why should anyone thank you? In what sense are you being noble?

Another common problem is a sense of detachment: you just cannot connect with the sense of another's pain, so the meditation practice feels like an empty, abstract ritual. It has no juice. Or perhaps you cannot connect to anything good in your own experience.

To work through detachment from other people's suffering, imagine that you experience the pain, suffering, or negativity that you are trying to take in. For instance, if you are taking in the pain of someone who is dying of cancer, imagine that you are dying of cancer. How would you feel? What would you be doing? What thoughts would be going through your mind? What worries and concerns would weigh on your heart? Step into the other person's shoes and you will soon overcome detachment from his or her pain and suffering.

To work through the difficulty of finding anything good in your own experience, recall an incident or event that felt even a little pleasant.

Hold the pleasant feeling in attention, and rest attention on the breath. Use the experience of sending this little bit of pleasure in your life to others as a way of opening to the experience of pleasure, goodness, and well-being in you. You will soon feel the operation of the habituated patterns that shut you down to your own happiness and joy. Now, use taking and sending, taking in from all beings the same patterns that shut down happiness and joy, so that you clearly experience the operation of the patterns in you.

Use everything you experience in taking and sending practice. Don't attach to any of it. For instance, if you feel overwhelmed at the prospect of taking in others' suffering, imagine taking in the feeling of being overwhelmed from all beings. If you feel afraid to take in a particular pain, illness, or behavior, imagine taking in fear from all beings. The same holds true for sending. If you are happy about a recent bit of good fortune, send the good fortune to others. If you notice that you want to keep the good fortune, take in selfishness. If you feel spacious and free when you send good fortune to others, send the spaciousness and freedom to others as well. Mind training, particularly taking and sending, is like a fire: the more wood you throw on it, the more intensely it burns.

USING TAKING AND SENDING IN SPECIAL SITUATIONS

Taking and sending can also be used to uncover and experience the undischarged emotions buried in reactive behaviors. Remember that the intention of practice is not to solve the problem, but to help you know the situation just as it is. For instance, the loss of a child is, for a mother, one of the most painful situations imaginable. Yet when a child dies, the child is gone. That is the hard, painful truth. Taking and sending can help you face such hard and painful truths.

> A woman came to Buddha with her dead daughter and asked him to restore her child to life. Buddha said, "To do so, I would need some mustard seed from a household in which no one has died." In India, mustard is one of the most common spices. Everyone has mustard seed.
>
> The mother went to every home in the town. When she inquired if the household was free from death, however, the answer was always no.
>
> Finally, the mother understood that death touches everyone and was able to accept the loss of her own daughter. Buddha, by sending her on this search, had led her to take in the losses of others.

Taking and sending works the same way. By taking emotional reactions from others, you open to the same reactions in you. The level of energy in your attention rises so that you experience the underlying feelings as feelings and stop identifying with them. They are released and the energy in them now powers your attention, uncovering the courage, empathy, understanding, and caring that were present in you all the time but had been obscured by emotional confusion and reactivity.

Relationship Difficulties

If you are in pain in a relationship, your partner is, too. Take your partner as the focus of taking and sending practice, taking from him or her the pain you imagine he or she feels. Send your own understanding and willingness to work on the relationship to your partner. Initially, you may feel superior or righteous because you are the one willing to open to the problems in the relationship. Such a proud posture usually fades quickly in taking and sending practice, and you relate more directly and more immediately to the other person's experience. You begin to see, understand, and feel what is going on in the relationship from your partner's perspective. In sending your own love and affection, you see what truly matters to you in the relationship, what you are holding on to, and what is or is not possible.

Taking and sending does not by itself resolve the difficulties in the relationship. Instead, it helps you become clearer about what is going on, and be less reactive and more empathetic. With greater emotional resources, you meet difficulties in a more responsive and appropriate way.

Trauma and Abuse

Trauma and abuse leave a person deeply disconnected from the world. You feel cut off from human understanding and caring, both because of the shock of the actual incident and because of the inability of others to understand what you experienced. Taking and sending can be used to re-establish a connection with the part of you that feels cut off.

Do taking and sending with yourself, not as you are now, but as you were just after the trauma or abuse. Take in all the suffering, shock, pain, humiliation, fear, and incomprehension. Give to the traumatized you all your understanding, caring, affection, assurance, and support. For instance, a woman who was raped when she was a teenager might imagine herself as she was right after the rape, with feelings of pain, violation, shame, rage, confusion, self-doubt, and powerlessness. The woman doing the practice takes in these feelings from the teenager and sends love, compassion, understanding, strength, and sympathy to the teenage girl in return.

Such a practice is very powerful and needs to be approached with care. In each meditation session take in only what you are able to hold in attention. Don't force the issue. Work consistently in the practice, respecting the extent to which you can open to the feelings of injury and pain. You will gradually be able to open more and more deeply. You will come to experience the feeling of disconnection as a feeling, not as the actual state of affairs—an important step in the healing process.

While taking and sending practice is powerful and effective, the strong energies present in cases of trauma and abuse require that extra care be taken in the practice. The most important point is not to let the strong energies released in the practice decay into reactive patterns and reinforce them. The presence of a knowledgeable and caring individual in the healing process is an important safeguard. I usually advise students working with such deep issues to use these techniques only if they are consulting regularly with a capable therapist or teacher.

CUTTING OBSESSIONS

An obsession is anything that consistently undermines attention and triggers the operation of habituated patterns. We have lots of obsessions. The Tibetan term for obsession, *dü,* carries the idea that a demonic or evil force takes over. A number of mind training practices were developed to exorcise obsessions. One of the best known and most popular is the practice of *chö,* cutting.

The word *chö* means "to cut." The name is taken from the *Diamond Cutter Sutra,* a text on the perfection of wisdom that elucidates the teaching of emptiness. Chö was developed in thirteenth-century Tibet by a remarkable teacher named Machik Labdrön. She enhanced many of the techniques of mind training and taking and sending with dramatic visualizations. With her profound understanding of the perfection of wisdom she developed a set of practices that cut through confusion to bring out presence directly, in pain or pleasure, suffering or happiness.

The full name means "the sacred ground that comes from cutting obsessions." The four classes of obsession in this tradition are

- Obsession with the external world
- Obsession with reactive emotions
- Obsession with pleasure and power
- Obsession with self

Cutting Obsession with the External World

What we call "the external world" consists of sensory impressions, sensations. We infer the existence of an external world from the sum of the sensations that we experience and then obsess on the inferred external world as what is real. The obsession arises at the level of perception and is strongly reinforced by social and cultural conditioning, so much so that we erroneously regard birth and death as a coming into and a leaving behind of a so-called objective world. We are barking up a tree that isn't there.

> Any piece of news, a harmless phrase, the headline in a newspaper: everything proved the outside world's existence and my own unreality. I felt that the world was splitting and that I did not inhabit the present. My present was disintegrating; real time was somewhere else.
>
> In spite of what my senses told me, the time from over there, belonging to the others, was the real one, the time of the real present.
>
> —OCTAVIO PAZ, NOBEL PRIZE ACCEPTANCE SPEECH

The perspective of Buddhism is the opposite: we are what arises in direct awareness.

When we are present and aware, we are not separate from what arises in awareness. We are what we experience—nothing more. In particular, we do not exist apart from what we experience. The objective world that we share with others and call real is an abstraction of our own direct experience. When you and I see a red book lying on a table, you have your experience and I have mine. I abstract the concept book and use it to refer to a wide range of experiences. You similarly abstract the concept book. Using trial and error, interaction and memory, we have worked out a system so that the set of experiences I associate with book corresponds with a set of experiences that you associate with book. This system provides the basis of communication and shared experience.

> Thus, as I heard words repeatedly used in their proper places in various sentences, I gradually learnt to understand what objects they signified; and after I had trained my mouth to form these signs, I used them to express my own desires.
>
> —*Augustine, Confessions, I. 8*

We only have to consider how we learn a new language or how we learn to communicate as a child to understand that language is a sophisticated abstraction of experience. We do not learn to speak "English," for instance. We create and develop our own language and, with it, our own way of viewing and describing objects and experience. We start imitating words and phrases as children, inventing, copying, creating, and experimenting with different usages. Different language systems gradually evolve in each of us. When your individual language system allows you to interact with the language systems used by your parents and siblings, you are regarded as having learned to speak English, but the language that has evolved in you is unique. It differs from the English language systems in other people in subtle ways, ways that enable you to be creative and have an individual style of expression even as the overall functioning is sufficient for communication.

The same process takes place in the way we describe our experience and what we regard as real or illusion. The more we rely on a particular interpretation of experience, the more real we take the interpretation and associated abstractions to be.

As we become adept in communication, we forget that the concepts and words that we use in language are abstractions. In other words, we fall asleep to what is real—actual experience—and take concepts to be real.

As with language, so with every other aspect of experience. We forget that thoughts are thoughts, feelings are feelings, and sensations are sensations. We instead take the contents of thoughts to be real entities, feelings to be what we are, and sensations to be external objects.

Think of an elephant, for instance. If you forget that you are thinking about an elephant, then you take the elephant you are thinking about to be an actual elephant. "Absurd!" you say, but isn't that exactly what happens when you are distracted in meditation? A thought of a dispute with a friend arises. You don't recognize it as a thought. In the next moment, you are engrossed in an argument with your friend. You forget not only your meditation practice but also where you are. Your world of experience has collapsed down to the dispute with your friend. You are completely obsessed with it. The only argument that is taking place, however, is the one in your mind.

What you experience is yours and yours alone. No one else can experience exactly what you do. Even when you express what you experience in poetry, painting, or writing, no one experiences what you experienced. The experiences elicited in them by the poetry are their experiences, not the experience that originally inspired you.

To help us awaken from the enchantment of the abstraction we call the external world, Buddhism applies a bit of common sense and calls the external world what it is—an enchantment, a dream.

The raw materials of the so-called external world are the sensory experiences that arise in awareness. To undo the obsession with the apparent reality of the external world, use the mind-training teaching

Regard everything as a dream.

When you dream, buildings, people, trees, and animals arise vividly. During the dream, you take the buildings and people to be real; that is, you regard them as an external world in which you move around. When you wake up, however, you know that the buildings and people are simply experiences that arose in the dream.

By carrying the idea that everything you experience in your waking life is like a dream, you undermine the conditioned tendency to project an external reality onto sensory experiences. In effect, you move into a more intimate relationship with sensory experience. Your experience of sensations becomes clearer and more vivid, and you are less likely to project emotional reactions onto them.

This instruction is often interpreted to mean that we should not care so much about what happens and not take things so seriously—a dangerous misinterpretation. When we regard everything that arises as a dream, we actually pay more attention to what we are experiencing and how that experience is arising. Instead of automatically interpreting sensory experience as independent objects, we perceive sensory experience for what it is—sensory experience, neither more nor less. Habitually, we regard awareness and sensory experience as separate and different, but sensory experience cannot be separated from awareness. By cutting through the sense of separation with the instruction "everything is a dream," we cut through the conditioning, interpretation, and reactivity that are ordinarily set in motion.

Thoughts, feelings, and sensations do exist—as thoughts, feelings, and sensations. But when the thought "Bill's behavior is offensive" arises, we tend to forget that it is a thought. We act as if the person really were offensive. We forget that the experience of being offended is arising in us and, instead, regard the thought as conveying an "objective" reality.

The instruction to regard everything that arises as a dream is intended to short-circuit our attachment to the "objective" reality of what we experience. Bill's behavior may be offensive to you, but the person next to you may not be offended by Bill's behavior—so much for "objective" reality.

Another way to understand that your life is just what you experience is to consider a difficult situation in your life, one with huge consequences. Imagine the worst case scenario—everything has gone wrong in the worst possible way—and ask, "Then what happens?"

When you imagine the worst possible case, you see that the statements "I can't handle this" and "This is too much" are expressions of feeling rather than fact. When push comes to shove, you will do what you have to do. You will handle the situation, one way or another. In the end, the worst case is just another experience. Even when the worst case leads to injury or even death, you see that your death is also an experience. Your concern for safety or survival leads you to ignore what is happening and prevents you from acting on what you truly value, that is, what you are willing to die for.

So, by considering the worst case, you see that life consists of precisely what you experience and that all other things—social values, conditioned values, what should be done, what is permissible or acceptable, what is regarded as important—are all elements of a dream, the dream of life in the world as we ordinarily regard it. The combination of considering the worst case and regarding everything as a dream enables you to die to the belief that you are only what the world sees you as being. Die to that belief, and you are no longer a passive participant in your life. Instead, you know that you are one with what you experience and that what you do is, in the end, up to you and you alone.

Concern for survival is the basis of the obsession with the reality of the external world. Survival means that we continue to experience being in a body that exists in a world of external appearances. The concern for survival is based on the belief that we are our bodies, but we are not—we are what we experience.

Cutting Obsession with Reactive Emotions

We not only take what arises externally as real; we also take what arises internally—thoughts, emotions, ideas, beliefs, and passions—as real. The obsession with thinking and feeling causes us to react to every thought and feeling that arises as if it presented what is actually happening. In meditation and in life, reaction results in distraction. The field of awareness collapses and the thought or feeling becomes all that we experience. In daily life, the obsession with thoughts and feelings prevents us from responding to situations. We act, not on the basis of what is actually happening, but on the basis of the patterns and projections that are associated with the reactive emotions. Suffering is the inevitable result.

The most important tool for cutting through reactive emotions is to understand that what the emotions are saying is not what is actually going on. For instance, your spouse or partner does something you asked her not to do and you become angry. As anger arises, the field of open awareness collapses and you perceive everything in terms of anger. Anger sees the world as hell and says that you are in danger. It says that you are being attacked and that you will be destroyed if you don't destroy the other (in this case, your spouse) or the situation (by leaving the relationship). The actual situation, however, while it may cause you inconvenience and unpleasantness, doesn't constitute a threat to your existence or to the relationship. Without awareness, you take both the anger and what the anger presents to you as real. You explode at your spouse or walk out of the room. In other words, you believe the anger.

The remedy is this instruction:

The trouble is that I believe my feelings.

As soon as you are aware that you are caught up in the world of the emotion, you have started to step out of it. Now take the second step: bring attention to what you are experiencing, and know it for what it is, a feeling. As you rest in the experience of the feeling, the feeling subsides and you are able to see more clearly what is really there, or the feeling shifts and you become aware of another emotional reaction at a deeper level. In either case, you step out of the world projected by the emotion.

This remedy is particularly effective in the case of strong reactive emotions that dominate significant portions of our lives—anger, neediness, or depression, for example. Whenever you recognize that you are caught up in a reactive emotion, say, "The trouble is that I believe my feelings." The phrase reminds you that both the feeling and your current perception of the world are the products of reactive patterns and conditioning. The shift temporarily breaks the obsession. In the gap, the feeling and the projected world are experienced as objects of attention, not as the way things are. Cut into the emotion again and again. Gradually, you come to understand that you are not the emotion and that the projected world of the emotion is not how things are. Other possibilities open up. When you die to the belief that you are your emotions, you have cut the obsession with reactive emotions.

This and other mind-training techniques are often described as ways of stepping back from the situation. You are not stepping back at all. You are stepping deeper into the situation by moving into a closer relationship with what arises in experience. By stepping out of reactive tendencies, you move closer to the reality of things.

Cutting Obsession with Pleasure and Power

As practice deepens, you experience periods of increasing pleasure. One source of pleasure is the subsiding of reactive tendencies in the body and mind, so the body and mind are both suffused with feelings of lightness, flexibility, and pleasure. Another source is the increased effectiveness of your understanding and behavior, which comes from the steady decrease in reactive behaviors. A third source of pleasure is the richness you experience in relationships and connections with others, again because of the decrease in reactive emotions.

You become obsessed with controlling the effects of practice. You become attached to the pleasurable or ecstatic states and try to stay in them as much as possible. You start to use the power of attention to get what you want from others.

You have lost presence, and the energy of practice now fuels old habituated patterns. The obsession with controlling experience is traditionally called the *god-child* obsession. Psychologically speaking, practice has penetrated down to an early level of conditioning (the child) that now tries to use the energy of practice (the god) to generate comfort and security.

To cut through this obsession, use the phrase:

May all suffering come into me.
May all happiness go to others.

This verse reminds us that the intention of our practice is presence and not the titan's obsession with enhanced abilities. Presence means that you are present with whatever arises in experience, whether it is pleasure or pain, happiness or suffering. In presence, you are not concerned with controlling experience. The god-child seeks to experience comfort and happiness and to avoid pain and suffering. As practice itself becomes the source of pleasure and power, keep the intention of presence in mind and let go of gaining ideas. Gaining ideas are any ideas about how we are going to benefit from practice. Suzuki Roshi, in *Zen Mind, Beginner's Mind,* reminds us again and again that our practice is in trouble when gaining ideas creep into it.

To cut through the god-child obsession, die to the belief that you can control what arises in experience.

Cutting Obsession with Self

The deepest level of obsession is obsession with a sense of self. A sense of self, generated as a reaction to non-referential space, lies at the core of every habituated pattern. A self is felt to be a permanent, independent unit. The feeling of permanence manifests in life as a feeling of dullness, of not being quite present. The illusion of independence arises as a feeling of separation. The feeling of being one thing arises as a feeling of incompleteness or dissatisfaction. Together, these three qualities obscure the mystery of being.

The sense of self does two things. It interprets what arises in experience to conform to its projections, and it presents the interpretations as the way things are, rather than as mere interpretations.

Because the actions of a pattern are based on projections, the actions eventually run counter to what is actually happening. Problems arise. The obsession with our idea of who and what we are causes us to ignore the problems or the signs of the problems. For instance, a person rises to a leadership position in an organization because of a remarkable ability to connect with people and involve them deeply in the organization's business. Because of his increased responsibilities as a leader, he is required to take clear stands on key issues, but the pattern of needing to connect compels him to avoid displeasing people.

Although he sets standards and objectives, people consistently fail to meet them because, with his style of leadership, noncompliance has no consequences. The organization begins to run into trouble. He is now perceived by others to be untrustworthy and unreliable, changing his mind on important issues and unable to hold to a definite course of action in difficult situations. Eventually, the perceptions of distrust and unreliability outweigh his ability to connect. He loses the confidence and respect of others and becomes ineffectual.

Similar mechanisms operate in all patterns, so when you encounter difficulties in your life, take difficulties as an indication that the obsession with a sense of self is operating. Use this phrase:

> *This is what you wanted.*
> *This is what you live for.*

In the previous example, the lack of direction in the organization is exactly what the pattern produces. The pattern works to degrade attention whenever the possibility of conflict arises. The person, operating under the pattern imperative, pours energy into connecting with people and making them feel good. The pattern imperative here is "Can't confront, must please others." This is what the pattern lives for.

The sense of self has very specific notions of how things are meant to be and ignores how things really are. The phrase brings attention to the world created by the pattern. When you see the inevitable contradictions between what the pattern generates and what the situation requires, you undermine the arrogance associated with the sense of self and cut the obsession.

In many discussions of compassion practices, we find the phrase

> *All sentient beings want to be happy,*
> *but all they create is suffering.*

On first reading, we usually understand these lines to mean sentient beings want to happy but keep doing the wrong things so they end up suffering. All of us know ways in which we (and others) have created suffering by trying to obtain something that was unattainable or trying to keep something whose time had passed.

A deeper reading, however, suggests that the effort to be happy is itself the reason we suffer. As Uchiyama Roshi points out in *Refining Your Life,* when you seek happiness, you assume that you are unhappy.

What you do, how you act, depends largely on how you see the world. You can look at the world in many different ways—through different lenses, as it were—but you quickly forget that you are looking through a lens. You go to sleep, a sleep induced by the lens through which you are looking, and take what you see as reality rather than the interpretation that it is.

When the lens through which you look at the world is formed from the assumption that you are not happy, then everything you experience through that lens necessarily reinforces the feeling that you are unhappy. Your search for happiness will be futile.

Mind training refines your experience of life by burning away emotional projections. Consequently, the practice of mind training feels like emotional suicide and the injunctions of mind training are hard to swallow. As Chekawa Yeshe Dorje writes, in *The Seven Points of Mind Training*:

Give up all hope for results.

Don't expect thanks.

Other injunctions from the mind-training tradition include

If it's better for me to be ill,
I pray for the blessing of illness.

Now that this trouble has arisen,
May it completely destroy "me" and "mine."

The fundamental insight of Buddhism is that what is called the self is, in fact, a pattern of misperception. We are so heavily identified with the sense of self that we do not question the thoughts and feelings generated by it. When we look directly at what we are, we see nothing. The phrase "This is what you wanted, this is what you live for" makes us aware that our reactions to difficulties and problems come from our obsession with being something or somebody. When we die to the belief that we are these reactions, we have cut through the pattern of self.

Behavior: The Ethics of Mind Training

True understanding carries an imperative to manifest what we know in action and in life.

The purpose of mind training is to stabilize awakening mind by refining the way we perceive and relate to what arises in experience. Awakening mind (Sanskrit: *bodhicitta*) is the intention to live awake—awake to the nature of experience (emptiness) and present in all that arises in experience (compassion). Awakening mind is the union of emptiness and compassion. The ethics of mind training are about how to manifest the union of emptiness and compassion in life.

To know emptiness means that you know directly that life is only what you experience. To know compassion means that you fully attend to what arises in experience because it is all you know and can ever know. Because mind training focuses on the expression of compassion, the primary ethical consideration is how to attend to what arises in experience.

The ethics of mind training come down to two key points to be avoided: rejecting others and corrupting practice.

Rejecting Others

The first aim is not to reject others, which means, in practical terms, to stop being unpleasant. The more deeply you train in taking and sending, the more clearly you understand that suffering is suffering, whether experienced by you or someone else. You naturally wish that others not suffer. Just as naturally, you see that unpleasantness toward others has no place in your life. Trying to get the best of someone, dwelling on their faults and failings, harboring grudges, retaliating against impoliteness, shirking responsibilities, and trying to benefit from someone's misfortune are examples of unpleasantness.

Bring attention to sore points.

What are the sore points in your life—an irritating colleague, a rebellious teenage son, a loud and obnoxious neighbor? Whatever the source of irritation, pain, or hurt, apply the technique of taking and sending. Take in and open to the experience until you can experience the irritation, pain, or hurt for what it is, a sensation. Send out your own happiness and well-being, understanding that, whatever the pain or difficulty, it is only an experience.

When we experience pain, attention often collapses and we just react. All we can think of is how to stop the pain. The pain becomes the enemy and we try to destroy it or whatever we, in confusion, think is causing it. We kill the messenger, who may be a colleague, neighbor, or even our spouse or partner. Practice taking and sending in the moment, and stop identifying with reactions to pain. Transform suffering into attention and awareness.

Don't seek pain to support your happiness.

"I hope he fails." Does this kind of thought ever cross your mind? The essence of compassion is wanting others not to suffer, but when situations arise in which you will benefit from another person's misfortune, you hope for the misfortune to happen or even do what you can to cause it.

At a retreat many years ago, an actor once asked my teacher, Kalu Rinpoche, how to approach auditions. "Because only one person can have the part," the actor asked, "am I causing other people misfortune if I compete for it?" Rinpoche replied that the matter really came down to intention or motivation. "If," he said, "your intention is to beat the other person, then, yes, you are intending to cause them pain from which you benefit. But if your intention is to do the best that you can, as an actor, then you are not seeking their pain for your happiness."

I once asked another Tibetan teacher about euthanasia. "This is very tricky," he replied. "Suppose you hear a screech of brakes and a thud. You go outside and you see that your dog has been hit by the car. His back is broken, his head is smashed, and he is whimpering and writhing, obviously in great pain. You go back into your house, take a gun and shoot your own dog. What's wrong with that? But if you hesitate for a moment, everything changes."

Don't put the horse's load on a pony.

This instruction is about assuming personal responsibility for difficulties in your life. Wash your own dishes. This instruction works on many levels. You have to lay off an employee. Don't delegate the job to another person. Speak to the employee yourself. This is what your life has brought you, so face it and bring all your attention to the matter. If you were in the employee's position, how would you want your boss to tell you? What help, assistance, or support would you like? What severance package would feel fair and appropriate? What can you do, within or even outside the company's policies?

On quite a different level, suppose that you have difficulty in handling your own anger. Instead of experiencing it, you fly off the handle at anyone who is around, whether that person is your spouse, your child, your brother, or a friend. Everyone knows this about you, and those close to you try not to take the tantrums personally, but you are still putting the horse's load on a pony. You are making them experience your anger instead of experiencing and releasing it in attention yourself.

Don't wait in ambush.

Because revenge is always based on the past, not on the present, it is totally contrary to the ethics of mind training. You cannot exact revenge without being marked by the action. So, when somebody injures you, address the injury as a matter of restoring balance, not as a matter of revenge. Revenge is the desire to cause pain to another in the mistaken belief that their pain will remedy your own. Take a moment to recall an incident when someone injured you, even intentionally. Now imagine taking revenge on that person. What motivates the action in you—anger or presence? How does that person's pain help you with yours? What are you setting in motion inside you by wishing pain on this person? Do you really want that dynamic operating in you? Now ask, "What needs to happen in order for me to be able to let go of the pain of this injury and move forward in my life?"

Corrupting Practice

The second key point is not to serve sleep or, alternatively, not to allow habituated patterns to corrupt practice. Holding a view of being an accomplished individual, trying to impress others with your achievements, anticipating how practice will make you a better person, and using mind training to relieve discomfort instead of experiencing it directly are all corruptions of mind-training practice. Corruption is a progressive process. Small compromises with habituated patterns make larger compromises more acceptable. Gradually, habituated patterns take over your practice and your life.

Don't reduce a god to a demon.

One of the most common pitfalls on the spiritual path is to develop an identity as a spiritual practitioner—"I'm a spiritual person." One teacher I met many years ago would introduce his students saying, "This is Jane; she's a great meditator" or "This is Jim; he has made great progress in his practice." Something is deeply amiss here. The practice of Buddhism is not about becoming a great this or a great that, but about being so completely in tune with what is that you move through life without leaving any traces, like a bird flying in the sky.

In mind training, you are deliberately giving victory to others and accepting defeat in order to generate friction with your habituated patterns of self-cherishing and self-importance. If you tell people that you are deliberately accepting defeat you undermine the whole enterprise. Telling another person how compassionate you are not only leaves a bad taste in the mouth; it is the antithesis of true compassion—the willingness to be with the other when he or she is in pain. Making an issue of your magnanimity, empathy, or patience just reveals that your so-called compassion is about maintaining a self-image. You've taken a "god," the practice of mind training, and reduced it to a "demon," a means by which you reinforce a sense of identity.

Change your attitude but behave naturally.

Another common pitfall is to try to impress others with your practice of mind training. You make a show of giving a better seat to another person, of waiting for others to be served first, of letting the other person have the last word. Such behavior is not only obnoxious; it reinforces the pattern of being special. The behavior that comes from mind training is completely natural and uncontrived, and so, unnoticed. I have a cousin in England, a dentist, who exhibits this quality wonderfully. Without any ostentation or manipulation, he is there, holding the door open for you. I didn't notice this trait at first, but as I observed his behavior, I saw how he naturally gave way to others, made others feel comfortable, without any effort or contrivance on his part. If I made a point of holding the door open for him, he just stepped through it, without comment or ceremony.

Bring your mind-training practice into how you move and how you speak. A person who practices mind training is a good listener—an active listener, to use a modern phrase—but the listening is completely natural and not forced. Mind training is basically a secret practice, a practice that you do unbeknown to others.

Don't revert to magic.

This instruction means that you don't use mind training to feel better. Many people use meditation to discharge the emotional tension of difficult situations, but the intention of mind training is different. When you encounter unpleasantness, use mind training to experience it completely, inviting in the same sort of unpleasantness from all beings everywhere. You aren't going to feel better. You are going to feel a lot worse! And you are going to feel worse and worse until you realize that an unpleasant experience is only an unpleasant experience, not the end of the world. Don't use mind training to make things better.

Whichever of the two arises, be patient.

Mind training is a very tough practice. Here you start relating to life as experience—what you experience is your life. Sometimes what you experience is very unpleasant, so you experience unpleasantness. Know it to be an experience and nothing more. Sometimes what you experience is very pleasant, so you experience pleasure. Know it to be pleasure and nothing more.

When you encounter adversity or unpleasantness, you usually think that something has gone wrong. You go to work, figure out what has gone wrong, and correct it if you can. In particular, you tend to work harder at spiritual practice when you encounter major difficulties and unpleasantness in your life. In the case of mind training, this is essentially a corruption of practice. When adversity arises, use mind training to experience it completely. Use mind training to burn up the patterns that try to resist or avoid what is arising in experience.

On the other hand, when you encounter pleasure, you are apt to take credit and feel that you have done something right. You are less motivated in spiritual practice and tend to go to sleep in the experience of pleasure. Mind training directs you to relate to pleasure in exactly the same way that you relate to discomfort—as experience. When pleasure arises, give it away to others. When discomfort arises, take the discomfort of others into you.

The mahamudra tradition refers to a stage of practice when the circumstances of life change dramatically. Sometimes the change is for the better—everything goes right. Your work goes better, you prosper, everyone gets along in your family and circle of friends, you become famous, respected, and honored. This is called *good fall*. Sometimes the change is for the worse. You become ill, you lose your job, your friends leave you, and people regard you as unreliable, stupid, or unsociable. This is called *bad fall*. Why some people experience a good fall and others experience a bad fall is a mystery, but the instruction is the same—both kinds of falls are just experiences. Ironically, those who experience a bad fall usually continue to make progress in their practice and those who experience a good fall often let their practice fade away.

The ethical principles in mind training provide a sounding board for us to be clear about what is happening internally. But for mind training to act as that sounding board, we must take as absolute our own intention to awaken to compassion and emptiness.

AWAKENING MIND

The intention of mind training and taking and sending is to refine the totality of knowing and experience.

What we are—pure being, empty awareness, buddha nature—is obscured by the presence of habituated patterns of perception, feeling, and thinking. The practice of mind training takes the raw ore of awareness and experience and refines it, progressively eliminating the impurities that cloud perception and trigger reactions. As impurities are removed, direct open awareness manifests more and more clearly. The sense of separation created by the subject-object patterns of perception begins to subside, and we enter into the mystery of being.

As the sense of separation diminishes, we know what arises in experience fully and completely. Our relationship with what we experience moves into balance, a movement that has two aspects: compassion and emptiness.

Emptiness refers to knowing what experience is—groundless, open, and indefinable. With this complete and accurate knowing, we are able to perceive balance and imbalance precisely.

What we do is not based on personal agendas or the need to maintain a sense of self. Instead, what we do arises from the direct perception of the direction of the present. At this level, compassion is the natural manifestation of awareness. The unity of compassion and emptiness is awakening mind.

Mind training is the process of refining our ordinary experience of the world into awakening mind. Awakening mind is intention, the intention to awaken to the way things are and the way they arise. The core of Mahayana Buddhism is the generation and cultivation of awakening mind, which has two aspects, awakening to what is apparently real and awakening to what is ultimately real. The former is the aspiration to wake up, to achieve buddhahood, in order to help others. The latter is the direct understanding of what is.

When intention is refined to the point of awakening mind, your whole life and experience of life change. Everything you do, even eating and sleeping, contributes to awakening.

When awakening mind arises, all concern about maintaining a sense of self separate from the world we experience drops away. We know that the sense of self is the source of suffering. From that knowing arises, naturally and powerfully, the intention to work to remove the basis of suffering wherever it occurs. This intention is known, in traditional Buddhism, as the vow of awakening mind. Taking and sending is one of the simplest yet most powerful methods for uncovering and refining this intention.

CHAPTER 9

Insight and Dismantling Illusion

Nasrudin was walking past a well, when he had the impulse to look into it. It was night, and as he peered into the deep water, he saw the Moon's reflection there.

"I must save the Moon!" the Mulla thought. "Otherwise she will never wane, and the fasting month of Ramadan will never come to an end."

He found a rope, threw it in and called down: "Hold tight; keep bright; succour is at hand!"

The rope caught in a rock inside the well, and Nasrudin heaved as hard as he could. Straining back, he suddenly felt the rope give as it came loose, and he was thrown on his back. As he lay there, panting, he saw the Moon riding in the sky above.

"Glad to be of service," said Nasrudin. "Just as well I came along, wasn't it?"

—IDRIES SHAH,
THE PLEASANTRIES OF THE INCREDIBLE MULLA NASRUDIN

In the early seventies, I served as the translator for a lama who was invited to teach in Whitehorse in the north of Canada. We arrived in the late afternoon, met the people connected with the center, and were taken to our host's home for the night. Although Whitehorse is a few hundred miles south of the Arctic Circle, it is sufficiently far north that in the summer the nights are no darker than twilight.

The next morning, the lama called me with some urgency. He was clearly shaken. "It didn't get dark last night," he said. "What's going on?" Using oranges and apples, I explained that the earth was round, orbits the sun, and is tilted on its axis, and I demonstrated how the sun does not set in the far north. He muttered that he had heard something about Westerners viewing the world as round when he came out of Tibet and had dismissed the notion as nonsense. Now he took the matter seriously. He had to face the fact that his experience of nights without darkness contradicted the view of the universe that he inherited from his culture. He was depressed for several months. The loss of his cosmology was like a death for him.

We may laugh and say that people who believe the earth is flat are wrong and do not know anything, but only a few hundred years ago, everyone in our own culture not only believed the world was flat; they "knew" that the world was flat. We cannot distinguish beliefs from knowledge except by direct experience.

The immense intellectual, emotional, psychological, and cultural investment in a worldview makes it immune to any challenge except direct experience. Even direct experience is not always sufficient. Inside we all have a bit of the politician who says, "I've made up my mind: don't confuse me with facts."

Insight is seeing—clear, direct seeing. It is experience, experience so direct and vivid that you know and that's that. It is not speculation, deduction, inference, or any other form of understanding arrived at through the intellect. It is not belief—holding to a concept or idea because it conforms with how you want things to be despite evidence to the contrary.

Insight practice is about dying, dying to the world defined by the operation of habituated patterns, so that you see. It requires faith, the willingness to open to the mystery of being as it is revealed in direct experience.

Consider how a family looks to a psychologist, an attorney, an accountant, a doctor, a sociologist, a physicist, a historian, a parent, or a child. None of the views of these individuals is the family. What is valued by the psychologist may be ignored by the attorney. What is meaningful and worthwhile to the parent may be regarded as unwise or irrelevant by the accountant.

We interpret experience through systems of thought and other structures. A father interprets his experience of the family in terms of the welfare and well-being of his children. The accountant interprets the experience of the family in terms of cash flow, savings, and debt. Finances paint one picture of the family. Relationships paint another. Both the accountant and the father take their pictures as how things are. In each case, the picture presented by the structure is taken as real. The father pays attention to relationships and the growth and development of his children. The accountant pays attention to income and expenses.

The father, limited by his concern with relationships, may not see the threat to the family from overspending. The accountant, focused on money, may not see the potential damage to family relationships that an austere budget could cause. Both are concerned with the family's viability, but attachments to their respective interpretations limit their effectiveness. Neither sees what is actually there. The family is what is and cannot be defined as this or that.

We often fail to appreciate how structures and beliefs limit what we see and what we value. Structures develop for good reasons. Money, for instance, was originally invented to facilitate trade and exchanges of work and material. Over time complex financial structures developed. Within these structures, money is the only thing that matters (because it is the only thing they address). Now something subtle but very important happens. We forget that we are looking at a picture and take the picture that money presents as what is real. We believe that money is all that counts. We believe that money defines value! In believing, we fall under the enchantment of the financial structure and lose connection with other facets of life.

Of course, money is only one example of a system that weaves an enchantment. Science is another self-justifying system, insisting that it is the unarguable, sole, and absolute truth. It is another set of beliefs and only appears to be direct experience to those who believe in it. That modern people insist that their assumptions—round earth, capitalism, representative democracy—are actual realities and not beliefs only confirms that they are beliefs. Other systems are law, medicine, emotional health, artistic expression, family values, relationships, and subject-object dualism.

Every system presents us with a picture of the world of experience. Each picture has the specific purpose of portraying experience in a way that preserves the functioning of the system. Aspects of experience relevant to the functioning of the system are assigned values according to the extent that they facilitate the system. Everything else is assigned the value zero in the picture. The economic system, for instance, assigns the value zero to activities that do not generate income, so child care that is paid for is valued more than good parenting. A system denies the existence of aspects of life that it is unable to represent in its picture, just as medical science, until recently, denied the existence of the power of loving care in healing. The usefulness of a system lulls us into dependence on it, and we end up believing that the picture the system presents is what life actually is.

Insight dismantles the illusion that the picture presented by a structure is what is real. When you practice insight, the picture is seen to be a picture. The picture is seen to have specific agendas associated with it—the agenda of money, the agenda of relationships, the agenda of subject-object separation.

These agendas may be contrary to your intention in life. You cannot find meaningful relationships when your world is defined by money. Neither can you experience the mystery of being when your world is defined by subject-object dualism.

INSIGHT AND DYING

Insight practice has two essential components: dying to the world of beliefs, and pointing-out instructions. In the story of the lama at the beginning of this chapter, the direct experience of night with no darkness caused him to die to the world of his beliefs. The explanation of the earth tilted on its axis and orbiting the sun was, in a way, a pointing-out instruction, pointing out how things are seen in a scientific context.

First you die. Then you see. You can't see before you die because patterns cloud seeing. Insight practice is, by its nature, frustrating, challenging, and frightening.

> A man looks for the hat he is wearing. He knows he has a hat, but he can't remember where he put it. A friend says, "It's on your head."
>
> "No," he says, "I put it down somewhere." His friend comes up to him, but he pushes his friend away, saying, "Just let me look for it." This is the first stage of dying: denial.
>
> He searches the room, opening closets and drawers, overturning furniture, even looking under the rug. Frustrated by his inability to find his hat, he grows more and more irritated. This is the second stage of dying: anger.
>
> He looks everywhere, but he still cannot find it. He starts talking to himself. "From now on, I'll always put it in the closet. I'll keep everything tidy and neat." This is the third stage of dying: bargaining.
>
> Eventually he collapses in despair. He does not know what to do. He gives up, sits down, and stares into space. This is the fourth stage: depression.
>
> His friend asks, "Do you want my help?"

"Yes," he says, "I don't know where it is." This is the fifth stage: acceptance.

Then his friend taps him on the head and says, "What's this?" This is the pointing-out instruction.

"My hat, my hat! I found my hat!" he cries. "Why didn't you tell me before?"

We don't die willingly. The more invested we are in the worlds projected by patterns, the stronger the denial, anger, and bargaining, and the despair of depression. Insight practice is inherently frustrating because you are looking to see where, at first, you are unable to see— beyond the world of the patterns.

Another way to look at insight practice is to see that the process has three stages: shock, disorganization, and reorganization.

The first stage starts when you see beyond illusion. You experience a shock. You react by denying that you saw what you saw, saying, in effect, "That makes no sense. I'll just forget about that." Unfortunately, or fortunately, your experience of seeing is not so easily denied. It is too vivid, too real, to ignore. Now you become angry because the illusion in which you have lived has been shattered. You know you can't go back, but you don't want to go forward. You are still attached to the world of patterns. You feel anxious, and the anxiety gradually matures into grief. You now know that you have to go forward. You experience the pain of separating from what you understood, just as the lama in the example experienced pain at the loss of his worldview.

You then enter a period of disorganization. You withdraw, become apathetic, lose your energy for life, become restless, and routinely reject new possibilities or directions. You surrender to the changes taking place but do nothing to move forward. A major risk at this stage is that you remain in a state of disorganization. You hold on to an aspect of the old world. Parents who have lost a child in an accident or to violence, for example, have great difficulty in letting go. They may keep the child's bedroom just as it was. Their views and expectations of life have been shattered, and, understandably, they cling to a few of the shards. They may stay in the stage of disorganization for a long time.

The third stage of insight is reorganization. You experience a shift, and you let the old world go, even the shards. You accept the world that you see with your new eyes. What was previously seen as being absolute and real is now seen differently. The old structures, beliefs, and behaviors no longer hold, and you enter a new life.

PRACTICE GUIDELINES

Initially, insight practice is very confusing. You feel as if you are staring into nothing, and you have no idea what you are doing. You probably have felt the same way in other practices, but insight practice amplifies these feelings considerably. In my retreat training, the whole group of us spent a peaceful and enjoyable month cultivating attention in preparation for insight. Then we received instructions for insight, and we all felt as if bombs had gone off inside us.

A month, by the way, is not a long preparation period. Rangjung Dorje, a Tibetan master, was required to cultivate stable attention day and night for three years before his teacher gave him instruction in insight. Stable attention is very important. Most difficulties in insight come from not having stable, strong attention.

For insight practice, make your formal practice sessions at least forty-five minutes. Spend the first five to ten minutes resting with the breath, letting the surface level of activity and tension dissipate.

Then spend another ten minutes doing the energy transformation practice described in the instructions. Because insight is about seeing beyond the limitations of patterns, you need a level of energy in attention higher than the level of energy in the patterns. The energy transformation practice raises the level of energy in your attention. Where resting with the breath stabilizes attention, energy transformation practice strengthens it.

Then spend twenty to thirty minutes working at insight. A cardinal rule for insight practice is "Work from a base of stable, clear attention." When you look at the nature of experience or the nature of mind, you will fall into confusion again and again. Thoughts and feelings will erupt in you, or you will fall into thick, dull states of mind. You will feel as if you can't meditate at all.

You can't do insight if your mind is either full of thoughts or thick and dull. You might as well try to see your reflection in a pond ruffled by a strong wind or in a pond filled with mud. Reestablish stable, clear attention by letting go of looking and returning attention to the breath. Then go back to the looking.

A friend once worked on a crew that was laying an oil pipeline in northern California. For several weeks, they worked in a valley far from any towns or highways. After a few days, they noticed that a man climbed up one of the hills every day at about the same time. Halfway up, he sat down facing the length of the valley. The man sat motionless for several hours, then walked down the hill. He repeated the same ritual day after day. During one of their lunch breaks, the crew climbed up the hill and approached the man. "You come up here every day," one of the crew said. "What do you see?"

The man replied, "I look. When I know how to look, then maybe I will see."

Looking involves three steps: exhausting experience, cutting the root, and resting in seeing. Each of the meditation exercises is divided into three sections in order to make clear what is being exhausted, how to direct attention to cut the root, and how to rest.

The insight practices given here use questions about the nature of mind such as "What is mind?" You may come up with logical or philosophical answers, but, for the purpose of developing insight, such answers are worse than useless. They reinforce your reliance on intellectual processes. Awareness, not the intellect, sees the nature of mind. You cannot think your way to it.

Use the question to direct attention to mind or experience. Hold the question. Attention forms and begins to penetrate habituated structures of thought and experience. Reactive patterns are triggered. Thoughts, feelings, and confusion arise. Hold the question in the face of the reactive mechanisms. Attention gradually penetrates the patterns, and you are able to look more deeply and for longer periods. Seeing often arises as soon as the patterns are penetrated. If it does not, then you need to cut the root of experience. How do you know

> Inconceivable,
> inexpressible,
> indescribable,
> The mother of all
> buddhas is beyond
> the intellect.
>
> —*Prayer to the*
> *Perfection of*
> *Wisdom*

whether you have experienced seeing? Generally, you will know, but you should have your experience examined by your teacher.

Cutting the root means turning attention to what is holding the question. In holding the question, you dissolve the clouding influence of the patterns. The question holds your attention, and reactive patterns are unable to function. Still, the pattern of subject-object fixation remains and prevents you from experiencing mind nature. Turn the attention back on what is looking, what is holding the question. Redirecting the attention breaks the subject-object fixation, and seeing can now arise.

At a certain point, the question and the looking dissolve into nothing. You feel as if the looking just fell to pieces. Now you see. Rest right there. Rest in the seeing. Don't make any more effort. Initially the seeing will last for only a short time, perhaps only a second or two.

Return to holding the question and cutting the root. If you become confused by dullness or busyness, stop making efforts at holding the question, and reestablish a base of attention. Insight practice is best done for short periods of great intensity.

For the last five to ten minutes, just relax and rest. Sit with your mind open and clear. Let the energy and effort disperse. Then go about your day.

Practice transforming energy for short periods throughout your day. At the same time, regard all experience, inside and outside, as a dream. Whenever you can, stop and look at what you are experiencing, posing the question, "What is this?" The effort keeps the practice alive in you and interrupts habituated functioning.

Throughout the practice of insight, regular interaction with a teacher is very important. The pitfalls are numerous. Very still or very clear states of mind are easily mistaken for experiences of seeing mind nature. Inconsequential experiences are commonly taken as important insights. You can also become fixated on certain states of mind and lose the intention to see. A capable and experienced teacher is often the only safeguard against these pitfalls.

In insight, you are trying to see what you cannot see. A teacher shows you how and where to look. Because you have to die to how you currently look at things, you need someone to hold the possibility of moving through death. To die, you have to let go, so you need someone who inspires the trust and confidence you need to stand in the fear and to let go.

Insight practice is based entirely on the arising of direct experience. You are not instilling an understanding, as in many of the previous meditations. Some people progress very quickly in insight and then turn to the practice of presence (see chapter 10). Others work long and hard before they see mind nature. If you are unable to connect with insight practice, then you need to work on the earlier meditations in greater depth. Once you have a direct experience of mind nature, you also return to the earlier meditations but in a different way, as described in the next chapter.

Meditation: Uncovering Insight

FOUNDATION: ATTENTION AND ENERGY

Base of Attention

Rest attention on the breath for a few minutes at the beginning of each session until attention becomes stable.

Ecstatic Practice: Raising the Level of Energy

Raising the level of energy has four steps: frame, field, expansion, and rest. It is called ecstatic practice because you experience a pleasurable shift in energy as you open to experience. It transforms the energy of experience into attention. Practice this ecstatic technique both in formal sessions and during the day.

Begin with sensory experience. Sit in front of a window or open door. The window frame or door frame is the *frame*. Let your gaze rest on the window until you can see the whole frame all at once. This step sets the frame.

Open to the whole field defined by the frame. The *field* is everything in your field of vision that falls within the frame, regardless of its distance from you.

Initially, your eyes will pick out an object in the field, and your attention will collapse down to that object. As soon as you notice that you are looking at only a part of the field, *expand* from that object to the whole field again. In ecstatic practice a collapse down to an object is analogous to being distracted by a thought in breath meditation.

You will soon be able to see everything in the frame simultaneously and will feel a shift. *Rest* in the shift. You relax, and a pleasurable feeling pervades your body and mind. Subject-object differentiation lessens.

Work first with a well-defined frame, one that is small enough that you can actually open to the whole field. Then extend your practice by using larger and larger frames until you can use the physical limits of your field of vision as the frame.

During the day, practice this energy transformation when you go for a walk, go shopping, or take a break in your workday. Shopping malls are good places to practice because they are full of visual objects, and the walls and ceilings provide natural frames. Sit in front of a waterfall until you can see every drop of water as it falls. Look at a tree, using the outline of the tree as a frame, until you can see every leaf and every branch at the same time. Look at a lawn, and see every blade of grass at once.

Once you have a sense of the shift in energy from working visually, work with the other senses. During the day, listen to a piece of music, hearing every instrument at the same time. Whenever your attention goes to one instrument or one strain, expand to include all the music and every instrument. Listen in the same way to people talking.

Extend the practice to the sense of touch so that you are aware of all the clothing you are wearing, what you are sitting on, and any stiffness or tension in your muscles, all at the same time. Then include taste and smell as well.

Finally, include thoughts and feelings, until you can open to everything that arises in the moment, internally and externally, and experience it all simultaneously. This step extends the practice to emotional sensations and transforms the energy of all experience into attention.

Needless to say, you won't do all this in your first session. Over time, however, you become more adept at the practice and can open to more and more.

In your formal meditation sessions, spend ten minutes doing this practice, resting in open experience and transforming energy into attention. Now you are ready to look.

INSIGHT: THE MAIN PRACTICE

Appearances Are Mind—Life Is but a Dream

Exhaust the Experience
Take a simple object—a book, a flower, or a stone—and look at it.

What is your experience? You say, "I see a book." True, but what do you experience? *Book* is a label you apply to your experience. What is your experience? A red rectangle. True, but again you are labeling your experience. The book may appear as a rectangle, a square, or a parallelogram depending on where you are positioned. The color likewise depends on available light, how it filters into the room, and whether you are wearing sunglasses. Again, what is your experience? Seeing is also a label. What is that?

Every time you answer the question, note the labeling and return to your experience. Keep looking past the labels to the actual experience of seeing the book—an appearance of shape, form, and color.

Where does this bare experience of shape, form, and color take place? Does it take place in the book? Probably not, because you are having the experience. Does it take place in you? Well, no, the shape, form, and color seem to appear outside you. In between? That doesn't seem right, either. Keep looking at the experience, asking again and again, "What is it?"

You can do this meditation with sound—a dripping tap, the noise of traffic, or music. Clear polyphonic music (such as Bach's *Brandenburg Concertos*) listened to with headphones is very effective.

> Nothing is like it seems, but everything is exactly like it is.
>
> —*Yogi Berra*

Where is the sound? Use the question to direct attention. Reason-ing, deduction, and inference are all distracting thoughts. Look with your mind to see where the sound is. With a good headset, you have the impression that some instruments are to your left and others to your right. Where is the sound, actually? Where is it experienced? Keep ask-ing questions to direct your attention to the experience itself. What is it?

You come to a place where there are no words. With the book, you come to place where the appearance of red shape arises, not in you, not outside you, just there. With the music, you come to a place where sound, music, is just there.

Practice cutting through labeling until you can hold attention in sensory experience itself.

Cut the Root
Now pose the question "What is experiencing this?" Keep the experi-ence, the color and shape of the book, and the seeing in attention and look at what is experiencing it.

If you start thinking or wondering about what experiences, you have fallen out of attention. Relax, go back to the pure experience, and again ask, "What is experiencing this?"

At some point you experience a strange shift. The usual framework of subject-object perception collapses for a moment. You *see* that what arises as experience is your mind!

You are clear, awake, and present, and perhaps a little awed and puzzled. The shift is to a different seeing, in which appearances, that is, what arises in experience, and mind, that is, experiencing itself, are not separate.

Rest
Rest in this seeing. At first, it will last for only a moment. When it fades, don't try to recover it. Instead, repeat the whole process. Look at the object, go through all the labels until the experience of the object arises as pure experience, cut the root by asking, "What is experiencing this?" and, again, rest in the seeing.

When your seeing shifts, rest in seeing. Don't do anything more. If you keep asking questions at this point, you spin meaninglessly in confusion, like a dog chasing its own tail.

Gradually, you will rest for longer periods in seeing, shattering the illusion that subject and object are independent and separate.

Recall the instruction "Regard everything as a dream." Now, perhaps, the instruction makes more sense. Appearances arise in experience. What arises in experience is not separate from what experiences, which we call "your mind," just as in a dream, what arises in the dream is not separate from the mind that is dreaming.

Mind Is Empty—
Examine the Nature of Unborn Awareness

Exhaust the Experience
Rest with your mind open and clear. Let your mind rest, and look at the resting mind. What is the resting mind? You start thinking, "What is mind?—Well, it's the source of experience, it's what I am, it controls everything." Such thoughts are distractions that take you away from looking. Just ask the question, "What is this, the mind that rests?" and look. Look and rest in the looking. You see nothing. You fall into confusion, and you wonder if you are doing the practice correctly. Your mind becomes thick and dull. Wake up! Go back to the clear, open, resting mind. Reestablish a base of attention. Then ask again, "What is this resting mind?" Look, and rest in the looking.

How is the resting mind? Does it have a color, shape, or form? Does it have a location? You may well think such questions make no sense, but look anyway. Even though we know intellectually that mind doesn't have shape or color, we still hold emotionally to the notion that mind is a thing. The question directs your attention to mind, and though you see no thing, the looking is what is important. Keep looking.

Now look at an object, a flower or a book. Look at your mind as sensory experience arises. Does anything change? What changes? How is the mind that experiences a flower different from the mind at rest? Again you see nothing. No matter, keep looking.

> Don't think; just look.
>
> —*Wittgenstein*

Let a thought or a feeling float up. Now your mind is moving. What is the moving mind? What moves? The same reactions of speculation and bewilderment arise. Let them go, return to a base of attention, let another thought or feeling float up, pose the question, and look again.

Cut the Root

Awareness operates in both the resting mind and the moving mind. You know when your mind is resting, you know when your mind is moving. You know when you are experiencing a flower and when you are not.

What knows? Look at that. Again you fall into thinking or confusion. Many ideas will occur to you: nothing is born, nothing dies; everything is empty; there is no one home. Don't confuse these ideas with direct understanding.

Again establish a base of attention, and then start the whole process over again.

Look again and again at what is aware. You don't see anything. Keep looking. Whenever any idea of the mind being this or that arises, look again. You don't see anything. Keep looking.

At some point, you again feel a shift and you *see* nothing.

Rest

Rest in the seeing. Practice this stage until you can rest awake and clear in seeing nothing. This stage is particularly frustrating because you keep coming back to no thing. You want to say, "Okay, I get the point," but that's not good enough. You have to keep coming back and looking until everything in you is exhausted, all the old habituations, all the desires for a definite reality, all the subtle ways you cling to a sense of self.

Emptiness Is Natural Presence— Let Go of Understanding, Too

Exhaust the Experience

Mind nature has three qualities. It is empty, clear, and unceasing. Look at each of these and their relationship with one another.

"Just look along the road, and tell me if you can see either of them."

"I see nobody on the road," said Alice.

"I only wish I had such eyes," the King remarked in a fretful tone. "To be able to see Nobody! And at that distance, too! Why, it's as much as I can do to see real people, by this light!"

—*Lewis Carroll*

The emptiness of mind is the "being nothing there" quality. You look at mind and see nothing, so you say, "Mind is empty." What says, "Mind is empty"? Look at that.

The clarity of mind is the ability to be aware. Mind is not just blank emptiness, like the space inside a box. You are aware, so you say, "I'm aware." Look at what is aware. What is that?

Experience-awareness arises unceasingly. It is always arising, whether as the thick torpor of sleep, the brilliant awake mind of insight, the confusion of reaction, the richness of emotional and sensory experience, the intricacy of the intellect, or the quiet and peace of an evening at home. What experiences everything? Look at that.

Look at the clarity and emptiness. Are they the same or different? What about the clarity and unceasing, the emptiness and unceasing?

Cut the Root

As you practice, ideas will arise: "mind is empty" or "in emptiness nothing is harmful or helpful" or "mind is total clarity." Look right at the idea, concept, or thought, and cut it with attention.

Cut through any concept of even the qualities of mind nature as existing in their own right. Cut through any concept that you have such and such understanding. Both tendencies reestablish the subject-object framework and pull you back into habituation.

Rest

As before, as soon as you have cut, rest. Relax and open, allowing the quality of presence to unfold in you, as a flower unfolds in the warm rays of the sun.

Natural Presence Is Natural Freedom—
Rest in the Nature of Things

This is the culmination of practice, the practice of presence—resting in the nature of things.

Exhaust the Experience
When you sit down to meditate, let everything go. Don't fall into distraction. Don't try to make anything happen. Don't try to cultivate anything. Relax and rest, vivid, awake, and open.

Cut the Root
Whenever you fall into distraction or the vivid clarity fades, relax and look directly at what experienced the disturbance. Whatever arises—whether thoughts, reactive emotions such as anger or greed, higher emotions such as equanimity or compassion, meditation experiences such as bliss, clarity, or non-thought, even visions or hallucinations—just recognize it and rest in clarity.

Since appearance is mind and emptiness is mind,
Since understanding is mind and delusion is mind,
Since arising is mind and cessation is mind,
May all assumptions about mind be eliminated.

—*Rangjung Dorje*

Rest
Rest in the state of just recognizing the nature of whatever arises. When left to itself, ordinary mind is utterly empty, vividly clear, and totally open. When left to itself, experience just arises and subsides on its own.

Commentary

Insight is about experience, not philosophy. Over the centuries, various schools of Buddhism have developed powerful and sophisticated arguments to "prove" that external reality does not exist, that all experience is empty, and that the nature of mind is sheer clarity or emptiness or something equally as wonderful and incomprehensible. For the practice of insight, however, these arguments and proofs are almost worthless. At best, such arguments open your mind to new possibilities. At worst, they lead to particularly intractable forms of belief.

Don't simply read the instructions and commentary and say, "Yes, that's interesting." Use these instructions to examine your own mind and how you experience thoughts, feelings, and sensations until you see how things are. Nothing else is important.

Raising the Level of Energy

In meditation practice, we raise the level of attention by transforming emotional energy into attention. For the practice of insight, that level of energy must be higher than the level of energy in the pattern of subject-object perception.

If you practice the ecstatic method consistently, the level of energy in your attention will rise and your insight practice will be more fruitful. You will also be more present and less reactive in your daily life.

Energy transformation techniques are basically advanced practices to be used when your intention in your practice is clear and stable and you are able to use attention to remedy any problems that arise.

An element of danger is inherent in all energy transformation methods. Reactions are triggered as higher levels of energy penetrate habituated patterns. There is no way of predicting which patterns will be triggered or how strongly the reactions will run. Consequently, the best course is to learn energy methods from a person who has experience with them and knows how to recognize and remedy the unpredictable effects of such practices.

Every Buddhist tradition has a set of practices that it uses to transform energy. In the Theravadan tradition of Southeast Asia, for instance, the four immeasurables are used to power higher and higher states of attention known as the jhanas, or meditative absorptions.

The refined states of mind developed in the meditative absorptions can be very pleasurable. If these practices are introduced too early, students run the risk of developing addictions to such states. You must be clear that the intention of practice is presence, not ecstatic states of mind.

In the Tibetan tradition, devotional practices, especially prayer to your teacher, are used to transform energy. The power of faith, the willingness to open to the mystery of being, is used to transform the energy of emotions into attention. The teacher is taken as the embodiment of original mind. In some traditions, you imagine your actual teacher, and in other traditions you work with a symbolic teacher. In either case, you pour emotional energy into devotion, praying to the teacher for understanding and insight and other qualities. You then imagine that the teacher's mind and your mind join.

This is a very powerful practice because it draws on very powerful energies: the energy of respect and appreciation for your teacher, the energy of love and connection, the energy of spiritual yearning, and the energies that define and maintain a separate sense of "I." All these energies are transformed into faith, which then powers attention.

In devotion practice, you form a deeply emotional relationship with your teacher. You see him or her as the source of everything you learn and understand. If you read the biography of Milarepa, for instance, you see how totally devoted he was to his teacher, Marpa. If devotion practice is introduced too early, however, students project their family patterns onto their teacher, reinforcing patterns of dependency, passivity, or unrequited love. For devotion practice, you must be totally clear in your relationship with your teacher and able to cut through or transform family projections as they arise.

Another widely used method of energy transformation is directing attention into the body and transforming the energies of the body using visualizations and special exercises. These methods are very powerful and should be learned only from a teacher, not from a book.

The danger in working with the energies of the body are physical and emotional imbalances that can result in insanity or death. You are working with the energies that your body depends on for functioning. If you are able to access the energy that keeps your heart beating and your attention wanders, your heart may stop beating. These practices must be taken very seriously.

The ecstatic opening method given in the meditation instructions above is simple, powerful, and effective. As energy practices go, it is also one of the safest. It raises energy only to the extent that you have the capacity of attention to stay present with any reactions that are triggered. Other energy transformations dramatically elevate the level of energy in your system and may trigger reactions that overwhelm your capacity in attention. The heightened energy then flows into the patterns, reinforcing them instead of dismantling them.

As the level of energy in your system rises, you may experience waves of emotions unrelated to what you are doing, inexplicable sensations or aches and pains, or sudden surges of energy in parts of your body. Generally, such experiences come and go, but if they occur with increasing frequency or intensity, you should practice dispersion to balance out the energy.

Sit quietly, and then bring your attention to a point in your body about two inches below your navel and about two inches in front of your spine. Gently imagine energy collecting there. Then imagine the energy dispersing smoothly throughout your body and extending out through the pores of your skin so that you sit in a field of energy that extends about three inches from your body. Sit quietly for a few minutes. Do this two or three times as necessary. The dispersion method is quite safe to practice and quite useful.

Insight practice can be upsetting, particularly in the initial phases. If you are overly agitated, unable to sleep, or generally unsettled, use the dispersion practice to balance your energy. You will probably feel calmer and less agitated, and your work in insight will go better.

When you work with energy transformation practices, start slowly and end slowly. Start slowly by doing them lightly for only a few minutes at a time. Gradually extend the amount of time and the depth of your work as your ability to stay present in attention increases. If you decide to stop doing energy transformation, do not stop suddenly. Decrease the time and depth of your practice over the course of a few weeks, tapering off and letting your body and mind adjust. If you stop suddenly, the energy in your system either will stagnate and cause illness in one or more places in your body or will flow into habituated patterns and make them stronger and less workable. In all energy transformation practices, continue to work with a teacher.

Step 1: Appearances Are Mind

Despite the prevalence of interpretations to the contrary, "appearances are mind" does not mean that everything that happens in the world somehow takes place in your mind, that everything that appears exists in your head or brain, or that what arises in your experience is "only" mental or psychological. All views that substantiate appearances even as mental objects are inaccurate. Equally, to say "appearances are mind" does not mean that what does arise in experience does not really exist, is not real, or is just a hallucination. Views that try to deny the validity of experience are also inaccurate.

Perhaps the confusion begins with the word *mind*. In English, it usually denotes the intellect or related phenomena. In Buddhism, *mind* means "what experiences." Kalu Rinpoche used to say that mind means experiencing. When you are given the pointing-out instruction "What is mind?" you are actually being asked, "What is experience?"

In *Refining Your Life*, Uchiyama Roshi returns again and again to the question: what is experience? I have my own life experience. You have yours. I cannot share any of my experience with you. Neither can you share any of yours with me. Even if we share a piece of strawberry pie, you have your experience of the pie and I have mine. You can describe your experience to me, but you cannot give me your experience.

Are you having fun? Good. Give some of your fun to another person. No matter how much fun you are having, it's yours and yours alone. You cannot give it or even share it with anyone.

What is reality? Reality is what you (or I) actually experience. You don't experience book, money, wind, or child. These are labels you apply to complex sets of thoughts, feelings, and sensations. Actual experience consists only of the thoughts, feelings, and sensations that arise in life. What thoughts are going through your mind right now? What emotions are you feeling? What are you experiencing through your senses? These are what your life consists of.

Consider the sense of touch. Rub your finger on a piece of cloth. You experience what is usually called the texture of the object. What is "the experience of the texture of the object"? Before you touched the cloth, there was no experience of texture. If you lift your finger away from the cloth even slightly, the experience disappears. If you examine your finger, you cannot find the experience in the finger. If you examine the cloth, you cannot find the experience in the cloth. The experience of the texture of the cloth only arises when your finger touches it. So, where is it—in the cloth or in the finger? When you look at experience this way, experience takes on a mysterious quality. It arises from nothing. It arises only when the appropriate conditions come together. As soon as those conditions are no longer present, the experience disappears. This is the mystery of being, that experience arises from nothing and subsides into nothing. Most of the time, we are so caught up in the fictions generated by labeling and conceptualizing that we never experience the mystery.

Whenever I teach this material in a class, at least one person argues vehemently that an external reality exists independently of experience.

You raise up your head
And you ask, "Is this
    where it is?"
And somebody points to
    you and says, "It's
    his."
And you say, "What's
    mine?"
And somebody else says,
    "Where what is?"
And you say, "Oh my
    God
Am I here all alone?"

Because something is
    happening here
But you don't know
    what it is
Do you, Mister Jones?

—*Bob Dylan*

The resistance to seeing appearances as mind has little to do with logic and philosophy and much to do with the emotional attachment to the idea of a world of shared experience. Intuitively, the student realizes that if the world of shared experience is only a construction, then each of us is alone. The vociferous arguments come from the fear of being alone.

Are we alone? The question itself seeks to avoid the mystery of being and to relegate experience to another category. Things are not what we think they are. Equally, they are not what we think they are not. Things just are.

Work with a teacher who can examine your experience and point you in the appropriate direction when you run into difficulty. You may well feel that your teacher is constantly tripping you up with tricky logic questions. He or she is showing you where you have stopped looking and started to interpret experience. Of course, you feel tricked, stupid and bewildered! Such feelings come from the operation of patterned perceptions that cannot see what the teacher is pointing to. Only you can see. Your teacher is trying to separate you from your patterned perception.

However, many people, including a few teachers, misunderstand this process and conclude that logic games and tricks are the point. They become adept at abstruse epistemological reasoning but completely miss the intention of the practice. They end up messing up both their own minds and the minds of their students. Stay away from such people.

Step 2: Mind Is Empty

Kangyur Rinpoche, one of the first Tibetan lamas to accept Westerners as students, gave regular teachings at his home near Darjeeling in India. On one occasion, he was teaching how mind has no origin, cessation, or location. A Western student objected, saying that the mind was in the brain. The discussion went on and on until Kangyur Rinpoche told the student to approach. The student bowed respectfully, and Kangyur Rinpoche punched him hard in the stomach. The student doubled over in pain, gasping for breath.

"Where is your mind now?" asked Kangyur Rinpoche.

Mind is not a thing. Mind is experiencing. Where does experiencing come from? That is the mystery of being. Recall the first time you fell in love—all those wonderful, powerful feelings you experienced. You couldn't imagine living without him or her. Every moment of separation was exquisitely painful. Whenever you thought of your lover, colors were brighter, your spirit lifted, and everything was right in the world.

Where did those feelings come from? Where are they now? Where did they go?

The great mystery of being is that all experience, thoughts, feelings, and sensations arise from nothing and dissolve into nothing. Stuck as we are in the habituation of subject-object perception, we think that experience consists of an "I" that exists on its own perceiving objects that exist on their own.

In the previous step—*appearances are mind*—you saw that what is experienced cannot be separated from experiencing. Now look at experiencing itself; call it mind or whatever you want to call it.

To know the nature of mind (and, consequently, the nature of experience), work through these seven questions in your meditation:

> Appearances, which never existed in themselves, are mistaken for objects;
> Awareness itself, because of ignorance, is mistaken for self;
> Through the power of dualistic fixation I wander in the realm of existence.
> May ignorance and confusion be completely resolved.
>
> —*Rangjung Dorje*

1. What is mind?
2. How is mind?
3. What is sensory experience?
4. What is movement?
5. What is the difference between mind and sensation?
6. What is the difference between the moving mind and the resting mind?
7. What is the nature of experience?

Thousands of pages have been written asking and answering these questions. The nature of experience has been exhaustively analyzed in Buddhist colleges and universities for centuries. Do you have to know all this philosophy to understand the nature of mind? Some traditions take the position that you cannot know emptiness without formal philosophical training. Nonsense! You might just as well say that you can't know acceleration without formal mathematical training. Get in a car, turn the motor on, put it in gear, release the brake, and put your foot on the gas pedal. Provided nothing is in front of you, you know acceleration immediately—and if something is in front of you, you know deceleration.

Kangyur Rinpoche's student with the stomachache knew emptiness, too, though whether he appreciated the lesson is not recorded.

Real understanding, real knowing, comes from direct experience. When you work with these questions, don't get distracted by logic, reason, or speculation. Go for experience. Observe what you experience. Really observe what you experience. Nothing else counts.

What is mind?
Stop reading for a moment and pose the question "What is mind?" Observe what happens in you.

You go through four states very quickly. The first state is in the first moment of looking. As soon as you ask the question, you feel a shift in energy and attention and you are *looking at nothing*. The state lasts only for a moment, and then you become *unsettled and disoriented*. This is the second state. Attention has decayed, and energy is flowing into habituated patterns. The "being nothing there" experience gives rise to the third state, *fear*. You do not stay in the fear for long. One of the elemental reaction chains quickly moves you into the fourth state, *thinking,* or *dullness*.

Stop reading again. Let everything go, relax for a few moments, reestablish a base of attention, and then pose the question again. *What is mind?* Look and rest. Can you rest in the looking a little longer, now?

Through consistent practice, you will be able to sustain looking for longer and longer periods.

You encounter distraction and dullness in insight practice, just as you did in basic meditation. Because you are now working at a higher level of attention, the distraction and dullness seem to be even more pronounced. You may think you have lost all ability to practice attention. Do not be disheartened. Every time you move to a new level of practice or penetrate to the next layer of patterns, you will experience disruption and disturbance in your practice. Remember that all the usual criteria of success and failure are unreliable; just because you feel that your practice is hopeless doesn't mean that it is.

As in basic meditation, relax when attention is distracted, and energize when attention goes dull. To relax, rest with the mind open like the sky, infinite in extent and undisturbed by winds or storms or clouds. To energize, rest with the knowing quality of mind like the sun, brilliant and radiant.

If busyness and dullness are persistent problems, spend more time on energy transformation to raise the level of energy in your attention.

Another effective method for dispelling distractions is to meditate on change and death. To dispel busyness, reflect on the certainty of death. Distractions and reactions lose their attraction. To dispel dullness, recall that death can come at any time, even at the end of the next breath. You will quickly become more awake and present.

Clear, awake attention is vital in insight practice. In the beginning, look intensely for short periods of time, perhaps one to two minutes. Look right at mind. When the quality of attention fades, relax for a few moments. Then look again. Gradually, you will be able to rest in the looking, clear, awake, and vivid.

Now, what is mind? When you look, you see no thing. You look, sitting through all the reactions that arise. What is it? The question grows heavier and heavier. Keep holding the question. Let its weight power your attention, and rest in looking at nothing. Sooner or later, you will be caught by a concept or idea or experience that you are unable to let go. Now is the time to check with your teacher. He or she will help expose your fixation and return you to looking at nothing.

Whenever your teacher pushes you back into nothingness, one of the five reaction chains will arise in you. You will feel that your world is being shaken, that a wave of something you can't describe is engulfing you, that you are being burned to a crisp by the practice, that you are falling and can't find anything to orient yourself by, or that you are totally bewildered and confused and have no idea what to do.

You react, projecting one of the six realms. You become angry and belligerent, seeing everyone and everything as your enemy. You become grasping and needy, complaining that you don't have enough to go on. You become dull and stupid, taking care of your physical needs and not much else. You experience surges of energy in your meditation, and your practice is corrupted by the desire for more. You become competitive, anxious to prove to your teacher or fellow students how good you are. You become proud and arrogant, letting everyone know that you are working at advanced practices and they should be so fortunate.

Recognize all these reactions for what they are, and keep in mind the advice of Jamgön Kongtrül, a nineteenth-century Tibetan master:

> Practice with little fanfare but great effectiveness. Remain natural in your interactions with others.

At some point the question "What is mind?" vanishes. You may feel that a wall has crumbled and you are suddenly free, or you have been washed up on an open beach after drowning in massive waves, or you have been completely burned up and there is nothing left of you, or you've entered the eye of a hurricane and the howling winds have suddenly disappeared. The question goes empty, and you are present: awake, aware, and unable to describe what you are experiencing. Rest right there.

Many people miss the shift or dismiss it as insignificant because they haven't found an answer to the question "What is mind?" The point of insight practice is to bring you to the experience of clear, open awareness. When it arises, rest right there. The horse that brought you there, the question, is dead. Heed the age-old adage: *Don't flog a dead horse.*

Initially, you may not recognize the open clarity. It is right in front of you, and you do not see it. One of the crucial functions of a teacher is to point it out to you. Keep working at the practice, and one day you will know it and understand what your teacher is pointing to.

How is mind?

You may have a direct experience of mind nature at any point in working through these seven questions. Once you have had a direct experience, you can use the other questions to deepen your understanding, or you can move directly to the practice of presence described in the next chapter. Check with your teacher to confirm that your experience is valid and not self-deception.

The question "How is mind?" takes you deeper into mind. When you rest in that indescribable, open, awake mind, is it stable and permanent, or is there something that comes and goes? If something comes, how does it come? What characteristics does it have? What color, shape, or form? Where is it when it is present—inside or outside the body? If it goes, how does it go? These questions direct attention to different aspects of mind. The method remains the same: hold the question in attention until the question disintegrates. Then rest in the seeing.

One recurrent difficulty in insight practice is the desire to escape from the practice. The practice tears down the framework of ordinary experience. Your teacher doesn't help matters because he or she keeps asking what you experience and you have no words.

A common escape route is to refer to the indescribable nature of mind. When your teacher asks about your experience, you confidently say, "It's indescribable. It's beyond words." Such responses do not do the job. You are avoiding standing in your own knowing. When you are asked about your experience, the conditioned sense of self meets the emptiness of mind. There is no ground. Your effort at this point is to stand where there is no ground and to speak in your own voice: to be present without being anything or anyone.

When you speak truly about your experience, you speak with a voice that is beyond conditioning because, in seeing, you have stepped beyond conditioning. To hide in concepts and words or the impossibility of expression does you no good. Your teacher is looking for the voice, the expression, that comes from beyond conditioning. When you see, stand in what you see and speak from there. If your seeing is not complete or is clouded, your teacher will point out the problem in his or her own way. For insight practice, step beyond conditioned knowing, and learn from what arises.

The next four questions direct attention to the nature of what we call external experience (sensory experience) and internal experience (thoughts and feelings), to what experiences external experience (the mind in which sensory experience arises), and to what experiences internal experience (the mind in which thoughts and feelings arise).

What is sensory experience?
In step 1, *appearances are mind,* you saw that our relationship with what appears as the external world is much more intimate than we suppose. Ordinary habituated perception, with "I" on one side and

object on the other appearing to be two things forever separate and distinct, is misleading. Consider the sense of touch—no sensation without connection. This is very intimate. The same holds for the other senses, even though the sense of direct connection with the object is usually not noticed in seeing and hearing and smelling.

What is sensory experience? Recall the example of the ice cube in the discussion of wisdom in chapter 2. Hold an ice cube in your hand until the cold becomes so intense that your hand starts to hurt. Look directly at the pain. What is it? It is a sensation, an arising in your mind. Is it anything more than that? Look, until you see.

What is movement?

Thoughts and feelings come and go: they constitute movement in the mind. Let a thought float up in your mind, and look at it. What is a thought? The content of the thought is not important. What is thought itself? What is it made of? You have hundreds of thoughts every day. They move through your mind, triggering actions and reactions. Until this meditation, have you ever wondered what a thought actually is? It's not an object, like a book or a house. When you look at a thought, it seems to come to your mind. Does it come from the outside? Try to see a thought the moment it forms in your mind. Try to catch it in the process of forming. Then try to catch it in the moment of dissolving.

Go through the same process for emotions, both positive and negative.

Keep looking until you see.

What is the difference between mind and sensation?

Let your mind rest, and look at it. Look at how it is when you are not looking at any visual object or listening to any sound or tasting, touching, or smelling anything. Just note how it is.

Now look at a car or a piece of clothing or any other object. Listen to some music or eat some food. Look at how your mind is when you experience sensation.

Is the resting mind different from the sensing mind? What's the difference? What changes?

What is the difference between the moving mind and the resting mind?

As before, let your mind rest, free from thoughts, and then look at it. How is it? Now float a thought in your mind and look at it. How is it now? How is the resting mind different from the moving mind?

With these last four questions, you have looked at all aspects of experience, resting, sensing, thinking, and feeling. Some thoughts and feelings, such as grief, love, and anger, are very powerful and consume all your energy so you are not aware of anything else. Some sensations, such as intense sunlight, beautiful music, and the tactile sensations of making love, absorb all available attention. Nevertheless, all experience is either the mind at rest, a thought, a feeling, or a sensation.

The point of these questions is to know that everything is experience. Most of the time, we are so caught up by the content of experience that we don't know whether we are experiencing a thought, a feeling, or a sensation.

We take the content of experience as real, as something that exists on its own, and miss the mystery of being, which is the arising and subsiding of experience. Money, beauty, fame, happiness, red, blue, melody, fragrance, anger, jealousy, pride, compassion, faith, and even knowledge are all arisings and subsidings. These questions point us to the fact that, no matter what the content, an experience is an arising in the mind, nothing more.

The only world you know is your world of experience. It arises when you are born and ceases when you die. You cannot share this world with anyone else. All you have is experience.

What is the nature of experience?
Experience is a mystery. Pick up a pebble and look at it. What is it? Every time you name the experience, let go of the name and look again and move into a deeper knowing of the pebble. Seeing stops as soon as you give a name. To know the pebble, you must step into the mystery of the experience.

The names we give to objects are not the experience of the object, whether it be a thought, feeling, or sensation. Language abbreviates and condenses experience for the purpose of communication. Because connection is a basic human need, we readily forget or neglect the world of our own experience (limited and conditioned by habituated patterns) and take the world defined by communication, the world of apparently shared experience, as what is real. To see what is, you must penetrate the limitations on perception imposed by conditioning and belief in consensus reality.

On the wall in my office is a piece of minimalist art that one of my students gave me. It is a small rectangular canvas covered with thick green-black paint that has been worked to an even texture. One small piece of canvas at the edge is unpainted. When students come to see me, they usually sit so that this piece of art is on the opposite wall in plain view. The painting has been there for years, but students do not see it because there is nothing to see. It either does not register, or, if it does, the registering is suppressed immediately because it involves looking at nothing. When a student asks me when I put that piece of art on the wall, I know that he or she can now look at nothing and stay present.

When you can look directly at experience and see nothing, then you have begun to see how things are. Can you hear the silence when music is playing? Without the silence, the music couldn't be there. Usually, however, we are so caught up in the music that we aren't aware of the silence that is always there. Put on some music and listen to it, but hear the silence at the same time. In the same way, we can't see unless space is present. Habitually, we focus on the trees, mountains, buildings, furniture, or people and ignore the space between them. Go for a walk in a park and notice the trees, grass, flowers, and people—and notice, too, the space in which all these appear.

> Joy, anger, grief, delight, worry, regret, fickleness, inflexibility, modesty, willfulness, candor, insolence—music from empty holes, mushrooms springing up in dampness, day and night replacing each other before us, and no one knows where they sprout from. Let it be! Let it be! It is enough that morning and evening we have them, and they are the means by which we live.
>
> —*Chuang Tzu*

Now look at the mind, which experiences everything. You look and see nothing, but there is not simply nothing there. A vivid, clear awareness is present, and experience arises unceasingly. That is how things are.

> *Look directly at your own mind.*
> *Look at it deeply.*
> *When you look and see nothing,*
> *That is the nature of things.*

Looking again and again, you see that there is nothing that you can point to and say, "This is mind." Yet you are totally awake and clear.

You see that experience just arises whatever you do. These three understandings make up the nature of unborn awareness: emptiness (nothing there), clarity (what makes awareness possible), and unceasing arising (experience comes and goes on its own).

Step 3: Emptiness Is Natural Presence

At this point in practice, cut the tendency to take even understanding and realization as real. Although you have experienced mind as empty, the tendency to take this understanding as something real moves you back into subject-object habituation. Cut this tendency by turning attention to the understanding itself. When a concept such as "mind is empty" arises, look right at it. As soon as you do, any notion of emptiness vanishes and you return to presence.

Do the same thing with clarity. As soon as you take clarity as something real in its own right, you are back in habituation. Cut the habituation by directing attention at the experience of clarity.

What is experience? Experience is energy moving from emptiness into form and form into emptiness. When experience-awareness arises in the presence of the habituated pattern of dualism, energy flows into either the subjective pole or objective pole of the pattern. When it flows into the objective pole, you experience a thought, feeling, or sensory sensation: energy is diffracted through confusion, and what arises is experienced as "other." When energy flows into the subjective pole, you experience a sense of self: energy is refracted in confusion, and what arises is experienced as a sense of "I." What you experience as awareness is the radiance of mind nature.

Nothing exists that is not experience, and all experience is empty of independent existence. To return to presence, redirect your attention to any reification of experience until it becomes empty again.

Step 4: Natural Presence Is Natural Freedom

The four steps in this practice of insight correspond to the four noble truths. *Suffering* arises when we experience what appears as other than mind nature (step 1). *The origin of suffering* is not knowing that mind nature and all experience are empty (step 2). *Suffering ceases* when we return to presence (step 3). *The path* is traveled by resting in presence and letting all experience arise and subside on its own (step 4). When the practice of presence is strong enough—that is, you have a sufficient level of energy in attention—even the deep-seated habituations of fear and the undischarged emotional cores of patterns can be experienced in awareness. Then even these long-blocked energies are released and subside on their own.

Bokar Rinpoche, Kalu Rinpoche's successor, once taught me the following verse:

> *After the awareness that there is nothing other than mind*
> *Comes the understanding that mind, too, is nothing itself.*
> *The wise know that these two understandings are not things.*
> *And then, not holding on to even this knowledge, they rest in the*
>   *realm of totality.*

These four lines describe the progression of insight practice. First look at appearances and see that they are not separate from mind. Then look at mind and see that mind is empty. The habituation of subject-object perception still takes understanding itself as an object, so cut through that. Then cut through the understanding that understanding is not an object so that there really is nothing left. Then, ironically, you enter the totality of experience and awareness.

In *The Message of the Tibetans* by Arnaud des Jardins, Kalu Rinpoche says to the author:

> You live in confusion and the illusion of things. There is a reality. You are that reality. When you know that, you will know that you are nothing and, in being nothing, are everything. That is all.

In the wake of Einstein and others, the notion of relativity has permeated our culture to the point that we often hear that there is no reality. The view is further reinforced by misinterpreting such traditional Buddhist phrases as "all phenomena are empty" to mean that everything is relative and hence unreal. From such a perspective, it is a short step to the attitude that nothing exists apart from subjective experience and that each person's subjective experience is equally valid. Such attitudes create horrendous problems in both our interactions with others and in our own spiritual practice. Moral relativism undermines any sense of right and wrong, reduces society to anarchy, and abandons society to those willing to have no sense of right or wrong.

In your own practice the same attitudes reinforce conditioned perceptions and render you impervious to any challenges to what you consider true or real. Kalu Rinpoche's statements that there is a reality and that we are that reality say that we can go beyond conditioned perception, see what is, and know that we are not different from it. The price for such complete and clear perception is to die to the sense of being a separate "I"—to know that we are one with what we experience.

TECHNICAL POINTS

You look at your mind and see nothing. You fall into confusion again and again. You can't see anything, and you can't understand why your teacher is being so insistent yet so uncommunicative. Nothing makes any sense. You feel like giving up, and, then, suddenly, your mind is completely clear and you see.

In the moment of seeing there is no confusion. Afterward, however, the doubts and questions come. What was that? Has anything changed? What did I actually see? What do I do now?

The evaluation of experience is always a tricky business, so a few guidelines are helpful.

Four Levels of Knowing

First, learn to distinguish four levels of knowing in spiritual work: knowing that comes from intellectual understanding, knowing that comes from surges of energy, knowing that comes from direct experience, and knowing that comes from being.

Intellectual understanding is the comprehensive understanding of philosophical perspectives or views. You develop intellectual understanding by study and reflection. It becomes yours when you have sifted through the viewpoints, arguments, and logic and they make sense to you. Even though you have a thorough understanding and may be able to explain things clearly to others, this level of knowing has insufficient energy to change behavior in any meaningful way. You may live by its principles, but you constantly have to remember to do so. You have to make an effort to overcome or step out of emotional reactions that take you in another direction. The danger of intellectual understanding is that it can be taken over by emotional reactions and habituated patterns, which then use the same viewpoints, arguments, and logic to maintain their functioning. In *Thirty Pieces of Sincere Advice*, Longchenpa, a great Nyingma master in the twelfth century, admonishes:

You collect a lot of important writings,
Major texts, personal instructions, notes, whatever.
If you haven't practiced, books won't help you when you die.
Look at the mind—that's my sincere advice.

As for the second kind of understanding, *energy surges* are experiences that arise in and out of formal practice sessions. The breaking down of habituated structures releases energy. Energy surges arise as openings into new ways of seeing and experiencing or as emotionally charged states reflecting the undischarged emotions at the core of the pattern. In the latter case, you may experience profound despair or loneliness or intense neediness or feel that you are falling apart or going insane. On the other hand, surges of bliss, clarity, or non-thought or a combination of these provide a powerful boost to your practice. In either case, the surge fades after a while (anywhere from a few minutes to several days), and you wonder where your upset or understanding went. In all traditions, students are warned against taking energy surges as indications of real understanding. For instance, my teacher used to say:

Meditation experiences are like flowers in alpine meadows—so many, so beautiful, and they last for such a short time.

Another piece of advice is

Meditation experience is like turnip soup. The first sip is sweet and delicious, but later, all you have is a bad taste in your mouth.

Everybody attaches to energy surges when they first arise. To stay attached, to hold on to them, or to seek them out, however, will take your practice in the wrong direction. Gaining ideas have crept in, and you are reinforcing subject-object dualism in seeking experiences to satisfy the sense of "I."

Direct experience, the third level of knowing, arises when you see. Whatever questions your teacher puts to you, you stand in your experience, even if it seems to make no "logical" sense. Your teacher's questions can't and don't shake your experience, so you don't fall into defensiveness or confusion. A pattern has been broken, and you may feel both joy in the freedom and grief at the loss of illusions. Direct experience is often accompanied by exhilarating energy surges and associated experiences, but, with direct experience, you understand the nature of such surges. You see that they are not the point of practice. Your practice becomes clearer and stronger, not because you want to gain something, but from knowing directly that life is just the arising and subsiding of experience. Your intention is to be present in the arising and subsiding, whatever comes. In "Aspiration for Mahamudra," the Tibetan master Rangjung Dorje says:

> *Attachment to good and fixation on experience subside on their own.*
> *Confusion and evil concepts vanish in the realm of totality.*
> *In ordinary mind there is no rejection or acceptance, no separation*
>   *or attainment.*
> *May I realize the truth of pure being, complete simplicity.*

The fourth level, *knowing at the level of being*, means that the knowing is present all the time: you live in the knowing. Unlike intellectual understanding, knowing at the level of being means you never have to remember to live by your principles. Indeed, you don't live by principles—you just respond to what arises. Unlike with meditation surges, knowing at the level of being means understanding and insight don't fade with time. Unlike with direct experience, here all sense of understanding something is gone. You just are.

The aim of pointing-out instructions is to precipitate an experience in which the possibility of open, clear, empty awareness is opened. At the lowest level, pointing out instills an intellectual understanding. At a middle level, it precipitates a surge of experience. Ideally, pointing out provides you with a seed of direct understanding. You then nurture the seed in your practice until it blossoms into understanding at the level of being.

Three Types of Meditation Experience

Three types of meditation experience deserve special mention: bliss, clarity, and non-thought. When the structure or operation of a pattern is disrupted, areas frozen by the pattern open up and energy flows into them. Meditation experience is the experience of these energy flows.

Bliss experiences are sensations of bliss that permeate body and mind. They include physical or emotional warmth, well-being, joyfulness, and lightness. They vary in degree from pleasant sensations to orgasmic waves of bliss that engulf you. Your whole body may vibrate or shake as energy flows through it. You may not be able to sleep because the experience is so powerful. Bliss experiences also take the form of physical and emotional pain. Parts of your body ache inexplicably. Intensely painful emotions unconnected with current circumstances flood you. Whether pleasant or unpleasant, such experiences can be very unbalancing. We tend to take the experiences as being real, and understandably so, because they can be so powerful. As best as you can, however, continue to do your practice, looking at the experience itself to see what it is—not what the content is but what the experience is. Intellectually regarding the experience as an arising in your mind is not sufficient. You must look and see it as such. Then you step out of the confusion, and the experience itself deepens your understanding.

Clarity experiences include extraordinary vividness, clarity, or both in sensory, emotional, or mental experience as well as experiences of sheer clarity with no reference point. Ordinary experience dissolves into clarity or is infused with a clarity and vividness you have not previously experienced. You may also experience periods of intense dullness in which you can't think or understand anything at all. A friend asks if you want a glass of water, and you can't put his words together to make sense of them. You may even experience clairvoyance, knowing what is happening in another room or what someone else is thinking. One of my teachers, Dezhung Rinpoche, always advised students not to explore or rely on such clarity experiences because, like all meditation experiences, they are inherently unstable.

In one teaching, he said, "Suppose you are sitting in your hermitage and you have an experience of clairvoyance. You see that a friend is coming to visit you. When he arrives, you tell him that you knew he was coming, and you tell him details of his trip. Naturally, he's very impressed. He goes and tells his friends, and they come to see you. But the clairvoyance has passed, and you had no idea they were coming.

"Now you don't look so good!" he chuckled.

As in bliss experiences, to transform the clarity into understanding, look directly at what experiences clarity.

Non-thought experiences include feeling completely empty inside, a total absence of any internal dialogue, an extraordinary sense of stillness, no movement in mind when sensory experience arises, or the feeling that there is no one home at all. They can also take the form of mental blankness, massive confusion, or disorientation. As with the others, look at the experience itself or at what experiences non-thought.

These and other experiences are not problematic in and of themselves. If, however, you seek them out or try to avoid them, you create problems. If you seek them out to confirm your practice or because you enjoy them, you reinforce the basic pattern of attraction. If you try to avoid them because they are disturbing or painful, you reinforce the basic pattern of aversion. If you try to ignore them, you reinforce indifference.

Generally, the painful manifestations of these three types of experience are temporary and subside as energy flows through body and mind. The explicit experiences of bliss, clarity, and non-thought increase in intensity and frequency. As the experiences grow stronger and more stable, don't attach to them. Instead, use the energy of the experiences in your practice. Direct attention at what experiences the bliss, clarity, or non-thought. In other words, as the experience arises, cut with attention, as described previously, not to end the experience but to know it completely.

Ascent and Descent

Ascent and descent are related pattern mechanisms that degrade attention whenever attention begins to penetrate the undischarged core of a pattern.

When you practice insight (or any other form of meditation) and repeatedly run into states of depression, withdrawal, helplessness, or dullness, you are experiencing *descent*. Recall that emotional patterns, triggered by your efforts in practice, react to degrade attention. In descent, the pattern mechanisms shift the energy of attention to a lower level. You become dull, immobilized, helpless, or powerless. The downward shift of energy drains all the juice out of your attention, and practice grinds to a halt. If you push harder in practice, the mechanisms operate more powerfully and you become more depressed. On the other hand, if you do nothing, your practice stagnates. Basically, you are caught between a rock and a hard place. The situation is made worse by the insistent voices associated with the patterns. Like the call of the sirens, they say that you will always be depressed, nothing will change, and you are powerless. You believe the voices because every time you make an effort in practice, you sink back into a black hole. Don't believe them. The voices are part of the pattern operation that degrades attention.

First and foremost, consult with a teacher. The human connection is very important in working with descent. You need solid guidance and support. Second, practice consistently and work at the edge, not so much that you are driven into depressed states, not so little that your practice is stagnant. You find the edge only by trial and error. Third, make a point of doing simple acts of kindness and virtue. Mark Twain once said that the best way to cheer yourself up is to cheer someone else up. When you are kind and generous, the patterns of depression and immobility can't hold. Space opens up. In the Tibetan tradition, people who encountered descent were encouraged to make hundreds of thousands of small devotional objects and then give them away to others. The giving to others was as much a part of the practice as the making of the objects themselves.

Ascent is the opposite phenomenon. When attention encounters emotional material, the mechanisms degrade attention by shifting energy to higher levels. You experience clarity, bliss, visions, dreams, or other psychic phenomena. You are likely to take these experiences as signs that your practice is going in a good direction. You are enthralled by the experiences and delve into them. You may even develop facility in special powers such as clairvoyance or healing. Whenever you return to the actual practice, be it insight or another form of meditation, the practice is dull by comparison. You plod along and feel a twinge of discomfort, a fleeting tug on your heart, or a flash of anxiety, as if you were on the edge of an abyss. Then you have more experiences reading people's minds, or your body is flooded with bliss, or you hear voices telling you the secrets of the universe, and you let your practice go yet again.

Most people who experience ascent are relatively impervious to advice or suggestions because they are convinced by the higher energy state that they know what is going on. Many spiritual groups actively support and encourage people who experience ascent. One way to distinguish ascent from real understanding is that ascent experiences are inherently unstable. They come when emotional material is aroused and disappear as soon as the pressure is off. Nevertheless, many spiritual groups and more than a few teachers encourage ascenders, holding them as role models for spiritual practice.

Ascent is more difficult than descent to work through, precisely because it is more pleasant. If you never have any confusion or bewilderment in your practice of insight, and you regularly shift into fascinating and enthralling states of mind but can't answer your teacher's questions about mind nature, then chances are you are experiencing ascent. When your teacher points you away from the enthralling mind states, you resent the suggestions and feel that he or she is wrong. You think you can use the mind states to gain understanding and don't see why you have to let them go. Eventually you will have to leave the god realms of extraordinary experiences because they are distractions. They take you away from the confusing and disturbing emotions at the core of the patterns you are trying to dismantle.

WORKING WITH A TEACHER AND THE POINTING-OUT INSTRUCTIONS

A lama in England once told me about his one and only interaction with a famous and somewhat controversial teacher in Tibet, Khenpo Gangshar. This lama had heard much about Khenpo Gangshar and yearned to study with him. Khenpo Gangshar came for a two-week visit to the monastery at which the lama was staying. The lama submitted a formal request for a meeting. When no reply, not even an acknowledgment, came back, he resubmitted his request. He hesitated to make a third request, but so deep was his yearning that he did so anyway. Again, no reply. Khenpo Gangshar was due to leave the next morning.

That night, the lama sat in his room wondering what to do. He desperately wanted to see Khenpo Gangshar, but he was hesitant to violate monastic protocols. He was so agitated that he couldn't sleep. A knock sounded on his door. He opened it, curious to see who would come to see him so late at night. One of Khenpo Gangshar's attendants told him to come. Elated, he followed the attendant and was shown into Khenpo Gangshar's room.

Khenpo Gangshar was busy in a conversation with another monk, so he sat down and waited. Eventually the monk left. Protocol demanded that Khenpo Gangshar initiate any conversation, so the lama waited for leave to speak. Khenpo Gangshar just looked at him but said nothing. The lama couldn't ask any of the questions that were burning in his heart.

The two sat in silence for about fifteen minutes. Then Khenpo Gangshar motioned for him to leave. He was devastated. He left and returned to his room, where he sobbed with grief and raged with anger. Eventually, totally exhausted, he fell asleep. When he awoke the next day, he started his morning meditation practice and found that his meditation had changed completely. To this day, he regards Khenpo Gangshar as one of his most important teachers, even though he had only this one meeting and they never exchanged a word.

Ananda was Buddha Shakyamuni's nephew. He was very close to Buddha, serving as his attendant. He studied and practiced under Buddha's guidance for decades. Ananda also had a phenomenal memory. He attended all Buddha's teachings and could repeat verbatim what Buddha had said on any occasion. Despite his close relationship with Buddha, despite the great number of teachings he had received, despite his own sincere and substantial efforts in practice, Ananda could not penetrate the mystery of being and remained caught in the web of emotional reactions and habituated patterns. When Buddha died, Ananda was grief-stricken, not only because his teacher was gone, but also because he feared that the possibility of his waking up had died with Buddha.

What happened next varies from tradition to tradition. The following account is taken from the *Cullavagga* of the Theravadan tradition:

> Then the venerable Ananda, thinking: "Tomorrow is the assembly. Now it is not suitable in me that I, being (only) a learner, should go to the assembly," and having passed much of that night in mindfulness as to body, when the night was nearly spent thinking: "I will lie down," he inclined his body, but (before) his head had touched the mattress and while his feet were free from the ground, in that interval his mind was freed from the outflows (asava) with no residuum (for rebirth) remaining. Then the venerable Ananda, being a perfected one, went to the assembly.

These two stories illustrate the tremendous range in the teacher-student interaction that is so vital to insight practice—fifteen minutes of silence that change everything or twenty years studying under the Buddha himself with no experience of insight. The teacher's role is to show the student the possibility of presence. The pointing-out instructions are the transmission: together the teacher and student create the conditions in which the student sees what the teacher is pointing to. In Ananda's case, the conditions came together only after Buddha died.

Insight practice is virtually impossible without a teacher. Because you are trying to see what you can't see, you need someone to show you how to look, to show you what to look at, and to show you how to recognize what you see.

Different Approaches

The interaction between teacher and student in which understanding arises in the student is one of the great mysteries of life. In the arena of insight, the process is subtle, almost magical, and, consequently, is much misunderstood.

A key element in the development of insight is the pointing-out instructions. As we have seen, they point out presence or direct awareness or original mind to the student. The effectiveness of pointing-out instructions depends on several factors. First and most important, the teacher must have direct experiential knowledge of what he or she is pointing out. Second, the student must be capable of a level of attention that can stay present with what is being pointed out. Third, conditions must be such that there is sufficient opening in the student to see what is being pointed out.

The need for the first is obvious. A teacher working only from an intellectual or inferred knowledge cannot evoke direct experience in the student or accurately assess the student's understanding. This is the teacher's responsibility. If you teach without having direct experience of what you are teaching, then, regardless of your motivation, you are knowingly misleading people who come to study with you.

> The story is told of a student who approached a Zen master and asked, "What happens after we die?"
>
> The Zen master said, "I don't know."
>
> "You don't know?" exclaimed the student. "But you are a master!"
>
> "That may be true," was the reply, "but I'm not a dead one."

The second factor, attention, is just as important and is the student's responsibility. Attention is the essence of practice. For insight practice, you must have a level of attention that can stay present with the arising of emotions so that you experience them as coming and going. You know what they are and are not disturbed, distracted, or dulled by them. In terms of the levels of attention described in chapter 3, you need to have some experience with stage 4, a lake with waves. Traditional descriptions of the level of attention necessary are that mind is radiant, like the sun in a cloudless sky, movement in mind arises like waves in the ocean, and attention is clear and open without clinging, like a child visiting a cathedral for the first time.

A third factor is responsible for much of the mystery that surrounds pointing-out instructions, empowerment, transmission, and awakening. The teacher either recognizes when conditions are present and takes advantage of them or creates the necessary conditions through the power of attention or other energy transformation methods.

Numerous stories abound in all traditions of instances when a teacher pointed out the nature of being to a student and the student had a moment of awakening. Is such a moment a matter of chance? Is there a common thread?

One way to understand what happens in the teacher-student interaction is to use the framework of the four ways of working: power, ecstasy, insight, and compassion. Each approach has its own way of raising the level of energy in the student. The raised energy goes into either attention or habituated patterns. When energy goes into attention, the student may see what the teacher is pointing out. When the energy goes into habituated patterns, no seeing takes place and the student reacts, projecting emotional material onto the teacher.

The warrior approach is connected with power. It uses the experience of conflict to raise the level of energy in the student. Direct and confrontational, the effort on the part of the teacher is to create conditions so that the student experiences going empty in conflict. The teacher is pointing out the emptiness of being. If the student's energy flows into habituated patterns, however, the student only experiences being threatened or attacked, and resistance is reinforced.

The conflict may be formal or actual. Formal conflict uses a ritual form to create the experience of conflict and enable the student to go empty. In actual conflict, the teacher takes advantage of situations in daily life to confront the student and precipitate understanding. The following story is taken from the *Record of Rinzai*:

> Rinzai, the founding master of the Rinzai tradition of Zen Buddhism, and his monks were hoeing the monastery's fields. When he saw his teacher Obaku approach, he stopped working and propped himself up on his hoe.

Obaku said, "Would this fellow be tired?"

Rinzai replied, "I have as yet not even lifted my hoe. Why should I be tired?"

Obaku hit him with a stick. Rinzai grabbed the stick and gave Obaku a good blow, knocking him over. Obaku called the superintendent to help him up. The superintendent, doing so, remonstrated, "Venerable, how can you permit the impudence of this madman?"

Obaku was hardly on his feet when he hit the superintendent.

Rinzai, having started to hoe again, remarked, "Cremation is the custom everywhere, but here, I bury alive with a single stroke!"

Later, Issan asked his teacher, Gyosan, about this incident: "What is the meaning of Obaku's beating the superintendent?"

Gyosan said, "The real robber ran off; the pursuer got the stick."

The second approach, ecstasy, uses the experience of opening through loving-kindness, devotion, or transformation of sensory experience to raise the level of energy in the student. The energy from opening enables the student to relax very deeply. Habituated patterns go empty in the relaxation, and the student opens to the nature of being.

In the Tibetan tradition, ritual forms are used to evoke powerful experiences of devotion. The emotional energy of devotion pours into the student's attention, and devotion arises as mind. The teacher then directs the student to look at the devotion itself, which now arises as empty. The energy of devotion has been transformed into seeing the nature of mind.

As in conflict, the teacher also takes advantage of moments of intense devotion, loving-kindness, or sensory experience to push the student into seeing. If the student is not able to open, the energy decays into dependence, into efforts to fuse with the teacher, or into addiction to energy states.

A large assembly of monks gathered around Buddha at Vulture's Peak to hear him teach about the nature of being. Buddha, sitting quietly, held up a flower and showed it to the whole gathering. Everyone sat in silence, but one student, the venerable Kashyapa, smiled.

The Buddha then said, "The one true teaching is beyond form and does not depend on words or letters. It is a special transmission outside all scriptures. I now entrust it to the venerable Kashyapa."

The third way of working, insight, uses the method of holding questions to raise energy in the student. The student is given a question that cannot be answered by intellectual reasoning but only by having a level of attention that can see what the teacher is pointing to. The structures that limit the student's interpretation of experience go empty as the student holds the question. If the student is not able to hold the question, the student disconnects from actual experience and tries to resolve the question through the intellect or logical tricks. The questioning and the moment of awakening may take place during the interaction between student and teacher, or the student may continue to practice with the question and later experience seeing and then confirm that understanding with the teacher.

> A friend of mine recalls an incident from her practice of insight with a teacher in Nepal. The teacher's English was minimal—a few words and no sense of English grammar. My friend's Tibetan was worse. "Look your mind," he told her. "What color?" For a week she practiced, looking at her mind to see its color, but she couldn't see anything and concluded that she didn't understand how to do the meditation. She returned to the teacher and told him about her failure.
>
> His face broke into a huge smile. "Not seeing seeing!" he said.
>
> "That's right. I don't see anything. What am I doing wrong?" she asked.
>
> "Not seeing seeing!" he said and smiled again.
>
> "You don't understand," she said, in tears. "I don't see anything!"
>
> "Yes! Yes! Not seeing seeing!"
>
> Then what he was saying hit her. Seeing no thing is really seeing. She wasn't doing anything wrong. The "not seeing" was the practice.

The fourth approach, compassion, is through obedience or service. The demands of the teacher or the demands of the needs of others are used to raise the level of energy in the student. When the energy goes into attention, the patterns of control go empty and the student sees what is being pointed out. If the energy flows into habituated patterns, the student becomes controlling—demanding obedience from others— or is compelled by a sense of duty to enforce obedience on others. Again, awakening or seeing may occur in the moments of greatest demand when the energy is raised suddenly, or it may arise in the course of service as attention is given to what is required. In the following mythical account, an act of service precipitates the realization of loving-kindness.

Asanga, a fourth-century Indian master, lived in a cave and prayed to meet the future buddha, Maitreya, whose name means "loving-kindness." After twelve years without so much as a vision or a dream, he gave up and left his cave. He came across an old dog covered with sores that were infested with maggots. The sight aroused such compassion in him that he sought to relieve the dog's suffering by removing the maggots—not with his fingers, for fear of killing them, but with his tongue. He bent over, extending his tongue, but he had to close his eyes to the revolting sores. His face hit the ground, and he ended up with a mouthful of dirt. The dog was nowhere to be seen. Directly in front of him was a pair of feet. Raising his head, he looked directly into the eyes of Maitreya.

"You're not very compassionate," Asanga said. "I've been praying to you for twelve years!"

"I was with you the day you began your retreat," Maitreya said, "but only after this last act of compassion are you able to know me."

Pointing Out: The Last Straw

When your teacher asks you a question that seems to make no sense in the circumstances or pushes you when you are already at your limit, emotionally or physically, pay attention! He or she is deliberately placing the straw that breaks the camel's back.

Questions or testing may be take place at the height of conflict, in a moment of relaxation, in the midst of confusion from your struggles with other questions, or when the demands of service or obedience have stretched you as far as you can go. The testing questions may be presented as challenges, observations, questions, or commands. How they are presented depends on the skill of the teacher and the condition of the student. Most teachers are trying to point out the nature of being most of the time. When the student is present, he or she experiences a moment of seeing. Otherwise, all the student experiences is a strange comment or an incomprehensible question. No seeing arises.

Questions are often given in the context of meditation practice, and they direct the student's attention to a specific aspect of experience. The teacher is looking not for a logical or philosophical answer but for a response that indicates you have directly seen or experienced what the teacher is pointing to. Insight is concerned only with direct experiential understanding. A teacher might ask a student, "How is mind present?" or "What is the essence of mind?" or "What is mind?" Answers such as "Mind is present as thinking and emotion" or "The essence of mind is the knower" or "Mind is what experiences things" indicate only that you have thought about what mind is. Insight takes you deeper.

The direct expression of experience is very difficult because direct expression requires that we go beyond Buddhist vocabulary, philosophical, psychological, or habitual forms of expression, or other familiar concepts. Direct expression is uncontrived, creative, accurate, and transformative. The teacher is looking for signs and indications that an opening has taken place and that the student sees what the teacher is pointing to.

A student described his experience to his teacher: "When I look at mind, I see nothing, but everything is very clear. Knowing is present, but I can't say that 'I' know."

His teacher asked, "This knowing, does it know itself?"

The student had studied a bit of Buddhist philosophy and "knew" the answer to this question. "Just as a sword cannot cut itself, so the mind cannot know itself."

His teacher replied, "Very clever! Your answer has all the life cooked out of it. Give me a response before you put it in that oven of yours."

When you direct attention to your teacher's instruction or question, you feel a shift in attention. That shift is the beginning of looking. Thoughts and ideas may come to mind, but these are just distractions. Keep coming back to the looking.

For instance, suppose the question you are given is "When your mind is at rest, how is it?" You look and you see nothing. You go to your teacher and say, "I don't know; there is nothing there."

Your teacher asks, "Is there really nothing there, no form, no color, no shape, no substance?"

A little doubt creeps into your mind, so you go back to the practice and look more deeply. Yes, there's nothing there: no form, no color, no shape, and no substance. It is definite. There's nothing there. You report on the practice.

The next question catches you by surprise: "How do you know there is nothing there?"

"Well, I do. I just know."

The next questions come quickly: "What is the knowing? Is the knowing nothing?"

You don't know what to say.

Often, the teacher can tell from the your demeanor or presence that something has taken place in your practice. In this case, the pointing-out instructions serve to catalyze your understanding.

Every direct awareness tradition has its own methods of guiding the student to seeing the clear emptiness of all experience and awareness. Seeing can arise at any stage of the process. When the teacher is satisfied that the pointing out has been effective, he or she then explains to the student the significance of what the student has experienced and what further effort the student should make in practice.

Pointing Out: The Teacher's Perspective

In order to clear up some of the confusion that surrounds the teacher-student interaction, let's take a look at a set of pointing-out instructions from the teacher's side.

In meditation, mind rests. In thinking, mind moves. Whether resting or moving, mind is aware. Are these three different minds or one mind? If one, how can the same mind rest, move, and know? These questions are at the heart of a set of pointing-out instructions named, aptly enough, *resting, moving, and knowing*. The sequence is used in both the Kagyu and Nyingma traditions of Tibetan Buddhism. The particular version presented here is based on Shamar Chokyi Wangchuk's commentary *The Ocean of Certainty*, an important training manual in the Kagyu tradition. I have paraphrased the often terse Tibetan and added expanded explanations to make the process clearer.

My intention in including this description is to help you understand what is happening in the teacher-student interaction. The teacher is interested in only one thing—direct experience—and will try to bring you to that any way he or she can. You won't be able to use the responses in this description to fool your teacher because he or she will easily tell that you are not speaking from your own experience. However, this description may help you understand better what is going on between you and what effort you need to make in insight practice.

Resting Mind

Instruct the student to let the mind rest and look at the resting mind.

Ask, "How is the resting mind?"

If the student responds that there is nothing, that the mind just rests, then direct the student's attention to what knows the mind is resting. Ask about the knowing: "Is the knowing cloudy or clear and vivid?"

If the student answers that it is clear and vivid, then he or she has seen something of mind nature.

If the student responds that mind is this or that thing, then use various questions and reasoning to point out the fixation and to show that the object of fixation cannot be substantiated as mind. Direct the student to keep looking at the resting mind.

When the student says that he or she sees nothing, inquire about the difference between nothing and knowing. If the student experiences the mind resting and clear and is unable to identify anything as mind, then he or she has seen mind a little.

If nothing comes from these efforts, the student needs to work harder at cultivating attention. His or her level of attention is not sufficient for insight practice.

Moving Mind
Ask about the moving, thinking, sensing mind, "How is it when activated? How is it activated?"

Tell the student to use a visual object or a sound to look at the moving mind. Ask, "Where is the mind that experiences the visual object or the sound? Is the knowing quality of experience in the body, in sensory stimuli, or in the projections of internal patterns that make up your experience of the world?"

Ask, "How is the mind when moving, and how is the mind when resting?"

If the student responds as described above, then the pointing out has been successful.

Cutting the Root
If the student has not been able to see into mind nature, then attention needs to be directed to the origin of perception. Perception is where subject-object duality is fixed in patterned reaction. Beginning with the resting mind, direct the attention to larger and larger differences between subject and object. Since mind is both subject and object, the student has to hold both simultaneously. The additional effort leads to the formation of a higher level of attention that penetrates the subject-object duality and leads to insight at the level of perception.

Ask, "What is the difference between the resting mind and the inquiring mind?"

The student looks at the resting mind and sees nothing. If the student is able to do this and does not recognize mind nature, then tell the student to direct attention at the inquiring mind, that is, that which is looking at the resting mind, and ask, "What is the difference between the two?"

Ask, "Where does the inquiring mind come from, where is it, and where does it go?" Whenever the student comes up with a philosophical or concrete response, use logic and reasoning to expose the fallacy, and return the student to looking.

These questions take the student's attention deeper into the inquiring mind, looking to see its nature. You can tell when the student is not able to hold attention because he or she will fall into confusion or start speculating intellectually about the nature of mind and experience. Direct the student to stop formulating answers and use the question to look. "Are the resting mind and the moving mind the same or different?"

The pointing-out sequence begins with what seem to be three different minds: the mind that rests without thought or movement, the mind that moves as experiences arise, and the mind that inquires into the nature of the other two. When the student experiences that the resting mind, the moving mind, and the inquiring mind are not different, pointing out has taken place.

A Zen story on the same matter appears in *The Gateless Gate,* a collection of koans compiled by Master Mumon in the thirteenth century.

> A monk once went to Daihogen of Seiryo before the midday meal to ask for instruction. Gen pointed to the bamboo blinds with his hand. At that moment, two monks went over to the blinds and rolled them up in identical manner. Gen said, "One has gained, one has lost."

Practice After the Pointing-Out Instructions

When effective, pointing-out instructions plant a seed of experience. In the Shangpa tradition, four additional instructions are given to prevent the student from falling back into habituated patterns.

> *Too close—you can't recognize it.*
> *Too profound—you can't appreciate it.*

Too simple—you can't believe it.
Too good—you can't accept it.

Too close—you can't recognize it

The first line tells us to show up and face what we are: mind nature, empty clear awareness. We are so caught up in trying to be someone or something that we ignore what we are.

Mind nature is like a mirror. Hold up a mirror and look at it. You don't see the mirror. All you see are the objects reflected in it. To see the objects as they are, as reflections, you have to recognize that the mirror is there, even though you can't see it. We habitually take the content of experience as real. To know what experience is, you have to recognize mind nature. The nature of experience, empty clear awareness, is right in front of us, closer to us than our own faces, and yet we never recognize it. As Rangjung Dorje wrote:

It doesn't exist: even buddhas do not see it.
It doesn't not exist: it is the basis of all experience.

Too profound—you can't appreciate it

The second line of the Shangpa instruction tells us to open to what we see, let it in, and appreciate it for what it is. The resistance is formidable. Mind nature is so deep and so profound. Facing infinite open space, with no inside or outside, the elemental reaction chains go into overdrive. Yet, when we open to the profundity, the reactions dissolve and pristine awareness arises.

All of us, in times of great stress, can suddenly shed the restrictions of habituation and do what needs to be done. Afterward, we wonder where the energy, understanding, or skill came from. They come from mind nature, from being one with what is arising in experience. That energy, understanding, and skill are present all the time.

Almost any moment of shock, embarrassment, relief, or joy temporarily disrupts habituated functioning. Mind nature shines out, but we do not appreciate it because we quickly fall back into reacting to the fright, embarrassment, relief, or joy.

Too simple—you can't believe it

The third instruction tells us to know what we are and not to rely on beliefs. Beliefs form the basis of habituated living. They are deeply habituated patterns that govern how we view and understand our lives. They may take the form of an explicit set of beliefs, as in some religions, but for most of us beliefs develop from a complex interaction of developmental experiences and cultural perceptions. The central belief is that there is some thing that corresponds to the word *I*. We believe that the "I" is an unchanging entity, independent of everything else we experience. Ambrose Bierce, in his send-up of Descartes, was closer to the truth than Descartes:

Cogito cogito ergo cogito sum:
"I think that I think, therefore I think that I am."

The illusion of "I" arises from layers of conditioning and complex interactions among habituated patterns. It is a swirl of reactive energy following a program of reaction that formed and froze a long time ago. We may believe we are the program, but that is not the case.

Most of us cannot imagine functioning without beliefs. They appear to be the warp and woof of life, and everything that we think we are is woven from them. The practice of insight, however, shreds the fabric woven from beliefs.

When attention penetrates patterns, we see no thing, no unchanging and independent entity. Only clear empty awareness is present, clear empty awareness, which arises as an unceasing flow of experience consisting of thoughts, feelings, and sensations. Unbelievable—things can't be that simple. Buddha Shakyamuni went into a state of profound shock when he came to this understanding. He was unable to communicate with anyone for seven weeks. So simple, and we cannot believe it.

All of us have had the experience of being unable to solve a problem, only to have a friend or a teacher show us a simple solution. "That's all?" we say. "There's nothing to it! It has to be more difficult than that." We could not see the solution before, and now that we see it we cannot believe it.

Too good—you can't accept it
The fourth line tells us to give up control, accept what is, and enter the mystery of being. Mind nature goes by many names: buddha nature, the perfection of wisdom, original mind, original purity, awakening mind, to name a few. Like it or not, nothing is fundamentally wrong with us. We are not condemned to a life of misery by original sin, past karma, or fate. We may have difficulty accepting the freedom and responsibility that come with knowing original nature, but acceptance is where the life of presence begins. You walk forward from this point

into the unknown, free from the fetters of illusion, free in the knowing that, whatever arises, it is your experience, it is your life.

STAGES IN WORKING WITH INSIGHT

Individual experiences in working with insight vary greatly. Each person has a different way of interpreting experience and different patterns that impede, block, or undermine the cultivation of attention and insight. Even though individual experiences vary widely, I have discerned six stages that most people encounter. The stages describe a process that also takes place in many other areas of life, so in this section, I take a broader view of insight and show how the process of looking into what arises applies to understanding difficulties in a relationship as well as to understanding mind nature.

Insight is a seeing into the way things work or a seeing through layers of interpretation to what is actually there. Such seeing may be brought about in a number of ways. Cultivating attention precipitates insight into the workings of mind for many people. Meditation on death and impermanence shatters socially conditioned notions of what life is and undermines our beliefs in the significance of conventional success and failure. Consistent attention always leads to understanding, whether in personal relationships, political and social dynamics, business challenges, scientific research, or other arenas. In all cases, insight involves dismantling the assumptions and interpretations currently in operation and moving into unknown territory where deeper seeing can take place.

The following chart describes the stages we go through whenever we move from one level of interpretation and understanding to a deeper one, whether the movement takes place in meditation practice, in problem solving, in learning a new job, or in coming to a new understanding of a relationship. The metaphor of the village is used to describe the current system of functioning. The dragon refers to the operation of the mechanisms that maintain the system. Every system presents at best a partial picture of what is, and by accepting one system, another aspect of reality is systematically ignored. In the case of the system of subject-object perception, the oneness of being is ignored. As insight develops and threatens to expose what the system ignores, the system reacts to degrade attention. It blocks, co-opts, destroys, or cancels efforts in attention and insight. Understanding emerges only when the system collapses or, in the metaphor, the dragon dies.

In the explanations that follow the chart I trace the emergence of insight in two different circumstances: seeing into a problem in a relationship and seeing into mind nature in meditation.

The Six Stages of Insight

STAGE	DESCRIPTION	SIGNS	EFFORT
stepping out of the village	confusion arises from not seeing anything	irritation, disorientation, confusion	stay in the confusion
feeling the dragon's breath	five element reaction chains	strong emotional reactions	transform the reaction chains into presence
seeing the dragon	you see how the reactions perpetuate themselves	sinking feeling, depression, strong inclination to turn away into one of the six realms	observe how the system operates, empty the realms
meeting the dragon	you see the system as a system that operates on its own agenda	raw emotional reactions, fear and uncertainty	stay present in the undischarged core emotions
cutting the dragon	you bring attention to the system	disorganization, alternating hope and fear	maintain practice and stay present in the transition
dying	emergence of insight	disturbances collapse and understanding arises	act on the understanding and accept the changes that follow

Stage 1: Stepping Out of the Village

Relationship

You know that your relationship is in trouble. You don't experience the kind of connection or rapport you used to have with your partner. The two of you seem to be going in different directions or just missing each other, even in simple exchanges. Your partner says that the two of you never spend any time together.

"I don't understand what you are talking about," you say. "We had dinner together last night."

"We hardly said a word," your partner replies. "We don't spend real time together anymore."

"I don't understand," you say again, but something is wrong. You are confused, irritated, disoriented, and a little sad.

Mind Nature
When you first look at mind, you quickly become distracted and confused. You look, but you cannot see. You are irritated or disheartened. You try to analyze or deduce what is meant to happen, but your teacher just sends you back to your practice. You feel incompetent, stupid, or hopeless. The practice makes no sense to you.

Effort to Make
The first stage in insight is to look at what you have not looked at before. You step out of the village of habituated interpretations of experience. At first you can't see anything, you don't know what to look at, and you can't understand what others are talking about. As far as you are concerned, they are speaking a different language. You are confused, bewildered, and disoriented. You want to go back to what you know. Resisting the temptation, you keep looking, even though you are bewildered and confused. Gradually, attention forms and you begin to see.

Stage 2: Feeling the Dragon's Breath

Relationship
You think about the last week or the last month with your partner. How much time have you spent together? You see each other in the morning; you usually have dinner together. Sure, you are tired and so is your partner. You both work hard. You open the topic up with your partner one evening. The longer you talk, the more anxious you become; until you say, "I can't talk about this anymore. I have to prepare a presentation for a meeting tomorrow."

"There, you see. Work is more important. You always have something to do," your partner says.

"But it's important. It's my job. It's what I do." You work on the presentation, but it's already in place, so you spend most of the time fussing with details.

Mind Nature

When you look at mind, you see nothing. As your level of attention rises to the point at which you can stay present in the confusion, you look more deeply. You still see nothing but you have an intimation of open space, a space so open and so limitless that you cannot conceptualize it in any way. You feel a little shaky inside (earth), you feel very alone (fire), or you feel another of the other reaction chains. In the earth reaction, you stick doggedly to the structure of the practice, working through every detail. In the fire reaction, you become angrier and angrier, until you can hardly sit still. These reactions, or the corresponding ones for the other elements, tell you that you are feeling the dragon's breath.

Effort to Make

The second stage is to experience the reaction to looking, to stepping out of the village. The looking has already begun to dismantle the structures that define your world. Even though you don't sense any change, you have begun to look at things a little differently. You are stepping into a world different from the one you have known. One of the five reaction chains is triggered. This is the dragon's breath, the emotion underlying your reaction and the fear underlying the emotion. Use the five dakinis meditations in chapter 6 to transform the reaction chains, and return to looking.

Stage 3: Seeing the Dragon

Relationship

The matter doesn't go away. You keep thinking about what's happening to your relationship. Every time you talk with your partner, your partner becomes upset. You become defensive, and you break off the discussion to start doing something—going over notes, fixing things in the house, picking up newspapers, anything to keep moving. You know you aren't getting anywhere, but some nameless fear prevents you from really sitting down with your partner. Right now, everything is in place. You both have your jobs. You have the money to do what you enjoy. You don't dare spend more time with your partner! If you do, your world will fall apart. Your work will suffer. You'll be fired, you'll lose your house and your cars, and you'll end up on the street. You're clear: keep things just as they are.

Mind Nature
When you look at mind, you see how you fall into the same reactive cycle again and again, doggedly clinging to the structure, perhaps, or seething about the injustice of it all. You also observe how you keep projecting the same realm: your teacher is out to get you, or he is never going to give you what you need. You are like a dog chasing its own tail, spinning around and around, faster and faster.

One of the most common mistakes in the practice of insight is to ignore the emotional reactions that arise in insight practice. The emotional reactions may be no more than emotions, but the reactions have to be unmade. To step over them or avoid dealing with them leaves them intact. Even if you manage to have a glimpse of mind nature, the ability to implement that insight in your life will be limited and corrupted by the emotional reactive patterns you have not dismantled.

Effort to Make
The third stage, seeing the dragon, begins when you see the self-perpetuating nature of the system of reactive patterns. You observe how you keep dropping out of attention, how you go through the cycle of reactions, and how each cycle reinforces the pattern. You see that the way you perceive things, the way you think, and the way you act are all part of the pattern. Intimidated by the size and power of the dragon, you feel the whole business is hopeless and you might as well give up. The sinking feeling is a manifestation of fear, the subjective experience that arises when the internal structures that condition your sense of physical, emotional, or spiritual existence are threatened. You react by projecting one of the six realms, but your projection is frustrated:

> You have to fight, but you can't find the enemy.
> You need something, but you don't know what.
> You are sure you are going to die, physically, but you can't name the threat.
> You feel terribly unhappy, but you don't know why.
> You are sure that you have to prove something, but no one is paying any attention.
> You feel everything is falling apart, and you try to keep it all together.

Fear is emotional energy pouring into the system's mechanisms of self-maintenance.

At this point, observe how the system operates, and keep looking into what is arising. Use the meditations on emptying the six realms in chapter 6 if you can't hold the reactions in attention.

Stage 4: Meeting the Dragon

Relationship
Tensions mount.

Your partner has less and less patience. "So what if everything falls apart," your partner says. "What's it brought us, anyway?"

You can't believe what you are hearing. Your partner is questioning your whole life, everything you've worked for, everything you've achieved together. You feel as if you are falling into the Grand Canyon. You try to stay busy, but you can't concentrate on your work. You are short with colleagues at your office. At night, you can't sleep, and when you do, you dream of being pushed out of a plane and you have no parachute. You feel completely helpless, even powerless, but you know that you have to face this matter.

Mind Nature
You look at mind, and all you see is the whole set of reactions. Practice becomes very personal at this point. Nothing you have read, studied, or heard is any help. You learned how to do the practice, step by step, but there are no steps in front you now. Neither does anger help. You just feel more alone. You stare into the darkness, not knowing what is ahead and fearing the worst.

Effort to Make
As the reactive patterns start to fall apart, the intimation of space grows stronger. Fear becomes more and more pronounced. You begin to see the whole picture. All the parts fit together—the elemental reaction chain and the projected world, and the attachment to a sense of self. The whole system is there, and it is your life. It is all you know. The situation is truly hopeless.

You are sometimes reduced to a primitive or infantile level of functioning, unable to articulate what you are feeling or experiencing, uncertain where to go or what to do. Reactive emotional patterns arise strongly and show up in reactive behaviors whenever you lose mindfulness. Attention is penetrating to the undischarged emotional core of the pattern, and you don't feel very good. Congratulations! You've met the dragon.

Stage 5: Cutting

Relationship

You now see how your relationship has suffered because you have not put enough time into it. You've been so focused on work, you ignored your partner. You first resolve to take time off, take a vacation together, but the old fear grips you and you postpone your plans. Your partner explodes, or, worse, she or he no longer takes you seriously.

You realize you have no choice. You take the vacation—and you really enjoy it. How could you forget how much fun your partner is to be with? When you come back, you are full of resolutions, but they quickly fall by the way and tensions mount again.

You see that the problem is not your partner but your own need to be busy so that you never have to feel any doubt about who you are. You want to let go, but you can't quite do so. Deep in your heart, you hope that things will get better, and at the same time you are overcome by fear, fear that your partner will leave you, you will lose your job, and your life will fall apart.

Mind Nature

Attention cuts into whatever arises in experience. The practice has developed its own momentum. Whatever arises, you look and it falls apart. Again and again you cut the root of mind. The energy locked in the old patterns of perception is transformed into attention. Powerful feelings of hope and fear wash through you. You keep cutting and looking at what experiences the surges. Looking goes deeper and deeper.

Effort to Make

One minute you are full of hope that your efforts will bear fruit, but the next minute you fall back into hopeless despair when the same old stuff comes back and carries you away. The system of patterns and structures has started to collapse, and now you see that the system has to go, but the patterns keep coming back.

You have entered the transition process. Keep making the same effort: look into what is arising, and rest there. On the one hand, you are cutting into the dragon of reactive patterns: it is dying. On the other, you are opening into what is: you are energized and begin to have glimpses of extraordinary possibilities. As the dragon dies, its energy becomes available to you. You catch the old reactions earlier, you see more possibilities, and you begin to explore them.

If you lose attention, you are immediately overtaken by the dragon's energy and fall back into habituated patterns. If the dragon revives, it is stronger than before, so teachers strongly warn against distraction at this stage.

Keep looking, holding on to nothing.

Stage 6: Dying

Relationship

Then one day, you sit down with your partner and ask, "What do you want our life to look like?" Your partner responds. She or he is very clear, and the ideas make a lot of sense. You wonder why you didn't ask before.

The old dynamic is dead. You feel pain—the pain of all the damage caused by the old pattern and the pain at the core of the pattern. Your relationship with your partner has changed. The old relationship is dead, and a new relationship is forming. You see also that nothing guarantees what will happen in the future, but you are prepared now to go forward.

Mind Nature

In looking at mind, you see nothing. The open space isn't just empty space because it is simultaneously clear and aware. The clarity and emptiness are not different, but there is absolutely nothing there. Yet experience arises: thoughts, feelings, and sensory sensations. Everything arises like a magical show. Nowhere is there anything you can identify as "I." Experience just arises, empty and clear. You go about your life, knowing this clear empty awareness in everything.

Effort to Make

The last stage is dying. The old structures fall apart, and you see clearly how things are. The dragon dies, though you may feel that you have died. Everything seems so obvious and straightforward that you cannot quite understand what all the struggle was about. You know you cannot hold on to the old structures, and you have little inclination to do so. You set about changing what needs to be changed and doing what needs to be done.

WHAT'S NEXT?

Many years ago, a cartoon by Gahan Wilson appeared on the bulletin boards of Buddhist centers all across the United States. The cartoon showed an old monk and a young monk sitting in meditation, both huddled in robes. The old monk, his face wrinkled with years of effort, has turned to the young monk. The caption reads, "What's next? Nothing—this is it."

I remember talking with a Tibetan teacher who gave up a senior position in the Tibetan hierarchy and worked for many years as an orderly tending to psychiatric patients. We were discussing the relationship between practice and life. "You see, Ken," he said, "meditation isn't the point of life. You work hard at meditation, very hard, to get a good result. Then you live your life."

All that we have is what we experience, right now. This, right here, right now, is our life. We will not know any other.

CHAPTER 10

No Separation

Nasrudin's tomb was fronted by an immense wooden door, barred and padlocked. Nobody could get into it, at least through the door. As his last joke, the Mulla had decreed that the tomb should have no walls around it. . . .

The date inscribed on the tomb was 386. Translating this into letters by substitution, a common device on Sufi tombs, we find SHWF. This is a form of the word for "seeing," especially for "making a person see."

Perhaps it is for this reason that for many years the dust from the tomb was considered to be effective in curing eye troubles. . . .

—IDRIES SHAH,
THE PLEASANTRIES OF THE INCREDIBLE MULLA NASRUDIN

In 1993, during a retreat in Santa Fe, Nyishöl Khenpo Rinpoche, a Nyingma teacher, taught me three lines:

Crack the egg of ignorance.
Cut the web of existence.
Open awareness like the sky.

This set of instructions embodies, in poetic form, the *Three Words of Garab Dorje:*

Wake up to your own nature.
Be absolute on one point.
Have confidence and be free.

Let's take a look at each of these.

Crack the Egg of Ignorance:
Wake Up to Your Own Nature

Everything in this book up to this point has been focused on the first line, cracking the egg of ignorance—waking up to your original nature.

Kalu Rinpoche often demonstrated the progression of practice by taking a crystal to represent mind nature, or original mind. He then covered the crystal with a fold of his robes, saying, "This is basic ignorance."

Then he took another fold of his robes and laid it over the first, "This is dualistic perception," then another, "and this is the obscuration of reactive emotions," and, finally, "this is the obscuration of karmic conditioning."

"And this is practice," he continued, peeling away the layers of cloth one by one until the crystal was revealed.

All through this book you have been peeling away layers. With the meditations on death and impermanence, you peeled away attachment to conventional success and saw the rigid structure of patterns and conditioning. Using the meditations on the five dakinis and the six realms, you peeled away reactive emotional patterns. The four immeasurables exposed and released raw, undischarged emotional cores. Insight cut through the fabric of dualistic perception and ignorance to reveal the crystal of original mind.

Now you know what presence is: knowing the whole and knowing that what you are is not separate from the whole.

A verse from Rumi also applies here:

> I have lived on the lip
> of insanity, wanting to know reasons,
> knocking on a door. It opens.
> I've been knocking from the inside!
> —RUMI

When you have cracked the egg of ignorance, everything changes. You now understand what practice is and what it is not. It's not a means to become happy, rich, famous, or respected. It's not about achieving this or that realization, experience, or understanding. It's not about becoming wise, compassionate, or powerful. It's a way to be completely present in each moment of life. You break out of the egg of ignorance into the world of presence.

Once you've had a direct experience of the nature of things, you know that nothing is real. You know, despite what conditioning continues to tell you, that you are not an entity existing separately, apart from what you experience. You know that what you experience is not an external world that exists independently of you. You have seen into the mystery of being, and you know what prevents you from living in it.

You see the functioning of habituated patterns much more clearly. When they run, you are not present, and you experience the difference. You see clearly how habituated patterns run on their own agendas that have little, if anything, to do with present circumstances or your intention in life.

The other day I had dinner with a woman, Carol. Though a kind and thoughtful person, she is tenacious in her intention and one way or another usually manages to get her way. Over dinner, she complained lightheartedly how her friends were always doing little things to get the better of her. The latest ploy by an old friend was not returning her phone calls, at least not immediately. Piqued, Carol had responded in kind, and tension was building up between them. A power struggle was under way. I asked Carol what calling her friend, that is, losing the power struggle, would cost her. "Well, she'd get her way," she laughed, but she saw how the pattern of having to win could cost her the friendship.

Cut the Web of Existence:
Be Absolute on One Point

The second phase is to *cut the web of existence*. You may feel that once you have had an experience of original mind or presence, your practice is finished. Such an attitude is extremely dangerous. While many habituated patterns are destroyed by even a glimpse of original mind, in truth, your work has just begun. Kalu Rinpoche wrote:

> These days, many people think that once they more or less understand mind nature or have had a moment or two's experience of presence, that's sufficient. They stop cultivating compassion, awakening mind, and respectful appreciation. They stop any formal practice and disregard moral principles. They end up with badly mistaken views and worse reactive emotions than before and think they are doing the right thing. Such people spin endlessly in their own confusion.

In your practice, you must not dissipate presence in any thought or action. Continually direct attention at mind and at what you do. Until your ability to rest in presence is stabilized, continue with the forms of practice to prevent habituated patterns from corrupting your experience.

Cut the web of existence means that you make one point, presence, absolute in your life. You cut the operation of habituated patterns whenever they arise. You cut through and return to presence. Everything else is just stuff.

Even if you have had only a glimpse of mind nature, you now approach practice differently, constantly returning to presence, to the experience of the whole in which self and other are known to be constructs. You return to the mystery of being in which there is no inside or outside, there is just what is.

You might suppose that understanding original mind makes cutting easy, but it really just makes cutting possible. The web of patterns that make up conditioned existence operates automatically. It is deeply entrenched. Up to now, it is all you have known about how to live and function in life. Cutting the web involves letting go of your reliance on habituated ways of functioning and returning to presence. In other words, you let go of your life as you have known it up to this point. You stop struggling to make things conform to the way the patterns tell you they should be, and you relate directly to what is.

> The range of what we think and do is limited by what we fail to notice.
>
> —*R. D. Laing*

When you have a fight with your husband or wife, dispense with concerns about who wins and who loses, cut the web, return to presence, and do what needs to be done. When you are aggressively pushing a business deal, cut the web, forget about driving the hardest bargain, and return to presence, knowing the place this business transaction has in your life. When you are confused in your meditation practice, cut the web, forget about achieving enlightenment or any other personal ambition, return to presence, and open to what you are experiencing right now. To borrow a page from Taoism, Chuang Tzu writes:

You can't discuss the ocean with a well frog—he's limited by the space he lives in. You can't discuss ice with a summer insect—he's bound to a single season. You can't discuss the Way with a cramped scholar—he's shackled by his doctrines. Now you have come out beyond your banks and borders and have seen the great sea—so you realize your own pettiness. From now on it will be possible to talk to you about the Great Principle.

Placing Attention in Original Mind

After you have had a glimpse of original mind, meditation practice changes and the emphasis shifts to resting in mind nature. First, place attention in original mind. Recall the key principle of basic meditation:

Return to what is already there, and rest.

You now apply this principle to original mind, which is what you already are but keep forgetting.

Sit in formal meditation practice. Sit with the back straight, with the chin brought in slightly toward the throat so that the head sits on top of the spine. Relax the stomach; let your back be soft yet straight. Place the hands either on the thighs or in the traditional meditation position, palms up, one on top of the other in your lap so that no tension is transmitted to the upper back and shoulders. Settle into the sitting posture, straight but not tense, stable but not rigid, relaxed but not limp. Keep your eyes open, looking straight ahead, as if staring into the open sky.

Breathe naturally through the nose with the lips closed but the teeth not touching. Natural breathing is very important in the practice of presence, as the breath becomes very subtle. Any attempt to control or manipulate the breath works against the practice.

To place attention in original mind, recall the instructions of Gampopa:

- Don't invite the future.
- Don't pursue the past.
- Let go of the present.
- Relax right now.

Sit straight and relaxed. Let go of any thoughts or concerns about the future. Thoughts and ideas may or may not vanish. Just stop focusing attention on them. When your hopes, fears, concerns, excitement, or other feelings about future events arise, let them go, too, which is to say, just let them be there, like clouds in the sky.

Let any thoughts or concerns about the past come and go. As you become aware of feelings of accomplishment, regret, shame, vindication, triumph, or defeat, let them go, too.

> Tenno asked, "What is the essential meaning of Buddhism?"
>
> Sekito replied, "No gaining, no knowing."
>
> "Can you say anything further?"
>
> "The expansive sky does not obstruct the floating white clouds."
>
> —*Shobogenzo*

At this point, you will naturally start thinking about the present, what you are doing in your life and why. Let these thoughts come and go, too, like leaves stirred by a gust of wind.

And then relax, letting body, breath, and attention just be.

You will experience a shift. That shift is the placing of attention in original mind. There is nothing else to do. Rest right there.

Resting in Presence

As you become used to placing attention in original mind, you move into the practice of presence. The instructions for presence are very simple. One set, from the mahamudra tradition, is:

- No distraction
- No control
- No work

No distraction means that you rest in attention. When a thought, feeling, or sensation arises, let it be there. Don't follow it or get involved with it. Just stay open and relaxed. Don't be distracted for even a moment. Start by placing attention in original mind for short periods so you are totally awake and present. Gradually lengthen the periods, keeping the clarity vivid and attention stable. The moment you are distracted, you fall out of attention and the energy of your practice flows into habituated patterns. Sit like an empty house. Thieves—thoughts and feelings—come, but the house is empty and there is nothing to steal, so they go away.

A teacher and a monk arrived at a junction of two roads about a mile from a small village. The teacher pointed to a tree and said, "This is a good place for you to practice. It's not too close to the village, so you won't be distracted. It's not too far, so you can receive support from the people in the village. Stay here and practice until I return."

The monk sat down under the tree, and the teacher went his way.

A couple of years later, the teacher decided to see how the monk was doing. As he walked through the village, it seemed to be much busier than it had been a couple of years earlier. The road he had taken with his student earlier was now bordered by buildings he didn't recognize. Cars and trucks trundled to and fro. Near the crossing was a large warehouse with its loading docks filled with merchandise. On the other side, a large factory was surrounded by workshops and tool sheds. Vendors plied their wares everywhere. A large office building, all concrete and glass, stood on the corner.

> Let what arises rise; take care not to follow.
>
> —*Milarepa*

Puzzled, the teacher asked a man about the whereabouts of the monk who practiced meditation. Smiling widely, the man pointed to the top floor of the office building. The teacher entered a magnificent marble lobby and took the elevator to the top floor. He walked into a spacious carpeted office with administrative assistants quietly busy at their desks. When he inquired about the monk, he was directed to an even larger office with a huge mahogany desk. Behind it stood his student dressed in an elegant suit in conference with an aide.

The teacher cleared his throat. His student looked up and staggered back with a look of astonishment on his face. He sank into his leather chair and started to sob. "It all started when I needed a new loincloth," he said.

In Mahayana Buddhism, the counterpart to the three marks of existence—impermanence, suffering, and non-self—are the three gates to freedom: no characteristics, no aspiration, and emptiness.

Good, bad, pleasant, unpleasant, big, little, open, closed, blue, red—these are all characteristics, and when your mind stops on any one of them, you fall into distraction. Mind stops on the content of experience, and you fall out of the mystery. When you maintain clear vivid attention without distraction, you enter the gate of "no characteristics." You stop grasping at such characteristics as good, bad, interesting, boring, stillness, or movement. Thoughts, feelings, and sensations come and go freely on their own.

The instruction *no control* means that you do not try to make something happen in your practice. This instruction is aimed at the misconception that presence is an ideal state of undisturbed equanimity or permanent bliss or total purity. In Dante's *Inferno,* the words "Abandon all hope, ye who enter here" are inscribed above the portal to hell. More apt, perhaps, is to inscribe these words above the portal to presence, because "no aspiration" is the second gate to freedom. Presence is knowing the whole, knowing that self and other are constructs, and living in the mystery of experience. That's it. The urge to control comes from the desire to create and maintain an experience different from what you are currently experiencing. In the practice of presence, you give up all hope, meet whatever comes, and do not try to change, control, or manipulate your experience in any way.

> Drukpa Kunlek was one of the famous mad hermits of Tibet. When a prospective student came to him for instruction, Drukpa Kunlek asked, "Are you afraid of experiencing rebirth in the hell realms?"
>
> "Yes," the student answered, "that's why I came to see you."
>
> "Do you hope to attain enlightenment?" asked Drukpa Kunlek.
>
> "Yes, that's why I want to practice."
>
> "Go away!" said Drukpa Kunlek. "With so much hope and fear, you can't possibly practice. I would be wasting my time giving you any instruction."

No work means that you don't try to cultivate any particular quality or understanding. In other forms of practice, you worked at accepting impermanence and death, dismantling the reaction chains, and cultivating the four immeasurables. In the practice of presence, do not try to cultivate any quality or ability. Don't try to make the mind calm and still. Don't work at compassion or faith or insight. Go empty. Just be.

> A Zen teacher came across one of his students meditating in the courtyard of the temple.
>
> "What are you doing?" the teacher asked.
>
> "I'm working at knowing original mind," the student replied.
>
> The teacher sat down beside the student, picked up a stone, and started to polish it with his robe. The teacher kept rubbing the stone with his robe, seemingly oblivious to the passage of time. Eventually the student could restrain his puzzlement no longer.
>
> "What are you doing?" he asked his teacher.
>
> "Making a glass tile."

"But you can't make a glass tile by polishing a stone."

"Nor can you know original mind by working at it!" said the teacher.

To rest without working at anything involves letting go of the beliefs that you have to be "somebody," that you need special qualities or abilities, or that you should be doing this or should not be doing that. When you release these beliefs, you become empty and enter the third gate to freedom, emptiness.

The Zen practice of shikantaza, the Tibetan practices of mahamudra and dzogchen, and the Theravadan practice of full mindfulness of breathing are all examples of the practice of presence. You need three qualities for this practice: appreciation of impermanence, compassion, and faith. A profound appreciation of impermanence and the suffering of human existence provides the motivation necessary to let habituated patterns fall apart. Compassion, because it manifests as deeply caring attention to everything that arises in experience, ensures that your practice embraces all aspects of life and does not reinforce the sense of "I." Faith, the willingness to open to the mystery of being, provides the emotional energy to stay present in the face of patterns until they naturally release in the open space of original mind. As Niguma sang to Khyungpo Naljor after pointing out mind nature to him:

> In this world of magical suffering
> We work at a magical practice
> And experience a magical awakening,
> Which comes through the power of faith.

Dispelling Misconceptions

We can't know what we haven't experienced. One of the most common problems associated with the practice of presence is our preconceptions about what presence is, what emptiness is, and what the mystery of being is.

A king, much impressed by the teachings of a sage, developed a deep attachment to truth. He decreed that all his subjects had to speak the truth in all circumstances. To enforce his decree, he instructed the guards at the city gates to determine whether people were telling the truth and to hang those who didn't.

The sage, disturbed by the turn of the events, took leave of the king and left the city. The next day he returned and was questioned by a guard, "What is your reason for entering this city?"

"I'm going to be hanged," the sage replied.

After a few moments' reflection, the guard realized that he was out of his depth. The conundrum and the sage were eventually referred to the king himself.

"Your Majesty," the sage said, "there is world of difference between truth and your concept of truth. Repeal your decree, and let us study the subject again."

Although this phase of practice is about being absolute on one point, you must be careful to understand exactly what is involved to avoid falling into the same kind of pitfalls as this king.

The first pitfall is to take emptiness as real and arrive at a nihilistic view of life. If emptiness is real, then nothing else matters because nothing else is real. You regard the functioning of patterns as unreal and pay no attention to them. You ignore what arises in experience, and your patterns run completely amok with nothing to check their operation. Saraha, an Indian master of the third century, said of this view:

> *Those who believe that what appears is real*
> *Are stupid, like cows.*
> *Those who believe that emptiness is real*
> *Are even stupider.*

Emptiness is not what is real. Emptiness doesn't exist. If it did, it wouldn't be emptiness. Nothing is real—not emptiness, not experience, not awareness. As Avalokiteshvara says in the *Heart Sutra*:

> . . . no suffering, no origin of suffering, no cessation of suffering, no path, no wisdom, no attainment and no non-attainment.

Mind nature is not a thing. It cannot be labeled as this or that. It does not come into existence. It does not cease to be. It is not made, and neither can it be destroyed. It is just what is present, and you know it when you are no longer confused or distracted by the operation of habituated patterns.

The second pitfall is to try to make disturbing thoughts, reactive emotions, or distracting sensations "empty." You can't *make* them empty, because they *are* empty. They appear to be real because you don't experience them completely. Your effort in practice is not to make thoughts and emotions empty but to experience them completely and know what they are. When you experience them completely, you experience them as empty because that is their nature.

In the previous chapter, I talked about the world of money. You can't make money empty. It's a part of life. You can try to ignore it, pretend it doesn't exist, or regard it as the source of all evil, but such approaches create only difficulties. Equally, if you take money as real, you see and value everything in your life financially, and your life is poorer, no matter how much money you may have. If, on the other hand, you understand exactly what money is—a collective agreement for exchanging your energy with others—then you can relate to money sensibly without losing your life to it. You may choose to exchange energy with others using money, or you may choose to exchange energy emotionally or spiritually—in ways not based on economic valuations.

Instead of trying to make experience empty, open to experience completely and know it for what it is. Then you will not be confused by what you experience. You will be clear and present in your life.

The third pitfall is to think that naming emptiness is enough. You have a disagreement with a colleague, and you are angry about what she said. "Ah, but anger is empty," you recall, and decide that labeling the anger as empty is enough. The anger, however, still festers inside you. You haven't experienced it completely, so it hasn't released. Not only is labeling not enough; it prevents you from directly knowing what does arise in experience. To be absolute about one point, mind nature, experience the anger completely without losing attention, neither dumping it into the world nor suppressing it in you.

The fourth pitfall is to take the attitude "meditate now, be enlightened later." The teacher who polished the stone was showing his student that this approach is not the practice of presence. Nothing exists outside the present moment of experience. Everything—the past, the future, the external world, the sense of self—is a construction, or interpretation, of what you experience right now.

Stop reading for a moment, and imagine that you are going to die in one minute. The last things you are going to experience are reading these pages, sitting in this room, wearing the clothes you are wearing, thinking and feeling what you are thinking and feeling right now. This is it. This is the end of your life. You have no time to do anything about it. You have no time to write a note or make a phone call. Your life is over. You will die in one minute. All you can do is experience what is, right now.

This is a very simple exercise, but it is quite profound. It brings you into presence very quickly. The projections of the six realms subside. You stop fighting, you stop needing, you stop being concerned with physical comfort, you stop wanting, you stop achieving, and you stop maintaining. Enlightenment, attainment, realization all become meaningless. You are just present. This is one way to cut the web of existence. Be absolute about this point.

Commentary: Cutting the Web

Four Approaches

Cut the web of existence comes down to a single principle: return to the direct awareness that is our human heritage. The web of existence is the web of habituated patterns that make up your personality and color your experience of life. Cut the web by experiencing completely what arises— the thoughts, feelings, sensations, the operation of habituated patterns, everything—in attention. What arises is released, and you know direct awareness in the moment. The process of cutting has four steps:

- Bring attention to what arises
- Let attention penetrate
- Hold attention in the reactive processes that are triggered
- Receive what is present when the reactive processes fall apart

Awareness is already present, but it is obscured by habituated patterns. Experience is what arises. You lose touch with mind nature when you lose touch with awareness and don't know completely what arises in experience. Start by bringing attention to what arises in experience, without judgment or evaluation. Just experience it. Attention penetrates the habituated interpretations of experience, and reactive mechanisms are triggered. Hold attention in the reactive process. Instead of being distracted and taking the reactions as real, experience them as they are, arising and subsiding in attention—awareness mixes with experience. You experience a shift at this point: you see and experience what arises differently. The final step is to accept and receive what you see and not try to change or control it.

The four-step process of mixing awareness and experience can be applied in each of four ways of working: power, ecstasy, insight, and compassion. These four approaches are subtly different. *Power* emphasizes going directly into what arises. *Ecstasy* emphasizes opening to what arises. *Insight* emphasizes seeing and knowing, and *compassion* emphasizes letting go. Of the four ways one will be more effective than the others in dismantling a particular reactive pattern. By becoming skilled in all four, you can cut the web of existence, whatever arises in experience.

For power, the process is called *standing up*. The four steps are

- Show up
- Open
- Serve what is true
- Receive the result

Show up means that you face what is happening. You don't ignore the pattern or pretend that it will go away on its own. *Open* means that you open to what is happening. You don't close down to any part of it. *Serve what is true* means that you act in accord with what is true to the limit of your perception—doing what is required by the situation even in the face of the resistance of reactive patterns. *Receive the result* means that you accept the consequences of your action or inaction. When you go through these four steps, you will be in a higher energy state because, in standing up, you cut through the operation of habituated patterns and their energy is transformed into attention.

Suppose, for instance, that you are a pack rat. You can't throw things away. You have one room in your home that you use for storage, and it is full. The growing accumulation of stuff is taking up living space in other rooms. To show up, you face the problem. You no longer ignore the accumulation. You don't deny, pretend that no problem exists, seethe, or fall into distraction or confusion. You make a decision: every day or every week, you go into this room and look at all the stuff. The next step is to open. When you are in the room, you open to what you experience, inside and outside. You don't edit, rationalize, decide to look through everything in detail, or pick up this item, then that. You open and experience it all.

What is all this stuff serving? What in this room have you used in the past six months, the past year, or the past five years? One way to serve what is true is to pick a time period, say three years, and throw out everything that you haven't touched for three years or more. Then you come across a letter from an old lover. You can't throw it away! What is being served by keeping it?

Receiving the result means that you accept the consequences of your action. If you keep the letter, how and where are you going to store it? If you throw it away, you feel the grief, the nostalgia, and the warmth of those tender memories as you recognize that the relationship is over and is no longer part of your life.

For ecstasy, the four steps in mixing awareness and experience are

- Focus
- Field
- Internal material
- Presence

Focus means to take one aspect of what arises in experience as the focus of attention. *Field* means to expand the range of attention to include everything that arises in experience. *Internal material* means to maintain attention by including the internal reactions that arise as you open to the field of experience. *Presence* means that you let those reactions play themselves out, staying present in the process. Because the reactive patterns arise in a field of attention, they are unable to maintain their functioning, and they fall apart.

As an example, suppose you are a great problem solver but have difficulty in connecting with people emotionally. When you meet someone, take his or her voice as the focus. Expand attention to include every sensation—all the other sounds, the colors of his or her clothes, eyes, and hair, the table, chairs, furniture, the walls of the room, everything. Then include your own reactions—all the ideas that flash in your mind as the other person speaks, the urge to take over the conversation, the discomfort or fear of just being with him or her. You may not be able to speak or converse the way you are accustomed to. So be it. You may feel vulnerable, uncertain, or anxious. So be it. Stay present in your experience.

For insight, the mixing process is called the *four gestures*. The four steps are

- Something happens
- A world is created
- Die to the world
- Shift a level

Something happens means just that—something happens. A thought arises or a person speaks to you. Immediately, *a world is created*. Reactive patterns, triggered by what happened, project one of the six realms. Open to it. As soon as the world is created, reactive patterns associated with that world start to run. *Die to the world* means that you hold the reactions in attention. You feel the pain of death as you experience the reactions completely and make no effort to maintain them or their world. Don't die passively. Be present as you die. *Shift a level* means that the effort in attention shifts the level of energy, cuts through the net of existence, and returns you to original mind. You see with new eyes.

A friend is having a hard time in his life. He calls to talk with you, and you have a pretty good understanding of his problems. You make a suggestion. He dismisses it and turns to another topic. You feel a sudden surge of anger. You have just moved into the hell realm. As the anger arises in you, you want to say, "Why did you call me if you are just going to dismiss what I say?" Hold the angry reaction in attention, and die to it and the world it projects. This person is not your enemy. This is a friend who called for help. Your survival is not at risk. You don't have to fight. Die to the notion that whatever you suggested was right for him. Die to the assumption that you know how to help him. Die to it all. You stop fighting, and you experience a shift, and you see what you couldn't see before—he just needed someone to talk to. He wasn't looking for advice or solutions. He was looking for human connection. Can you provide that, or does the insight trigger another round of reactions in you?

For compassion, the process of mixing awareness and experience is called *breaking chains*. The four steps are

- Enter
- Take
- Empty
- No separation

Enter means to enter into the experience of what is arising. *Take* means to take in what is happening and experience it directly. *Empty* means to disrupt any reactive involvement with what is happening. Drop into non-thought, take a breath, go empty, or just stop for a moment. *No separation* means to join with what arises right at the moment you go empty. By joining with what arises, you return to mind nature.

To continue the last example, you just saw that your friend wants and needs to feel connected. That is what is arising. A friend is in need. You enter into the interaction. You take in what is happening, the pain and fear in his voice, the uncertainty in you. Reactive tendencies start to arise: you will be buried, engulfed, burned up, or destroyed. Take a breath. Breathe out. The reactions stop. You go empty for a moment. Now join with what is. Your friend is in need, and he called you. You and he are here right now, and that's it.

Use these four approaches in meditation and in daily life. All four are important. We all have our strengths and weaknesses, but to rely only on our strengths is to create weakness. Some people are good at going right into things, but they can't open or they can't let go. Others can open, but they can't understand. Learn all four because to neglect any is to ignore a part of your life, and that part, if not addressed, will take over everything.

Energy accumulates in what is not cut. If what accumulates power is not cut, then the accumulated power cuts everything external to it. This is the dynamic of exploitation and often arises in politics, organizations, and cults. A person accumulates power but does not cut into his own need for power. Initially, he rationalizes his accumulation of power as being for the greater good, the good of the organization, or for some other lofty ideal. As time goes on, his activities serve the organization less and less, even as he accumulates more power. Yet he still demands greater sacrifices from his employees or followers. In the case of cults, if the cult doesn't fall apart, it inevitably ends in death, because the leader's craving for power eventually demands the lives of those who follow him.

> All animals are equal. Pigs are more equal than other animals.
>
> —George Orwell, Animal Farm

Similarly, if you don't open to every aspect of your life, energy fuels precisely what is not open. This is the dynamic of addiction. At the heart of most addiction is a core of shame. As long as you don't open to that shame and experience what it is—a self-image trained into you by a family or cultural system—it runs your life. In meditation practice, people, intoxicated by meditation states of bliss, clarity, or non-thought, cling to a projected reality, taking these experiences as what is real and not opening to their empty nature. Their practice degenerates into the maintenance of idyllic states, which they mistake for presence.

In the case of the perversion of insight, the ability to see into and understand what is happening is used by the parts of you that you have not seen into. More than a few spiritual teachers have fallen into this trap, seeing deeply into the working of things but being unable or unwilling to see into their own patterns. They end up manipulating their students, patrons, and communities to gain money, power, sex, or fame.

Finally, when you don't let go, what you hold on to ends up ruling your life and everyone around you. This is the dynamic of control. Think of bureaucrats who establish elaborate structures to control every aspect of an organization. Eventually, the structures themselves control the organization, and the bureaucrats are as much prisoners of their creation as the people they sought to control.

> Benevolence, courage, trust, and integrity are fine human qualities, but it is possible to plunder the benevolent, to incite the courageous, to deceive the trusting, and to intrigue against those with integrity.
>
> —*The Book of Leadership and Strategy*

Dismantling Patterns

In addition to the four methods described above, use the tools you learned in the earlier chapters: the meditations on death and impermanence, the dynamics of habituated patterns, the five dakinis and emptying the six realms, the four immeasurables, taking and sending, awakening mind, and insight.

Use these practices to cut the web of existence and return to mind nature. In death meditation, become very clear about the reality of death, and then ask, "What dies?" When you are ill, ask, "What suffers?" Look again and again into what you experience until you know it to be mind nature arising as appearance-emptiness. Do the same with loving-kindness and compassion and every other mental state, thought, feeling, or sensation.

In particular, cut consistently into the web of your personality. Identify a number of patterns that operate in you, and make a list of them. Then, by trial and error, pair each pattern with a technique that works on it effectively. For instance, suppose you observe that you constantly criticize yourself. Whenever the critical attitude arises, evoke the meditation on joy, cutting into the trained values that you take as absolute. Perhaps the power approach isn't effective, but you discover that opening to the critical attitude is, so just open to it ecstatically, raising the level of energy in attention to the point that you experience the trained values but no longer hold them as absolute.

Once you have paired each pattern with a technique, work on just one pattern for a week or more so that you cut that pattern whenever it arises. Then add another pattern, and work on that for a week while you continue to work on the first. Keep adding one pattern a week until you are working with four or five. This number is not too many to remember but enough to keep your conditioned personality out of balance so that you constantly experience coming back to mind nature. When a pattern collapses, begin working with a new pattern so that you are always working with four or five at any given time.

How, you might ask, do you identify and study patterns? Here are four ways.

First, *observe what you don't notice, what you don't question, and what you don't laugh about.* What you don't notice tells you where patterns keep you in ignorance. What you don't question tells you what patterns assume. What you don't laugh about tells you where your identity is invested.

Become aware of what you don't notice by noting what other people—your teacher, spouse or partner, friends or colleagues—see. Become aware of what you don't question by noting the assumptions that operate in your thinking and interpreting of events. Become aware of what you don't laugh about by noting what is not funny for you and questioning why. In all three categories, you will discover fixed points in you. Those fixed points are where the patterns are fixed, and by following the threads from the fixed points, you will be led into the patterns.

Second, *study your life history.* In the first meditation on change in chapter 4, you studied your life at five-year intervals to see what changes took place in your personality, your worldview, and your relationships as you grew older. Studying your life history reveals how patterns developed and shaped your life. Study your family history as well, since patterns are transmitted all too faithfully from generation to generation. Look at your parents and look at your children to see what patterns operate in you.

Third, *look at the five circles of your life.* The first circle is where you live—your home and what you do on your own. The second circle is your immediate support system—your immediate family, intimate friends and colleagues, and how you interact with them. The third circle is how you earn your livelihood—what activities you engage in, the people with whom you interact, and how you handle money. The fourth circle consists of your social relationships—your parents, siblings and relatives, friends, and acquaintances. The fifth circle is the social and cultural realms—where you fit in the socioeconomic system, what cultural values you hold, and the nature of your relationship with society. Study each of these circles, and you will have a good idea of the patterns that shape your life.

Fourth, *practice alternation*. Alternation is both a method for studying patterns and a method for cutting the web of existence. Take the six realms, for example. Suppose you identify with the hell realm. You see and experience the world in terms of opposition. Everything is a fight for you. So, for one day, fight everything imaginable. Exaggerate the operation of the pattern. Deliberately invite conflict over the slightest disagreement. Observe the patterns that seek and invite conflict. Observe how far they will go. Observe what stops them. Observe what they want and what world they create for you. The next day do the opposite. Nothing is a problem. Don't oppose anything. Be the most agreeable person in the world. The day after, return to fighting. Continue alternating, one day fighting, one day agreeing. Do the same thing in your meditation, fighting everything that arises one day, going along with it the next.

Very quickly, you will become aware of how patterns operate—in you and in people around you. You may be astonished to discover that others don't notice any change in your behavior, or you may be astonished by how little tolerance they have for any deviation in your behavior. One side of the pattern may feel very familiar, while the other side is forbidden territory.

A student, unable to recognize the god realm, used alternation. One day he acted like a god, assuming that everyone in the world existed only to serve him, and that everything he thought and everything he did was right and true simply by virtue of who he was. He fostered an attitude of such superiority and entitlement that the suggestion that he could do anything wrong was ludicrous. His only concern, on the god realm days, was to maintain his position of superiority.

On the alternate days, he was the lowest of the low. Nothing about him was good or honorable. He behaved as though he deserved no deference, honor, or service. If anybody complimented him, he apologized for being noticeable. If anybody thanked him, he replied that what he did was just a reflection of his subservient place in the world and that no gratitude was necessary.

After his first attempt he said that the alternate days were easy, but the god realm days themselves were out of the question. "I can't act like that," he said. "It's not right. It's impolite. It's inconsiderate."

These protestations revealed the first layer of patterning that prevented him from being present. He was habitually more concerned with behaving properly—behaving according to trained values and looking good—than with doing what was required by the situation.

When you practice alternation, the patterns scream, telling you every imaginable reason why you can't do this practice. Remember, what you don't notice, what you don't question, and what you don't laugh about are all indications of patterned material.

After repeated efforts, this student did manage to play the god role for a couple of days. He was aghast—this is what he really wanted. This was how he actually felt inside! He realized he was angry at the world because the world did not treat him as the god he felt himself to be. The practice had revealed a pattern in him that he hadn't even suspected.

A third result from alternation is that it opens up a gap between the two poles of the pattern. You find mind nature in that gap. Practice alternation, cut the web of existence, open the gap, and return to original mind.

Deliberate Behavior

These and similar practices fall under the general classification of *deliberate behavior*. In its most general interpretation, deliberate behavior refers to the volitional adoption of any form of behavior for the purpose of observing and cutting the web of existence.

The discipline is dangerous and damaging if you are unable or unwilling to maintain attention. At best, you will only suppress or reinforce problematic patterns of behavior. At worst, you will hurt others and yourself mentally, emotionally, and possibly physically.

All spiritual practices are forms of deliberate behavior and consequently are not immune from the dangers. Monastic vows and the vow of conduct for an awakening being are examples of deliberate behavior. In monastic vows, dangers include suppressing internal material and insensitively imposing literal interpretations on others. In the awakening being code, suppression is also a danger, as is the ignoring of appropriate boundaries. To avoid suppression, you must be clear about your intention: why are you doing this? With clear intention, power flows into your practice of deliberate behavior. If you take monastic vows, you own the decision, and everything you experience as a consequence becomes fuel for your practice. If you do a month's retreat and are hit by loneliness, futility, or illness during the retreat, the clarity of your intention gives you the power to meet these experiences with presence. Don't pursue spiritual practice, and especially don't engage in deliberate behavior to improve your life. The objective of spiritual practice is presence, not improvement. The objective of deliberate behavior is to dismantle those parts of your life that are based on habituated patterns.

In *The Lamp of Mahamudra*, Tsele Natsok Rangdröl uses five metaphors to describe forms of deliberate behavior associated with the practice of presence: a wounded deer, a lion playing in the mountains, the wind in the sky, a madman, and a spear stabbing into empty space.

A Wounded Deer: Renunciation When a deer is wounded, she retreats into the forest or into the mountains, avoiding dangers and distractions so that her body can rest and recuperate. Through renunciation, let go of the dangers and distractions of life based on habituated patterns and reactions. Just as the deer is determined to heal from her wounds, be determined to be free from habituated patterns.

A Lion Playing in the Mountains: Outlook A lion in the wild runs free, without fear, anxiety, or trepidation. In the practice of presence, all experience is an arising in awareness, and awareness itself is like the sky, clear, empty, and open. Even the difficulties you encounter in practice are experiences. With the confidence this outlook provides, fearlessly bring attention to whatever arises in experience, and know it for what it is.

The Wind in the Sky: Practice The wind adheres to nothing. It is movement and nothing more. It touches and moves on. Everything that arises in experience is movement, whether it is a thought, feeling, or sensation. The patterns of habituation attach to the content of experience, stopping the movement. Be like the wind in the sky: attach to nothing, and let experience arise and subside in the open space of awareness.

A Madman: Behavior The conventional notion of success is to be happy, wealthy, famous, and respected. Failure is to be unhappy, poor, obscure, and disdained. Only a madman doesn't care about whether he is happy or sad, wealthy or poor, famous or obscure, respected or disdained. The only way to reclaim your life is to recognize that life consists of precisely and only what you experience. To act on what others judge as success or failure, or according to what habituated patterns tell you is success or failure, is to ignore what you are. Be like a madman, disregarding the conditioned notions of success and failure. Pursue only the understanding of what you are until you are truly present in your life.

A Spear Stabbing into Empty Space: Result A spear stabbing into empty space and striking nothing describes how attention penetrates the layers of confusion. Direct attention into habituated patterns, and the patterns dissolve like clouds in the sky. You strike nothing. The more deeply attention penetrates what arises in experience, the more completely you know that thoughts, feelings, and sensations simply arise and that there is no self or "I" at the center. When you rest in mind nature, experience flows freely. Unrestricted by dualistic fixation, it is released in open awareness.

Deliberate behavior is a much-misunderstood area of practice and has given rise to the justification of bizarre behavior as the expression of "crazy wisdom." Any action that is not the expression of presence is the operation of habituated patterns and acts only to strengthen and reinforce them. You can tell what is the expression of presence and what is the operation of patterns. Presence is alive. Patterns are mechanical. Presence transforms. Patterns reinforce. Presence leaves no traces. Patterns leave a trail of disturbance.

Three Steps in Deliberate Behavior
The three steps are recognize, observe, and change behavior. The first step is to study the operation of patterns so you recognize where you fall into reaction. In other words, when do you lose attention? You lose attention because circumstances are difficult and overwhelm your ability in attention. You also lose attention when circumstances are so familiar that you just slip into habituated behavior.

In a class on insight practice, I asked students to listen while I read a poem. I read "The Jabberwocky" from Lewis Carroll's *Through the Looking Glass* because it is full of strange words and odd images. I wanted them to observe their reactions. No one observed anything. They all slid into a warm, comfortable feeling, recalling how they had been read to when they were young. Habituation took over completely; attention went out the window.

The second step in practicing deliberate behavior is to observe the mechanical quality of habituated behavior—how it is lifeless, unspontaneous, limited, and automatic. The range of mechanical behavior can be very wide. Some people can paint, draw, or sing beautifully, but their actions are all automatic. Other people teach or do therapy mechanically. Just because you do something well does not mean you are awake and present while doing it. A friend of mine, a concert-level flautist, told me he could play whole concertos without ever mentally being in the concert hall. The sheer force of habituation took him through the whole concert without a moment's presence.

The third step is to deliberately change behavior, at first in small ways and then in bigger ways. If you are used to working independently, you might ask someone to help you in a task, however difficult asking for help may be for you. If your habit is to go along with whatever anyone else suggests, try expressing your own thoughts and opinions. A person who is used to being competent might experiment with being incompetent to observe the reactions that arise.

Engage in deliberate behavior only if you are prepared to receive the results. For instance, if, like the student described above, you act like a god one day, you may lose a friend, your job, or your spouse. The risks are very real. You cannot and do not control the reactions of others. You are breaking internal structures and possibly external structures, too. The intention of these disciplines is not to behave in strange ways for the sake of being strange. The intention is to dismantle ingrained patterns of behavior so that natural awareness can manifest fully in your life. Remember, you do not engage in deliberate behavior to make your life "better." You engage in it to cut the web of habituated patterns and return to original mind.

Obstacles as Practice

Everybody encounters obstacles in practice and in life. "Do not worry about your difficulties in mathematics," Einstein once wrote to a student. "I can assure you that mine are still greater."

In many fairy tales, the hero searches for a magical amulet, a bright sword, or a life-giving elixir. Often, he finds the desired object relatively easily, but then his troubles begin. In one story, a young man enters a castle. Lining the path are huge dragons, but they are all asleep. Inside the castle, guards are posted everywhere, but they are all asleep, too. He goes deep into the castle, into the treasury, where he finds what he is looking for—the bright sword of awareness. It lies on a table, and an old man guards it. He's asleep, too! Around the room stand soldiers in armor, and they are all asleep. So the young man picks up the sword—and nothing happens. He then looks for a scabbard and can't resist taking one finely wrought of silver. As soon as he sheathes the sword, everybody wakes up. The old man thumps the table, yelling to the soldiers to stop the thief. The castle guards wake up and aim their weapons at him. The dragons wake up and start belching fire. Now he has a problem!

Problems worthy
of attack
Show their worth
by hitting back.

—*Piet Hein*

Imagine for a moment that you encountered no obstacles in your practice. What would that mean? Either you are already fully awake and present, or else your practice never touches a pattern. In the former case, you don't need any advice. In the latter, your practice is not changing any habituated area of your life. Obstacles and resistance are signs that your practice is effective. You are hitting something (your habituated patterns), and they are hitting back.

Obstacles are experience, too. Use the tools you have learned to cut through reactions to obstacles until you can see them as the arising and subsiding of experience. This is very difficult, mind you. Obstacles are the manifestation of a pattern. They can persist for years or even decades. At times you will feel that your practice is totally stagnant and futile. Don't underestimate the power of persistence. As you study your experience and the manifestation of the pattern, you will see that the obstacle is not consistent after all. It fluctuates, perhaps only a little, but you can work a little deeper here and a small opening opens up there. So you proceed, and one day a piece of the pattern falls apart. All your effort was not in vain.

Obstacles are useful. They help you understand the nature of experience in ways nothing else can. In the face of powerful obstacles, you have to give up your hope of being a spiritual person. You have to give up your hope for happiness and comfort. A powerful obstacle completely shreds your patterns of achievement, identity, and superiority. Dharmakirti writes:

> Adverse conditions are spiritual friends.
> Devils and demons are emanations of the buddhas.
> Illness sweeps away evil and obscurations.
> Suffering is the dance of what is.

Tough instructions, perhaps, but keep them in mind.

Open Awareness Like the Sky: Have Confidence and Be Free

As your experience of presence stabilizes, you enter the third phase of practice according to Nyishöl Khenpo Rinpoche's teaching at the opening of this chapter: *open awareness like the sky.* This phase is marked by increased confidence and trust in your original nature, a confidence that allows you to let things be as they are. Whatever arises in experience, you are not separate from it, and you experience completely its arising, unfolding, and subsiding. To many people, this phase of practice seems very passive, but it's not. You see clearly the direction of the present and move in it, not caught up and confused by spurious distractions. Again, Chuang Tzu writes:

> Great wisdom observes both far and near, and for that reason recognizes small without considering it paltry, recognizes large without considering it unwieldy, for it knows that there is no end to the weighing of things. It has a clear understanding of past and present, and for that reason it spends a long time without finding it tedious, a short time without fretting at its shortness, for it knows that time has no stop. It perceives the nature of fullness and emptiness, and for that reason it does not delight if it acquires something nor worry if it loses it, for it knows that there is no constancy to the division of lots. It comprehends the Level Road, and for that reason it does not rejoice in life nor look on death as a calamity, for it knows that no fixed rule can be assigned to beginning and end.

Here, you are not separate from what you experience. Thoughts, feelings, and sensations arise and subside, not separate from the awareness that experiences them. You have no sense of gain or loss, victory or defeat, only the play of what is. This extraordinary way of living is the fullest expression of the meditation instruction *mind like the sky* from chapter 3.

Mixing Awareness and Experience

Original mind is empty and clear, and experience arises without impediment. The difference between ordinary consciousness and original mind or pristine awareness is not in what arises in experience, but in how experience is released.

Practice consists of resting in the open space of pristine awareness, the direct awareness that is original mind, so that knowing and what arises in experience are not separate.

Initially, of course, you have to make an effort to mix awareness and experience. The practice has four steps:

- Look at what arises.
- Look at what experiences what arises.

- Rest in emptiness.
- As experiences arises in emptiness, do not separate.

Whether in formal meditation practice or during the day, apply the four steps to everything you experience. Look at a tree until the sense of "tree" collapses and you are left with pure sensation. Then look at what experiences sensation, that is, your mind. It arises as empty. Rest right there, and open to the experience of the tree again. At first, experience arises from pure being. Then you see it as the play of pure being. In the end, experience releases into pure being, leaving no trace.

Do the same with all thoughts, emotions, and sensations. When powerful states of clarity, bliss, or non-thought arise, do the same. When compassion or devotion arises, do the same.

In *open awareness like the sky* practice, do not fixate on any experience. As soon as you feel the tendency to fixate, whether on bliss, clarity, the dreamlike nature of experience, or emptiness, look directly into what is aware, what knows. The fixation releases, and you return to free and open awareness.

At the highest level of practice, experience releases itself, just as a snake tied in a knot releases itself.

ENERGY TRANSFORMATIONS

We now take another look at the process of practice, looking at it from the perspective of energy transformation. This formulation is a comprehensive summary of what we have considered in the last two chapters. It sets out the progress in understanding from penetrating the illusion of an external reality to experiencing what is.

The three stages correspond roughly to the three instructions at the beginning of this chapter. *Crack the egg of ignorance* corresponds to penetrating the illusion of subject-object perception and discovering the direct open awareness that is original mind, or mind nature. *Cut the web of existence* corresponds to understanding that awareness doesn't constitute an internal absolute that simply replaces the external absolute of an independently existing world. Finally, *open awareness like the sky* cuts through the notion that practice itself is an absolute. The instructions come from *The Hundred Thousand Teachings on Om Mani Padme Hung (ma.ni.bka.bum)*, a compendium of teachings on the mantra of Awakened Compassion attributed to Tsong-tsen Gampo, a Tibetan king in the eighth century.

The energy transformations, using the same form as in the four immeasurables, can be diagrammed as follows:

Energy Transformation in Insight and Presence

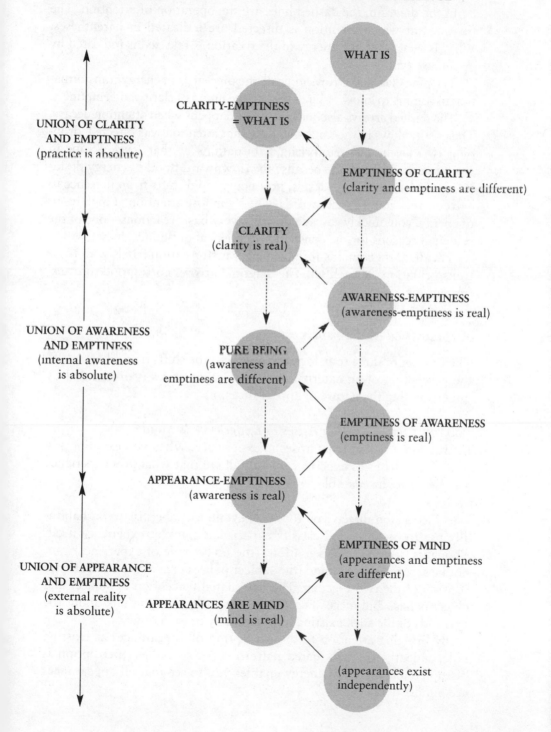

In the diagram, the dashed lines are the operation of attention. The fixations at which attention is directed are indicated in parentheses. What is seen when the energy in the fixation is released is indicated by uppercase type.

The nine diagonal arrows indicate the nine steps of energy transformation in coming to know original mind—the union of clarity and emptiness.

The dashed arrows also indicate what happens when attention decays. The energy flows in the same direction that attention was directed, dropping two levels and reinforcing habituations at that level. Drops in attention tend to cascade because the downward flood of energy destabilizes attention at lower levels, producing rapid shifts from presence to extreme reaction. In other words, when you lose attention at high levels of energy, you quickly cascade down to very basic reactions—one of the principal reasons for the constant reminders about mindfulness.

The diagram contains three sets of transformation triads with three transformations in each set. The diagonal arrows correspond to transformations.

Appearance and Emptiness

The first set of three transformations tracks the shifts that take place as the perception of an external reality of appearances is dismantled by understanding the nature of appearances.

Pointing Out That What Arises in Experience Is Mind
Instruction: Look at what arises in experience. When you examine any object that arises as experience, you will see that what you experience as objects are inseparable from mind.

This instruction directs you to look beyond the labels that you habitually use to organize and classify experience. Look at experience itself. Thoughts, feelings, and sensations (the object pole of experience) cannot be separated from mind (the subject pole of experience). Experience consists of the two together. The habituated perception of subject and object is false and misleading. Imagine a stick. Can you talk about the two ends of the stick existing independently of each other?

By bringing attention to the perception of appearances as existing independently, the habituated pattern of subject-object perception is disrupted and the freed energy enables you to see that all appearances are mind.

Pointing Out That Mind Is Empty
Instruction: Everything that arises in experience comes from mind. Look at mind, and see that it has no substance and no defining characteristics and that there is no thing you can point to and say, "It is that." Mind, in essence, is empty.

Once you see that all experience comes from mind, you become aware of a deeper fixation—that mind is real, that is, that it exists separately and is a thing. This instruction directs attention to that fixation. Look at mind to see what it is, to see how it exists. You see nothing. When sufficient energy develops in attention, the fixation on the existence of mind breaks up, and the released energy arises as the understanding that mind is empty, that is, it is not a thing.

Thinking, conjecturing, reasoning, and deducing do not have sufficient energy to break up the mind-is-real fixation. Only direct experience, the experience of seeing nothing, is sufficient.

Pointing Out That Appearance and Emptiness Are Not Separable
Instruction: Appearances arise, seemingly out of nothing. They are, in essence, empty. In empty mind, the play of awareness is free and unceasing. When appearance and emptiness are pointed out as inseparable, appearances do not stop arising, and emptiness does not become a thing. Empty appearance is naturally free.

On the one hand, appearances arise. On the other, mind is empty. Appearances seem to arise out of nothing, stay for a while, and then subside. A subtle dualistic fixation is revealed: you see appearance and emptiness as different. This instruction directs attention to the fixation on difference. Look directly at appearance. It is empty. Look directly at emptiness. It is not a thing. There is no separate emptiness out of which appearances arise and then subside. Appearances are empty in and of themselves. Appearance and emptiness are inseparable and arise together as the play of natural awareness.

Awareness and Emptiness

The second set of transformation triads tracks the shifts taking place as the perception of an internal reality of awareness is dismantled by understanding the nature of awareness.

Pointing Out That Awareness Is Empty
Instruction: Look at awareness. Awareness is moment-to-moment knowing. It is not a thing. It is empty, too.

Having understood that all experience is appearance-emptiness and arises as the play of awareness, you fixate on awareness as real. This instruction directs attention to that fixation. What is awareness? As in looking at mind in the earlier set of transformations, you find nothing. All that is present is moment-to-moment knowing.

Pointing Out Emptiness as Pure Being
Instruction: Look at emptiness. The nature of awareness is pure being: this is the totality of experience.

Seeing that awareness itself is empty, you then tend to fixate on emptiness as what is real. When you look at emptiness, however, you experience a shift, and you see the pure being of all experience. You step into the realm of totality when you see that all experience, appearance, awareness, confusion, and understanding have this same quality of being empty and being experienced.

Pointing Out That Awareness and Emptiness Are Inseparable
Instruction: Look at awareness-experience. It arises unceasingly. It is empty yet arises as thoughts, feelings, and sensations. Although these experiences arise, they are empty. They arise, are present, and subside freely on their own.

Awareness-emptiness does not mean that experience stops arising. It does not mean that emptiness blocks everything out. That awareness and emptiness are inseparable points out that experience is free.

The experience of pure being reveals another level of dualistic fixation, that awareness and emptiness are different. In every moment of experience, look to see what it is. You see that awareness is present in every moment of experience. It never stops. When you look at awareness, you see nothing: it is empty. Yet, as soon as you take the position that nothing is there, you are immediately confronted with the vivid awareness of experience. While not any thing, awareness arises as constantly changing thoughts, feelings, and sensations. You see that awareness, the vividness of experience, and the emptiness, the "being nothing there" quality, are not separate. So, awareness-emptiness does not mean that you reach a state where all movement in the mind stops and you do not experience anything. It means that you know that awareness and experience are not different. In awareness-emptiness, experience arises and subsides freely on its own.

Clarity and Emptiness

The third set of transformation triads tracks the shifts that take place as the perception that practice is an absolute is dismantled by understanding the nature of clarity.

Pointing Out That Mind Nature Is Clarity

Instruction: Look at mind nature. Mind nature is just what is and arises naturally. Clarity is the uncontrived vastness of pure being.

Turn attention to mind nature, which is awareness-emptiness, to dismantle the fixation that it is real. It is not made or produced. Mind nature does not come from anything, and it is not produced by anything. Mind nature refers to what is present when all confusion and patterning have been dismantled. There is nothing to be made, changed, or fixed. Though empty of intrinsic reality, it is not nothing because clarity, the ability to know, is present. It is the infinite natural clarity of pure being. This is the mystery of being.

Pointing Out That Emptiness Is Unobscured

Instruction: Look at what is empty. Reality is not a thing. The totality of being is open and groundless.

The patterns of dualism die hard. Even at this point, you still have a subtle tendency to take clarity as one thing and emptiness as another. Look at the clarity of mind nature and see that clarity, too, is not a thing. The infinite openness of emptiness is the totality of being. In this open vastness all experience arises. Experience is emptiness expressing itself in form and dissolving.

> There is no thing that is spread throughout the universe and permeates all beings. Buddha nature is just what is present when all the confusion and distortions of pattern-based existence are cleared away.
>
> —Jamgön Kongtrül Lodrö Taye

Pointing Out That Clarity and Emptiness Are Inseparable
Instruction: Look at clarity and emptiness. Vividness, clear and unobstructed, and openness, empty and unobscured, are just there. The notion of practice as an absolute collapses since there is nothing to be done.

When attention penetrates all confusion, all experience is vivid and arises freely. The empty nature of experience is also clear. The two aspects of experience—vivid clarity and being no thing, or awareness and emptiness—are not different. This is how things are, so there is nothing that needs to be done. Even when a person has dismantled the illusions of an absolute external and internal reality, he or she may still hold that the practice is real. The final pointing-out instruction is that the practice itself is an arising in experience. Practice is not absolute, either.

In the end, practice is not a form or a specific activity. It is a way of living through which we accumulate momentum in attention and in our willingness to open to the mystery of being. Many people latch on to the idea of practice not being an absolute to justify not making an effort in practice or to justify aberrant and harmful behavior. These people are only fooling themselves. They are either turning away from the discipline of effort or rationalizing their lack of mindfulness as energy spills into reactive behaviors. Real learning, real understanding, and real mastery come only through great effort and great faith.

Transformation of Consciousness

In transforming your experience of life, attention necessarily transforms the functioning of consciousness. *Ordinary consciousness* refers to how you experience the world when the direct open awareness of original mind is obscured or distorted by the operation of habituated patterns. Direct open awareness is like the sky, open, infinite, clear, and unobstructed. Ordinary consciousness is like a storm, and you take the storm to be what you are, unaware that the storm itself is the arising and subsiding of original mind.

Traditionally speaking, ordinary consciousness operates at three levels: basis consciousness, emotional mind, and sensory consciousness. *Sensory consciousness* refers to consciousness of seeing, hearing, tasting, smelling, touching, and thinking. "I see a cup," for example, is an instance of seeing consciousness. "I have a good idea" is an instance of thinking consciousness. Ordinarily, everything that arises at the level of sensory consciousness is taken as a real object. Thoughts, sounds, sights, smells, touch, and tastes arise as "other" in opposition to a felt sense of self. We formulate this duality in our language with such phrases as "I see what you mean" or "This tastes good to me." The felt sense of self is the *emotional mind*. When, in meditation, you have developed a level of attention that is undisturbed by the arising of thoughts, sensations, and feelings, you still experience a clear sense of self, "I am." A sense of self is an emotional attachment to a projection, but it operates at a deeper level than ordinary reactive emotions. The sense of self is taken to be more real than thoughts, feelings, or sensations. When attention begins to penetrate the projection, you often encounter intense fear since letting go of a sense of self feels like a direct threat to survival. When you can maintain attention and let go of the sense of self, you do not die—you experience *basis consciousness*. In basis consciousness, no explicit sense of self arises. It is experienced as empty clarity and is often mistaken for original mind. Basis consciousness is essentially passive. The structures of self and other and the patterns of emotional reactivity are not explicit but remain latent in basis consciousness. Consequently, it is also called *store consciousness* because it stores the seeds of patterned existence.

The difference between basis consciousness and original mind is that basis consciousness immediately moves into the dualism of emotional mind and the reactivity of the sensory consciousnesses as soon as experience arises. In basis consciousness, the awareness we call original mind is obscured. In original mind, when experience arises no duality or reactivity arises. Experience arises and releases itself in awareness, like figures drawn on water.

The transformation from ordinary consciousness to the pristine awareness of original mind is traditionally described in terms of the different aspects of pristine awareness, which we have already met in chapters 6 and 7. When you know original mind, the ice of basis consciousness melts and the energy, dynamism, and radiance of original mind are freed. Basis consciousness transforms into *mirrorlike awareness*. When you look in a mirror, you do not see the mirror. You see only the reflections. Without the mirror, no reflections would arise. If the mirror were not totally clear, the reflections would be partially obscured or distorted. Although you do not see the mirror, you know it is present because you see the reflections. In the same way, when the confusion and dullness of ordinary consciousness have been cleared away, basis consciousness becomes mirrorlike awareness. Experience continues to arise, vividly and clearly, but original mind, as such, is not seen because it is empty. Recall the pointing-out instruction from the previous chapter: so close you can't see it. Like a mirror, mind nature is right in front of you and you can't see it. And just as a mirror can reflect everything and anything, the clarity of original mind can know all that arises in experience.

The arising of experience in open awareness does not trigger the projections of self and other. All experience is known for what it is, just experience. This quality of sameness is often referred to as *one flavor,* the one flavor being that experience in and of itself is just experience and is empty of such qualities as being this or that, bad or good, helpful or harmful. The emotional mind, the level of ordinary consciousness that holds a sense of self as a special aspect of experience, is transformed and becomes *sameness pristine awareness:* all experience shares the same quality—emptiness. With the absence of the sense of self, the natural ability of awareness to distinguish one experience from another operates freely. *Distinguishing pristine awareness* arises. Experience is no longer edited and interpreted by a sense of self and the reactive patterns associated with it. Each arising is distinguished and known as it is.

Finally, the sensory consciousnesses based on subject-object duality are transformed. You know directly what arises. What is experienced is not separated into subject and object. Without the editing and discrimination of the emotional mind, everything is known fully and completely. Sensory consciousness is transformed into *effective pristine awareness.* You know what is, you know what to do, and you know how to do it because you are not separate from what is experienced.

The fifth aspect of pristine awareness, *totality pristine awareness,* is the totality of the other four. It is the realm in which they function.

LIVING PRESENCE

In *The Unfettered Mind,* Takuan Soho writes:

> There is such a thing as training in principle, and such a thing as training in technique.
>
> Training in principle is this: when you arrive, nothing is noticed. It is simply as though you had discarded all concentration.
>
> Training in technique is practicing over and over again until the technique is one with you.
>
> Even though you know principle, you must make yourself perfectly free in the use of technique. Even though you know technique, if you are unclear about the deepest aspects of principle, you will likely fall short of proficiency.

Although Takuan was writing to a sword master, his words apply equally to living presence. You need both technique and principle. Techniques are methods, things that you do or ways that you move. Principles are formulations that capture how things work and guide you in the use of technique.

In this book, you have learned many techniques—how to cultivate attention, how to dispel busyness, how to bring attention to death and change, how to use reflections on death to cut through cultural distractions to presence, how to use attention to transform the elemental reaction chains into pristine awareness, how to uncover the four immeasurables, and how to use attention to cut through dualistic perception. Your work is to make these techniques your own. Learn all the methods, and practice them until you experience the intention of each method and how each method works. Then choose which methods work best for you, and make them so much a part of you that they naturally come into play when situations warrant. One of the teachings from mind training is:

You are proficient when you practice even when distracted.

During a kayaking lesson, one of my instructors was caught broadside by a large wave. She immediately dug her paddle deep into the wave, tipped her kayak into the wave, and road it safely to shore. Her movements were smooth and effective even though she was definitely in danger of being rolled under the wave. That kind of proficiency comes only through practice. Work the techniques you choose until they become how you live and interact with others.

You have also learned principles on which practice is based: patterns are automatic structures that operate mechanically, attention is emotional energy, awareness is naturally present when the confusion of pattern-based functioning is cleared away. Learning principles is a deeper and subtler process. As you train in technique, look for what is common and for what is different among techniques.

> In theory there is no difference between theory and practice. In practice there is.
>
> —*Yogi Berra*

You will see the principles of practice with your own eyes. You will see how things work in a deeper way. Your application of techniques will become subtler and more effective. You will expend less effort in fighting patterns and accomplish more in undermining their operation.

Here are two more sets of instructions that together summarize everything that has gone before. The first is known as *Separating from the Four Attachments*. It comes from Sakya Pandita, a Tibetan teacher of the twelfth century, who received these teachings in a vision of Manjushri, the bodhisattva of awakened intelligence:

> *When you attach to this life, you do not practice the way.*
> *When you attach to habituated patterns, you are not free.*
> *When you attach to your own welfare, you don't have awakening mind.*
> *When you attach to a fixed position, you do not see how things are.*

When you attach to this life, you do not practice the way is put into practice through meditating on death and impermanence, which severs attachment to social conventions and ordinary values and particularly to the accepted notions of success and failure in life.

When you attach to habituated patterns, you are not free is put into practice through meditating on the functioning of habituated patterns, including the six realms and the five elements. These meditations bring out the restricting and self-perpetuating nature of reactive emotional patterns and the impossibility of freedom as long as you are subject to them. In the meditations on the five dakinis and emptying the six realms, you learn how to step out of and transform reactive patterns.

When you attach to your own welfare, you don't have awakening mind is put into practice through meditating on the four immeasurables and taking and sending. These meditations shift you from conditioned emotional reactions that are based on self-interest to free, open, emotional energy that is available for whatever needs to be done.

When you attach to a fixed position, you do not see how things are is put into practice through insight meditations, which penetrate the patterns of subject-object perception and open you to presence.

A second set of principles, *The Four Steps in Joining with What Is True*, is found in the mahamudra tradition. Here the four stages are

- Single mind
- Simplicity
- One flavor
- No cultivation

Single mind means to know original mind. Look at the resting mind. What rests? Look at the moving mind. What moves? Look at the mind that knows resting and moving. What knows? What rests, what moves, and what knows are one—original mind.

Simplicity means experiencing original mind in all experience. Cut through the complications of habituated patterns by recalling original mind. Know original mind in everything you experience, and return again and again to its simplicity.

One flavor means knowing that everything you experience in your life is original mind; there is nothing else. Everything in your life is experience—powerful, vivid, possibly painful and difficult, but, in the end, experience—that arises from no thing, abides nowhere, and subsides into no thing.

No cultivation means resting in original mind, not separate from the arising and subsiding of the experience that is your life.

In 1970 I was on my way to India, though I didn't know it at the time. Crossing Turkey, I caught a ride with a Swiss truck driver who was the spitting image of John Wayne. I rode with him for three days as we navigated the frighteningly narrow roads in the Turkish highlands. Not infrequently, he closed his eyes as he turned the steering wheel to round a curve, with a sheer, thousand-foot drop on one side and a mountain wall on the other. "It's best if I close my eyes," he said. "Then I don't freeze up."

He had made more than thirty trips across these highlands and the deserts of Iran and Afghanistan and had had more than a few adventures. All those hours alone, however, had also given him time to reflect on life and the nature of things.

"I have a friend," he said, one day, "who lives in a small village in Switzerland. We are about the same age. She has never traveled outside her village. And I've been all over Asia and Europe. I'm not sure which of us has had the better life."

I went on to study Buddhism, do the three-year retreat, and a few other things. Nevertheless, his comment has always stayed with me, pointing me away from concern about the content of life back to the importance of being present in the experience of life itself.

Put this book down for now—you've come to the end of it. Take what you've read and bring it into your life. Find a teacher to help you. Cultivate attention in everything you do, and, until your last breath, live in the mystery of being.

Sources

My principal teacher, the late Kalu Rinpoche, gave me complete trans-
missions of the essential teachings of the Karma Kagyu and Shangpa
traditions of Tibetan Buddhism as well as the authorization to trans-
mit these teachings to students and to guide them in their practice.
From Dezhung Rinpoche, I received detailed instructions in the cultivation of attention, mahamudra and dzogchen teachings, and many
valuable instructions on the bodhisattva vow. I have also received
instructions in a wide range of topics from other Kagyu teachers,
including H. H. Karmapa XVI, the late Jamgön Kongtrül III, and
Thrangu Rinpoche. I'm indebted to my retreat director, Lama Tenpa,
who patiently guided me in my practice during the three-year retreat. I
also received instruction in the Nyingma tradition from Khyentse
Rinpoche, Dudjom Rinpoche, and Nyishöl Khenpo Rinpoche. From
Gangteng Rinpoche, I received the Padma Lingpa transmission of
dzogchen.

The primary source for chapter 2 is oral teachings I received from
Kalu Rinpoche in India in 1970–71. I also incorporated Stephen
Batchelor's perspectives on the four noble truths from *Buddhism
Without Beliefs* (New York: Riverhead, 1997).

Chapter 3 is largely based on meditation instructions I received
from Dezhung Rinpoche in 1972.

Chapter 4 is based on a five-point meditation from the Kadampa
tradition (thirteenth century C.E.) that appears in Jamgön Kongtrül the
Great's *The Torch of Certainty,* translated by Judith Hanson (Boston:
Shambhala, 1977). The commentary relies on oral teachings I received
from Kalu Rinpoche.

Chapter 5 is a compilation from several different sources. The meditation on the six realms is an adaptation of a classical meditation on the
suffering of cyclic existence. The five-element reaction chain is derived in
part from the work of Ngakpa Chögyam in *Rainbow of Liberated*

Energy: Working with Emotions Through the Colour and Element Symbolism of Tibetan Tantra (Dorset: Element Books, 1986). The view of conditioned karma as the evolution of complex systems of patterns begins with Kalu Rinpoche's presentation of karma as a process of evolution. The formulation presented here is a combination of perspectives I learned from Jon Parmenter and from my own investigation into chaos theory, complex adaptive systems, artificial life, and evolution theory. Sources include *Chaos: Making a New Science* by James Gleick (New York: Viking, 1987), John H. Holland's *Hidden Order: How Adaptation Builds Complexity* (Reading, MA: Addison-Wesley, 1995), Stuart A. Kauffman's *At Home in the Universe: The Search for Laws of Self-Organization and Complexity* (New York: Oxford University Press, 1995), and *The Collapse of Chaos: Discovering Simplicity in a Complex World* by Jack Cohen and Ian Stewart (New York: Viking, 1994).

The material in chapter 6 comes from various sources. The five dakinis meditations are based on a transformation technique that appears explicitly and implicitly in many meditation practices in the Tibetan tradition. I adapted parts of a long practice ritual of chö (cutting) and incorporated dzogchen perspectives from Ngakpa Chögyam in *Rainbow of Liberated Energy*. The section on the six realms is an adaptation of methods from a meditation practice focused on Avalokiteshvara (Tibetan: Chenrezi), the embodiment of awakened compassion, as taught by Kalu Rinpoche.

The material in chapter 7 comes from a wide range of sources. The meditation on equanimity, from which I developed the other meditations, appears in Longchenpa's *Kindly Bent to Ease Us,* translated by Herbert V. Guenther (Emeryville, CA: Dharma Publishing, 1975–1976). I adapted Guenther's representation of the dynamics in the four immeasurables for the section on decay. I also drew on *Distinguishing Ordinary Consciousness and Pristine Awareness* by Rangjung Dorje, Angeles Arrien's *The Four-Fold Way: Walking the Paths of the Warrior, Teacher, Healer, and Visionary* (San Francisco: Harper San Francisco, 1993), and Robert Moore and Douglas Gillette's *King, Warrior, Magician, Lover: Rediscovering the Archetypes of the Mature Masculine* (San Francisco: Harper San Francisco, 1990), as well as perspectives from *Refining Your Life: From the Zen Kitchen to Enlightenment* by Uchiyama Roshi, translated by Thomas Wright (New York: Weatherhill, 1983), and *The Buddhist I Ching* by Chih-hsu Ou-I, translated by Thomas Cleary (Boston: Shambhala, 1987).

Chapter 8 consists of traditional treatments of chö and the bodhisattva vow as well the teachings on taking and sending published under the title *The Great Path of Awakening* by Kongtrül, translated by Ken McLeod (Boston: Shambhala, 1987).

Chapter 9 is based on mahamudra and dzogchen teachings from the Kagyu and Nyingma traditions, respectively. In particular, I relied on a Shangpa text, *The Three Settlings,* and a Kagyu text, *The Ocean of Certainty,* for the instruction in insight practice.

Chapter 10 is based on the *Three Words of Garab Dorje,* which I first learned from Dezhung Rinpoche and later through oral instruction from Nyishöl Khenpo. The description of energy transformation is adapted from *The Hundred Thousand Instructions on Om Mani Padme Hung,* attributed to Tsong-tseng Gampo. Some of the material on deliberate behavior comes from *The Lamp of Mahamudra* by Tsele Natsok Rangdröl, translated by Erik Pema Kunsang (Boston: Shambhala, 1989).

Permissions

Idries Shah, *The Exploits of the Incomparable Mulla Nasrudin* (NY: E.P. Dutton, 1972), p. 112

Thomas Cleary, *Book of Leadership and Strategy: Lessons of the Chinese Masters* (Boston, Shambhala, 1992)

Idries Shah, *The Exploits of the Incomparable Mulla Nasrudin* (NY: E.P. Dutton, 1972), p. 52

Idries Shah, *The Exploits of the Incomparable Mulla Nasrudin* (NY: E.P. Dutton, 1972), p. 108

John Le Carre, *The Spy in His Prime* (audio edition)

Idries Shah, *The Pleasantries of the Incredible Mulla Nasrudin* (NY: Penguin Arkana, 1993), p. 53

Idries Shah, *The Pleasantries of the Incredible Mulla Nasrudin* (NY: Penguin Arkana, 1993), p. 42

John Stevens, *One Robe, One Bowl: The Zen Poetry of Ryokan* (NY: Weatherhill, 1977), p. 14

The Zen Teaching of Rinzai, translated by Irmgard Schloegl (Berkeley: Shambhala, 1975), p. 81

Idries Shah, *The Pleasantries of the Incredible Mulla Nasrudin* (NY: Penguin Arkana, 1993), p. 218

Guide to Meditations
and Commentaries

Chapter 7: The Four Immeasurables

Chapter 8: Mind Training

Chapter 9: Insight and Dismantling Illusion

Chapter 10: No Separation

Index